Network and Netplay

Network and Netplay

Virtual Groups on the Internet

Edited by Fay Sudweeks,
Margaret McLaughlin and Sheizaf Rafaeli

Foreword by Ronald Rice

AAAI Press / The MIT Press

Menlo Park, California, Cambridge, Massachusetts, London, England

Copublished and distributed by The MIT Press, Massachusetts Institute of Technology, Cambridge, Massachusetts and London, England.

Library of Congress Cataloging-in-Publication Data

Network and netplay : virtual groups on the Internet / edited by
   Fay Sudweeks, Margaret McLaughlin, and Sheizaf Rafaeli.
       p. cm.
   Includes bibliographical references and index.
   ISBN 0-262-69206-6 (pbk. : acid-free paper)
   1. Computer networks. 2. Virtual reality. 3. Computer networks--Social
aspects. 4. Telematics. I. Sudweeks, Fay. II. McLaughlin, Margaret L.
III. Rafaeli, Sheizaf.
TK5105.5N4647 1998
302.23--dc21   97-43441
                                                                    CIP

Printed on acid-free paper in the United States of America.

Contents

Foreword / xi
Ronald Rice, Rutgers University

Introduction / xv
Sheizaf Rafaeli, Hebrew University of Jerusalem;
Margaret McLaughlin, University of Southern California;
Fay Sudweeks, University of Sydney, Australia

Smile When You Say That: Graphic Accents as Gender Markers in
Computer-Mediated Communication / 3
Diane Witmer, California State University, Fullerton, USA;
Sandra Katzman, Interac Co, Japan

In the gender-bending world of computer-mediated communication (CMC), is it possible to determine the gender of a message sender from cues in the message? This study addresses the question by drawing on current literature to formulate and test three hypotheses: (1) women use more graphic accents than men do in their CMC, (2) men use more challenging language in CMC than do women, and (3) men write more inflammatory messages than do women. Results indicate that only the first hypothesis is partially supported and that women tend to challenge and flame more than do men in this sample group.

Frames and Flames: The Structure of Argumentative Messages
on the Net / 13
Edward A. Mabry, University of Wisconsin-Milwaukee, USA

This chapter assesses the use, in computer-mediated communication, of the strategic message structuring tactic known as framing. It is hypothesized that framing strategies are related to the emotional tenor of a disputant's message and that a speaker's emotional involvement with an issue should be curvilinearly related to the appropriation of framing as an argumentative discourse strategy. Results provided support for the primary hypothesized relationship.

Telelogue Speech / 27

Alexander E. Voiskounsky, Moscow University, Russia

Mediation processes form the basis of human psychological development. Speech signs play a crucial role in the internalization of mediating means. In the computer-mediated communication (CMC) field, speech has its own peculiarity, thus modifying the possible directions of the internalization process. The analysis in this chapter shows the specifics of CMC speech, i.e. telelogue speech.

"Hmmm ... Where's That Smoke Coming From?" Writing, Play and Performance on Internet Relay Chat / 41

Brenda Danet, Hebrew University of Jerusalem, Israel and The Smithsonian Institution, USA; Lucia Ruedenberg, Ben Gurion University of the Negev, Hebrew University of Jerusalem, Israel and New York University, USA; Yehudit Rosenbaum-Tamari, Hebrew University of Jerusalem and Ministry of Absorption of Immigrants, Israel

This chapter is a study of writing, play and performance on Internet Relay Chat, known for short as IRC, a network program that allows thousands of users all around the globe, at any hour of the day or night, to talk to each other in real time by typing lines of text. We adopt a textual, micro-sociolinguistic approach, informed by recent work in discourse analysis, the study of orality and literacy, and the anthropology of play and performance.

Media Use in an Electronic Community / 77

Steve Jones, University of Tulsa, USA

This study examines one facet of the penetration of personal computers into everyday life. It seeks to discover how members of a Usenet newsgroup value and use news sources. Electronic news sources predominated. An important finding is that media use was not tied to the user's local geographic. The study raises several questions for future research: What are the rhetorical dimensions of media use in electronic communities? How might our understanding of readers and communities be affected by new patterns of media use in electronic communities?

From Terminal Ineptitude to Virtual Sociopathy: How Conduct is Regulated on Usenet / 95

Christine B. Smith, Margaret L. McLaughlin and Kerry K. Osborne, University of Southern California, USA

This chapter explores standards of conduct across a representative sampling of Usenet newsgroups. Established newsgroups, those with a core cadre of regular posters, can be characterized as common place where group standards for acceptable and unacceptable behaviors regulate discourse. These standards differ from group to group and in many ways reflect the underlying goals and purposes of the group as well as its demographic makeup. This chapter raises and addresses several interesting behavioral questions and gender issues in the development of so-called online communities. It highlights a critical research question that remains in this area: Are standards for conduct a symptom of or an inevitable consequence of community?

Investigation of Relcom Network Users / 113
Alexander E. Voiskounsky, Moscow University, Russia

Relcom is the most intensively used network available of the former Soviet Union, and its users form a sample of highly active and educated citizens of the newly-formed independent states. To describe this newly-formed sample, surveys of the users were conducted via the network. The results include data on demographic characteristics of users, their attitudes, motivations, and typical ways of network usage. Attitudes towards possible social monitoring service functioning in the network are also investigated, and the potential directions of its functioning are rated by the respondents.

Practicing Safe Computing: Why People Engage in Risky Computer-Mediated Communication / 127
Diane Witmer, California State University, Fullerton, USA

This chapter defines the basic types of computer-mediated communication (CMC) and contextualizes them as electronic counterparts to other forms of communication. It then discusses the ways in which message privacy and security can be compromised in the electronic environment and reports a survey study of individuals who engage in potentially embarrassing forms of CMC via USENET newsgroups. The questionnaire asked respondents how risky they perceived their communications to be and why they felt secure enough to engage in risky communication. Survey results were equivocal on the question of user perceptions of privacy, but indicated that the perceived risk was low in the sample group. Finally, the chapter discusses implications and proposes an agenda for future research.

The Social Construction of Rape in Virtual Reality / 147
Richard MacKinnon, University of Texas at Austin, USA

The current social construction of rape in virtual reality is not a worthwhile endeavor in that it forces theorists to adapt an undesirable concept in order to import it into virtual reality. Rape exists as such in real life because of the social construction of women relative to the social construction of men. The relationship of these constructions is not and does not have to be analogous in virtual reality because virtual reality presents an opportunity for social reordering. Among these opportunities is the exploration of the ramifications of bodies presented arbitrarily. Given these opportunities, theorists seeking to pursue positive constructionism ought to endeavor to develop virtual-reality specific constructions which empower rather than import real life constructions which victimize.

Interactivity on the Nets / 173
Sheizaf Rafaeli, Hebrew University of Jerusalem, Israel; Fay Sudweeks, University of Sydney, Australia

> This chapter proposes that one useful perspective for studying group computer-mediated communication (CMC) is interactivity. Results indicate that the content on the net is less confrontational than is popularly believed: conversations are more helpful and social than competitive. Interactive messages seem to be more humorous, contain more self-disclosure, display a higher preference for agreement and contain many more first-person plural pronouns. This indicates that interactivity plays a role in the social dynamics of group CMC, and sheds a light on comparing interactive messages with conversation. The focus should be on the glue—that which keeps message threads and their authors together —and what makes the groups and their interaction tick.

It Makes Sense: Using an Autoassociative Neural Network to Explore Typicality in Computer Mediated Discussions / 191
Michael Berthold, University of Karlsruhe, Germany; Fay Sudweeks, University of Sydney, Australia; Sid Newton, University of Western Sydney, Nepean, Australia; Richard Coyne, University of Edinburgh, Scotland

> ProjectH, a research group of a hundred researchers, produced a huge amount of data from computer mediated discussions. The data classified several thousand postings from over 30 newsgroups into 46 categories. One approach to extract typical examples from this database is presented in this paper. An autoassociative neural network is trained on all 3000 coded messages and then used to construct typical messages under certain specified conditions. With this method the neural network can be used to create typical messages for several scenarios. This chapter illustrates the architecture of the neural network that was used and explains the necessary modifications to the coding scheme. In addition several typicality sets produced by the neural net are shown and their generation is explained. In conclusion, the autoassociative neural network is used to explore threads and the types of messages that typically initiate or contribute longer lasting threads.

Modeling and Supporting Virtual Cooperative Interaction Through the World Wide Web / 221
Lee Li-Jen Chen and Brian R. Gaines

> The development of the Internet has been very rapid, with little central planning. Despite its widespread use, there is little information about the social dynamics of Internet technologies. Many systems have been developed to cope with the information overload generated by direct access to the Internet. One common feature among the wide variety of indexing and search tools now available is the support they provide for selective attention and awareness in the communities using the net. It would be useful to analyze the design issues and principles involved in these tools in terms of the knowledge and discourse processes in the communities using these tools. This chapter provides a model of the virtual cooperative interaction on the World Wide Web in terms of discourse and awareness and uses it to classify the types of support tools existing and required.

Guided Exploration of Virtual Worlds / 243

Patrick Doyle and Barbara Hayes-Roth

In this chapter, we introduce Merlyn, an intelligent computer agent whose purpose is to guide children in their discovery of such worlds, and by so doing, to increase both their enjoyment and the effectiveness of that discovery. Merlyn is an autonomous agent that also has an integrated personality and emotional model, since he is intended to be a companion rather than a reference. We describe a particular kind of virtual world, the MUD (or multi-user dimension), that Merlyn is designed to interact with. We explain how he makes decisions in such a world, and how these places can be annotated with information to help him understand why they are there and how to use them. Merlyn can use these annotations to learn more about the world as the children travel, and this allows him to explain the world to the children, to suggest activities that may interest them, and to participate with them — in playing games, for example. We describe two prototype implementations of Merlyn, and describe future additions for a full-featured version. With Merlyn as a companion, children can be guided into strategically-chosen learning activities while having a friendly, entertaining experience in the virtual environment.

Appendix: ProjectH Overview: A Collaborative Quantitative Study of Computer-Mediated Communication / 265

M. Sheizaf Rafaeli, Hebrew University of Jerusalem, Israel; Fay Sudweeks, University of Sydney, Australia; Joe Konstan, University of Minnesota, USA; Ed Mabry, University of Wisconsin-Milwaukee, USA

A large group of people from several countries and many universities collaborated for two years on a quantitative study of electronic discussions. Members of the group include researchers from several dozen universities, representing numerous academic disciplines, who used the net in order to study use of the net. This report documents the design of the study and the methodology used to create the first, and possibly, representative sample of international, public group computer-mediated communication.

Bibliography / 283

Index / 309

Foreword

In 1984, in the introduction to *The New Media: Communication, Research and Technology,* I argued that the development and diffusion of computer-mediated communication (CMC) would not only stimulate new research approaches and theoretical perspectives, but should also be the focus of familiar approaches and perspectives. While it is true that, as some claim, some writing on CMC still lacks analytical rigor and theoretical grounding, there has been a gratifying growth in serious, innovative, and rigorous studies of CMC. This is partially due to the groundbreaking conceptual and survey research by the pioneers of CMC studies, the increasing acceptability of multiple approaches (such as triangulation, use of computer-collected usage and content data, in-depth interpretive studies, communication flows and content), and the recent widespread access to and use of the Internet. *Network and Net Play* represents one of the best examples of this generation of research.

Network and Net Play involves a creative and challenging variety of foci, data sources, analyses, discussions, and examples of how CMC fosters scientific communication and collaboration.

Some of the primary areas emphasized in this collection of related studies include the growth and features of the Internet and the nature of networks (such as demographics of online users, and styles such as graphic accents, signatures and "flaming"). Other chapters consider network norms and experiences (such as CMC features that influence the development of electronic community and use of traditional news media, online behavior at virtual parties, why some people persist in "unsafe" computing practices, how online social norms and communication conventions arise and are debated, and how the "virtual" nature of online interaction uncovers some of the deepest assumptions about what otherwise might be considered to be rape in a "real" situation). And a third set of chapters considers conceptualizations of the essential nature of network communication (telelogue compared to monologue and dialogue, "typical" messages represented by sets of highly associated message aspects, and patterns and flows of interaction across messagers, messages, and time).

The studies in *Network and Net Play* should also stimulate readers to become better aware of the wide array of data sources available to students of new media. A variety of online services, such as electronic messages, bulletin boards, newsgroups, listservs, real-time "chatting," and gaming environments provided the sources for a wide range of data types. These include online transcripts, usage statistics, online surveys, follow-up online and personal interviews, ethnographic participation, massive message databases, use of graphic accents and message signatures, use of editing and insertion features, case studies of use of CMC systems in recent political events, relationships between other media forms such as music CDs and online communication behaviors, message threads or messages that refer to prior messages, discussions about offending postings, demographic differences among users, and frequency probabilities of message characteristics. Any researcher who shuns the study of a medium that can provide all these (and more!) sources and forms of data, on the grounds that CMC is "faddish" or "just technology," is like those who avoided studying the "technological toys" we know as the telephone, radio and television.

Further, access to such a wide variety of data sources and to such large bodies of message and usage data requires more innovative and complex ways to retrieve, store, and analyze such data. These include various functions available in most systems to search, request, and retrieve particular files, usage data, messages or discussion groups, and database programs for qualitative analysis, style analyzers, and indexing capabilities. Other approaches included here include coding large message databases for theoretical, technical, and emerging aspects of online communication; neural network analysis of typical associations among these aspects across thousands of messages; grouping and interpretation of non-textual content such as graphic accents and signatures; and the development and distribution of online interactive surveys. Just as with all research methodologies—from analysis and representation of ethnographic field notes, to statistical analyses, to summaries of focus groups—one must become well-trained and familiar with appropriate ways to obtain, organize, analyze, represent, and summarize evidence and argument.

The range of disciplines, data sources and types, and analytical approaches, naturally leads to discussions. Some of the topics considered include: the extent and role of gendered communication in online contexts, rhetorical devices such as recounting and reframing in online arguments, formal and informal representations of personal and organizational identity through signatures and graphic accents, and how online cross-national networks interact with changing geo-political boundaries and tensions. Other topics include: the salient dimensions of listserve usage, the tensions between mass and community societies and the very nature of "media use" in such contexts, aspects of CMC that foster playfulness—and perhaps "online" rape—and alter frames for interaction, tensions between security/standards and freedom/privacy in online communication, possibilities for definition and enforcement of offending online behaviors, how teleologic communication differs in nature from traditional as well as other online communication forms, and how and why "interactivity" perhaps represents the essential nature of network communication.

Finally, there's a sort of recursive discourse implied, and sometimes explicit, throughout *Network and Net Play*. This occurs on two levels.

First, the research reported here used the medium that was studied as a way of obtaining samples and collecting data. Thus, as I argued in a 1987 *Journal of Communication* article, CMC can be considered both in a traditional way as a communication medium, but also as the content itself of the process being studied—such as diffusion of innovations, or online communication. So, for example, studies that use CMC to obtain usage or content data can also be studies of the nature of CMC systems, and vice-versa.

Second, *Network and Net Play* represents a significant implication of CMC and online networks. That is, as described in the introduction, these (and other) reports were conducted by groups of researchers, across the globe, communicating through the very systems they were studying. The data were collected, organized, coded, re-organized, analyzed, debated, summarized, written-up and edited, and co-authored through the Internet. Indeed, the editors are from Australia, the United States, and Israel, and the authors range from Russia to Southern California. I, for example, obtained the draft manuscripts from Fay Sudweeks from Australia while in New Jersey, discussed the book with her at the International Communication Association conference in New Mexico, prepared and emailed suggestions from Utah, received her responses during her trips back to Australia and then Mexico, and provided my finished draft while back in New Jersey. As Hiltz and Turoff, Lievrouw and Carley, and many others have suggested, the very nature of invisible colleges and scientific communication is being transformed through CMC and global communication networks. It's clear, from discussions with the authors of *Network and Netplay* that such capabilities have both positive and negative aspects. It's equally clear that people can engage in both work and play, in traditional and new ways, using the Internet and similar networks.

Ronald E. Rice
Rutgers University
New Brunswick, New Jersey

Introduction

Sheizaf Rafaeli, Margaret McLaughlin, and Fay Sudweeks

A vast, international web of computer networks, the Internet offers millions of users the opportunity to exchange electronic mail, photographs, and sound clips; search databases for books, CDs, new cars, and term papers, take part in real-time audio- and video-conferencing, and run software on distant computers. In recent years, the fastest growing Internet application is the World Wide Web, which engages users in a rich environment of text, graphics, animation and sounds. The Web integrates most of the Internet tools. With a graphical user interface browser, the most naive computer user is able to "point and click" to retrieve information from around the globe. From a home computer, it is possible to read the New York *Times,* order chocolates from Belgium, check the weather in Australia and book a flight to Albania. This huge conglomerate of links, hyperlinks, and virtual links is not just a technology for linking computers, it is a medium for communication.

The convergence of computer and communication technologies is a social convergence as well. In global neighborhoods, people congregate and meet in chat rooms and discussion groups, conversing on topics from auto mechanics to zoology. McLaughlin, Smith, and Osborne (1995, p. 91) comment on the social implications of the new medium in their examination of Usenet newsgroups:

> The global reach of the Internet not only facilitates communication among members of existing distributed groups and teams, but perhaps more importantly it provides a medium for the formation and cultivation of new relationships through virtually instantaneous access to thousands of potential contacts who have compatible interests and spheres of expertise.

Network users can turn to more than 13,000 newsgroups (Smith, McLaughlin, and Osborne, 1997), or electronic bulletin boards, to ask for advice on parenting or to express their opinions about the Communications Decency Act, to argue about Foucault and exchange tips on fly fishing.

Furthermore, new coteries are easily created. Networked groups form virtually and on-the-fly, as common interests prompt. The computer mediated groups crystallize and disband seemingly without traditional deference to time or space differences. How much respect is offered other customary parameters of group communication? Like interpersonal communication, these networks are participatory, their content made up by their audience. Like mass-mediated communication, they involve large audiences. But the networks are neither pure mass nor purely interpersonal; they are a new phenomenon.

The emergence of computer-mediated groups poses a variety of communication issues. What is the ecology of these networks? How much do we know about the content? As with the emergence of any new medium, the question of substitution or complementation arises. And what about broad, macro-social effects of these nets: the sociology of knowledge, the social control of the manufacturing, consumption, ownership, and storage of information? And more specifically, how do the use and content of the new medium fit within the general landscape of all mediated communication? How does the mass-interpersonal-mediated-group process work?

The Internet ignites many metaphors.

Turkle (1984, 1995) uses the mirror and the screen. MacKinnon (1997), refers to Leviathan. Danet (1997) speaks of a stage. Umberto Eco (1994), in a now famous essay, invokes religious sacred texts as his driving image. Among the analogs and similies others have used are mosaics, television, the newspaper, spider-woven webs, rodent-dug tunnels, college sports-team mascots, the modern metropolis, traditional villages, the town square, democracy, anarchy, toys, serious tools, classroom, museum, marketplace, the telephone network, family, tribe, collection of overheard conversations, cocktail party, mass movement, liberating technology, slavery and substance addiction.

Something must be going on.

In our title, we choose to focus on the juxtaposition of work and play, so typical of all talk; because this book is about the Internet from a communication angle; because, paradoxically, all the metaphors used by others are appropriate; and because evidence suggests the Internet is a new way of merging the seeming opposites of mass and interpersonal, local and global, serious and frivolous, spoken and written, real and "virtual," peril and promise.

In a famous FAQ (frequently-asked-questions file) circulating on the Internet, there is an interesting attempt to define Usenet. In this file, Usenet is defined in the negative. It is defined as being "not" 13 different things. Though commonly understood as an organization, protocol, public utility, network, or software package, Chip Saltzenberg (1994) argues Usenet is none of these. In a now famous rebuttal, also circulated as a news.answers FAQ, ample arguments are provided that Usenet is, in fact, all of the things used to define it in the negative.

Worldwide, legislative and judiciary action on defining the Internet continue to escalate (see, e.g., *The Journal of Computer-Mediated Communication,* Volume 2, Whole. No. 1 and Whole No. 2). Issues such as intellectual property, decency, flaming, educational efficiency, utopian feasibility, etc. continue to capture the public's imagination. Over recent years, we've witnessed a public scandal erupting almost predictably every several weeks over one press report or another about the Internet. See, for instance, the flurry of activity surrounding a cover story in *Time* magazine about "cyberporn." This cover story in June of 1995 sparked numerous other stories in almost all news publications during the summer and fall of that year. The following year brought headlines of the debates over ratings, the Clipper chip and "Decency" legislation in the United States. Most countries are undergoing a major legislative overhaul in laws relating to communication ownership, oversight, and content regulation. Much of this legislative effort is related to the appearance of computer-mediated communication.

Whatever is going on, is interesting. However, it has so far been represented more in the popular press than in serious scholarly scrutiny.

Speaking as a self-described "uncredentialed social scientist" (p. 16), Howard Rheingold provided a "first-person word picture" of the varieties of life to be found on the Internet. He points out the importance of examining behavior on the Internet. Such study is interesting intellectually. It is important as an exercise in historical documentation, to learn how human-beings, communities and democracies are changing, to forestall vertigo and disruption, and to help cope with the emerging norms and legislation. But, Rheingold says, "all arguments about virtual community values take place in the absence of even roughly quantified systematic observation." (Rheingold, 1984, p. 64).

These chapters attempt to fill this void.

We take neither a technology-centered, nor a social-deterministic perspective. In studying new communication environments there is always the temptation to make causal claims about the effects of a particular tool or protocol. Such claims are often influenced by the marketing rhetoric of those intent on selling new devices. Or they can have roots in an idealistic zeal to oppose the ills of an innovation. We avoid making claims that the Internet "does" such and so. Instead of focusing on what the Internet *does,* the research reported here examines what the Internet *is.* On the other hand, much of the critical response to technological determinism tilts too sharply in the other direction. Often, this position argues that the real determinants of communication processes are eternal, that all new technologies flow along the same relational lines that have existed earlier, and that innovations are just new manifestations of the familiar. We do not accept this view either. One cannot ignore major new vistas opened by the Internet. New topics, audience reach, distribution and size, and the ratios of passive and active participation in conversations have all changed. The notions of "virtual communities" and "virtual communication" are no longer oxymorons.

At first glance, the enormity of the Internet, its growth and its audience almost defy study on a normal, scholarly schedule. Furthermore, the Internet has been evolving away from conversation, toward demonstration. The recent appearance of the World Wide Web, splashy multimedia uses of the Internet, and the virtual explosion of voice, color, picture and motion seemed to overshadow plain ASCII traffic in ideas and emotions, which are the subject of this volume. But the first glance is, of course, deceiving. The essence of the Internet remains mostly a medium for conversation (see McLaughlin, 1984). Interactivity is still one of the more exciting qualities of communication made possible by computer-mediated forums (Rafaeli, 1988). Interactivity remains a defining feature for conversations generally, and an especially curious one when the conversations are not held in physical proximity. Newhagen and Rafaeli (1996) discuss how the concepts of interactivity, hypertextuality, packet-switching, and asynchronicity are just as important as the multimedia, demonstration splash that seems to get so much popular attention. The social processes involved in virtual conversation continue to merit center stage. We predict that conversation, the exchange of information, ideas, views and emotion will continue to be the main thrust of communication, even as it becomes more computer-mediated.

Are we civil in using computer-mediate networks? (Mabry and Witmer address the issue of flaming in their respective chapters.) What happens when transgressions occur and we are not civil? How does the community enforce decorum? (See the chapters by MacKinnon; Smith, McLaughlin, and Osborne.) In what ways should we and do we reinterpret the social construction of real crime? Are we realistic in our expectations? (The issue of efficiency is addressed by Voiskounsky and Jones) Is virtually social as social as we used to be? (Berthold and Rafaeli and Sudweeks explore interactivity in their chapters.) How *do* we use networks, who are *we,* and how does the communication context shape a sense of community? What is the international nature of computer mediated communication? (See Voiskounsky's and Jones's chapters for discussions of Russia and Yugoslavia.) Are our genres of talking and writing evolving? (Danet, Smith, McLaughlin and Osborne, and Witmer and Katzman explore this topic in their chapters.) Last, or perhaps first, how doe we know? How do we study this new phenomenon?

In the newest perspectives on the Internet, human users and intelligent agents interact seamlessly in virtual discursive learning environments, and the community of Internet users is reconstructed as a distributed network of experts. Doyle and Hayes-Roth describe their work in integrating an autonomous agent, Merlyn, into the plain-ascii world of the multi-user dungeon (MUD). In this world, Merlyn, in his role as companion and guide, queries annotated MUD environments to fit his actions and moods to learning activities in the virtual world.

Chen and Gaines, in their chapter, construe the Internet as an expert system characterized by an incipient virtual cooperative interaction. Usenet is viewed as a form of socioware, a computer-mediated environment that supports and provides tools for community-wide information sharing and social networking.

We have collected, in this book, a set of chapters that address the mutual influences between information technology and group formation and development. Employing a variety of perspectives, and drawing on a spectrum of disciplines, the contributors search for a new theoretical middle ground between the traditional treatments of interpersonal and mediated modes of communication.

Taken together, the chapters in this book consciously steer away from the pitfalls of previous work on network mediated communication. Multiple epistemologies and methods and numerous data sets are used, mutually tolerated and considered. The chapters include content analysis, survey data, sociolinguistic case studies, and other types of data and analyses. An explicit effort is made to avoid novelty effects. Hawthorne effects of this sort threaten new communication technology studies. Early experimental studies of computer mediated communication (CMC) are obviously loaded with novelty effects because the groups for the most part are formed by the experimenters. The network users we study obviously must have at least a minimal familiarity with the technology in order to be on the Internet in the first place. Serious study of computer-mediated communication ought, therefore, to make statements about non-ephemeral phenomena that are here to stay.

Specifically, these chapters concern the communication process among large groups. Both synchronous and asynchronous groups are represented. The units of analysis encompass non-verbal, verbal, process, and social dimensions. The theories discussed refer to the communication qualities of argumentation, collaboration, and performance, tying these to group properties such as regulation and interactivity.

Many of the chapters in this collection are, in fact, a product of ProjectH, a communication process among members of a large group (see the appendix for a detailed description of this project). ProjectH was an electronic collaboration among more than one hundred scholars. Our origins as a virtual group can be traced to our common subscribership to several computer-networked mailing lists, and the subsequent creation of one of our own. Demographically, the ProjectH list consisted of scholars from twenty-one different academic disciplines, and fifteen different countries.

The project was a novel approach to groupwork as the participants had never met, either online or offline. Electronic mail, both public and private, was used for participant recruitment, distribution of information, coordination, formulation of policies, decision making, encouragement and technology transfer. Over a two-year period, we used network-supported group activity, collected data and references, and discussed these to study network-supported group activity.

Network and Netplay

CHAPTER ONE

Smile When You Say That:

Graphic Accents as Gender Markers
in Computer-mediated Communication

Diane F. Witmer and Sandra Lee Katzman

On "the Internet, nobody knows you're a dog." Thus reads the caption of a Peter Steiner cartoon (July 5, 1993, p. 61). The cartoon depicts a dog at a computer, commenting on the anonymity of computer-mediated communication (CMC). The dog's words express awareness of a key characteristic of virtual reality: that CMC can mask personal characteristics and identities of cyberspace travelers to create personal anonymity in a public arena.

Every day, millions of people collapse time and space as they travel the information superhighway, measured in nanoseconds rather than miles. They communicate via the Internet, electronic bulletin boards (BBSs), wide-area and local-area networks, and subscription services like CompuServe, America Online, GEnie, and Prodigy with synchronous and asynchronous exchanges. In their virtual travels, computer users engage in research, scholarly discourse, and social interaction, including gender-bending encounters that take advantage of the ways in which the medium can enable individuals to hide their identities.

Impersonating a member of the opposite sex is a fairly common practice in the world of CMC. Bruckman (1993) reports that both men and women are aware of extra attention female personae attract in virtual communities called MUDs (multi-user domains). As a result, men often log onto MUDs as women (Bruckman, 1993), and Curtis (1992) reports that the most sexually aggressive of the "female" MUD inhabitants often are men. How does one know whether electronic exchanges are occurring with a man or with a woman? This paper considers the possibility that the ways in which men and women communicate via computers may differ, a concept that has made the cover of *Newsweek* (Kantrowitz, 1994; Tannen, 1994), and that those differences may be discernible in the typed symbols through which computer users attempt to create shared (or unshared) meaning.

A growing number of scholars are investigating the discourse processes that seem unique to a reality constructed through CMC (e.g., Carey, 1980; Asteroff, 1987; Blackman and Clevenger, 1990; Reid, 1991; Danet and Reudenberg, 1992; MacKinnon, 1992). One of the more interesting scholarly discussions concerns how computer users create community (Sproull and Kiesler, 1991; Reid, 1991; Rheingold, 1993) or "pseudo-community" (e.g., Beniger, 1987; MacKinnon, 1992; McLaughlin, Osborne and Smith, 1995). Users create relatively consistent personae (McLaughlin, Osborne and Smith, 1995) and assume social or organizational roles (e.g., Barlow, 1990; Matheson, 1991; Reid, 1991; MacKinnon, 1992; Herring, 1993; Kramarae and Taylor, 1993), perhaps not always intentionally. Herring (1993), for example, reports gender differences in the discourse of academic computer news list participants, including quantity (males tend to send long messages), topic selection (men most frequently discuss issues; women most often contribute to personal discussions), and style (e.g., strong assertions by males, attenuated assertions by females; self-promotion by males, apologies by females; challenges by males, supportive remarks by women). Might computer-mediated discourse, then, enable a reader to discern the gender of an author in CMC?

Ever since linguist Robin Lakoff's (1973) work indicated that women use a language that is powerless, scholars have scrutinized the verbal communication styles of women and men. Quina, Wingard, and Bate (1987) confirm Lakoff's feminine language, and characterize it as higher in social warmth than masculine language. Mulac and Lundell (1986) indicate that certain language features potentially serve as linguistic gender markers, including aesthetic quality and emotional expressiveness. Bate (1988) summarizing the work of Eakins and Eakins (1978), DuBois and Crouch (1976), and Berryman-Fink (1978), concludes that gendered language styles include adjectives and adverbs to qualify or equivocate feminine discourse, and active verbs without qualifiers in masculine language (p. 95). Tannen (1990), too, indicates that women's communication tends to be more supportive and rapport-building. In contrast, she states that men typically are more report-giving and informative. Do these differences exist on a computer screen or printout? If so, they might be manifested in some of the specialized symbols that are familiar to those who engage in CMC.

Most of the literature that concerns communicative gender differences focuses on face-to-face verbal or written language, but relatively little deals with CMC. Beniger (1987) posits that technological advances are blurring the distinctions between interpersonal and mass communication, and Herring (1993) extends the concept of gendered interpersonal discourse to CMC. It is obvious, though, that in the context of a computerized medium, social structures and discursive practices are created with a narrowly-defined set of symbols. CMC systems usually support only a "low-end ASCII" character set. This means the communicator is restricted to American upper and lower case letters and numerals, and some commonly-used mathematical and punctuation symbols (e.g., "\$," "%," "()," "+," etc., omitting umlauts and other European characters). As a result, users have developed a variety of conventions, including truncated language and acronyms, many of which are unique to the medium (e.g., "PITA," representing "pain in the ass" or "FWIW" meaning "for what it's worth"), artistic or directional symbols (e.g., @>—>——- represents a rose, and <—— commonly points to the sender's name). Other textual devices (e.g., upper-case letters, asterisks, or repeated punctuation marks), co-opted from written discourse, may add emotion or color to the electronic message. Some of the aggregate symbols are called "emoticons" or "smiley faces," which are intended to represent a human face, using a colon for eyes, a hyphen for a nose, and a parenthesis for a smile or frown:

   :-)   :-(

Smileys have become widespread and diverse enough to spawn a commercial "smiley dictionary" (Sanderson and Dougherty, 1993) and a variety of electronically exchanged lists.

   Grappling with terminology for these new symbols, Stanford doctoral candidate in communication Dennis Kinsey suggested the phrase, "graphic accents" (GAs), to one of the authors (personal communication, 1993). Since the term subsumes all of the phenomena described above, it is used in this paper to refer generically to emotional, artistic, and directional devices. Because of their potential to add expressiveness, emotion, and aesthetics to written discourse, GAs are the focus of this study as possible gender markers in CMC.

Hypotheses

The research on gender differences in verbal communication is methodologically and paradigmatically uneven, but often written from a critical theory perspective. This study distinguishes between sexist discourse, which often focuses on power imbalances or domination, and discourse that simply may disclose or indicate the gender of the author. Quina, Wingard, and Bates (1987) report that nonfeminine linguistic style is perceived as lower in social warmth than feminine discourse, but Epstein (1986) proposes that gender differences are context-specific and superficial. Ganong and Coleman (1985) posit that feminine-stereotyped communication is more expressive of emotion than masculine discourse, and Ivy and Backlund (1994) support the idea that women are more expressive both verbally and nonverbally than men. Herring's (1993) findings of gender differences in academic CMC are congruent with Bate's (1988) synthesis of gendered language. Herring (1993) proposes that in general, women's computer-mediated language includes "attenuated assertions, apologies, explicit justifications, questions, personal orientation" and supportiveness (p. 8). Men, on the other hand, communicate with "strong assertions, self-promotion, presuppositions, rhetorical questions, authoritative orientation, challenges [to] others, and humor/sarcasm." An additional dimension of feminine language is aesthetic quality, (Mulac, Bradac, and Mann, 1985; Mulac and Lundell, 1986), which is identified, in part, as evidence of beauty or ugliness in the discourse. GAs, then, may serve as methods of adding emotional or emphatic expressiveness to the computer-mediated text. In aggregate, they might be used to help express emotion, equivocate, and (perhaps) add an aesthetic element to feminine discourse. This evidence leads to the hypothesis that

H1: Women use more graphic accents than men in their computer-mediated discourse.

Because the nature of an e-mail message may affect the extent to which GAs are used, it also is useful to look at other message characteristics. If men's language is more assertive than women's (Tannen, 1990; Bate, 1988), we may see more challenges or "flames" (hostile or abusive language) in their e-mail messages. If so, challenging or flaming messages may include fewer GAs. This evidence suggests the following hypotheses:

H2: Men use more challenging language than do women in computer-mediated discourse.

H3: Men flame more often than women in computer-mediated communication.

To test the hypotheses, data were collected and statistically analyzed as described in the next section of this report.

Development of the Study and Methodology

This study originated as both part of the creation and the result of an international computer-supported collaboration called simply "ProjectH." In 1992, a number of strangers converged via Bitnet around an offhand question posted to Comserve's CMC "hotline," or news list. Within weeks, the group had developed its own hotline. The first 30 members grew to a relatively stable cadre of 100-120 members, representing 15 countries and 30 academic disciplines (Sudweeks and Rafaeli, 1996). Individuals posed research questions and coding schemes; committees hammered out reliability issues, a statement of ethics, a copyright statement, and sampling techniques; and a variety of individual and collaborative studies was born. Sudweeks and Rafaeli (1996) outline the goals of ProjectH:

1. To randomly sample a sizable chunk of publicly available, archived computer-mediated group discussions.

2. To content analyze the messages contained in the sample.

3. To focus on the single message, authors, aggregate thread, and the lists as units of analysis.

4. To empirically test hypotheses of interest to members.

5. To collect descriptive data to document the state of the medium and the communication over it.

6. To conduct research in a manner unprecedented so far—working with a group of people diverse in interests, time, age, status and location.

Sudweeks and Rafaeli (1996) explain that a quantitative methodology was chosen in an effort to dovetail with laboratory-based CMC studies. ProjectH members purposely created a codebook that was as broad as possible, to accommodate a diverse range of research questions and hypotheses. To some extent, then, this study is method driven (Rafaeli, Sudweeks, Konstan, and Mabry, 1994), although one of the authors was interested in GAs early on and helped write the portion of the ProjectH codebook that focused on GAs. The codebook included, in part, three questions on GAs, the gender of the message senders (where discernible), and codings of message content.

Only individuals who actively engaged in coding the raw data were permitted access to the processed data (that is, data coded and ready for statistical analysis with computer software), which was made available via anonymous FTP. Once the data were collected, analyses of variance (ANOVAs) were used to determine whether there were differences between messages written by males and females.

Sampling

Rafaeli, Sudweeks, Konstan, and Mabry (1994) provide a detailed description of the sampling process in the ProjectH Technical Report. In brief, the data were collected over a period of months, beginning with a randomly-selected Monday (March 15, 1993), from publicly-posted newsgroups and special interest groups on the Internet and CompuServe. After excluding groups that were inappropriate for study (e.g., languages other than English, extremely low volume, etc.), groups were selected at random, and 100 messages or three days' worth of postings, whichever was greater, were gathered from each group, starting on random Mondays. ProjectH members collected a total of 3000 messages, with the intent of having each block of 100 messages coded by two coders, in order to determine reliability. Rafaeli, et al. (1994) describe the outcome:

> For various reasons, 40 per cent [sic] of potential coders were unable to code. Of
> the 37 lists (batches of 100 messages) distributed, 20 were single coded, 12 were

double coded, and 5 were not coded. Of the 32 coded, 4 were unfinished, giving a final tally of 20 single coded and 10 double coded lists. The database(s), therefore, has a total of 4000 messages from fully-completed lists, of which 3000 are unique.

Since no single person coded all the messages, and since only 1,000 of the messages were coded by two persons, it was necessary to infer interrater reliability. Ten pairs of ProjectH members coded 100 identical messages, totaling 1,000 messages from ten lists, which comprised one-third of the 3,000-message sample. The GAs were coded as three types: The first type was the "emoticon," which was defined as an icon that might express emotion, such as a smiley face or "stage direction" (e.g., <grin>, <sigh>, etc.). The second was called "emodevice," and included an irregular use of punctuation or capitalization to add drama or color to a message (e.g., !!!!!!! or #^*$@). The third type of GA that was coded was the "articon," which was strictly artistic or directional in nature, such as the arrow (<——) or rose (@>->——). Although coders originally recorded the presence and number of GAs in each message, these were recoded to indicate presence or absence of the GA. Other variables included whether or not a challenge was present (yes or no), the gender of the message author (female, male, or indeterminate), the presence or absence of a flame, and the degree to which the signature was stylized (none, simple, or complex).

Cohen's kappa was computed for each pair of coders on the variables of interest to this study. Kappa ranged from extremely low (approaching zero) to 1.0, and empty cell rows or columns in the contingency matrix rendered kappa incalculable for several variables. For gender, kappa ranged from .12 to .78, with the median .64 (STDev. .21). For the coding of emoticon across the 20 coders, kappa ranged from .03 to .88, with a median of .68 (STDev. .38). For signature, kappa was .11 to .92 with a median of .65 (STDev. .32). In coding challenge, articon, and flame2 (the second of three categories on flaming), the ten pairs of coders had high levels of agreement, often approaching 100 percent, but the empty cells produced unreadable kappa values. In general, however, the coding for these variables seemed to be the most consistently reliable between individual coders. These six variables were the only ones retained for analysis. Low interrater reliability required that a number of potentially useful variables be discarded, including emodevice and categories intended to determine levels of humor, apology, and degree of formatting in the messages.

While the method of determining interrater reliability was unorthodox, it nonetheless provided a reasonably good picture of the general reliability of the coded data. The double-coded lists represent one-third of the data set; they are well-distributed, in terms of the natures of the lists; and they represent the work of half of the total number of coders. Once reliability was determined, the duplicate sample batches were randomly eliminated from the database, leaving a total of 3000 unique messages.

Results

Descriptive statistical analysis revealed that of the 3,000 messages, gender could be determined in only 2,599. Of these, the overwhelming majority of message authors, 83.6 percent, were male, and 16.4 percent were female. Of the 3,000 messages, 396 (13.2 percent) included GAs (emoticons or articons). The genders of 53 authors (13.4 percent) of GA-containing messages were unknown. Of the remaining 343 messages that contained GAs and for which the gender of the author could be determined, females posted 102 (29.7 percent), and males posted 241 (70.3 percent).

To test the hypotheses, a 2(gender) x 2(flame) x 2(challenge) factorial ANOVA and t-tests were conducted on the 343 GA-containing messages for which the author's gender could be identified. Since there were unequal numbers of males and females, and because a similar imbalance occurs naturally in the general population of online users, the technique of randomly deleting cases to yield equal n's was discarded. Instead, the "regression approach" in SPSS was used for the ANOVA, which is the most conservative method of adjusting for unequal n's (Tabachnick and Fidell, 1989, pp. 339-342).

Results of the t-tests are summarized in table 1. The findings indicated that females used GAs significantly more often than males [$t(341) = 4.51$, $p = .0000$], included more challenges in their messages [$t(341) = 5.66$, $p =. 0000$], and flamed more than men [$t(341) = 6.45$, $p = .0000$].
Results of the factorial ANOVA on GAs indicated significant main effects for flaming [$F(1,335) = 36.724$, $p. = .0000$] but not for gender [$F(1,335) = 3.361$, $p = .068$] or challenge [$F(1,335) = 2.857$, $p = .092$]. It also revealed a two-way interaction between gender and flaming [$F(1,335) = 8.950$, $p <.001$] and a three-way interaction between gender, flaming, and challenge [$F(1,335) = 7.041$, $p = .0000$].

Discussion

The first hypothesis, that females use GAs more than males, is partially supported by the data. Neither males nor females use GAs to any great extent, as indicated by GAs being identified in only 396 of the 3,000 messages—13.2 percent of the total sample. The results indicate, however, that the computer users who do include GAs in their discourse tend to be women. The use of articons and emoticons primarily by females suggests that the aesthetic quality reported by Mulac, et al. (Mulac, Bradac, and Mann, 1985; Mulac and Lundell, 1986) and (possibly) expression of emotion translates to the computer-mediated environment.

The data do not support the second and third hypotheses, that men use

Variable	t	p
Use of GAs	4.51	.0000
Inclusion of challenges	5.66	.0000
Use of flames	6.45	.0000

Table 1. Summary of Results (N=343) Gender Differences in CMC.

more challenging language and flame more often than women. Although the literature indicates that men might be more likely to flame or challenge, the opposite is true in this sample population. The unexpected difference between women and men in flames and challenges may be a result of a status-leveling effect of CMC (Sproull and Kiesler, 1991). One explanation for this might be that women feel more at ease in the relatively anonymous electronic environment. Another possibility is that the women who currently engage in CMC already are involved in male-dominated endeavors such as high-tech organizations and academia. These women may not represent the discursive praxis of women in general nor their places in a still male-dominated power structure. Finally, it is possible that if women are more expressive of emotion than men, a comparison between their uses of supportive or equivocal language also will indicate significant differences. Since the interrater reliability for apology was not high enough to include it in this study, we don't know if women apologize as well as challenge in CMC.

This study has several limitations. First, because of the way in which ProjectH evolved, many of the research questions and hypotheses arose during the process of data collection. The codebook, sampling method, and ethics statement were each collaborative efforts that involved compromise. Furthermore, not all ProjectH members were involved in all phases of the data collection or codebook development. As a result, the data do not include codings for some variables that might inform this study. Second, while a content analytic approach has the advantage of being unobtrusive and permitting the collection of a large sample, it also has the disadvantage of forcing the researcher to guess or infer why some phenomena occur (e.g., are emoticons used to attenuate or emphasize message content; are they simply manifestations of playfulness? do they serve as a form of shorthand? are they substitutes for writing skills?). Third, interrater reliability remains problematic. While many of the paired codings seemed respectably congruent, the unprecedented ProjectH collaboration presents new methodological challenges. Coder training consisted of a detailed codebook, but the training and clarifications were conducted exclusively via e-mail. This method had the advantage of automatically providing coders with documents they could print out for later reference, but also limited the early discussions and clarifications that occur when coders are trained in face-to-face settings.

In spite of the limitations, this study raises some questions about the ways in which women and men communicate in the computer-mediated environment. Why do women tend to challenge and flame in this group of CMC users, rather than use the supportive and qualifying language we expect in face-to-face settings? What purpose, beyond being cute, does the smiley serve? How do keyboard, writing, and computer skills affect the use of graphic accents? It seems clear that the information superhighway is paving a road to new forms of discourse, offering communication scholars a rich field for study.

CHAPTER TWO

Frames and Flames

The Structure of Argumentative
Messages on the Net

Edward A. Mabry

This study represents an exploratory investigation of how message texts generated in computer-mediated groups reflect applications of stylistic tactics and related choices in message construction when communicators disagree or argue. The primary message convention of interest was the use of the argumentative technique known as argument framing; that is, juxtaposing previous arguments with new refutational arguments in counterargumentative messages. A diverse sample of messages obtained from computer-mediated discussion groups active on the Internet (e.g., Bitnet, Usenet, Compuserve) were examined. The aim of the study was to investigate how differences in communicator goals, as evidenced by perceived differences in the affective-linguistic intensity of a message, were related to message construction decisions like those used to assert or counterargue a stance, to induce a change in the position held by another, and other correspondingly appropriate subjective and objective message characteristics (e.g., confrontiveness, references/quotations of preceding messages, propensities to resolve or intensify a dispute).

Participation in Computer-Mediated Groups

Growing use of computer-mediated communication (CMC) is being fostered by the increasing popularity of and expanding access to the global computer communications network known as the Internet (or, net). The popularity of the Internet network is due to the inexpensive and efficient means of relaying electronic files (containing correspondence, documents, catalogs, or databases) and multimedia images (video and audio signals) for users of desktop computing equipment with network access.

Internet use has increased as network members have created and maintained a wide variety of specialized discussion groups for exchanging messages using electronic mail. These electronic groupings vary in their formality and conversationlike continuity of message exchanges (Sudweeks, Collins, and December, 1995). Group membership and participation is dynamic. Some function as electronic mailing lists—or bulletin boards—for distributing and seeking information (often used by professional and technical organizations). Many list groups are rather structured and formal using volunteer moderators that screen contributions for topical appropriateness and politeness. The majority of list groups are loosely structured, unmoderated entities created as a vehicle for exchanging information and opinion on a specific thematic issue. Topics run the gamut of interests ranging from computer security encryption programming to entertainers (e.g., Madonna). While most communication in list groups is prescribed, some groups can be rather experimental, personal, and permissive—either by design or through the concerted influences of members.

Many of these affinity groups represent relatively open communication environments that only loosely conform to the topical identities originally projected by their organizers, whose computer facilities often support the message distribution system (Rheingold, 1993). Permissive environments tacitly, if not actively, encourage the airing of controversies and usually evidence substantial tolerance in supporting ongoing arguments and disputes.

Argumentative exchanges among net group members are quite prevalent. The intensity and deviancy of such disembodied exchanges can become so heated and destructive (Hiltz et. al., 1989) that norms of network usage (referred to as netiquette), inculcated and reinforced among net users, specifically address the diligence users should display in how they write argumentative messages. These norms stress obligations for group and self-monitoring to insure that members maintain civility and communicative relevance (Kiesler et al., 1985; Lea et al., 1992). One frequently sanctioned breach of netiquette involves flames: messages that are precipitate, often personally derogatory, ad hominem attacks directed toward someone due to a position taken in a message distributed (posted) to the group (Siegal, Dubrovsky, Kiesler, and McGuire, 1986).

Argumentative Message Structure

The apparent acceptance, if not cultivation, of argumentative discourse in computer-mediated discussion groups stands in sharp contrast to the conventions of ordinary social conversation. Conversation theorists and researchers convincingly demonstrate that conversants typically display a "preference for agreement" in social interaction (Brown and Levinson, 1978; Holtgrave,

1986; McLaughlin, 1984). This paradox is compelling. Mediated groups are susceptible to more extensive, and often more intense, amounts of argumentative discussion than face-to-face groups (Kiesler and Sproull, 1992; Weisband, 1992). Conversely, routine social practices governing conversation are grounded in taken-for-granted assumptions of agreement and conciliatory behavior. And there is little reason to doubt that computer mediated messaging emulates primary linguistic characteristics of face-to-face interactions (Selfe and Meyer, 1991; Spitzer, 1986). The question arises as to how mediated groups manage this more adversarial communication context while retaining the discursive coherence and cohesiveness necessary for enacting socially appropriate rational discourse.

A strategy that has been proposed for maintaining the structural coherence of conversational arguments in face-to-face interaction is the practice known as recounting (Govier, 1985; Snoeck Hankemans, 1989, 1991). Recounting is the restating or summarizing of an opponent's position (including supporting or refutational stances) in the construction of one's own refutational or counter-refutational message. Snoeck Hankemans (1991) proposed that recounts may act to strengthen argument either indirectly or directly. Indirect advantage is gained by linking a refutational claim to the opponent's argument (should the claim be successful) with a reassertion of one's own stance. This combines a potentially successful attack with a potentially successful argumentative defense. Direct contribution to refutations of argumentative claims advanced by others is made in the juxtapositioning of counterclaims and supports. This structure amplifies the arguer's counter-refutation. It serves to punctuate an arguer's role-switching in moving between being the defender of a position and an attacker of the claims and counter-claims advanced by the other disputant.

Enactment of such strategies is interpretively similar to Bateson's (1972) conception of the perceptual "framing" that individuals engage in as they construe social situations. Bateson analogized this phenomenon to the principle of figure-ground separation in perception. He claimed perceivers make distinctions between the stream of interaction and specific elements in the stream they believe warrant separate and/or immediate interpretation and response. Thus, a frame-of-reference is the perceptual differentiation called into use by drawing the social landscape (background) against which particular people, events, behaviors (figures) are compared. According to Bateson, frames provide important and unique bits of social information and contribute to metacommunication.

Aside from Snoeck Henkemans' theoretical explication, there has been little direct examination of argumentative framing. Indirect support for its plausibility is evident in studies of interlocution and conversational arguments (Antaki and Leudar, 1992). For instance, Holtgraves' (1986) examination of speech acts has shown that conversational rejoinders interact with speakers' face needs. Assertive rejoinders (moves aimed as directing the speaker's attention back to a question not coherently answered) were perceived as more likely to occur in non-face-threatening episodes. Accepting rejoinders (non-confrontational moves in the presence of discoherent enactments) were more probable in face-threatening situations. Predictably, accepting rejoinders were always perceived as more polite than assertive rejoinders.

Studies of small group influence recognize the importance of discussants' reactions to decision proposals, task opinions, and similar issues that often lead to arguments and group conflict. Alderton and Frey (1986) proposed using argumentative responses as an index of the impact of group arguments. Mabry and his colleagues (Mabry, Jackson, McPhee, and VanLear, 1990; Mabry, VanLear, Jackson, and McPhee, 1991) created and tested a method for analyzing group arguments that explicitly measured the extent of responsiveness to a preceding message that was present in a succeeding speaker's argumentative message.

Research comparing computer-mediated groups to face-to-face groups also provides indirect clues to message strategies that may be in play when members attempt to influence group outcomes. Weisband (1992) has shown that advocacy sequences produce different outcomes in mediated versus face-to-face groups. Advocates in face-to-face groups, and early advocates in mediated groups, were significantly more likely to converge toward a group opinion. Third advocates (the final person in three-person groups) in computer-mediated groups were more likely to retain and express their pregroup opinions regardless of how discrepant that stance had become by the time it was made public.

Kiesler and Sproull (1992) noted similar processes in their assessment of mediated decision-making groups. They interpreted such patterns to be a concomitant of the more complex social organization required of mediated groups. Members often are simultaneously inputting messages. Some advocacy effects ultimately appear to be the result of asynchrony. However, mediated groups also strive to accommodate diversity of participation. Thus, members may not initially respond to primacy effects while they are enacting turn-taking sequences. Therefore, time or other response latencies may dilute the primacy effects of first advocates and significantly increase the likelihood that later advocates will influence group thinking.

The Human-Technology Interface in CMC

One aspect of participating in CMC systems could be unique with respect to its impact on the structure of argumentative discourse. Virtually all systems software supporting the electronic mail (email) function on which network communication is based includes so-called "cut-and-paste" message editing features. The combination of electronic filing, making it possible to save exchanged messages, and efficient keyboard editing utilities affords computer-mediated interactants access to very powerful message construction tools. These tools, however, are not uniform in the amount of knowledge or physical effort (e.g., keystrokes) they require.

An arguer can easily create a new message, say a counterargument to a position advanced in a previously distributed message, by inserting segments of the disputed message along with counterclaims the arguer wishes to advance. In this way, edited insertions (when they are used) function as strategic recounts and frame the arguer's discursive moves.

The following is an example of a brief, modestly confrontational exchange of email messages, employing cut-and-paste editing:

#: 312513 S14/Chatter
16-Mar-93 13:54:29
Sb: #312252-#Babylon 5
Fm: <Pseudonym *A*>
To: <Pseudonym *B*>

>>>The "logging arc" had a rather curious creative problem, being that at its heart is was a parody of something which the general public had not seen yet.<<<

Do you think that arc was an out and out parody of TWIN PEAKS? It had some of that flavor, I agree, but I didn't see it that way.

>>>But, it did have David Straithairn, which is a positive point in anything.<<<

Which player was he?

Note. Text segments in >>><<< are cut and pasted inserts from a message received from B by the message sender A. The message is an actual message taken from the database used in this study.

The arguer *(A)*, in the context of an exchange of messages regarding impressions of television programs, disagrees with an interpretation of a plotline advanced by another discussant *(B)*. The left (<) and right (>) angle brackets are used as graphical markers by *A* to display the segment of *B's* message that *A* wishes to counterargue. *A's* counterclaim, in ordinary sentence formatting that visually sets it apart as a separate—yet concatenated—message act, follows immediately below *B's* bracketed text.

Also interesting to note in this example is *A's* use of cut-and-paste editing to accomplish a different goal. A second bracketed text segment of *B's* message is followed by a question from *A* seeking clarifying information from *B*. Both of *A's* reactions function as inducements for *B* to send a responding message to *A* on this topic. Thus, *A's* message signals both an interest and a willingness by *A* to continue the mediated dialogue with *B*—even if there was a point of contention on the floor.

Research Objectives and Hypotheses

Little is known about communicators' uses of software supported message framing devices in the enactment of online arguing. Especially interesting are the implications of this form of message construction in the management of interaction involvement and maintenance of rationally versus emotionally driven argumentative stances. Message editing is a rationalistic activity requiring concentration and attention to the content of arguers' language and reasoning choices. Conversely, emotionally intense messages, especially negative ones that are often perceived as flames, seem ill-suited to the cognitive demands of message editing. Enacting highly rationalized argumentative strategies, juxtaposing claims and counterclaims in a complex message, requires a deliberateness that would escape most arguers in the heat of battle.

It is assumed a message's relational implications, particularly argumentative convergence (or divergence), is related to message structure. Positive or negative emotional overtones should evoke less internally structured messages. Likewise, rational and emotional message characteristics ought to be linearly related to the confrontational intensity. These assumptions lead to the following hypothesis:

- *Hypothesis 1:* Message framing and message continuity evoking strategies should be curvilinearly related to message intensity.

It follows that message structure and coherence should be related to other message characteristics like compositional style and purpose. Message structure is only one facet of message content. Different message content strategies could be used in conjunction with varying levels of emotionality. In general, message content like appeasement, conciliation, or aggressiveness, should be linearly related to message emotionality. Thus, the second hypothesis of the study asserts:

- *Hypothesis 2:* There is a positive (negative) linear relationship between message connotativeness and message intensity.

Methods

This study was conducted as part of an international project in computer-mediated collaborative research. The project, initiated in May 1992, was the outgrowth of a mediated group discussion on organizational communication over the Comserve system's Internet "hotline" (sponsored by the Communication Institute for Online Scholarship). Over a period of months, basic research objectives and methodological practices were decided. The principal goal of the project was to facilitate the investigation of actual computer-mediated messaging activities in Internet computer-mediated discussion groups. A thorough explanation of the project is contained in Sudweeks and Rafaeli (1996).

Message Sampling

A complete discussion of sampling is available in Rafaeli et al. (1994) and will be abbreviated here. Various computer bulletin boards, lists, and newsgroups were canvassed for a period of approximately one month. Messages were randomly sampled across days and times. Sampling of a given group terminated when a target of 100 messages was collected. Messages were sampled beginning on a randomly chosen Monday (March 15, 1993), and took, in some cases, up to six months before the target number of messages was reached. Only lists in English were retained for the message pool. Approximately 3000 messages, from 30 different online discussion groups, have been coded and comprise the project's database.

Message Coding

A standardized message content analysis coding protocol was collaboratively developed by participating project members in the first year of their work together. The content analysis scheme measured 46 message variables of which 40 were hand-coded and 6 were machine coded. The coding protocol required trained coders to read the literal text of a message and apply all code variables to each message (wherever possible). A message was evaluated on whether it contains content descriptive of facts, opinions, humour, challenges, metacommunications, presence of graphic art, formality of composition, quoted material, emotional tone (or flames), and sender characteristics (e.g., gender, status) (see Rafaeli et. al., 1994, for more on message analysis categories).

More than 40 people participated as coders. Coders were furnished with a codebook (distributed electronically) and provided with on-line training activities and guidance. Training involved coding a set of sample messages chosen to cover the range of code variables. Coders rated the messages and returned their results via electronic mail. Low concordance on the training sample of messages led to additional coaching and more training messages being sent for test coding.

High agreement with the preferred responses to training messages qualified the person as coder for the purpose of receiving messages to be analyzed in the main study. Coders were sent sets of 100 messages. Along with a message set, coders were supplied with various reporting style formats for submitting their work and a post-task questionnaire requesting impressions of the list coded and information about their coding and reporting practices. Completed sets of formatted codes were returned via electronic file transfer to a host computer system. Work was automatically screened using custom software to debug technical errors (e.g., off line formats, typographical errors) and any rejected codes were sent back to the coder for correction.

Reliability

Given the methodological approach taken in the project, coding reliability is important and rather difficult to assess. Online discussions among researchers indicated that initial efforts at establishing reliability proved inconsistent. Primary difficulties were encountered as both listwise (sampled group) and variable-specific results yielded outcomes with high variances and, for some variables, modest to low reliability values.

Two conventional methods for assessing reliability were used: Brennan and Prediger's (1981) modification to Cohen's kappa, $k(n)$, coefficient and Cronbach's (1951) alpha coefficient. The $k(n)$ coefficient permits an assessment of interrater reliability under conditions where marginal values of an n x n coding matrix are free to vary. Kappa was computed for all variables used in this study. Alpha was computed for items that were treated as scaleable. Reliability and descriptive information for variables needed in testing study hypotheses is contained in table 1.

A sample of 1,000 messages comprising 100 messages from each of 10 computer-mediated discussion groups/lists, were double-coded and thus constituted the data for computing reliability analyses. Because coders were not fixed across lists, reliability calculations were performed on a listwise basis (for each 100 cross-coded message sample) and averaged. Listwise alpha coefficients could not be computed for conciliation and challenges variables due to attentuated variances caused by high percentages of agreement among coders (in excess of 90 percent). Bracketed entries in table 1 show the number of lists used in deriving mean alpha coefficients. Two variables, opinion and fact, did not attain acceptable $k(n)$ coefficients and were dropped from the analyses. Both items were related to the test of hypothesis 2. However, neither item was deemed critical to an adequate test of the hypothesis as salient information from other variables was available for the analyses.

Statistical Analyses

The primary analytic strategy was to assess the influence of a message's emotional tone (its level of argumentativeness) on message structure and attribute variables. Consistent with hypothesis 1, it was expected that emotional tone would not be linearly related to message variables measuring argumentative framing tactics. The framing tactics are reflected in message dependency (referencing of previously distributed messages) and length of quotations (the amount of previous message material inserted into a coded message). The hypothesis was tested using univariate trend analyses with

Independent variables			Dependent variables						
			Hypothesis 1						
Emotional tone			*Message dependency*			*Quotations (lines)*			
	n	%		n	%		n	%	
Neutral	1765	58.8	None	907	30.2	None	2115	70.5	
Friendly	767	25.6	1 message	1600	53.3	1-10	666	22.2	
Diverging	205	6.8	2+ messages	178	5.9	11-25	163	5.4	
Disagreeing	125	4.2	Series	302	10.1	26+	49	1.6	
Tension	65	2.2	k(n) = 0.592			k(n) = 0.882			
Antagonism	46	1.5	alpha(8) = 0.609			alpha (7) = 0.833			
Hostility	20	0.7							
k(n) = .525			*Hypothesis 2*						
alpha (6) = .670			*+/- Coalescence*			*Apology*			
				n	%		n	%	
			Strong agreement	156	5.6	None	2802	93.4	
			Mild agreement	229	7.0	Mild	139	4.6	
			None	2087	69.6	Full	52	1.7	
			Agree/Disagree	141	4.7	k(n) = 0.940			
			Mild disagreement	254	8.5	alpha (6) = 0.778			
			Strong disagreement	126	4.2				
			k(n) = 0.525						
			alpha (7) = 0.749						
			Conciliation			*Challenges*			
				n	%		n	%	
			None	2865	95.5	No	2877	95.9	
			Avoids tension	60	2.0	Yes	116	3.9	
			Reduces tension	68	2.3	k(n) = 0.950			
			k(n) = 0.948						

Note. Percentages may not sum to 100 percent due to missing data. Numbers in [] are number of online groups for which Cronbach's alpha could be computed. Emotional tone is the only independent variable tested in hypotheses 1 and 2.

Table 1. Reliability and descriptive statistics for variables analyzed .

emotional tone as the independent variable (Kerlinger and Pedhazur, 1973).

Hypothesis 2 asserted that message attributes consistent with seeking positional convergence or divergence should be linearly related to emotional tone. This hypothesis also could be tested using univariate trend analyses with emotional tone as the independent variable and coalescence, apology and conciliation as dependent variables. Additionally, a measure of verbalized challenges in messages was judged as too range restricted for entry into the trend analysis. It was addressed in a chi square analysis that compared it with the emotional tone variable.

Results—Hypothesis 1: Message Framing

Hypothesis 1 tests for curvilinearity in message dependency (continuity with past messages) and amounts of quoted material (necessary in argument framing) as a function of message intensity.

Emotional tone	Message dependency		Quotation	
	Mean	SD	Mean	SD
Neutrality	1.71	0.78	1.26	0.54
Friendliness	2.23	0.87	1.40	0.64
Diverging	2.27	0.78	1.78	0.87
Disagreement	2.37	0.85	1.74	0.83
Tension	2.39	0.93	1.89	1.00
Antagonism	2.89	1.04	1.97	0.95
Hostility	2.05	1.05	2.05	1.32

Table 2. Means and standard deviations for variables tested in hypothesis 1.

Message Dependency

The trend analysis confirmed the hypothesis concerning a curvilinear relationship between emotional tone and message dependency. The weighted quartic ANOVA was significant (F [1,2980] = 30.62, p < .0001). Multiple range tests using the conservative Scheffe method (Winer, 1971) revealed a significant ($p < .05$) increment in the amount of references to prior messages between affectively neutral messages compared to messages observed to be diverging, friendly, disagreeing, evoking tension; message referencing also was significantly higher in antagonistic messages compared to neutral, hostile, diverging, friendly, and disagreeing messages. As the pattern of means in table 2 indicates, dependency increased as a message's emotional tone became increasingly negative but tended to flatten out between disagreement and antagonism, ultimately dropping off at the point where a message was overtly hostile.

Quotation

A similar relationship between Eemotional tone and quotation linage could not be established. The weighted linear ANOVA trend model was highly signficant (F (1,2986) = 266.95, $p < .0001$). The distribution of means corroborates the ANOVA results (table 2). The upward trend for increasing length of quoted material insertions into messages is broken only by a plateauing between diverging and disagreement after which the linear trend re-emerges and continues unbroken.

Results—Hypothesis 2
Message Content Characteristics

The shape of relationships between message characteristics and emotional tone were tested using four message variables: positive and negative coalescence, conciliatory statements, apologies, and challenges.

Positive/Negative Coalescence

The ANOVA trend analysis results for coalescence were curvilinear, rather than linear as predicted, thereby failing to confirm the hypothesis. The value of the weighted quintic term was $F (1,899) = 18.32, p < .0001$. The shape of the trend, as reflected in the patterns of significant Scheffe comparisons between means showed a double-bend, or wave, pattern across levels of emotional tone (table 3). Messages rated as neutral, friendly, or hostile were also more likely to contain bids for agreement or convergence in positions compared to diverging, disagreeing, tension-evoking, or antagonistic messages. The mean for coalescence returned to a point of mild agreement from nearly a plateau point of strong disagreement. As might be expected, coalescence means for emotional neutrality and hostility explained most of the variance in significant Scheffe comparisons of mean range distributions. Hostile messages containing agreements, capitulations, or compromises are relatively complex messages. Thus, these results indicate greater message complexity is being signaled in the coalescence scale than was initially predicted.

Conciliatory Statements

Results for the trend analysis of the relationship of emotional tone with communicators' use of conciliatory statements also were not in the expected direction. The ANOVA analysis resulted in a significant weighted quadratic trend: $F (1,2987) = 37.90, p < .0001$. The pattern of significant Scheffe pairwise mean comparisons emulated a classic arching configuration showing greater intensity of conciliation as emotional tone turned more negative. Emotional neutrality and friendliness were associated with significantly fewer expressions of conciliation than divergence, disagreement or tension containing messages. However, the intensity of conciliatory behavior again significantly increased as message content also included tense, antagonistic, or hostile argumentative statements.

The result parallels findings on face needs and message rejoinder positiveness (Holtgrave, 1986). Apparently, the presence of norms regulating latitudes of verbal aggressiveness and/or invectiveness between Internet communicators does produce a self-vigilant attitude. Interlocutors showed a clear tendency to craft messages that combine assertives with cues to indicate that seeking convergence or agreement is a preferred relational state. And, consistent with findings for coalescence, message complexity indicated that rather dissimilar levels of affectivity were being enacted in the same message.

Emotional tone	Apology		Coalescence		Conciliation	
	Mean	SD	Mean	SD	Mean	SD
Neutrality	1.06	0.27	2.17	1.01	1.01	0.15
Friendliness	1.06	0.28	2.37	1.15	1.05	0.29
Diverging	1.10	0.37	3.57	0.81	1.18	0.53
Disagreement	1.12	0.41	4.24	0.98	1.16	0.50
Tension	1.34	0.67	3.83	1.40	1.43	0.72
Antagonism	1.35	0.71	4.10	1.22	1.61	0.88
Hostility	1.80	0.83	2.16	1.27	1.75	0.79

Table 3. Means and standard deviations for variables tested in hypothesis 2.

Apology

ANOVA trend analysis results for the use of apology revealed a strong quadratic trend (F (1,2986) = 56.55, $p < .0001$). Inspection of means for level of Apology (table 3) included in the composition of a message clearly indicates that apologizing intensity escalates with message confrontiveness. The quadratic form of the results points to a clear interaction between emotional tone and apology that is supported by the pattern of Scheffe mean comparison results. Mean rates of apologies did not register significant changes until the emotional tenor of a message reached at least a perceived state of tension display. Thus, the perceived affect level of a message probably must shift towards a more negative bias before apologizing seems warranted.

Challenges

The chi square analysis of emotional tone and Challenges did reach statistical significance: $X2(6) = 250.89$, $p < .0001$. However, contrary to the implicit rationale of the hypothesis, Challenges decreased as emotional tone shifted from positive to negative poles. Thus, for instance, there were three times as many challenges in messages rated "friendly" ($f = 31$; 26.7%) compared to messages rated "hostile" ($f = 10$; 8.6%).

Discussion

This study was an initial investigation into the efficacy of applying conceptualizations derived from the study of oral conversation and discourse practices to messages exchanged among members of computer-mediated discussion lists and groups. Specifically, it focused on strategic message structuring tactics used in explicitly and symbolically framing arguments that a communicator attempts to counterargue. Additionally, the study hypothesized that certain message content enhancements ought to be linearly related to argument and confrontation and would be present in the CMC messages studied.

Framing strategies have unique and powerful applications in argumentative discourse. It was observed that computer-mediated communicators have unique systemic resources that allow the use of framing in mediated discourse. Furthermore, it was hypothesized that framing strategies were most likely related to the emotional tenor of a disputant's message. The speaker's emotional involvement, argumentativeness, was hypothesized to be curvilinearly related to framing strategies. Framing was expected to rise and rational disputation increase, but plateau, and then decline, as a speaker's emotional involvement transgressed beyond appropriate levels of affect and discursive moves.

The results of an analysis of 3000 messages obtained from a diverse sample of computer-mediated discussion groups and forums, provided partial support for the hypothesized relationships. A communicator's emotional involvement and use of message framing devices (making pointed references to prior messages and quoting from those messages) are systematically related.

The study also tested hypothesized relationships between the communicator's emotional involvement in their communication goals and their use of communication practices that can facilitate or impede the development and strengthening of personal relationships. Although not linearly related to a message's emotional tone as hypothesized, being conciliatory and apologetic increased as message affect increased. Thus, there is some reason to believe that communicators try to neutralize the effects of negative emotional spirals when they arise. However, the study also found evidence that communicators are just as likely to move towards polarizing sentiments in a dispute. Messages seeking positive or negative coalescence on an issue were significantly related to a message's perceived emotional tone. And, in a somewhat surprising finding, communicators used more confrontive challenging messages when a message was low in affective tenor.

The implications of these findings are intriguing. First, they clearly indicate that computer-mediated discourse contains message structuring devices similar to those found in (or recommended for use in) face-to-face interaction. Conversational and argumentative structuring is apparent in mediated groups. Technologies supporting mediated groups appear to offer certain resources that facilitate the use of complex and adaptive message strategies for enacting social argumentation. Moreover, face-to-face communicators often appear to have only weak command over similar strategic tactics or experience less powerful outcomes when the applications are solely reliant on orality versus textuality.

Second, as Antaki and Leudar (1992) cogently reason, there is an apparent duality in discourse that is also found in both face-to-face conversations and computer-mediated interactions. Dialogues of all sorts often turn from platforms for agreement to exchanging of claims (contentions) and counterclaims. These moves are accomplished as cooperative, but argumentative, dialogue games. The dynamic tension between constructing a dialogue versus constructing an argument, when it is played out between the same interactants, sets constraints on the emotional tone in messages. One device for recognizing these constraints is juxtaposing polarized claim-making with moves for conciliation or tension reduction. These message patterns may have two very different implications. On the one hand, they may reflect a threshold-setting tactic where a disputant claims the most radical position and uses its extremity as a negotiating lever. Conversely, juxtaposing interaction intensity with opportunities for argumentative convergence (requisite for moving back to a dialogue) may be a necessary pragmatic move that signals a recognition that the emotional tone of an exchange of messages is moving towards, or has reached, unacceptable levels.

Third, results support the efficacy of applying conceptual models of communication developed for explaining face-to-face interaction to mediated environments. This is another instance of corroboration for the utility of mediated communication providing communication resource opportunities similar to those expected from face-to-face interaction. And it adds validity to the notion of including mediated environments in the range of social contexts for which communication processes need to be accounted (Kiesler and Sproull, 1992).

Finally, as was apparent in the discussion of producing satisfactory reliability analyses for this very unique database, there is a need to revisit underlying assumptions of currently popular methodological practices. Clearly, the nature of the team effort responsible for obtaining these data also created unique problems in ensuring empirical consistency without an inordinate loss of efficiency. These are more than practical problems of execution. They speak to the inherent complexities of collaborative enterprises that are only beginning to emerge in and out of academia (Galegher, Kraut, and Egido, 1990). Understanding both the adaptive potential and constraints that confront users of CMC systems is integral to competent performance as a communicator. Seeking out new ways to compare and benchmark communication in CMC seems essential for developing insights about the effective use of the technology and the impact it will have on human relationships.

CHAPTER THREE

Telelogue Speech

Alexander E. Voiskounsky

Human psychological development is strongly based on the mediation and remediation of actions performed. New technologies give birth to (or at least transform) accompanying sign systems needed to administer or to use new complicated products. This is especially evident if we take into consideration emerging telecommunication technologies, as they transform human-to-human contacts and connections. Of all mediation tools, speech signs are the most natural and significant, promoting mental transformations and development. The description of specific attributes inherent in the new ways of adapting to new technologies precedes the purely psychological research of human mental development. The aim of this chapter is to explore the attributes of computer-mediated speech usage.

The most common usage of computer mediated communication (CMC) systems is for exchanging messages (e-mail). E-mail messages include printed texts plus graphic images and sometimes sounds (music, voice, etc.). Messages can be sent both to a single receiver, and to world-wide distributed groups of network users. Speakers of numerous ethnic languages are involved in CMC, and for inter-ethnic communication English is mostly used. The existing status of English as a universally adopted medium of communication has thus been approved once more.

There are two possible reasons for the choice of English as a universal computer-mediated language. First, CMC originated in an English speaking country, namely the USA. Second, network communication facilities were enhanced in the R&D community which, for decades, purposely used English as a common language. Other significant factors might be noted. From the very beginning, the majority of network community members were, and still are, North Americans (mostly native English speakers) who could afford computers and connection expenses more easily than citizens of many other countries. Next, representatives of small nations never expect that their ethnic language will be universally understood, so they use English readily. Non-English speaking nations do not expect that the international community will adapt numerous keyboards and drivers to monitor hieroglyphs (as in Chinese or Japanese), or non-Latin alphabetical signs (as in Russian or Arabic), or accents, umlauts, and other diacritical marks (as in Spanish, French, or German). Thus, for many reasons English happens to be an optimal option.

The new media influence sign systems, even quite traditional ones, used to generate and comprehend messages. These systematic influences are being thoroughly analyzed by communication researchers. Computers mediate human communication and at the same time influence it. Mediated communication via computer networks has been called *telelog* (Ball-Rokeach and Reardon, 1988). Telelog (or telelogue) is an apt term since it refers to both *distant* and to *communication,* and it was originally a new term for denoting communication processes. The term is therefore adopted in this chapter to refer to CMC.

Mediation Problem in Psychology

CMC research is in the same tradition as the cultural and historical lines of psychological investigation, formulated first by Vygotsky (1962). Complex psychological processes and functions might be represented as mediated mental acts, and the development of mental processes means that they are mediated and remediated. Vygotsky stressed that mental development is a social and historical (in the context of individual history) process, as a child acquires mental skills in a social environment. Thus both social and material (nonsocial) environments induce the development and enrichment of mediating processes, forming higher mental functions.

The mediation process consists of using and acquiring tools, instruments and (mostly) signs, as well as semiotic systems. The signs were taken to represent internal tools mediating human behavior. Vygotsky described rather primitive ways of mediation, such as the use of knotted ropes as a mnemonic device practiced by the Incas (South American Indians), and the use of ritual sticks discovered among the Australian aborigines. These external tools lead to the functioning of an internalization process, which is a means of forming higher mental functions. Thus the process of acquisition of new tools (being performed in inner or external activity processes) is taken as a major factor of psychological development. External tools (both material objects and ideal signs) being internalized make the core of inner mental mechanisms.

The sociocultural school founded by Vygotsky (1962, 1978) is highly regarded in general and developmental psychology. Vygotsky paid much attention to the role of speech in mental development. Prominent research on verbal signs as mediating and regulative mental mechanisms was performed by his disciples (Luria, 1961; Luria, 1976). For decades the psychologists were preoccupied with the investigation of the intricacies of the internalization processes. Now it is equally important to investigate the exteriorization processes. This need is based on major new trends in high technology development, and mostly in telecommunications. The mediation process is escalating and accelerating.

Quite new (and modernized old as well) mediator tools are vying for individual and/or group forms of activity. Restricting oneself to communication processes, these tools include audio and video conferences, e-mail, voice mail, Usenet newsgroups, videotex service, and interactive media. All external tools and sign systems modify the behavior and, more broadly, the activity a person performs changes (in a way, enriches) underlying mental mechanisms. Working in the sociocultural paradigm, Griffin, King, Diaz, and Cole (1989) investigated the remediation process, which consists of changing the way a mediator regulates the coordination of individuals with their environment.

Remediation is rapidly escalating, thus giving rise to a kind of "futurological" research in cognitive and developmental psychology. The internalized features and sign systems characteristic of some special samples (i.e. users of high technology systems) will be quite common for the majority of future generations. The potential of "being smarter" through the use of sophisticated devices is thoroughly and eloquently analyzed by Norman (1993). It should be noted, though, that the potential is highly indirect; "the power of mediational means in organizing action is often not consciously recognized by those who use them" (Wertsch, 1991, 37).

Mediation Analysis in the Telecommunications Field

In the communication theory field, Cathcart and Gumpert (1983, 270) proposed that "each new technology not only extended the reach of human communication, it also altered the ways in which humans related to information and to each other." Being interested in describing new communicative effects, Cathcart and Gumpert analyzed *media simulated interpersonal communication* (the so-called parasocial interactions, broadcast and teleparticipatory communication), *human-computer interpersonal communication,* and *unicommunication* (the utilization of artifacts like T-shirts or bumper stickers for interpersonal interaction), along with *interpersonal mediated communication.*

Another simulated effect of a rather different nature includes, for example, the animation or personification of the mediator. The animation problem raised by Piaget (1929) was revived with the appearance of simulating devices, mainly in the artificial intelligence (AI) field. In the AI context, the problem is raised in full and analyzed using somewhat different experimental data (Collier and Berkeley, 1982; Colby, 1975; McGuire and Stanley, 1971; Turkle, 1984; Weizenbaum, 1976). When seeking explanations of the peculiar phenomena inherent in mediated human-to-human interactions, researchers refer to the effect of responsiveness and investigate it thoroughly (Bresler, 1990; Rafaeli, 1988). It must be taken into consideration, though, that responsiveness effects may lead to simulations (Werner and Latane, 1976). Simulations are not to be taken as an artifact. In Turkle's (1984) stimulating research it was shown that "identification stage" children (mostly preschoolers) with access to computers may reach more sophisticated conclusions concerning living/nonliving, animate/nonanimate, and emotional/rational differences, compared with previous generations of children who used as a basis for their reflections on animation and personification matters the differences between plants, animals, humans, and mechanical toys.

Telecommunications gave rise to numerous types of mediated communication. The research in this field deals with the exteriorization process. The earlier research in mediated communication was concerned mostly with assessing groupware and moderating strategies, working out the procedures for efficient discussions, measuring attitudes towards conferencing devices and equipment, comparing discussions mediated by different communicative tools, and so forth. Working conditions were, for example, frequently analyzed from the perspective of sociology and management theory in the research field of computer-supported collaborative work (CSCW) (Schmidt and Bannon, 1992). Rather little attention was paid to sign systems which turned out to be specific for mediated communication. Recently this line of research has been given more attention by researchers.

In the psychology of telecommunications field, thorough research has been conducted on various dimensions: the use of speech variables during dyadic problem solving; specific lexical and grammar features of verbal communication via different mediators; the typology of dialogical speech units; the preferred (in mediated communication) ways of deviating from strict rules of linguistically correct behavior (Ford, Weeks, and Chapanis, 1980; Stoll, Hoecker, Krueger, and Chapanis, 1976). In the computer mediated communication field, new artificial sign systems dealing with emotive communication (Arndt and Janney, 1991) consisting of graphic accents (smileys or emoticons) have been analyzed (Katzman, 1993; Witmer and Katzman, 1998; Rice and Love, 1987; Sproull and Kiesler, 1992).

An analysis of speech patterns made by CMC adepts supported the conclusion that CMC speech resembles a telelogue style of communicating (Ball-Rokeach and Reardon, 1988). The reference to distant communication surely differentiates telelogues from the somewhat more familiar (although not intensively investigated) polylogues. The latter refers to face-to-face communication patterns in small groups. Polylogues seem to be extensions of dialogues between more than two participants. Polylogue communication patterns differ and include both formal and regular patterns with special rules for holding the floor, interruptions, leadership or moderatorship, or free and informal ways of self-expressions, such as chatting with a group of close friends.

The use of graphic accents, for example, indicates the difference between telelogues and polylogues is quite substantial; surely, many other distinctive features differentiating polylogues and telematic polylogues (i.e. telelogues) might be investigated.

Forms of Speech

In recent research (Griffin et al., 1989), a hybrid form of speech patterns was observed that included features and attributes common to both oral and written forms of speech. The oral speech features were colloquial forms of speech, incorrect syntax, attempts to interrupt the partner, and sometimes (in children's verbal exchanges) rhyming, which is close to a *rap,* i.e. spoken (more correctly, sung) genre of speech. The written speech features included sophisticated phrases, use of passive and causal verbal constructions, corrections of drawbacks, and efforts to disambiguate partners' word choices (Griffin et al., 1989).

The distinction between oral (or spoken) and written speech is obvious. Written speech is devoid of extralinguistic cues (e.g. gestures, mimics, facial expressions, intonations, etc). Spoken speech, on the other hand, can be elliptical and rich in extralinguistic cues. "The differences between spoken and written speech are of considerable psychological interest..." (Luria, 1976, 36-37). The psychological mechanisms of acquiring these two types of speech are entirely different. As a rule, written speech is taught to articulate children. Moreover, these children are not always motivated to learn written speech (Vygotsky, 1962, 1978).

Curiously, in the speech pathology field, the opposite sequence is known as well: those engaged first in special forms of written speech acquire some motivation to speak orally. CMC has been found to be useful for that type of therapy. Indeed, there is evidence that autistic and emotionally disturbed children might benefit from using the written form of CMC (Hilf et al., 1971; Zimmerman, 1987). It is widely known that there is an urgent need for versions of software for the disabled.

Taking these research data into consideration, it must be assumed that an investigation of the speech specifics of CMC is of the utmost importance. Speech is the most significant sign system that mediates human mental processes. Quite often, new signs and sign systems are formed on the basis of natural languages; thus, acquiring a new semiotic system means that the inner mediation and internalization processes have been somehow changed and altered.

The distinction between monological and dialogical forms of speech is as important as the distinction between written and oral forms of speech. The real inherent nature of human communication is in the dialogical exchange of views and messages; monologues, on the other hand, are a taught and thus rather artificial (in a sense nonnatural) way of communicating (Bakhtin, 1984; Wertsch, 1991). Dialogical and monological forms of speech are widely investigated in almost all branches of psychology, in education theory, in psychotherapy, in rhetoric, in communication theory, in hermeneutics, and so forth. In most instances, dialogues are associated with democracy, and monologues are associated with an authoritarian style of management and ruling. The distinction is not entirely strict, though, as there are significant exceptions.

Polylogue speech usually attracts less attention than monologue or dialogue speech. In analyzing group discussions and group decision-making processes, researchers are primarily interested in specifics of forming and changing opinions, in channels of information exchange, in the safeness and reliability of group decisions, in the bias to extreme and risky decisions, and to the groupthink phenomena. The speech structure of polylogical discussions is rarely analyzed. In the CMC field, polylogues (more strictly telelogues) take place in discussion groups (newsgroups, lists), echo-conferences, forums, and teleconferences. As complete transcripts of group discussions are easily saved in computer files and archived, a content analysis of the typology and inner structure of polylogues is possibly the most feasible methodology. Research of this nature has already been performed by members of the ProjectH research group (Rafaeli et al., 1994; Sudweeks and Rafaeli, 1996).

Pidginized Speech

In CMC, English is widely used and thus it functions as a world esperanto. Unlike esperanto, which is an artificial language, computer-mediated English takes some attributes of a lingua franca, or a pidginized or creolized language. The distinctions between them, their formation and acquisition, are intensively investigated in the field of sociolinguistics (e.g. Bell, 1976; Trudgill, 1983). "A pidgin language, then, is a lingua franca which has no native speakers. Chronologically speaking, it is derived from a "normal" language through simplification: most often reduction in vocabulary and grammar, and elimination of complexities and irregularities" (Trudgill, 1983, 179). Pidgin languages traditionally are a prerogative of spoken or oral communication.

There are obviously some attributes that bring together CMC research and sociolinguistic research of pidginized languages. In a sense, in CMC there appears to be an emerging continuum (Bell, 1976) of different styles of English language usage. Nonnative English-speaking networkers usually simplify linguistic constructions, and certainly they can, at best, guess the meanings of a great many nonsimplified phrases produced by natural speakers of

English. Stylistic, laconic and metaphorical English texts may be impractical, as there is always a chance that they will not be understood adequately. For the comprehension of important messages, the simplified nonnative style of English may be the most effective style of English.

There are several ways that pidgin languages develop. The most common principle in pidgin formation is a situation in which there are speakers of three languages and there is a need to form a lingua franca. Trudgill (1983) gives an example of two children—Dutch and Swedish—who have learned English at school for a short period, suddenly finding themselves on a deserted island. In this case, only one of the three languages—English—is common so a nonnative form of English will develop in order for the two children to communicate. Another way that pidgins are formed is when two languages come into contact. These two languages might be cognate ones, and the linguistic communities share some geographical area. As a typical example, the pidginized or creolized versions of the Bantu languages in Central and Southern Africa (e.g. Swahili) include a reduced number of verbal forms and noun classes, and phonological (tone) simplification. Finally, pidgins are formed when two noncognate languages come into contact on a permanent basis. The two languages are usually a local and a European one and the pidgin that is developed includes features and characteristics of each.

Rather similar to the mechanisms by which pidgin/creole languages are formed is the English language usage of nonnative speakers in computer networking. Speakers of different languages, and even different language groups, usually communicate in English. By simplification and by mistakenly introducing some features of their native languages (different word order, for example), Internet users could be considered to be actively developing a new form of English. This would-be form is a pidgin, not a creole, as there certainly will never emerge native speakers of network English.

The process is, in some ways, analogous to the adaptation of English as a means of professional communication in numerous technical fields but with radical differences. First, millions of network users cannot be treated as representing any single profession and, second, for the first time an entirely written version of a pidgin has a chance to emerge. The differences mentioned are strong enough to consider the adaptation of English to the CMC field as unique. This kind of uniqueness is somewhat close to Wertsch's (1991, 124) notion of privileging:

> Privileging refers to the fact that one mediational means, such as a social language, is viewed as being more appropriate or efficacious than others in a particular sociocultural setting.

One must admit that privileging leads to changes in the internalization process, and is thus worthy of being analyzed.

Research Aims and Methodology

The experimental data analyzed in this chapter are excerpts from several Usenet newsgroup discussions and from several Russian-language teleconferences. The excerpts to be analyzed were singled out while participating in different newsgroups and teleconferences, or while reading actual messages of the participants. Additionally, Russian network users were interviewed, participants of mediated discussions were consulted (both face to face and via computer networks), and questionnaires were administered (both paper-and-pencil and computer-mediated). Pilot research was performed to analyze the modes of speech usage of users of local and wide area networks in research institutions in Moscow.

The aim of this research is to define basic characteristics of the telelogue form of speech. The typology of characteristics common to telelogue speech and other existing sign systems is analyzed. An earlier stage of this research, with an analysis of newsgroups discussions, was published elsewhere (Voiskounsky, 1992).

Results

The research results are presented in terms of commonality between attributes of CMC and known speech forms. The known speech forms include written and oral speech, dialogical and monological speech, and polylogue (telelogue). The features of self-communication and pidgin forms of language usage are also analyzed.

Attributes of the Written Form of Speech

The attributes of written forms of speech in common with CMC that are worthy of mention are as follows. First, message senders control text composition while recipients are unable to intervene. Second, messages often have complicated syntax structure, e.g. subordinate clauses. Third, messages characteristically define the reason(s) for addressing the recipient. Fourth, authors can use rough notes and have the advantage of pre-editing and post-editing. Fifth, in written communication, senders have multiple opportunities to check misspellings and to correct the errors. Many mail and conferencing programs allow users sending messages via computer networks to correct their messages by using spell checkers, although this opportunity is very often overlooked. As I learned from the interviews, only a few network users said they use spell checkers frequently. Most of them, if they do use spell checkers, use them for important messages only.

Attributes of the Oral Form of Speech

People who use CMC frequently acquire a nonofficial style of conversation including attributes such as using first names, treating colleagues in an unceremonious manner, adopting specific kinds of slang expressions and various types of jokes (verbal and graphical). Interestingly, network users do their best to devise some e-mail equivalent of interrupting, perhaps due to the necessity to reduce traffic (in Russia it is necessary to pay for both received and sent messages). Lengthy messages may be returned to offending authors with a comment that half (or even less than half) of the message would have been sufficient to be understood. Certainly this kind of behavior is not equivalent to easily observed interruptions in face-to-face communication. The reasons for attempting to perform CMC interruptions are, though, quite similar and have the desired effect of stopping the message attaining process, and expressing dissatisfaction.

Oral speech is usually more emotional than written speech. Although in written speech there are quite effective means of expressing nuances of human affect and feeling, not many people are sufficiently skilled to use these means adequately. Many users engaged in CMC are not native speakers of English so they find themselves incapable of expressing affects in the foreign language. So, to make CMC closer to speech, users have agreed on and use, where necessary, the smiley symbol system.

Attributes of the Dialogical Form of Speech

A quick response factor is one of the main attributes of dialogues. In CMC, the regular time lag between a request and a response is often within 24 hours, which is unprecedented for postal mail. The short lag time and the question-answering procedure lead to a kind of alternating between composing a message and waiting for a reaction of the recipient. The only real obstacle is the diversity of time zones throughout the globe.

Another attribute relates to users expressing opinions on a particular topic and each new argument bringing new reactions generated by those newsgroup and/or teleconference members who did not participate in earlier discussions. This is characteristic both for chained dialogues and polylogues. The latter might be spontaneous or might be voluntarily initiated by participants. Both processes are inherent to a dialogical form of speech. The initiations usually take the form of addressing special questions to those who were not participating in the discussion. Questioning, of course, is highly characteristic of dialogues, not monologues. However, it is the answers, not the questions, that lead to dialogical discussions, otherwise the questions would turn out to be rhetorical ones, which is not an attribute of a dialogue.

A third attribute might be referred to as a dialogical attitude of CMC users.

For example, participants of a computer conference expressed their willingness to answer short auxiliary texts which were automatically printed on their screens and which had nothing to do with the content of the conference (these texts were just citations, changing each day). When the technical moderator explained how to switch off the auxiliary texts, the users argued that their aim was to answer them, not to get rid of them. Taking these facts into consideration, it can be concluded that users' dominant attitudes are dialogical.

Attributes of the Monological Form of Speech

The monological style of computer-mediated discussions may be revealed sometimes in an authoritative attitude of some participants. Although this style is not common, there were some instances of orders being given. This style of CMC may be characteristic of newcomers to the networks, as network users traditionally alter their communicative style for a more democratic one as they gain competence. Computer-mediated discussions also lack the nonverbal cues inherent in oral dialogical speech. Obviously, turn-taking hints and holding-the-floor signals have no equivalents in written speech.

When discussing attributes of the dialogical form of speech, it was mentioned that not only frequent questions, but also the question-answering process characterizes CMC dialogues. However, in some types of newsgroups (e.g. educational and research-oriented groups), the lack of responses to questions is characteristic of a monological form of speech. The reasons for not answering might be as follows. First of all, some questions are poorly formulated, incomprehensible, rhetorical, irrelevant or ask for information no one knows. Second, to give answers to certain know-how questions sometimes requires an explanation of an entire project. Surely a small proportion of these unrealistic questions have a dialogical status: the most courteous users replied that they needed additional time to give a full answer to the question. Third, certain questions are so specific that no newsgroup participant is capable of answering them.

Another class of monological messages is represented by verbal components of combined nonverbal-verbal dialogues. That is, the content of these verbal components is devoted to giving orders and consultations, asking for a copy of an article, or asking to pass on best wishes and regards to coworkers who are not online. The nonverbal part of these dialogues is outside the realm of the exchange of computer-mediated messages. Finally, another factor for not answering some messages is the carelessness and unpunctuality of users, their operational mistakes (incorrect replies), or problems with their telecommunication equipment. Sometimes this mode of communicative behavior is induced by a sensitivity to rank, where network users answer messages from higher-ranking colleagues swiftly and ignore messages from lower-ranking ones. Obviously, this manner of communicative behavior might be regarded as undemocratic, even though CMC is considered by some participants as having an equalizing effect.

Attributes of Self-Communication

Self-communication is understood as a process of addressing messages to one's own account, not as saving a copy as outgoing mail. The self-communication type of CMC is characteristic primarily of LAN users. For example, in an analysis of e-mail system usage in the Institute of Mechanics and Computing, Russian Academy of Science (Voiskounsky, 1985), of a mean number of 62 messages per month, 10 were self-addressed. These self-addressed messages remained in mailboxes from 1 to 48 days (mean 8.6 days) and were read many times.

Possible motivations for self-addressing are many: (1) a procedure for self-learning; (2) a mnemonic operation; (3) an act of communication with coworkers, when a group of colleagues uses the same account; (4) a component of managerial role functioning, e.g. systematically collecting information and placing portions of the information into e-mail boxes in order to summarize and generalize on a regular basis. Thus self-communication processes constitute an essential part of both communicative and noncommunicative actions.

Self-communication might be characteristic not only for LAN or WAN users, but for global network users as well. A professional who works in different geographical regions, for example, may prefer not to carry hard copies of necessary documentation between locations, but to telecommunicate it addressing their own e-mail boxes. This version of self-communication is considered to be useful and efficient.

Attributes of the Pidginized Form of Speech

As the pidgin attributes are the most disputed, I shall mention them only briefly. First, the CMC field is sometimes assumed, by both newcomers and strangers, as a sort of secret language and secret way of communicating. According to some observations, this assumption occurs partly because the body of messages are preceded by headers which are completely alien to nonnetwork users. The tradition of reading texts from top to bottom pays poor service, as the actual message is between.

Two kinds of communicative situations that seem to be quite common for CMC give perspectives of pidgin English formation. First, native English speakers have to simplify speech constructions when e-mailing nonnative English speakers. This is also the case when nonnative English speakers of different ethnic backgrounds communicate in English. We expect that quite analogous processes might take place in other sites where network users speak different languages. It is argued, therefore, that computer networking has all the characteristics for forming a pidgin "network English": nonnative English speakers born in diverse geographical regions and under diverse sociolinguistic settings, communicating in a simplified version of English.

The possibility of a network pidgin English seems unprecedented given sociolinguistic data. The selective process of pidgin formation begins with an English vocabulary layer of expressions used in computer programming and computer networking. This layer of computing terms is contradictory to the usual layers of pidgin formation, namely, trading and daily life. Still more unusual is that it began in a written, not oral form of communication. The network pidgin English still requires many years to be developed.

Interestingly enough, English influences language usage even when network users communicate in national languages. Let us restrict ourselves with the influence of English on Russian language usage in the CMC field. In Russian-language teleconferences, Latin and cyrillic alphabets are intermixed. Foreign names, for example, are usually inserted in the Latin alphabet. The same might occur with certain terms which have no optimal Russian equivalents, or with citations that were produced originally in Latin alphabet.

The intermixed alphabets are also used in other contexts, such as making messages more elaborative and argumentative, or more humorous. An example of the latter is the signature which very often includes maxims and/or witty phrases in foreign languages (mostly in English) functioning as a kind of motto/logotype that characterizes the networker who chooses the phrases.

Perhaps the most difficult style for nonnative English speakers to master is laconic, metaphorical speech. Quite often, nonnatives produce lengthier messages than native English speakers. These lengthy messages are composed according to the rules of a written, high-school textbook style and they lack metaphorical expressions. Curiously enough, English phrases and words are used in national-language computer conferences in order to shorten the messages. Two ways of shortening might be noted. First, foreign phrases are inserted into Russian messages, sometimes as abbreviations. For example, a popular foreign abbreviation is IMHO (in my humble opinion), used mostly in Latin notation but sometimes in cyrillics as well). Second, English words, in cyrillic notation, are used as a kind of stem. Combined with adequate Russian prefixes and endings, the following English terms were used in a teleconference during a two-week period in June 1994: message, link, PC, mail, crosspost, hub, signature, origin, voice, routing, host, source, node, sysop, login, telnet, direct, flame, user, programmer, and point. It is interesting to note that "postmaster" was the only correct English term used in Russian in the computer networking field, though there is an adequate and familiar Russian term which denotes a person in charge of a mailing service. In fact, few of the terms mentioned have no adequate Russian language equivalents. The insertion of English words, phrases and abbreviations into cyrillic messages, in cyrillics or in Latin, is a step towards an adaptation of pidgin English for regular usage by Russian networkers.

Thus, the reasons for the uniqueness of the pidgin English now being formed is that it is, first, in a written speech (as opposed to oral), and second, in the area of computer networking as opposed to the more usual field of market bargaining and trading.

Telelogue Attributes of the Polylogue Form of Speech

Due to the lack of special research procedures dedicated to telelogue and polylogue speech analysis, I am able to mention only some of characteristic features, and to refer to those relevant attributes mentioned above. Attributes of telelogue speech embrace all the abovementioned characteristics of the CMC contacts in addition to some special attributes.

First, in telelogue communication, no time zones are assumed; in other words, it might be argued that CMC never stops, it has no brakes. Next, as already mentioned, turn-taking is not assumed in CMC. In a sense, everybody holds the floor at any time. Altercations are characteristic for e-mail communication, but for newsgroups, it might be hypothesized that all participants are producing messages independently and simultaneously. Unlike face-to-face communication, this kind of egocentric speech, investigated in depth by Piaget (1929) and Vygotsky (1962), is a real way of communicating and is not considered an aspect of self-communication or internal speech.

Telelogue speech supports the communicator's initiative both in sending messages (the ease of holding of floor) and in receiving. The latter process includes the willingness to receive, to read, and/or to ignore the message. Subscribers to newsgroups and teleconferences, for example, usually browse headers to select messages for reading. Even when ignoring a portion of a message, a netter is aware of their existence and has some impression about content, interconnections, and relevance. Thus, awareness and initiative are characteristic of a telelogue way of communication.

Quotes from previous messages are highly characteristic of telelogue speech. Quotes are usually preceded by special auxiliary marks (e.g., >) and inserted into the corresponding response. This attribute is perhaps the most characteristic of CMC being a sort of "social invention" of experienced users and is helpful when opposing views are being discussed. Thus, the unprecedented new culture of publicly debated statements is inherently telelogue speech.

Repeating opponent's views is not a feature of face-to-face discussions, and in discussions using other media. The careful quoting of opponents' statements are thought to be necessary for professional and specialized interactions (i.e. contract negotiations, legal applications to a court, thorough reviewing of articles). This professional style of communication is usually considered more argumentative than the familiar one, where the opposition's arguments are not repeated. The culture of quoting, which had almost disappeared, is now reappearing as a feature of CMC.

As mentioned above, chained dialogues and polylogues, and attempts to initiate polylogues, are telelogue attributes. A more subtle attribute concerns the formation of the group style of CMC. In different newsgroups, echo-conferences, forums, and teleconferences, the real elements of this style might differ a lot, but observation shows that in each of them the specific style is formed. Taking into consideration new forms of speech originating in a new communicative medium, we usually give them the attributes of a style mode. For example, the terms "telephone conversation style" or "telegraph style" are used widely. Thus we try to validate that a CMC style is now being formed. The new kind of speech is far from being completely formed. It is syncretic in origin.

CMC, of course, is not limited to written texts but has expanded to include graphics, sounds and animation. Telelogue speech is intensively used in multimedia and World-Wide-Web (WWW) navigation. Most WWW texts, both written and voiced, and instructional multimedia products are being adapted for use by the less educated population, and especially by nonnative English speakers.

Conclusion

Telelogue messages generated in CMC sessions, including texts, voice, and graphics, have the attributes of written and oral speech, of dialogical and monological forms of speech, and they often serve the functions of self-communication. Telelogue messages form the basis of a new kind of pidgin English. As the newest and highly syncretic external tool of communication being internalized, telelogue communication will cause a profound evolutionary effect on human psychological development. The effect is similar to the effects caused by some other technological inventions but the artificial tools mediating human communication transform the existing and familiar semiotic systems that are in the core of the human mind.

Acknowledgement

Financial support for this research was given by the Russian Foundation for Basic Research, Grant #96-06-80515.

CHAPTER FOUR

Hmmm...Where's that Smoke Coming From?

Writing, Play and Performance on Internet Relay Chat

Brenda Danet, Lucia Ruedenberg, and Yehudit Rosenbaum-Tamari

C omputer-mediated communication (CMC) is strikingly playful. Millions of people are playing with their computer keyboards in ways they probably never anticipated, even performing feats of virtuosity—with such humble materials as commas, colons, and backslashes. Not only hackers, computer "addicts," adolescents and children, but even ostensibly serious adults are learning to play in new ways. This chapter is a study of writing, play and performance on Internet Relay Chat, known for short as IRC, a network program that allows thousands of users all around the globe to "talk" to each other in real time by typing, at any hour of the day or night. We adopt a textual, micro-sociolinguistic approach, informed by recent work in discourse analysis, the study of orality and literacy, and the anthropology of play and performance.

Playfulness in Computer-Mediated Communication

To borrow Turner's (1967) metaphor, written interaction on IRC is a veritable "forest of symbols"—typographic symbols. Phenomena that we have observed on IRC partially resemble real life (RL) genres of play such as charades, a carnival or a masked ball, having a party, and putting on a show. Yet most of what happens consists only of text—letters and typographic symbols dancing on a computer screen. Most events on IRC are a form of disembodied "virtual play" (Aycock, 1993), floating freely in cyberspace, an abstract domain consisting only of information and electronic pulses and existing in live links between millions of computers around the world (Gibson, 1984; Benedikt, 1991; Biocca, 1992).

The computer keyboard is something like a piano keyboard. On the piano, in addition to playing individual notes to create a melody, one can also produce chords by playing several notes together, much expanding the expressive possibilities of the instrument. On the computer keyboard, creative individuals sometimes produce amazing effects merely with the mundane options of upper and lower case, numbers, and typographic symbols.

"Emoticons" on computer screens are icons for the expression of emotion, or for marking one's intent as nonserious. They are composed of clusters of typographic symbols, and are popularly known as "smiley" icons or "smileys" (Raymond, 1991, p. 142-143; Godin, 1993; Sanderson, 1993; Witmer and Katzman, 1997). The best known ones are :-)   ;-)   :-(for a smiling face, a wink, and a frown, respectively; to view them, tilt the head toward the left shoulder. Some initiates to digital writing reject emoticons as in poor taste, or in conflict with standards of good writing associated with literate culture; for others, using them reflects or signals socialization to the new culture evolving in cyberspace. Although we produce these symbols sequentially, they are experienced almost simultaneously, as a *gestalt,* both when producing and when reading them. Thus, the effect is somewhat similar to that of a chord in music. In the exploitation of these and other possibilities of the computer keyboard, playful digital messages have fascinating affinities with graffiti, comics, the language of advertising, jazz, and improvisational theater.

Pioneering researchers on CMC in the late 1970s and early 1980s were slow to notice playfulness in the new medium, and to consider it worth investigating. Primarily interested in the instrumental, rather than the expressive aspects of communication , early research was concerned with the effects of the new medium on organizational functioning. The terms "teleconferencing" and "conferences" were frequently used (Short, et al., 1976; Hiltz and Turoff, 1978, 1993; Johansen, et al., 1979; Hiemstra, 1982; Kiesler, et al., 1984), and are still quite common today among researchers on organizational communication, developers of the technologies, and in popular discourse about CMC. Ordinarily, the term "conference" refers to a work-related meeting; thus, many people may have expected the general frame of messages exchanged to be "serious." The perception of the medium itself as cold, anonymous, and lacking in social presence because of the absence of nonverbal cues such as facial expression (Short, et al., 1976; Kiesler, et al., 1984; Rice and Love, 1987; Walther, 1992) also contributed to this expectation.

Persons who use computers for communication only sporadically may not necessarily have noticed or even been exposed to playful phenomena of the kind analyzed in this chapter. There is, in fact, an extraordinary amount of playfulness on the "Net," as it is called— the worldwide system of commercial and noncommercial computer networks and gateways that includes the Internet, BITNET, USENET, FidoNet, Freenet, CompuServe, GEnie, America Online, Delphi, BIX and The WELL, and so on (Quarterman, 1990;

LaQuey, 1993; Rheingold, 1993). Children and adults log on to read and post to bulletin boards (BBSs), participate in recreational and work-related discussion groups, and talk to each other through chat programs such as IRC or in text-based virtual realities known as MUDs (multi-user domains or dungeons) and MOOs (MUDs—Object-Oriented; Curtis, 1996; Marvin, 1995; Turkle, 1995). In the last five years or so, researchers have begun to pay close attention to linguistic and other features that appear in these modes, including those that pertain to playfulness and expressivity.

The classic theorists of play, Huizinga (1955) and Caillois (1961), saw it as activity set apart in time and space from ordinary life. Digital play shares with RL play many important characteristics: it too is voluntary, intensely absorbing, done for its own sake, and, as we shall see, more or less rule-governed. However, in cyberspace it makes no sense to ask "What time is it here?" or "Where on the globe are we?" (Gibson, 1984; Barlow, 1996; Benedikt, 1991; Biocca, 1992; Strate, 1995). Cyberspace provides perfect insulation to maintain a play frame. Even when ostensibly at work, individuals seated at their computers can be engrossed in deep play.

Like other forms of playfulness, that in digital writing takes place in the subjunctive mode of possibility and experimentation. It is a liminal activity that engenders *communitas* (Turner, 1974; Turner, 1986a; Handelman, 1976). As many have pointed out (e.g., Hiltz and Turoff, 1978, 1993; Kiesler, et al., 1984; Poster, 1990), the medium has a democratizing influence. For example, faculty and students who in RL would probably observe norms of asymmetrical address quickly fall into reciprocal first-naming.

Like other forms of play, those to be examined in this chapter are also amoral; they communicate about "what can be" (Handelman 1976: 186). By conventional criteria, playfulness in CMC can easily be viewed as threatening to the social order:

> [Play] is defined as "unserious," "untrue," "pretend," "make-believe," "unreal," and so forth, precisely because it is a fount of unorder against which the social order must be buffered. By definition it cannot be permitted to define a moral community, since...the directions of its transformative capacity are uncharted (Handelman, 1976: 189).

Thus, the breaking down of social barriers in digitized communication can, in certain circumstances, have a negative effect. People can go out of control, lose their tempers, get involved in sudden incidents of "flaming" (Raymond, 1991; Lea et al., 1992; Danet, in press). Communication is also volatile: the play frame can break down at any moment, if participants become disturbed or offended by what is happening, and particularly when dramatic RL events such as death, war, or natural disasters like earthquakes impinge on players' consciousness. Then the medium is mobilized for the dissemination of late-breaking news, online expressions of solidarity, and so forth.

Cyberspace as the New Frontier

Another factor fostering playfulness is the frontierlike quality of this new world, which is highlighted in the title of Rheingold's (1993) book, *The Virtual Community: Homesteading on the Electronic Frontier*. Hackers are sometimes called "computer cowboys" (Hafner and Markham, 1991: 10), or "digital explorers" (Levy, 1984, Preface). Barlow suggests that

> Cyberspace, in its present condition, has a lot in common with the 19th Century West. It is vast, unmapped, culturally and legally ambiguous, verbally terse..., hard to get around in, and up for grabs. Large institutions already claim to own the place, but most of the actual natives are solitary and independent, sometimes to the point of sociopathy. It is, of course, a perfect breeding ground for both outlaws and new ideas about liberty. (Barlow, 1996, p. 461).

Users of IRC treat the medium as a frontier world: a virtual reality of virtual freedom, in which participants feel free to act out their fantasies, to challenge social norms, and exercise aspects of their personality that would under normal circumstances be inhibited (Reid, 1991).

Melbin's (1987, chapter 3) analysis of night and night culture is also highly suggestive. Like the American West, he finds, night is characterized by uneven stages of advance; organized sponsorship rather than solo activity of individuals; sparse and homogeneous population; chances for escape and opportunity; a wider range of tolerated behavior than in daytime life; fewer status distinctions; novel hardships; decentralization of authority; lawlessness and peril. The similarities are striking, indeed!

An Inherently Playful Medium

Digital writing is inherently playful, first of all, because the medium, the computer, invites participants to fiddle, and to invoke the frame of make-believe (Bateson, 1972; Goffman, 1974; Handelman, 1976). When this frame is operating, participants understand and accept the meta-message "this is play" (Bateson, 1972; Handelman, 1976). Schechner suggests that:

> Playing is being loose with rules and bits of existence....[it] is what happens when humans get hold of actions or things that are apparently "set." We turn them upside down, use them in unexpected and unplanned for ways, make them into what they were not at first intended to be.[2]

Four interrelated features of CMC foster playfulness: ephemerality, speed, interactivity, and freedom from the tyranny of materials. The prominence of playfulness grows as we move from basic word-processing of author-absent texts (Heim, 1987; Bolter, 1991), to hypertext and interactive fiction (Delany and Landow, 1991; Bolter, 1991, chap. 8; Lanham, 1993) and e-mail and discussion groups (Myers, 1987a, 1987b; Ruedenberg, et al., 1995; Aycock, 1993, 1995; Kozar, 1995; Baym, 1992, 1995a, 1995b), to synchronous communication (Reid, 1991, 1995; Bruckman, 1992, 1993; Curtis, 1992; Danet, 1995; Jacobson 1996; Turkle, 1995). It is in the latter genres that writing is most intensively experienced as talking, and the distinction between process and product breaks down (Kirshenblatt-Gimblett, 1976, Introduction). Thinking primarily of word-processing, Heim (1987) notes that digital writing is inherently playful:

> My stream of consciousness can be paralleled by the running flow of the electric element. Words dance on the screen. Sentences slide smoothly into place, make way for one another, while paragraphs ripple down the screen. Words become highlighted, vanish at the push of a button, then reappear instantly at will. Verbal life is fast-paced, easier, with something of the exhilaration of video games (Heim, 1987: 152).

Thus, playfulness is present even when there is no apparent partner to play with. One is playing with the program and the machine, not a person. Similarly, with electronically composed literature—hypertext—in mind, Bolter argues that:

> Playfulness is a defining quality of this new medium. Electronic literature will remain a game, just as all computer programming is a game. [Hypertext]...grows out of ... computer games.....the impermanence of electronic literature cuts both ways: as there is no lasting success, there is also no failure that needs to last. By contrast, there is a solemnity at the center of printed literature—even comedy, romance and satire—because of the immutability of the printed page. (Bolter, 1991: 130).

Interactivity. Synchronous modes also invite playfulness because they offer an engrossing flow experience in which action and awareness are fused (Csikszentmihalyi, 1977). Interaction of all kinds with computers is often felt to be totally absorbing; computers are experienced as a second self (Turkle, 1984). An important factor which fosters this sense of flow is the magical quality of instant efficaciousness in interaction with the computer—even when no human partner is involved. We receive instant feedback to our own feedback. This characteristic has come to be called interactivity (Rafaeli, 1988; Laurel, 1992). The sense of flow may be even greater when participating in synchronous modes than when interacting only with the computer, or even when reading and composing e-mail. People often lose all sense of time, suddenly discovering that hours have passed.

Release from the Tyranny of Materials. Yet another aspect of digital writing which fosters playfulness is the release from dependence on physical materials. From the dawn of human efforts to make marks on the world, to encode information in graphic form, there has been a struggle with materials, both to prepare materials to write on and to do the writing itself. Writing was invented in the ancient Near East some 5000 years ago, in Mesopotamia and in Egypt (Gaur, 1984; André-Leicknam and Ziegler, 1982; Gelb, 1963). For thousands of years, the dominant materials were clay and stone—not very easy materials to work with! (Andre-Leicknam and Ziegler, 1982; Gaur, 1984; Walker, 1990). Over the course of history, materials requiring somewhat less physical effort came to be used, e.g., papyrus in Egypt and parchment in medieval Europe. However, even these lighter, somewhat more flexible materials still required endless, backbreaking toil (Gaur, 1984; Troll, 1990; Avrin, 1990; Olmert, 1992; de Hamel, 1986, 1992).

Many of us tend to read-and-delete e-mail, and to send messages without making either an electronic record or hard copy of them (though some e-mail software automatically makes copies even if we don't want them.) Similarly, in synchronous modes, we do not ordinarily make a record of the interaction. While it is often possible to log a chat session, as in IRC, we suspect that individuals do not generally take advantage of this feature. The game's the thing—not the outcome: like speech, typed interaction is fast-paced and as ephemeral as the wind. People who can type fast can "fly," though, of course, no one can type as fast we speak.

Playfulness in Hacker Culture

Playfulness is not only inherent to the medium of computers but has come to be cultivated and valued by the pioneers in its creation and use—the hackers (Raymond, 1991; Barlow, 1996; Meyer and Thomas, 1990). "Dry humor, irony, puns, and a mildly flippant attitude are highly valued—but an underlying seriousness and intelligence are essential" (Raymond, 1991: 20). Hackers love to play with words and symbols (Raymond, 1991; Barlow, 1996). "They often make rhymes or puns in order to convert an ordinary phrase into something more interesting," as in "Boston Glob" for "Boston Globe" (Raymond, 1991: 9), or "snail-mail" for ordinary mail services (Raymond, 1991: 325-6).

Many of the emergent conventions of digital writing originated in hacker usage (Raymond, 1991: 15-16). Thus, entire messages in CAPITAL LETTERS are interpreted as shouting. There is a preference for writing all in lower-case, even for the beginning of sentences and names. While this practice may have originated out of considerations of speed, it has spread from hacker subculture to the rest of us, and is frequently found both in informal email style and in typed real-time chatting. Another common feature is the use of asterisks to emphasize words denoting actions (*grins*) or sounds (*bang*).

Some forms of playfulness are familiar from earlier genres of writing. Thus, the use of capital letters to emphasize a word or phrase, as in "I REALLY LIKE THAT!" is familiar from the comics (Abbott, 1986; Inge, 1990) and from personal letter-writing. Children and young people are naturally quite richly expressive in handwritten personal letters; this expressivity tends to be suppressed by the teaching of literacy in the schools. Other forms of playfulness, however, such as the use of nicknames, virtually *de rigueur* on

IRC (Bechar-Israeli, 1995), and of evocative names for one's character on MUDs and MOOs (Reid, 1991; Curtis 1996; Bruckman, 1992; 1993; Turkle, 1995)—have more in common with certain oral, not written forms of communication. Thus, the use of nicknames has been a regular feature of Citizens' Band radio for years—participants are known by their "handle" (Powell, 1983; Kalcik, 1985).

The Masking of Identity

In all play there is reduced accountability for action (Handelman, 1976; Honigmann, 1977; Turner, 1986b, 1986c). In the material world, the releasing effect of masks and costumes at carnival time is the paradigmatic example (Turner, 1986b). In the present textual form of CMC, it is the ephemeral, nonmaterial medium and the typed text which provide the mask (Danet, 1996). The absence of nonverbal and other social or material cues to identity frees participants to be other than themselves, or more of themselves than they normally express. This is especially so when participants adopt nicknames or handles (Reid, 1991; Bruckman, 1992, 1996; Rheingold, 1993, chap. 5; Leslie, 1993; Bechar-Israeli, 1995; Turkle, 1995; Danet, 1996).

Stylization, "Orality" and Performance

Linguistic features previously associated with oral communication are strikingly in evidence in this new form of writing (cf., e.g., Maynor, 1994; Ferrara, et al., 1991; Murray, 1991; Yates, 1992, 1996; Bolter, 1991; Collot and Belmore, 1996; Leslie, 1994). "Electronic text is, like an oral text, dynamic" (Bolter, 1991: 59). Although simplistic notions of the differences between (pre-CMC) speech and writing have generally been dismissed in the last decade (e.g., Tannen, 1982a, 1982b), we have tended, in literate culture of the last 500 years, to think in terms of two contrasting models of communication: the contextualized, ephemeral oral conversation, which may be deeply personalized and concrete and is in varying degrees a performance of some kind, versus the decontextualized, author-absent written text—frozen in print, an entity of physical and symbolic integrity (Ong, 1982).

Just as performance tends to be highly stylized in oral cultures (Bauman, 1975, 1977; Finnegan, 1977; Ong, 1982; Edwards and Sienkewicz, 1990), textual and typographic art are prominent in CMC (Reid, 1991; Danet, et al., 1995), not just in the incorporation of ASCII art originally composed offline, but in spontaneous online improvisations. Participants in electronic communications are conscious of their audience and pay special attention to the display of communicative competence, to how their messages are packaged (Bauman, 1975, 1977). In other words, the poetic function of communication is dominant; formal aspects of language are foregrounded (Jakobson, 1960).

The need to say in writing what we have been used to saying in speech calls attention to the communicative means employed in formulating the message. The reduced transparency of language heightens meta-linguistic awareness, and leads us to treat words as objects and to play with them (Cazden, 1976).

A "Virtual Party" on IRC

We turn now to an analysis of a "virtual party" which took place on IRC in December 1991. The analysis focuses primarily on three interrelated, yet analytically distinct types of play—play with identity, play with frames of interaction, and play with typographic symbols. Play with identity and with frames of interaction are each discussed in specific sections of the chapter; play with typographic symbols is so prominent in our material that it appears almost at every turn in our analysis. We chose this sequence for analysis because it illustrates in concise form a number of features which characterize IRC more generally.

The party began when Lucia Ruedenberg logged on from Jerusalem, about 1:30 AM local time and made contact with a system operator (sysop) nick-named <Thunder>, a student at a university in New York state with whom she had developed on ongoing electronic relationship. During the one and one-half hours or so that Ruedenberg was logged on and present, six other persons joined them, for varying amounts of time. All were geographically dispersed, except for one player who was <Thunder>'s fellow student at the same university. Apart from the sysop's previous RL acquaintance with this fellow student and his evolving relationship with Ruedenberg, all were, to the best of our knowledge, strangers, not only in RL, but on IRC as well.

Play with Identity: "Nicks"

Who are the players at this virtual party? The nicks—IRC-ese for "nick-names," of the eight persons who took part are listed in table 1. Note that all nicks are displayed in angle brackets, just as they appear on IRC.

On many grounds there is no apparent need for researchers to disguise the identity of participants any more than participants have done so themselves. IRC is by definition a public space. Anyone with an electronic address and access to a server can log on. Moreover, all have the option of making a log of interaction. In addition, a distinction between public and private channels is built into the program, and a channel operator can make any channel private at any moment, and anyone objecting to being a part of ongoing proceedings in a public channel can instantly leave the channel. While participating in public channels, individuals have the option of exchanging private

Nick	Userid and Address	Additional Material
<Lucia>	soulr@vm1.huji.ac.il	
<Thunder>	root@xxxxxxxxxxxxxxxxx	(-: Raam / Chundeung :-)
<Kang>	GENGHISCON@xxxxxxxx	(<Drax the D>)
<Rikitiki>	rpa3@xxxxxxxxxxxxxxxxx	
<BlueAdept>	dlahti@xxxxxxxxxxxxxxxxx	
<Jah>	miksma3@xxxxxxxxxxxxxx	(Baba)
<Lizardo>	lizardo@xxxxxxxxxxxxxxxxx	(Doctor Lizardo)
<Teevie>	ssac@xxxxxxxxxxxxxxxxxxx	

Table 1. The players at a virtual party on IRC.

messages. Moreover, prior to logging on, participants can change information other than the address itself which is displayed when others check their address on screen.

Taken together, all these considerations argue for treating displayed material in a log as public and therefore not ethically problematic for researchers. However, what is perceived by participants as private or public, on IRC and in cyberspace in general, may be quite another matter. Therefore we sought and obtained permission to publish this analysis from the (former) sysop who plays an especially prominent role in the log, and at his request, have deleted details about the mainframe computers through which all participants except Ruedenberg were logged on. In addition, we refrain from using <Thunder>'s real name—the only one actually known to us.

As for the nicks themselves, we feel there is no ethical need to disguise these disguises. There are two great principles of design in nature, *the principle of camouflage* and the *principle of conspicuous marking* (Gombrich, 1984: 6). The use of masks and costumes at carnivals and masked balls brings these two principles together (Turner, 1986b). Masks are meant not only to hide players' real identity, but also to call attention to the person, and to the mask and its expressive power, imaginativeness, capacity to instill fear, evoke humor, and so on. Similarly, textual masks—online nicknames—are not only a means to disguise RL identities but a form of online plumage.

There is a certain amount of risk in the interpretations of nicks which we develop below since we did not interview the players, except for <Thunder>. In this respect however, we are actually in the same position as the players themselves, who must develop their own interpretations of the textual mask presented by any given player.

The Masking of Gender. Perhaps the most striking thing about players' nicks is that it is impossible to know if the players are male or female. Retaining her RL name, Lucia is the only obviously gendered individual in the group, though only we could know that this was also her real name and that her RL gender was indeed female. Those knowing that Kang is a male character in Star Trek or that Genghis Khan was a notorious male, medieval conqueror could at least assign a gender to the nicks <Kang> and <Genghis-con>, if not to the player behind them. Since mainly males participate in modes like IRC, we believe that most if not all of the other players were male. <Thunder> once telephoned Ruedenberg while she was in Jerusalem, so we could confirm from his male-sounding voice that he, at least, is male.

This sequence illustrates in miniature the tendency to play with gender identity in synchronous chat modes: either players cross-dress, impersonating a person of the opposite gender (not obvious for any of the players in this particular case), or they choose a gender-neutral strategy, at least in nickname or persona, if not in actual behavior (Bruckman, 1992; Turkle, 1995; Dickel, 1995; Cherny, 1995; Reid, 1995; Danet, 1996). This is a new phenomenon in the history of human communication. Until now, we could contemplate the notion of gender-free personhood only in science fiction, e.g., in Ursula LeGuin's *The Left Hand of Darkness* (LeGuin, 1969; Dickel, 1995; Danet, 1996). A fifth of over 7,000 characters registered on LambdaMOO in February 1996 were assigned unconventional genders, and about a third of the 1000 or so on MediaMOO (Danet, 1996).

Nicks and Student Culture. As for the age of players, there are no overt clues, though the ease with which they move into a simulation of smoking marijuana, and their knowledge of terms associated with it (e.g., "ghanja" for a certain type of hashish), analyzed below, suggest that they are college students, or at most in their early thirties. From the addresses now deleted, we learned that except for Ruedenberg, an American in Israel at the time, and one person in Finland, all the participants were in the United States, though quite dispersed geographically.

Nicks on IRC often appeal to fantasy and the fictitious in one way or another—to nature, mythology, the occult, comics, children's literature, science fiction, films, etc. (Bechar-Israeli, 1995). Some of these themes from popular culture or student culture find expression here too.

Analysis of Individual Nicks. The nick <Thunder> evokes power, loud noise, even, perhaps, an intention to instill fear in one's interlocutors—certainly the control that is indeed his as sysop. But according to <Thunder> himself, "Thunder" was chosen for personal reasons:—to commemorate his RL dog of that name, that had died. <Thunder> omitted his real name from his electronic address. The term "root" appears to refer to something in nature; however, this is the standard superuser userid for a sysop on a UNIX mainframe, and thus only a technical term . <Thunder> appends to the address a sequence which includes two smiley icons, facing each other, within which are two other apparent nicks: "Raam" and "Chundeung." We soon realized that *ra'am* is Hebrew for "thunder," and <Thunder> confirmed that *chundeung* is "thunder" in Korean. He was playful with his calling card in still another way. The insertion of the smiley icons is a visual or graphic pun: the end-brackets serve both as the smile on the smiling face and as conventional brackets for the text enclosed within them! He thus recycles the smiley back to its originally functional character as abstract typographic symbol, all the while retaining its playful use as emoticon.

For <Kang>, the next person listed in table 1, we have no less than three nicknames. From information now deleted we know that he was logged on from a mainframe computer in the state of Florida. As we just mentioned, <Kang> is the name of a Klingon character in the television series Star Trek. The userid GENGHISCON is obviously a play on Genghis Khan, the Mongol conqueror. In American pronunciation, "Khan" and "con" are homonyms, words that are pronounced the same though they are spelled differently. Thus <Kang> is playing with the relation between spoken and written language. Constraints imposed by the number of characters allowed in one's userid might also have influenced his choice—"con" having fewer letters than "khan." Nevertheless, the choice of "con" rather than "kon" or "kan" suggests that playfulness is present here too.

"Con" invites other readings too. It is reminiscent of "con" as in "convict." Is <Kang> pretending to "con" us into thinking that he is Genghis Khan? Then there is "con" as in "console"—the computer keyboard. This is the "con" intended in the "copy con" command in DOS. Finally, the "con" suffix can also be read as "convention," a conference or meeting. Conventions for fans of science fiction, Star Trek, and Dungeons and Dragons, as well as computer culture conventions are often referred to as "cons." Very likely, <Kang> also has a predilection for certain sounds: /g/ and /k/ recur in <Kang> and in "Genghiscon." Finally, <Drax the D> may be a reference to a character in Dragons and Dungeons. Dragon imagery is very popular in interactive genres, especially on MUDs and MOOs, which were developed from the original offline game Dragons and Dungeons.

<RikiTiki> is <Thunder>'s fellow college student. This nick also plays with sound. It contains reduplication: two components which rhyme. There are at least three possible associations to this nick. One is to a character in Rudyard Kipling's *Jungle Books* (Kipling, 1994), a second to Tom Lehrer's song, "Rickity-Tickity-Tin," popular with college students in the late 1950's and early 1960's, and a third to George Bernard Shaw's play *Man and Superman*, in which the heroine, Ann, disparagingly calls a character called Octavius "Ricky Ticky Tavy." We think the association to the *Jungle Books* is the most likely. Today's college students may no longer be familiar with Tom Lehrer's cynical songs; Kipling, on the other hand, may still be favorite childhood reading. Kipling's Rikki-tikki-tavi is a little mon-

goose whose war-cry was "rikk-tikk-tikki-tikki-tchk!" (Kipling, 1961).

<BlueAdept> is the name of a novel by the science fiction writer Piers Anthony. This nick also plays with typographic conventions, eliding two words which are normally written a space apart, and capitalizing them when normally they would not be capitalized except at the beginning of a sentence—of course they would be capitalized in the original novel's title. Technical constraints are at work here too. A nick on IRC may have up to nine characters; thus eliding "Blue" and "Adept" allows this person to have both words in his nick. This nick also invites associations to characters in the comics, such as "The Green Hornet." We surmised from the portion of the address now deleted that <BlueAdept> was in California.

<Jah>, located in Finland, has chosen a one-syllable nick . We have no way of knowing if it has substantive associations for him, or whether he just liked the sound of it. This might be a playful spelling of "ya" as in the German or Finnish for "yes." <Jah> has another nickname, "Baba," inscribed in his/her electronic address. Here too we find reduplication, of the syllable /ba/. <Jah> seems to like the sound of /a/, since it appears in both nicknames.

<Lizardo> is a briefer version of "Doctor Lizardo," which appears in the full address. Both play with the English word "lizard," adding an /o/ to make it sound foreign—say, Spanish or Italian. Thus <Lizardo> is playing with the codes of language, mixing the grammar of one with the lexicon of another. His use of a mock title—Doctor—is, of course, also playful and ironic, especially in combination with the name of an animal, rather than a person. From the mainframe address we learned that <Lizardo>was logged on to a computer in Texas.

Finally, <Teevie> appears to be a playful spelling out of "TV," that household word in contemporary America. It is also playful to adopt the name of an inanimate object as a nick, something rarely done in RL, but quite common on IRC.[3] We could not determine in which state <Teevie> was located but surmise that he was in the United States at the time.

Frames and Play with Frames

One of the most fascinating aspects of encounters on IRC is the nature and complexity of the frames of experience which are invoked and sustained. The activation of frames is something like the notion of multitasking in contemporary computer programming. In computerese, multitasking is "loading and running several applications at the same time" (Sheldon, 1992: 13). In the simplest terms, multitasking means being able to do more than one thing simultaneously, and to switch back and forth between them, keeping them all running. In ordinary life we do this without thinking: we may write while listening to music, or cook a meal while carrying on a conversation with someone.

When using multitasking software, one opens up one or more windows to be kept running simultaneously, but not necessarily visible on screen at the same time. Technically, only one frame at a time is foregrounded or available for action; all others are running in the background. In contrast, human beings can operate in more than one frame at a time, and action within one frame can also have meaning within the larger frame that incorporates it.

Five Frames and the Relations Among Them. We identified five frames in our virtual party: (1) REAL LIFE; (2) the IRC GAME; (3) the PARTY frame; (4) the PRETEND frame; and (5) the PERFORMANCE frame. Influenced by Victor Turner's (1986c) analysis of the frames invoked when he and his students experimented with performing ethnography, we too see the various frames as nested within one another (figure 1).

The PARTY frame is nested within the basic IRC frame; within the PARTY frame lies the PRETEND frame, and within that lies the PERFORMANCE frame. From within any of the four inner frames, participants can step "out of frame," and into REAL LIFE, momentarily, while still logged on and interacting with the others. Of course, they return to REAL LIFE when they log off.

Frame One. Real Life. By dint of being alive and functioning, the IRC players are already in the real life mode, which in Western culture is dominated by the expectation of serious activity in the workaday world (Goffman, 1974; Schechner, 1988). Adopting Bateson's (1963) and Handelman's (1976) notion of meta-communicational frames, we suggest that the meta-message of this frame is, "Everything inside this frame is everyday life, grounded in physical space and time; actors are accountable for their physical and verbal actions, for the well-being of their bodies, and for their social commitments." This frame continues to be activated but is moved to the background when participants log onto IRC, thereby activating frame two, the basic IRC GAME. Within frame two, <Thunder> initiated the PARTY frame—frame three, when he invited Ruedenberg to join him in a novel channel called *#weed*.

In multitasking terms, REAL LIFE was kept hidden in the text most of the time during this sequence—running but not visible on screen. Only rarely did it pop into the interaction overtly. At the same time, the players may have been busy with all kinds of REAL-LIFE activities which they were conducting simultaneously while logged onto IRC—eating, talking to someone, listening to music, writing in another window, and so forth.

Participants stepped out of the PARTY frame, or out of the nest of frames two–five shown in figure 1, to talk about things that are happening or that they have to do in REAL LIFE. For instance, at the beginning of the log, <Thunder> sends <Lucia> a private message, using the */msg* command:[4]

Line 9   *Thunder* I am gonna shower soon

In a return private message, she comments , "first laundrey (sic), then shower..." [you're going to be a] clean boy:" Later, <BlueAdept> types:

Line 381 <BlueAdept> beback , gotta locate some coffee

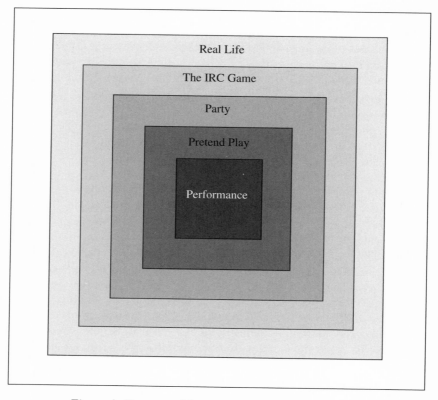

Figure 1. Five nested frames at a virtual party on IRC.

Participants also bring in other kinds of REAL LIFE content, which may or may not be an accurate portrayal of what is happening in their lives. Thus, <BlueAdept> comments,

Line 296 <BlueAdept> Nothing like a fat ganja spleef[5] to brighten one's day

and complains that his girlfriend had "dumped" him the previous night:

Line 310 <BlueAdept> yep... she couldn't relate to my usage of vegetables...

All this may or may not have happened. The point is not whether he is telling the truth, but that the material is presented as if it represents some event in the physical world of REAL LIFE.

Other examples illustrate how REAL LIFE floods the playful interaction. There is a very long stretch where <Rikitiki> discusses at length the voice mail system at his university ("I got a new Rolm phone today.. my old one died;" line 271). <Rikitiki> tells <Thunder>, his fellow student on a New

York campus, that Burger King is selling hamburgers for just $0.99 (line 360). In another instance, <Kang> has a long interchange with <Lucia> in which he tries to get factual information about how Jews get citizenship in Israel. And <Rikitiki> asks <Lucia> about politics in the Middle East and the state of the intifada (lines 686-696).

Frame Two: LET'S PLAY IRC. To log on to IRC is to activate the second frame, that of "LET'S PLAY IRC," or, simply, "Let's talk." There is no pretense or fooling around at this level, just as there is no necessary pretense or fooling around when people play chess. "Chess" is what they are doing. Any interaction made possible by the constitutive rules, the commands of IRC, occurs by definition within this frame. The content of the interaction may be playful, or it may be serious, as when a group of scientists discuss their research on IRC. Therefore the meta-message of this frame is "Anything may be said in this frame; participants enjoy reduced accountability if they choose to communicate in a playful mode."

If the talk on IRC can be serious, can we still say that IRC is a game? In the broadest sense, the answer is yes. Wittgenstein's famous notion of language as a tool kit is very a propos:

> Think of the tools in a tool box, there is a hammer, pliers, a saw, a screw-driver, a rule, a glue-pot, glue, nails and screws—The functions of words are as diverse as the functions of these objects (Wittgenstein, 1968: para. 11)

Just as language provides the tools for a series of spoken (and, secondarily, written) language games, IRC provides a set of tools for many different kinds of writing-based language or symbolic games. The meta-message of the IRC GAME frame is, then, "Anything may be communicated in this frame."

Frame Three: LET'S HAVE A PARTY. The third frame opened up and running in the log is one whose meta-message is, "Let's have a party; let's have fun; participants enjoy reduced accountability; action and utterances are primarily in a playful mode." This is the first of three frames or windows in which three different genres of culturally constituted, playful activity are activated—PARTY, PRETEND-PLAY, and PERFORMANCE. All messages communicated within the PARTY frame enjoy reduced accountability; anything goes. The players get acquainted, chat, fool around, drink, flirt, and generally have a good time.

The party got started when <Thunder> created the channel in which it could take place. He proposed different whimsical names or themes, finally settled on one, and set a playful topic to go with it:

```
Line  53   *** Thunder invites you to channel 16
           *** Thunder invites you to channel 2
      55   *** Thunder invites you to channel 3
           *** Thunder invites you to channel 4
           *** Thunder invites you to channel 5
```

```
        *** Thunder invites you to channel 6
        *** Thunder invites you to channel 0
60      *** Thunder invites you to channel hmmm this is confusing
        /msg thunder hmm so much to choose from ! hehe
        *** Thunder invites you to channel -)
        *** Thunder invites you to channel \
        /msg thunder hahahaha
65      *** Thunder invites you to channel -)
        *** Thunder invites you to channel \
        /msg thunder no way!
        *** Thunder invites you to channel ok..I will stop now
        *** Thunder invites you to channel +bagelnosh
70      *** Thunder invites you to channel +noshbagel
        /msg thunder oh yeah?
        *** Thunder invites you to channel +hsonlegab
        ***Thunder invites you to channel +kinky sex with riding crops
        and handcuffs
75      /msg thunder I'll think about it.
        *** Thunder invites you to channel +weed
```

<Thunder> starts the party by playing with different nonsense names for his channel, first numbers, then typographic symbols which hint at the "smiley" collections circulating on the Net (Godin, 1993; Sanderson, 1993), or which may indicate that he was planning to perform for Ruedenberg in some way typographically. He changes the channel names so quickly that she cannot join any of them.

"Bagelnosh" was a channel that Ruedenberg and Madeline Slovenz-Low, another graduate student at New York University at the time, had often created on IRC. It had become a hang-out where regulars chatted daily. Play with the word "bagelnosh" continues to signal PARTY. First, <Thunder> reverses the two components as "noshbagel" (line 71), and then he types the word backwards, yielding "hsonlegab" (line 73). The next channel name proposed is "kinky sex with riding crops and handcuffs" (line 74). Suddenly the PARTY may be turning into dark play (Schechner, 1988). <Lucia> coyly says just, "I'll think about it." Finally, in line 76, <Thunder> settles on the channel name #weed which is to hold throughout the sequence, issuing the invitation to this channel five times—repetition being in itself, of course, playful. She immediately joins the channel . For anyone familiar with American student or youth culture, weed immediately signals marijuana, relaxing, having a good time together. Perhaps because she was past the age of youth culture, or was never much into smoking pot anyway, <Lucia> didn't get it at first.

<Thunder> further elaborates the PARTY frame by setting a topic:

Line 90   *** The topic is: ssssssssssssssss hmmm wheres all that smoke from?
        +weed

Play with symbols now becomes more sophisticated. <Thunder> anticipates the form of play which eventually becomes the highlight of this sequence. From the juxtaposition of *sssssssss...* and the phrase, "where's all that smoke from?" we realize that *sssss...* is meant to simulate undulating smoke, as well as—on further reflection—the sound made by the person smoking the weed, and, to boot, *s* even happens to be the first letter of the word "smoke" in English! Ruedenberg still doesn't get it. She thought "weed" referred to "garden."

> >the water is warm
> Line 95   \<Thunder> water?
> >smoke?
> \<Thunder> smoke yes
> \<Thunder> look at the channel name
> >silly me
> 100   >I imagined an overgrown garden
> >haha

Finally, \<Thunder> makes his intentions explicit:

> \<Thunder> I was thinking more of grass, herb, pot, marijuana :-)

The PARTY is now on, no matter who joins them, though if the others decline to share the marihuana too, maybe it won't be much of a party! We should be careful, of course, of reifying the frame. On the contrary, it is a fluid, dynamic thing, highly contingent. It can change at any moment, and needs constantly to be ratified.

As we mentioned earlier, another activity that signals PARTY in modern urban culture is drinking—alcoholic drinking. Soon after \<Lucia> and \<Thunder> finally settle into their "channel" and "topic," \<Kang> joins them (line 123). Later on, \<Rikitiki> and \<BlueAdept> arrive. \<Kang> takes on the role of party "host" when he offers \<BlueAdept> a drink:

> Line 336   \<Kang> icewater or rum blue?

Not receiving any clear acknowledgement of the offer, he expands the range of choices to include wine and coca cola (line 342). \<BlueAdept> asks for beer (line 344), but then changes his mind and asks instead for "peppermint schnapps line 336), saying that it has a better taste (line 350). \<BlueAdept> is parodying the repertoire of student culture, in our opinion. In RL, students don't drink much peppermint schnapps! Eventually even herbal tea is added to the list of options.

Another range of content which signals PARTY is flirtation and sexual innuendo. This is typical for IRC, MUDs and MOOs. Spotting a female-sounding name, players immediately begin to flirt, and even to harass the individual (Leslie, 1993; Turkle, 1995). \<Kang> is very curious about \<Lucia>:

> Line 592 \<Kang> lucia=female as i suspect?
> ...
> 637 \<Kang> so lucia single long?

Not getting any answer, he says it a little louder, but <Lucia> plays coy:

Line 656 <Kang> SO LUCIA SINGLE LONG?
      >oh my....

      ...

      661 >SINGLE ALL MY LIFE

      ...

      667 <Kang> how long has your life been thus far.

Not getting anywhere, he tries again, addressing his question to the group:

Line 695 <Kang> how old are y'all?

<Jah> quickly answers "18," and <Kang> follows this with the query "lu-cia?" (line 698). But no reply is forthcoming. Much later, when <Kang> leaves, he asks:

Line 810 <Kang> are we engaged?
      >huh?

      ...

      <Jah> IRC-engaged?
      >I don't think so
      <Kang> just kidding never did get your age lucia

But it is late. Ruedenberg is sleepy (it is between 2:30 and 3:00 AM Jerusalem time) and signs off.

In addition to overt flirting there is subtle sexual innuendo in the log, as in:

Line 538 <Kang> here lucia *hands bong*[7] long reach (over ocean)
      >oh
      540 >I don't smoke
      >thanks
      >I just watch
      >and enjoy your games
      <Kang> must be pretty funny
      545 >can't handle the stuff myself
      >yes it is cute
      <Kang> who can?
      >well you haven't seen me
      >I don't go up
      550 >I go down
      >badly
      <Kang> eh?
      >I curl up into a little ball and don't speak
      <Kang> I'll be kind and not razz about that one...
      555 >no fun at all
      >razz?
      >razz if you want
      <Kang> good thing we're not on +hottub!
      >up and down?
      560 >haha

The action dies down when <Lizardo> says to <Lucia>

Line 790 looks like you and me are the only ones left.

<Kang> reappears briefly and, as we saw, tries to flirt with <Lucia>. But <Lucia> logs off, and the PARTY is over.

Frame Four: LET'S PRETEND. The highlight of the party was a virtuoso simulation of smoking marihuana, that took place within frame four: "LET'S PRETEND," and culminates in a performance in Frame five (figure 1). All symbolic activity in the PRETEND frame contains the meta-message "Let us make-believe; let us suspend belief" (Handelman, 1976).

In RL, extended pretend-play of this type is unusual for adults, confined to specialized contexts such as the theater, charades, improvisation, masked balls and carnivals. Extended pretend-play is usually the province of children, who play doctor, Mommy and Daddy, riding a horse, and so on. Just as children improvise with props created from objects around them in the physical world, the participants in our log improvise with the only means available to them on IRC—those on the computer keyboard. They simulate the various stages of smoking marihuana via words which depict or represent action and experience, and via pictorial means—smiley icons that act out these actions, in a kind of typographic pantomime. The full explication of how this is done is presented in the next subsection on the PERFORMANCE frame.

Textual and typographic simulation is something like mime and charades in the physical world. Charades is a game in which individuals use their bodies and gestures to act out, nonverbally, some verbal content or idea. At least in the early stages of the simulation in our log, the situation is something like charades, in that <Thunder>, the person who initiates this aspect of the interaction, in essence makes virtual moves, which the others must decode. They quickly figure out the game of pretense being played, and begin to make contributions of their own. The activity becomes a collective enterprise.

In *Mime: A Playbook of Silent Fantasy*, Kay Hamblin (1978) asks her readers: "Would you like to fly? Would you like to be two people? Would you like to own a magic lamp? You can.... All you need are your body and your imagination"... (Hamblin, 1978: 15). This passage fits our log wonderfully well: all the players need are their fingers, a computer keyboard and their imagination.

Frame Five: PERFORMANCE. The final frame activated in the log is a PERFORMANCE frame. The meta-message of this frame is "Let's show each other what we can do with the keyboard." The players do their stuff, show off, improvising individually and collectively. Many features which we have known in oral performance in the past are present in this new variety of written interactive communication. Bauman (1975; 1977) suggests that performance represents a transformation of the basic referential uses of language. Performers say, "Look at me!" or "Look at us, and at what we can do!"

Fundamentally, performance…consists in the assumption of responsibility for a display of communicative competence…Performance involves on the part of the performer an assumption of accountability to an audience for the way in which communication is carried out, above and beyond its referential content….the act of expression…is thus marked as subject to evaluation for the way it is done, for the relative skill and effectiveness of the performer's display of competence…. Performance thus calls forth special attention to and heightened awareness of the act of expression and gives license to the audience to regard the act of expression and the performer with special intensity (Bauman, 1977, p. 11).

The PRETEND and PERFORMANCE frames are not necessarily both activated simultaneously, as they happen to be in the present case. Children can pretend to play doctor without any concern with showing off to each other. Here, the players show keen interest in showing off, and, as we shall see, they also explicitly demonstrate admiration for each others' skills, and even for their own performance.

The PERFORMANCE frame was activated from the very beginning of the log. <Thunder> was very conscious of the fact that <Lucia> wants to log their interactions. They had a rather long conversation about this, with <Thunder> expressing a good deal of ambivalence. He knew that she had the capacity to make the log, since he was the one who had set up an account for her on his computer through his university.

Line 15 /msg thunder I have to ask yo if you mind my logging sometimes or ever, if yo're on it.
Thunder I just watch what I say :-)
/msg thunder ever since you asked me what I planned to do with that log I need to know
Thunder if there is something I don't want logged that I said.. I merely run program and it disappears
/msg thunder I will not log if you do't want me to
20 *Thunder* it does not matter..I will not say anyghint[8] I don't want logged since I assume your log is always on anyway
/msg thunder but don't do that if it will kill whatever else I have done before you talk
Thunder it will do nothing to the rest of your log.. it will merely remove the lines with <Thunder> in them
/msg thunder all you have to say is - don't log me.
…
25 /msg thunder I turn it off.
Thunder ok :-)
…
45 *Thunder* whatever lucia..it does not matter
/msg thunder well…okay

In the end <Lucia> says, "You have the power to do what you want, meaning that she knows that he can erase himself from a log, or even cancel her capacity to make a log at all. But he allows the action to proceed.

This passage makes it clear that <Thunder> is super-aware of being watched by <Lucia>. While there may be reasons why he objects to being logged, he also recognizes that there is a favorable side to being observed: he can show off to an appreciative audience. His playful suggestions as to names of channels are the first signs that he is indeed performing for her. Later, he sends her a private message:

Line   511   *Thunder* so have you been loggin all this?

         ...

         514   *Thunder* I have been trying to make your log very colorful

The simulation and the performance actually begin when <Thunder> types:

Line   107   <Thunder> sssssssssssssss *passes joint to lucia*

Once again, he draws on the sequence of *s*'s to simulate the undulating smoke and the sound made when smoking the joint. Notice the use of the third person verb "passes," to describe his action, marked with a pair of asterisks. This is a striking and very common feature of communication in synchronous and even some nonsynchronous modes (Blackman and Clevenger, 1990; Godin, 1993; Sanderson, 1993). In the past we have encountered such forms only in authors' directions to actors or directors in the scripts of plays, and in comics as a means to add a dynamic quality to the representation of action. Abbott (1986: 156) points out that "there are three main types of language in comic art: narration, dialogue and sound effect." In the comics, the narrative portion of the individual frame of action is usually graphically marked off, appearing at the top or the bottom of the frame in a separately demarcated space. Here, the narration is inserted in the dialogue, making the experience of decoding it somewhat disconcerting for those unfamiliar with it.

When <Kang> joins the interaction, he also easily mobilizes third-person descriptions of his own actions (*puff*, *hold,* *exhale*), to simulate the acts of inhaling the smoke and keeping it inside one's body. *Puff* and *hold* may be either nominalizations or infinitives—the names of the actions, or even first-person verbs with the pronoun "I" deleted. <Thunder> keeps the simulation going by commenting whimsically that smoke is "filling the channel" (line 145). In the next line he sets the topic to "ssssssssssssssssssss." At first, this seems to be just a repetition of line 90. However, there are more *s*'s than before—an invitation for all to become even more deeply involved in the game, or else a way to express the meta-comment that they are "really getting into it." <Kang> responds appreciatively with a midget "smiley" (the nose is omitted— :)), and he remarks that they had better be careful—the smoke will "spread to other channels." <Kang> further simulates the effect of the drug on him by intentionally misspelling "suspicious":

Line   156   <Kang> they might be *sushpishus*, huh? :-) ...(italics added)

The intentional online representation of infelicities of pronunciation is new too: in the past we encountered it only in dialogue in comics, fiction and drama. As we have already seen, online conversation is full of unintentional misspellings, because people are trying to type very fast (as noted in footnote 10, these misspellings are retained in all examples cited in this chapter). Here, however, the misspelling is clearly intentional.

When <Rikitiki> and <BlueAdept> join the party, the verbal simulation of smoking marihuana continues. Sometimes the participants use third person verbs, as in

    Line 204 <Rikitiki> *inhales deeply*
          214 <Rikitiki> *exhales slowly*
          386 <BlueAdept> <tosses 1/4oz of red sense on the end table

<Thunder> does this too, repeating his *ssssssssssss* sequence yet again:

    Line 291 <Thunder> *exhales* ssssssssssssssssss

There is also use of the gerund, in

    Line 335 <BlueAdept> (packing a fat bongload)

In yet another variation on the theme of *sssssss*'s, <Thunder> continues to inhale and exhale, representing the gradually dissipating smoke by reducing, line by line, the number of "*s*'s."

              <Thunder> sssssssssssssssss
    Line 370 <Thunder> sssssssssssssssss
              <Thunder> ssss
              <Thunder> ss
              <Thunder> s
              <Thunder>
          375 <Thunder> wow

<Thunder> is obviously pleased with himself, commenting "Wow." <Rikitiki> and <BlueAdept> then depart, one saying he'll "be right back," abbreviated to "brb" (line 379), as is customary on IRC, (but <Rikitiki> does not return), and the other to get coffee (line 381).

The verbal simulation of action continues with new material: at line 387, <Thunder> "throws seeds into channel +hottub" and says "look they are floting (sic) in the tub hehe" (line 391); "maybe they will root" (line 393). Then, we have an unexpected, serendipitous pun. Now that <BlueAdept> has "thrown" some new dope, red sense, on the "end table," <Thunder> contributes:

    Line 397 <Thunder> need to pack a new bowel heheheheh hehehehehe...

<Thunder> has had a slip-of-the-finger: instead of "bowl" he typed "bowel." "What a typo!" he chortles, in line 400. Kang is quick to pick up on his mistake:

    Line 401 <Kang> not bowel!!!! bowel?

<Thunder> corrects himself, "laughing" at his mistake:

Line   403   <Thunder> need to pack a new bowl hehhehehehe

Kang packs the bowl for him. Then Thunder offers:

Line   408   <Thunder> that is shitty pot I would say if it was packing a bowel

At the risk of stating the obvious, <Thunder> is introducing "shitty" as his chosen negative adjective because it goes with "bowel." This word play is all the cleverer because, unlike other examples discussed so far, it is the spontaneous byproduct of a typo—a typing mistake. Typing mistakes in the mad rush of getting one's contribution onscreen are an important source of humor on IRC. Considering that all of this improvisation is taking place on the fly, <Thunder>'s performance is impressive, indeed.

<Lucia's> contribution to the simulation is "cookies." At line 228, <Thunder> had asked her:

Line   228   lucia guess what is on for tonight

At line 230 she replied "cookies." <Lucia> knows from a previous conversation on IRC with a friend of <Thunder> that he has friends coming over and that they plan to make cookies later that night. <Thunder> is thus referring to REAL-LIFE activity in his apartment, outside the IRC frame. Later on, <Lucia> asked:

Line   247   you will make cookies while you're on irc?

<Thunder> replies, "no lucia," again a reference to REAL-WORLD plans. Much time goes by with no further talk about cookies, till line 406, when <Lucia> comments,

> bake it into the cookies

Here, Ruedenberg attempts to draw the REAL-WORLD activity of making cookies into the play world of IRC, recalling the practice, a generation back, of putting marihuana into cookie or brownie dough. But this suggestion fails to capture the others' imagination. Apparently, putting pot into cookies and brownies is a thing of the past, something flower children did in the 1970s. Besides, <Thunder> replies, a few lines later, that he doesn't have enough pot to do so.

We said earlier that one of the signs that a performance is going on is the presence of audience behavior, of giving compliments, and so on. Although the audience can't clap in this silent world, they can demonstrate their appreciation in other ways. Even though only <Thunder> and <Lucia> know that a log is being made, the others also make many meta-communicative comments. Although <Lucia> declines to smoke dope at the beginning of the log, she shows appreciation for <Thunder>'s whimsical suggestions for channel names. She laughs at his silly suggestions (lines 61, 64, cited above in the section on the PARTY frame). And when <Kang> joins them and immediately begins simulating smoking dope, <Lucia> smiles appreciatively at his performance.

    Line 126 <Thunder> sssssssssssss *passes joint to kang*

            ...

            <Kang> thanx dude *puff* *hold*

            >:-)

            <Kang> comments on his own action:

  Line 138 <Thunder> kang exhale.. you will die :-)

            <Kang> *exhale*

            <Kang> ;)

<Kang> winks with pleasure at his performance and at the terrific simulation game they are playing.

Now we are ready to have a look at the passage which is really a tour de force, shown in table 2. A new stage of the simulation begins at line 419. <Kang> and <Thunder> start playing with icons as a means to simulate and represent the various stages of inhaling, exhaling, and so on.

This clever improvisation begins when <Kang> draws from his digital repertoire an icon which is not widely used in ordinary e-mail: :| . He performs it twice, then adding another icon.

    Line 419   <Kang> :|

            <Kang> :|

            <Kang> :\

            <Thunder> heheheh

            <Thunder> heheheheh

            <Thunder> that was great

Neither <Kang> nor <Thunder> need to say explicitly what the icons mean or why <Thunder> is laughing and complimenting him. The sequence means something like "puff, puff, hold the smoke inside." Inspired to continue, <Kang> improvises further:

  Line 425 <Kang> :/

            <Kang> :)

            <Thunder> hehehehehe

            <Kang> *exhale*

            <Kang> :0

Again, one can follow quite easily what is happening: in lines 425-6, <Kang> smiles after inhaling. He tries to improve on the improvisation, reverting momentarily to the verbal *exhale*, but then, once again, he zips out from his repertoire of icons the one using the figure for "zero." So now the entire sequence has been depicted pictorially.

This inspires <Thunder> to improve on <Kang>'s improvisation. Beginning in line 430, he tries to put the whole sequence together in one line:

    Line 430 <Thunder> :| :| :\sssss :)

Line 416	<Kang> *inhale* *hold* ....
	>why?
	<Thunder> :-)
	<Kang< :|
Line 420	<Kang> :|
	<Kang> :\
	<Thunder> heheheh
	<Thunder> heheheheheh
	<Thunder> that was great
Line 425	<Kang> :/
	<Kang> :)
	<Thunder> hehehehehhe
	<Kang> *exhale*
	<Kang> :0
Line 430	<Thunder> :| :| :\sssss :)
	<Kang> hheeeheee
	<Thunder> :-Q :| :| :\sssss :)
	<Thunder> heheheh
	<Kang> ever ... mmmmmmm.... heard of Gainesville Green?
Line 435	>:-) cute
	<Kang> my hometown!
	>never heard of it
	*** Thunder sets the topic to: \:-Q :-| :-| :\sssss :-)
	<Kang> ha!
Line 440	<Thunder> uggg
	*** Thunder sets the topic to: \ :-Q :-| :-| :\sssss :-)
	<Thunder> there we go
	<Thunder> the : was a problem I needed a \

Table 2. The representation of smoking marihuana with emoticons.

<Kang> laughs appreciatively, and <Thunder> continues:

Line 432 <Thunder> :-Q :\| :\| :\sssss :)

Here, like <Kang>, <Thunder> has retrieved a seldom-used icon from the collections circulating around the globe— :-Q —whose meaning is usually given as "man smoking a cigarette," the cigarette being the tail in the letter "Q." Now the sequence is perfect, and one can read it as "I put a joint into my mouth; I inhale twice, exhale, let the smoke out, and then experience pleasure." <Thunder> laughs with delight at his own performance, and <Lucia> compliments him too (line 435: " :-) cute"). The improvisation has now reached such heights that <Thunder> adopts the sequence as the topic of the channel (line 438).

Line 438 *** Thunder sets the topic to: \:-Q :-\| :-\| :\sssss :-)

He puts one final touch on the sequence, in line 441, separating the joint from the act of putting it in one's mouth:

Line 441 *** Thunder sets the topic to: \ :-Q :-| :-| :\sssss :-)

This is the high point in the PERFORMANCE frame. As we have seen, the players have been improvising with great relish, and have been very generous with compliments and encouragement to one another. Once again, we have to remember that all of this is done on the fly. To examine the text retrospectively as we are doing is to reify it; as observers we have difficulty imagining the moment-to-moment surprises which the players deliver, or see zipping across their screens. Presumably, they are experienced, and have acquired such skills from the many hours they have been spending on IRC, not necessarily with each other. As noted earlier, except for <Thunder> and <Rikitiki>, who know each other both in REAL LIFE, the others are all strangers, as far as we know, not only in REAL LIFE but even on IRC.

Playful Blurring of Frames

The players not only operate within frames; they blur the boundaries between frames in playful ways. Thus <Thunder> comments

Line 145 <Thunder> *as smoke fills the channel again*

He says that smoke is filling the channel—reversion to the terms of frame two, the IRC Games, and even perhaps to frame one, REAL LIFE, rather than referring to the imaginary room they have collectively constructed in which the action is taking place (frames three and four, figure 1). Another good example is the following, which we cited earlier:

Line 387 <Thunder> *throw seeds into channel +hottub*
391 <Thunder> look they are floting in the tub hehe

By mentioning channel <Thunder> is overtly referring to constitutive elements of the virtual IRC GAME as if they are physical places within the frame four simulation. Or, alternatively, we might want to say that frames three and four are being blended with frame two components. *#Hottub* is an imaginary place which is a longstanding, popular channel on IRC.[9]

A fine example of the blurring of frames is <Kang>'s remark

Line 538 <Kang> here lucia *hands bong* *long reach (over ocean)*

Here <Kang> partially steps out of the PRETEND frame. The "bong" from the PRETEND frame is suddenly mixed with REAL LIFE—<Kang> takes explicit account of where <Lucia> is in the REAL WORLD, geographically! So she is, somehow, both in the imaginary playroom where they are having the PARTY and pretending to smoke dope and yet, paradoxically, sitting somewhere in Jerusalem at a computer screen.

Further Aspects of Play with Frames

Figure 1 provides a useful representation of the dominant frames in the log, and of the experience of the group as a whole. However, the actual experience of individuals is much more complicated than this, and would require another kind of graphic presentation which incorporated more than one dimension. For one thing, players can at any time exchange private messages with others, both within the same channel and even between channels. These messages appear only on the screens of those sending and receiving them. There are many such private messages between <Thunder> and <Lucia> in this log. Logs made by other participants would probably reveal the exchange of other private messages, thus producing a quite different text. To illustrate the polyphonic nature of the encounter, with private messages interspersed with public ones, here, again, is a passage cited earlier to make a different point:

Line   511   *Thunder* so have you been loggin all this?
                <Kang> *puff* *hold*
                ...
                Thunder I have been trying to make your log very colorful
                <Kang> ouch!
                <Kang> *koff* *koff*
                /msg thunder well you have been very cute

In lines 511 and 514 <Thunder> has sent Ruedenberg private messages, and in line 517 she sends him one.

It should be apparent that private messages can themselves be in any of the five frames, just as public ones can be. <Thunder>'s questions are in the REAL-LIFE frame—he wants to know if she has been logging and tells her he is trying to make her log colorful. Her message is in the performance frame: "you have been very cute." Still another way in which participants can maintain complex multiple frames is by being in more than one channel at the same time. <Lucia> did not take advantage of this option during this virtual party.

Afterthoughts

The 75 minutes or so of interaction analyzed in this chapter constitute but a tiny fragment of the millions, perhaps billions of words have been written, performed, danced, if you will, on IRC since its introduction in 1988. The textual party analyzed here revealed a remarkable degree of structure and coherence. Like REAL-WORLD parties, it had a clear beginning, middle and end; when the last guests left, the party was over. No doubt, it owed its structure in part to the previous contact between <Lucia> and <Thunder> and to his awareness that she had an ongoing interest in his ability to perform on IRC. However, as indicated earlier, except for <Rikitiki>, whom <Thunder> knew both in REAL LIFE and on IRC, we believe that the players had not interacted with each other before on IRC.

Like many REAL-WORLD parties, this virtual one had a featured activity which engrossed participants intensely, not dancing or drinking or flirting, but a textual form of virtuoso collective mime—not smoking pot but improvising a typographic simulation of it. The double agenda of play and performance was evident in the meta-comments that participants made about the simulation—they gave themselves and others compliments for their performance.

In addition to play with identity and with frames of interaction, we found a rich array of forms of play with writing itself: with spelling, typographic conventions, language as code, homonyms, and other aspects of sound—phonetic contrast, reduplication, etc. We also discovered verbal and visual puns, both intentional and serendipitous.

IRC and the Theory of Play

From the material analyzed in this chapter, we can see that playful interaction on IRC contains many important components of Caillois's (1961) classic typology of types of play and games. In its moment-to-moment quality as a textual "happening," our material has clear affinities with the phenomena of tumult, agitation, immoderate laughter, improvisation and joy that Caillois associates with *PAIDIA*—letting oneself go through the spontaneous manifestations of the play instinct (Caillois, 1961: 28).

At the same time, *LUDUS*, "a taste for gratuitous difficulty," as expressed in games of all kinds (Caillois, 1961: 27), is also strongly present, not only at the level of the constitutive rules of the basic IRC game, but at the level of emergent regulative but optional conventions of expression, such as those for the depiction of physical action. Perhaps even more important, *LUDUS* is dominant when the participants are conscious of performing for one another, because it is here that skill comes to the fore. As we saw, this self-consciousness was most evident during the simulation of smoking marihuana, when the players frequently complimented one another on their clever improvisations.

Caillois distinguishes between four categories of play, each of which has a *PAIDIA*-dominant set of play forms, on the one hand, and a *LUDUS*-dominant one, on the other. Caillois's famous typology is presented in figure 2. Types of play shown in the first row are closest, in his view, to the *PAIDIA* end of the continuum. Those in the second and third rows are closer to the *LUDUS* end. For *agon* or contest, Caillois contrasted the turbulent activity of racing and wrestling with football and chess, both heavily constrained, indeed constituted by rules. To illustrate *alea*, or chance, his second type of play, he distinguished between counting-out rhymes at the *PAIDIA* end and betting and roulette at the *LUDUS* end. For *mimicry*, or simulation, children's tag and the use of masks are contrasted with theater and spectacles. Finally, *ilinx*, or vertigo, characterizes horseback riding and waltzing at the *PAIDIA* end, and skiing and tightrope walking at the *LUDUS* end.

Where among all these types of play does interaction on IRC fall? At the level of the text, two are prominent, as we have seen—*agon* and *mimicry*. *Ilinx* and *alea*, on the other hand, are probably not usually discernible in the text itself, but rather are part of the experience of the players.

Contest is prominent in participants' tendency to show off, to perform for one another, as in sports and other RL forms of competitive play such as verbal dueling (Huizinga, 1955; Caillois, 1961; Labov, 1972; Gossen, 1976) and playful modes of "flaming" online (Danet, in press). In this respect, interaction on IRC seems to fall midway on the continuum between *PAIDIA* and *LUDUS*: contest is neither totally unregulated nor totally stylized or dictated by the rules. Second, *mimicry* is rampant in IRC, not only in specific instances of the representation of action (as in *puff* *puff* *hold*), but in more extended sequences like the simulation of smoking marihuana in the present case.

Third, we suggest that there is also a component of *ilinx*, of losing oneself, in IRC. While this is not directly evident in the text, we know from our own experience that sitting for hours and hours in front of the keyboard while on IRC can indeed be addictive. This aspect of IRC is discussed further in the next section.

As for *alea*, or chance, at least superficially, IRC and other synchronous modes of digital communication appear to have little in common with card games or lotteries, for instance. In face-to-face encounters, chance alone is not ordinarily the basis of interaction; on the contrary, usually, we exercise some choice in those with whom we interact. At the same time, there are some settings where chance is actually sought out, for instance, singles bars, pubs, large private parties. On closer inspection, there is an element of *alea* in IRC encounters, too. For one thing, it is a matter of luck who is already logged on when an individual joins the crowd in a particular channel, especially when visiting an established channel for the first time, or when creating a new one which others eventually join. Similarly, if a channel is left open or public, participants have no prior knowledge or control over who will join them (though a user can type */whois channel_name* to see who is on a channel before joining it). Finally, in any given encounter, it is also a matter of chance how skilled the other participants are in manipulating symbols in cyberspace—thus contest and *alea* are linked, here as elsewhere. In this particular case, <Thunder> and <Kang> were particularly well matched, and stimulated each other to reach increasingly greater heights.

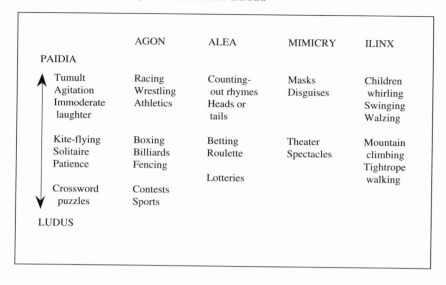

Figure 2. Caillois's typology of types of play and games.

Virtual Pubs and Cafes and the Art of Conversation

The phenomena discussed in this chapter also have wider cultural significance. Stylized online communication in real time is rapidly becoming a new form of leisure activity for the young, educated, and computer-literate. In the four years since this virtual party took place, dozens, probably hundreds of channels on IRC have become stable gathering places for online conviviality, relaxation, small talk, and virtuoso wordplay and use of the computer keyboard—each with its own regulars. These virtual pubs and cafes have become a new kind of third place—places lying somewhere between home and work where people can engage in relaxed conviviality (Oldenburg, 1989; Coate, 1992; Rheingold, 1993; Kirshenblatt-Gimblett, 1996).

> Third places exist on neutral ground and serve to level their guests to a condition of social equality. Within these places, conversation is the primary activity and the major vehicle for the display and appreciation of human personality and individuality....Since the formal institutions of society make stronger claims on the individual, third places are normally open in the off hours, as well as at other times. The character of a third place is determined most of all by its regular clientele and is marked by a playful mood. (Oldenburg, 1989: 42).

Many channels now have regular RL gatherings, which may be annual, biannual, monthly, and so on. For instance, regulars on *#gb*, a channel mainly populated by persons living in Great Britain, gather once a month in a London pub.[10] *#TahitiBar,* a channel for Finns, holds RL beach parties; other festivities include an October Fest and a Winter Sports Day. Dozens of channels now have Home Pages on the World Wide Web, complete with photographs of regulars, reports of past group gatherings along with photographs of those present, news about upcoming RL social events, and so on.

While each channel has no doubt developed its own subculture, unique in some respects, it is very likely that artful communication style is valued in all of them. Few make this explicit, however. Thus, the *#CoffeeHouse* Home Page advertises a "general conversation room," and announces simply that "Anyone desiring light conversation and good company should feel right at home here." Another channel, *#thecafe,* is a bit more explicit. This channel's Home Page declares, "Our channel on IRC is dedicated to the idea of *good conversation* and the belief that everyone is welcome to our channel, unless you prove to us differently."[11]

These developments can be viewed as a partial return to artful communication patterns characteristic of cultures without writing (Ong, 1982; Bolter, 1991; Lanham, 1993). But will virtual cafes and pubs remain merely a venue for light-weight chit-chat by young people? Might there even be in time a more profound revival of the art of conversation, as it flourished in 18th-century England (Kernan, 1987: 206-208; Broadhead, 1980), when not only form but substance was cherished? Perhaps this is an overly idealistic expectation, since we will never be able to type as fast as we speak, and online typed contributions will always share some of the same infelicities as spontaneous, unplanned conversation.[12]

Expanding the Expressive Possibilities of IRC: The Hamnet Players

More or less unplanned online improvisation is the typical pattern on IRC. A group called the Hamnet Players has taken the expressive possibilities of the IRC software and the computer keyboard a giant step further, in an attempt to create *virtual theater,* or an online performance art forum. Founded by Stuart Harris, an Englishman now living in California and a computer professional with a good deal of theater experience, the Hamnet Players have scripted and performed three hilarious parodies thus far.

Harris wrote an 80-line send-up of *Hamlet,* called "Hamnet" ("hamming it up on the Net"); this was followed by "PCbeth—An IBM Clone," a parody of *Macbeth* with obvious play on the contemporary tension between fans of the PC and the Macintosh, respectively. Finally, the most recent production was a takeoff on Tennesee Williams' *Streetcar Named Desire,* called "An IRC Channel Named #Desire." The main source of humor in these partly scripted, partly improvised productions, which take place—of course—in a channel called *#hamnet,* is the incongruous, outrageous juxtaposition of canonical plot and language with IRC and other computer jargon and various types of content from contemporary culture. In addition to being a form of virtual theater, Hamnet productions are extravagant carnivals of wordplay and other forms of typed online improvisation. Many of the phenomena discussed in this chapter recur in even richer form than in the material analyzed here (Danet, 1994; Danet, et al., 1995).

Playfulness and the Invention of Writing

Treatises on the invention and history of writing (e.g., Gelb, 1963; Gaur, 1984; André-Leicknam and Zeigler, 1982) seem to imply that pioneers in the development of writing systems went about their business with a seriousness of purpose which contrasts sharply with the playfulness highlighted in this chapter. In our view, this research invites speculation about the very earliest stages in the history of writing. The fun of inventing and using smiley icons, as well as the entire panoply of play with writing that we have discussed here suggest that inventors of writing systems, thousands of years ago, must have had marvelous fun while creating them.

The Light and Dark Sides of IRC

Synchronous and even nonsynchronous modes of CMC occasionally generate quite moving forms of cooperation, as when group members who may never have met, except electronically, mobilize to help individuals in very serious REAL LIFE trouble, in some cases providing far more than just moral support. Rheingold (1993, chap. 1), describes several such examples for the WELL. During the Gulf War, along with electronic discussion lists, IRC was a means for Israelis to communicate directly from their sealed rooms during missile attacks (Werman, 1993). And during the earthquake in the Los Angeles area in January, 1994, emergency channels with names like "Earthquake" were set up on IRC. Some provided up-to-date information on damage and aftershocks; another, run by ham radio operators, offered a volunteer relay service—to telephone friends and family, check on them, and report back to those sending requests.

But we should not be misled by dramatic events of this kind or by the charmingly playful tenor of the log analyzed in this chapter. Cyberspace is by no means wholly benign, and IRC is no exception (cf. Reid, 1991; Dibbell, 1996). The synchronous modes of CMC can release aggressive, even shockingly malicious behavior, including sexual harassment of females. Moreover, people can get themselves into fairly unpleasant RL trouble. One striking example, by now well known on the Net, is the case of the New York male psychiatrist who misled a number of coparticipants on the CB channel of CompuServe into believing he was a woman (cf. van Gelder, 1986). Perhaps the most dramatic instance, to date, is a textual rape on LambdaMOO and the genuine shock and furor it generated (Dibbell, 1996; MacKinnon, 1997).

In short, along with the exhilaration, sheer fun, zany inventiveness, and sense of flow that participants enjoy on IRC, there is a fair amount of extremely offensive, downright provocative aggressiveness, none of which is evident in the log we studied. In part the potential for it is built into the game, which includes such commands as /kill and /kick, which offer, respectively, the possibility of removing another person from the channel or from IRC altogether (one can use the /ignore command to prevent contributions from a certain person from appearing on one's own screen). The channel operator can use the command /kick to remove another person from a channel, but only IRC operators can actually /kill a person—bumping them altogether from IRC (participants can, if they want, immediately log back on, with another nick).

Ironically, although these commands were originally created to control the behavior of aggressive persons, they are used, in fact, as a means of aggression. Two members of our research team, Haya Bechar-Israeli and Tsameret Wachenhauser, were witnesses to such aggression online. Three individuals who appeared to be Neo-Nazis logged on from Munich addressed grossly anti-Semitic remarks to them, racing from channel to channel to repeat them.

Another aspect of the dark side of IRC and other synchronous modes is its addictiveness, mentioned above. This is a special case of the more general addictiveness of interaction with computers (Turkle, 1984). Strictly speaking, one should be wary of labeling it as a psychological addiction in the full sense. Nevertheless, computers *can* have a destructive influence on one's life. Rudy Rucker writes:

> As one of my fellow teachers at San Jose said to me, "Computers are to the nineties what LSD was to the sixties." With cool graphics and virtual reality, we can pursue the dream of the pure, nonphysical software high. (Rucker, 1992, p. 11).

Participants on IRC often speak of addiction not just metaphorically—admitting that they spend long hours at the computer at the expense of their physical and mental health, social life, studies or occupation. In November-December, 1991, around the time that the log analyzed in this chapter was made, Ruedenberg experienced a "totally irrational fascination with the medium and the people," often going to sleep at 5:00 or 6:00 AM after chatting for five hours or more. This fascination was eventually rationalized into a research interest in the topic. Madeline Slovenz-Low, a friend and fellow student at New York University, who also logged onto IRC today describes herself has having been obsessed. Her behavior was so extreme that her husband was worried about her, seated in the middle of their living room, in front of the computer for hours on end, head phones blaring the blues in her ears, slightly tipsy from drinking Southern Comfort. We have also heard of cases of students that report marathons of 24 hours and the need for alt.irc.recovery, a support group on USENET for those seeking release from their addiction.

IRC, Technology and the Human Spirit

Because synchronous modes like IRC and MUDs and MOOs have this addictive quality, they have the potential to cause breakdown in computer services, or so the managers of these services claim. Thus, MUDs have actually been banned in some places. In Israel, only four of the seven academic institutions allow direct access to IRC via local mainframe computers. IRC is banned at the Hebrew University; we gained access to it via another university server only after submitting a request to use it for research and teaching purposes. After four years of research, we are still fighting for recognition of the legitimacy of IRC and of our research on it.

It is not hard to argue that chat modes can be counter-productive for individuals, given that the majority of participants are, apparently, male 19- or 20-year-old computer science students who may be neglecting their course work. The potential for subversive behavior on IRC and other chat modes is similar to that of comics and graffiti, both in the diversion of the medium to other uses, and in the actual content produced (Estren, 1974; Sabin, 1993; Abel and Buckley, 1977; Castleman, 1982). This was well illustrated by the log analyzed in this chapter, whose highlight was, as we saw, the simulation of an illegal activity. Players' delight could only have been enhanced by the knowledge that they were simulating something illegal!

Although endless hanging out on IRC might, for example, tie up telephone lines, thereby blocking access of faculty members to their data and e-mail on mainframe computers, nevertheless, we see regulars on irc as pioneers experimenting with new forms of human expression. Contrary to the pessimism about the alienating effects of computers so often heard in the media, and to the position of technological determinism adopted by academics like Ong (1982) and Heim (1987), among others, our work identifies some of the ways that people domesticate, transform, and subvert these new technologies to make them their own. Just as the natural response of a kitten to a ball of knitting wool is to tap it, roll it around with its paws, fiddle with it (Schechner, 1988), so millions of people of all ages and all walks of life are now fiddling with their computers, modems and keyboards. Meyer and Thomas (1990) have written of the computer underground that "It is this style of playful rebellion, irreverent subversion, and juxtaposition of fantasy with high-tech reality that impels us to interpret the computer underground as a postmodern culture (Meyer and Thomas, 1990). The log we have analyzed in this chapter strikingly illustrates the postmodern nature of digital writing and speech play in chat-forms like IRC (Poster, 1990: 128; Meyer and Thomas, 1990; Reid, 1991).

Notes

1. We would like to thank Barbara Kirshenblatt-Gimblett, Tamar Katriel, Irit Katriel, and Hagai Katriel, for help and encouragement, and Fay Sudweeks, Sheizaf Rafaeli, and Margaret McLaughlin for feedback on earlier versions of this chapter, and for the opportunity to be honorary members of ProjectH. Nachman Ben-Yehuda and Noit Meshorer provided information on terms associated with the culture of smoking marihuana. We owe a special debt to <Thunder>, the central figure in the "virtual party" analyzed in this chapter, for faciliatating Ruedenberg's entrance into the world of irc and for making this virtual party possible.

2. Personal email communication from Richard Schechner, August, 1993.

3. See Bechar-Israeli (1995), the corpus of 260 nicks.

4. The asterisks around <Thunder>'s message are an indication from the irc software that this was sent as a private message; that is, he has typed /msg lucia I am gonna shower soon. The asterisks around his nick would show up only on the screens of all others logged onto the channel.

5. Ghanja is a kind of Indian hashish. This information was supplied by Nachman Ben Yehuda.

6. Lines marked with three asterisks are acknowledgements by the software of execution of commands; thus <Thunder> had typed, /invite lucia #weed.

7. Noit Meshorer informed us that a "bong" is a bottle with water in it, something like an improvised nargila pipe, for smoking marihuana.

8. All typos and other forms of infelicitous expression which occurred during the interaction and are preserved in the log are reproduced here as in the original

9. Like many channels with a well-developed collective identity on IRC, #hottub now has its own Home Page on the World Wide Web, complete with photos of "regulars," reports of past RL gatherings and plans about future ones. See footnote 11 for URLs (Universal Resource Locator, address on the World Wide Web) of #hottub and other virtual pubs and cafes on IRC. See also URL http://www.yahoo.com/, entries for IRC under Computers-Internet. For a large inventory of cybercafes generally, see the Cybercafe Guide at URL http://www.easynet.co.uk/pages/cafe/ccafe.html.

10. Personal communication from Haya Bechar-Israeli, a regular on this channel, though residing in Israel.

11. Here are just a few examples of virtual cafes and pubs on IRC with Home Pages on the World Wide Web:

   #nicecafe URL http://www.cs.utk.edu/~hill/nicecafe/cafe.html

   #thecafe URL http://www.lava.net/~eddiaz/index1.html

   #hottub URL http://www.fff.ccc.mn.us/kevin/hottub/hottub.htm or http://tech.west.ora.com/hottub/

   #tahitibar URL http://www.jyu.fi/tahibitar/

   #CoffeeHouse URL http://www.cyberenet.net/~cusumano/coffee.html

Many channels with geographically based names, e.g., *#gb* (Great Britain) and *#england*, function as virtual pubs and cafes too. Note that the World Wide Web is extremely dynamic, with new sites appearing and old ones disappearing every day; thus some of these addresses may be obsolete by the time this chapter appears in print.

12. Note that those who cling to the norms of formal good writing associated with literate culture decry, e.g., the syntactic sloppiness and spelling mistakes in postings to listserv lists and Usenet newsgroups, thereby failing to take account of the oral nature of the medium. In our opinion, this medium is much too new to make predictions one way or another as to what patterns will emerge, though the return to a preference for stylization, as opposed to one for ostensibly transparent meaning in written prose, seems quite stable. The increased available of video conferencing and sound might make virtual cafe conversation (spoken, not typed) a more serious possibility than it is today.

CHAPTER FIVE

Media Use in an Electronic Community

Steve Jones

The dichotomy between mass society and community permeates the discourse concerning mass media and mass culture. A significant thread in that discourse concerns the transformation of mass society into tightly-knit communities by way of electronic communication. J. Carey finds this to be "an increasingly prevalent and popular brand of the futurist ethos, one that identifies...computers and information with a new birth of community" (1989). An important element in the futurist ethos is the penetration of personal computers and their concomitant communication technologies into everyday life. And it is equally as possible that computer-mediated communication will separate participants and content by way of compartmentalizing messages and users, as well as disinhibiting users, thus leading to heightened interpersonal (computer-mediated) conflict, thereby playing a role in the death of community.

This study examines one facet of the penetration of personal computers into everyday life. It seeks to discover how members of a Usenet newsgroup value and use news sources. At a time when the news media are making efforts to have an online presence, and communication service providers are working to bring online services to consumers, an important area of study is the nature of news in the context of computer-mediated communication (CMC).

This study of media use in soc.culture.yugoslavia brings together ideas from two separate research strands: the study of media use, and the study of new communication forms. The most developed tradition of media use research relates media use to community ties. The Minnesota community research program (Tichenor, Donohue and Olien, 1980 and 1970; Donohue, Tichenor and Olien, 1975; Olien Donohue and Tichenor, 1978) concluded that "strong community ties are major forces leading to reading the local newspaper" (Tichenor, Donohue and Olien, 1980, pp. 57), though subsequent studies showed fewer direct ties (Stamm, 1985). The Minnesota research tells us about how communities use the media. They offer one account of how media are linked to communities. It also investigated how mass media are used as means of social control by powerful elites in the community. In the research cited definitions of community play a lesser role than the news media, and in some instances (most notably Tichenor, Donohue & Olien, 1980) community goes undefined. A new type of community, an electronic, or virtual community has been forecast, and one can see some form of it in the variety of computer networks (Internet, Usenet) and electronic on-line services (CompuServe, America Online) now available (Jones, 1995). In regard to this study, definition of community as "a variable of social relations...a complex of ideas and sentiments" (Calhoun, 1980, p. 107) is most appropriate.

Another thread in media use research is related to the choices people make when faced with an array of media to use for their own communication (Fulk, Steinfield, Schmitz, and Power, 1987).

As N. K. Baym notes in the context of another newsgroup,

> the ways in which people have appropriated the commercial and noncommercial networks demonstrate that CMC not only lends itself to social uses but is, in fact, a site for an unusual amount of social creativity (1995, p. 162; see also Rice and Love, 1987 for discussion of creativity).

New communication forms problematize the concept of "media use." In previous research, such as Tichenor's, media use is largely considered reading, and that activity is tied mostly to newspapers. CMC users have appropriated news sources for their own purposes. Schweitzer (1991) includes in media use other media consumption activities, such as television viewing. Delener and Neelankavil (1990) consider media consumption behaviors solely on the basis of time spent attending to a particular medium. Garramone et al. (1986) provide a more active view of media use insofar as it is connected to consumer choice of media for communication (rather than solely for consumption), but even in that case, attention is not paid to the actual uses to which a medium may be put, beyond the gathering of political information.

Indeed, there is something profoundly alienating about traditional definitions of media use. Though they may provide opportunities for measurement of audience activity related to the media, they paint, overall, a generally passive picture of the consumer, leaving out the active processes of meaning-making in which people engage. It is necessary to consider media use a particularly active process in electronic contexts, in part because CMC provides hypertextlike discourse and also because traditional media (newspapers, television, etc.) are fodder for conversation and discourse via CMC (one glimpse at Usenet provides ample evidence). Indeed, as Rogers (1986) claims, computer- mediated communication is distinctively interactive when compared to traditional media. Thus, to put it another way, media content becomes part of CMC content, and "readership" is not nearly as interesting an issue as is authorship based, in turn, on readership.

In essence, media users in an electronic community choose to redistribute (or reauthor) news stories. A study of personal computer owners and media use showed that "adopters of new information technologies do not necessarily give up more traditional communication media in order to adopt the new communication forms" (Schweitzer, 1991, p. 689). Because a wide variety of electronic news sources are available to computer users, including the AP, UPI, Reuters news wire, as well as *USA Today*'s Decisionline, will members of an electronic community predominantly use electronic news sources? It is important to discover what news sources matter to network users. What are the implications of changes in users' valuation of news and its redistribution?

Jeffres, Dobos and Lee (1988) made some effort at answering a similar question, as related to television and, again, only as regards the consumption of a media text. If media use is redefined to include the consumption *and* production of texts, and those activities occur on a worldwide scale thanks to the Internet and Usenet, how does this use of news affect our ideas about media use and community ties?

The Newsgroup

The group I studied is soc.culture.yugoslavia on Usenet, a "set of machines that exchanges articles tagged with one or more universally-recognized labels, called *newsgroups*" (Kehoe, 1992, p. 29). The reasons for the selection of soc.culture.yugoslavia are several. First, it is a group mired in conflict, mirroring the wars in the former country of Yugoslavia. The electronic messages that were captured from the group for this study were collected daily between June 1991 and July 1992, during a time of escalation in the ethnic wars there. Group members would therefore be likely to desire more information about the status of the war, especially since until June, 1992 when the war commanded international attention, coverage was relatively sparse.

Since reporting of that conflict had been limited, information about the situation in the former Yugoslavia was often passed from person to person, or from one person to many, electronically. Its passage, by way of citation and comment, reflects the attitudes toward media, and related information sources among community members.

For instance, postings of news stories can precipitate antagonistic discussions of both individual bias and media bias. One typical exchange was initiated after a letter to the Toronto *Globe and Mail* was published in early 1993. A portion of that letter was posted to the newsgroup:

> The blanket condemnation of the Serbian nation and the misrepresentation of the Serbian position would not be so deeply trenched in the media if people like my friend were not so willing to endorse any position or stereotype, as long as it

ostensibly leads to peace. An unreflective and sensational press—the electronic media in particular—has provided a well-meaning public with simplistic solutions to a complex situation.

The person who posted this message claimed the letter "explains rather well Serbian position" [sic]. However, the ensuing exchange in message threads related to that posting focused on media representations of the sides in the war, typified by comments like this one:

> I have seen plenty of new stories about Serbs civilians being victimized. But please, Bosnian Serbs are not the main victims, unless CNN, ABC, NBC have it all wrong.

What is particularly interesting about these postings is that they point to an active readership making clear its constructions. In that regard, soc.culture.yugoslavia is a site at which to view how audiences interpret media. Lindlof (1989) finds two conceptions of meaning in relation to media audiences: presented meaning and constructed meaning. The former is text-based; that is, it claims that meaning is found in content. The latter is interpretive, and claims that meaning is controlled through interpretation. This study seeks to attend particularly to the concept of constructed meaning in relation to the interpretive community that is soc.culture.yugoslavia.

Newsgroup Content

A total of 6,192 electronic messages were collected from the soc.culture.yugoslavia group on Usenet during the period June 1991 to July 1992. Although some messages were duplicated, first sent and perhaps re-sent to confirm delivery, only original, and not duplicate, messages were analyzed. Some messages were sent from other groups by way of "cross-posting," a form of sending one message to multiple groups. Cross-posted messages were included in the analysis as they were considered part of the discourse on soc.culture.yugoslavia. While there is the possibility that some messages were misrouted by the numerous computers in the Usenet chain and are missing from this analysis, the chances of this are very slim. It is likely that few messages suffered such a fate, and since all messages were analyzed and no form of sampling was involved, any such loss should be acceptable. Duplicate messages created by group members unsure of how to use Usenet software were discarded.

A content analysis of soc.culture.yugoslavia messages was undertaken following methods established by Krippendorf (1980), Holsti (1969), and Rosengren (1981). The procedure followed was to capture messages in ASCII text form on an IBM-PC. Each message was read to determine whether or not it contained reference to a news source. In all, 6,087 messages were analyzed; 1,120 messages mentioned a news source. These 1,120 messages were then coded using the following categories: news source name; news source type (print, broadcast, electronic); news source location; message sender location (determined from the sender's electronic mail address). Each message that contained mention of a news source, information directly attributed to a news source (paraphrased or quoted), or text re-posted directly from a news source was coded. A news source was defined as any institutionalized, mass-mediated source of information. The news source was coded once for each message in which it was mentioned. If a news source was mentioned multiple times in a message it was only coded once. If a message posted in the newsgroup quoted a previous poster's message referencing a news source, the quoting in the second message was not considered a new instance of a news source mention. The content analysis was performed by the author.

The 1,120 messages analyzed were posted by 131 individuals. A check of all messages analyzed revealed that 211 individuals contributed messages to the newsgroup. Because it is possible to hold more than one electronic mail address, it is also possible that these numbers are inflated. It should also be noted at the outset that members of this particular group are part of a larger social group of business people, academicians, independent scholars, college and university students, and computer professionals who use computer network services. Nevertheless, since what is of interest is media use situated in electronic discourse, the number and type of individuals should not be a primary concern, though study of group members may be of interest for future research. Because this study uses content manifest in posted messages, it is important to remember that it reflects media use among those who post messages, and not among those who read the newsgroup without posting their own messages. It is also important to note that the posters set the discourse agenda for the (presumably) larger audience of "lurkers" (that is, those who read the newsgroup but do not themselves post messages).

Results

An analysis of news sources mentioned in messages on soc.culture.yugoslavia showed that *Vreme*, an electronic digest of a Belgrade, Serbia-based periodical, led all sources with 141 messages in which it was mentioned, representing 12.59 percent of total news sources mentioned (figure 1). *Vreme* is available to those with Internet access, and copies of some of the stories from it were regularly posted on the newsgroup.

An aggregated analysis of news sources illustrated in figure 2 showed that electronic news sources predominated among those mentioned on soc.culture.yugoslavia (46%), followed by print news sources (36%) and, lastly, broadcast news sources (18%).

In light of the electronic nature of the newsgroup this spread is not surpris-

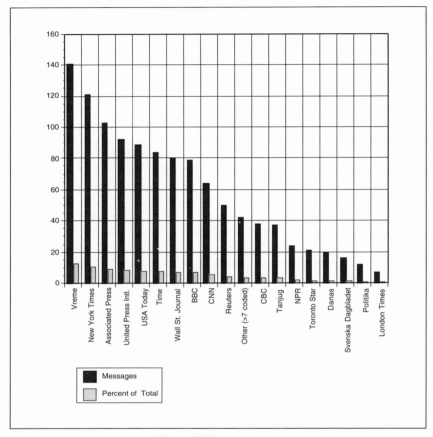

Figure 1. News sources.

ing. It does point, however, to a heavy, or at least heavier, use of electronic news sources like news wires available on the Internet or other BBSs. This finding supplements Schweitzer's assertion that personal computer use "did not lead to radical changes in use of traditional news media" (1991, p. 689) because it shows that, while users did not abandon traditional media, they did adopt new media as news sources. Although Schweitzer based his claim on analysis of readership surveys and not on analysis of news sources mentioned in, say, conversation, rendering comparisons problematic, these findings do point to a change in use of traditional news media.

Figure 3 breaks down the location, or geographic origin, of news sources mentioned. A comparison with message sender location reveals that most news sources mentioned originated in US media centers (New York and

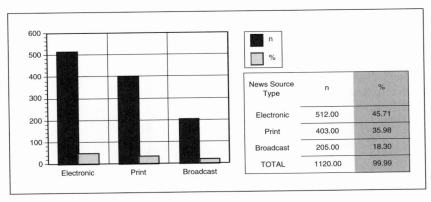

Figure 2. Types of news sources.

Washington). Most (just over two-thirds) of the individuals posting messages mentioning news sources are based in the US as well (figure 4). However, upon closer examination it is clear that there is little similar connection between message sender location and news source location, and a further breakdown of message senders by state (figure 5) reveals that news sources are not linked to geographic location of the message sender. The analysis of messages with news sources mentioned demonstrated no significant correlation ($r = .021$) between message sender location and news source location.

Newsgroup Users

A questionnaire was posted to the newsgroup in November, 1993, initially in an effort to gain demographic information about its users once data had been collected for content analysis. 128 responses were received. It is difficult to discern a response rate in this instance, insofar as the questionnaire was publicly posted. Information that has since been compiled about many newsgroups is not available for the time during which the questionnaire was posted on soc.culture.yugoslavia. Moreover, though the questionnaire was posted well after the sample of messages was taken for the previous section of this study, it is believed that the high proportion of nonstudents among posters means that user turnover was infrequent.

The information in figure 6 was compiled from the responses. Given the general availability of the Internet, and hence Usenet, to academic communities, these results are only relatively surprising. The results suggest cautious use of the data since the population is ill-defined, and the response rate may be very low. Yet the population does likely represent both posters and lurkers.

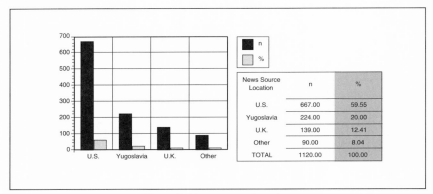

Figure 3. News source location.

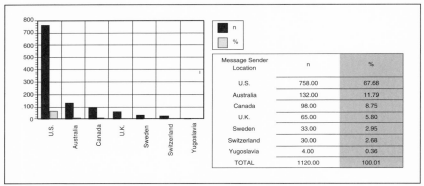

Figure 4. Message sender location.

From the questionnaire responses a random sample of 14 respondents was chosen for on-line interviews. It was at this point that attitudes toward news sources and their usefulness became most clear. Most of the respondents interviewed stated that the Internet had become a major news source in its own right. One respondent, for instance, said, "I really appreciate the electronic mail sources for news," in reference to being able to reach *USA Today*, and that "the Usenet newsgroups are a second source of news." Another respondent stated that he would not know very much about events in the former Yugoslavia were it not for Usenet. Still another stated that Usenet is useful because it "digestifies" news reports, often including ones unavailable locally (via newsstands or subscription) to many people. This can account, too, for the high number of messages with reference to *Vreme* and other electronic news sources.

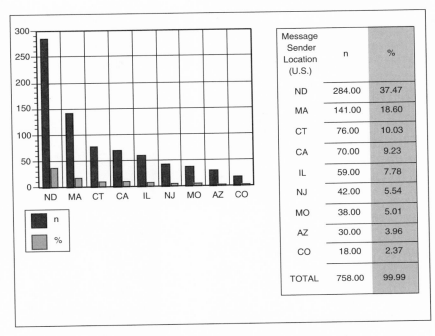

Message Sender Location (U.S.)	n	%
ND	284.00	37.47
MA	141.00	18.60
CT	76.00	10.03
CA	70.00	9.23
IL	59.00	7.78
NJ	42.00	5.54
MO	38.00	5.01
AZ	30.00	3.96
CO	18.00	2.37
TOTAL	758.00	99.99

Figure 5. Message sender location—US only

Making clear their critical reading of the news and newsgroup, all 14 respondents believed that the media were biased in their coverage of the war. They also believed that those posting messages to the newsgroup that contained stories from traditional news sources were doing so less to inform the newsgroup but rather to use the traditional stories to convince others that their arguments were correct. However, as one person said,[1] "even though I usually get angry reading many people's postings, it helps me understand how people see themselves (especially the ones from other regions in Yugoslavia from me) and where may be the roots of...propaganda."

Perhaps indicative of the predominance of PhD.s among the newsgroup's posters, some respondents were critical of objectivity itself, as expressed by one user who identified himself as a poster: "If a source appears objective, that only means that it best approximates the reader's opinions or else the average viewpoint of all the other sources the reader sees." For this user the mass media were reinforcers of already-held beliefs. One respondent claimed that the term "objective opinion" is an oxymoron.

Another respondent said that the newsgroup "helps to cross- check infor-

Education	n	%
Ph.D.	80.00	62.50
Master's	32.00	25.00
Bachelor's	16.00	12.50
Sex	n	%
Male	112.00	87.50
Female	16.00	12.50
Ethnicity	100% White	
Mean age	33.6 years	
Mean Usenet use	6.5 hours/week	
Mean	3.1 hours/week	

Figure 6. Soc.culture.yugoslavia degraphic information.

mation from different sources." One respondent's comment typified those of the others who believed that by having access to wire service reports they thus had access to a more objective news source than if they had to rely on those reports as edited and altered by local media.

Discussion

It is possible that the predominance of electronic news sources stems simply from the relative ease with which their text can be captured by a computer and redistributed to other users and communities, as opposed to the (relatively) laborious process of transcribing a broadcast news story or a newspaper story. But the nature of data used in this study, made manifest in discourse, may nevertheless provide a more profound and penetrating measure of media use than the type of self-reports generated from questionnaires and surveys in traditional media use studies. Moreover, the mention of particular news sources in the newsgroup points to their value (whether positive or negative) and tells us about which news sources were worthy of mention.

In the case of the Usenet newsgroup soc.culture.yugoslavia there is both a local aspect to media use as it has been defined in earlier studies (Tichenor et al., 1980) and evidence of desire for nonlocal media, particularly insofar as it appeared that users believed that wire services were more objective than local media. There is thus a tension between desire for knowledge of local "angles" other than ones available to newsgroup users in their own local (geographic) region and a desire for more objective news stories.

An important finding is that media use was not tied to the user's local geographic community, an important finding and one opposite to expectations one might have from previous studies like Tichenor et al. (1980), Stamm (1985), and Schweitzer (1991) that did not examine media use in CMC groups. And, in what may be the most important finding, we have evidence of cosmopolitan media "elites" (Rogers, 1962). Tichenor et al. (1980) also find that media "elites" are implicated in information flow in communities, though they defined those "elites" as community leaders and news professionals. In the case of soc.culture.yugoslavia it may be argued that posters are community leaders and lurkers community members, but the ability to join the information flow is unrestricted, and thus lurkers may at any time "cross over" to become posters, a highly unlikely scenario in traditional media use studies.

As a *Times-Mirror* survey showed, "computer-users tend to read more newspapers, books and magazines than others" (Davis, 1994, p. 24) and indeed there seemed to be quite an appetite among newsgroup users for news and information. It is absolutely imperative to note that these same users are not simply "consuming" news but are engaging in its critical analysis as well as passing it along as part of their own postings, often in service of their own opinions. Consequently, they fit the description of an "interpretive community" actively constructing meaning (Lindlof, 1989). Interestingly, during that process, few breaches of Usenet standards of conduct (McLaughlin et al., 1995) are found, even when particularly vehement criticism of a posting occurred. Indeed, "flame wars" (MacKinnon, 1995, pp. 129-130) were largely absent. Tichenor et al. (1980) also investigated the use of mass media by powerful elites, and in particular noted that:

A large portion of the information available...depends on an information delivery system which reflects the pluralistic organization and vested interests of the society in which it exists. Information appears to be generated and disseminated as a result of joint activity of professionals within the mass media channels and professionals who have advocacy functions for interdependent special interest groups (p. 15).

One of the ways to interpret newsgroup user interest in varied forms of information is to break through this form of joint activity and engage in media activity of their own. Interestingly, this action leads to the type of social control Tichenor et al. identify, as each user utilizes news and news sources to express and augment their opinions. However, given the nature of CMC, and the "personae" (MacKinnon, 1995) created on Usenet, the exchanges in the newsgroup critical of news sources, messages, and so forth, provide a kind of dialogue for which traditional social control paradigms, which focus on the one-way quality of news media, do not account.

It is possible that the news sources represented in this newsgroup are simply ones of sufficient international stature to be of interest to the group. However, how would one then explain the absence of newspapers like the Washington *Post* and Los Angeles *Times*, or the absence of the three U.S. broadcast networks? One would indeed expect major international newspapers to have greater representation, and yet they do not. It is apparent that members of the newsgroup made greater use of electronic news sources like *Vreme* and directly accessible wire services over other news sources. Newsgroup users posted little if any news from local sources such as newspapers in their hometowns.

These findings provide a basis for the assertion that local media are unimportant to readers except for reporting of local news. The heavy use of electronic news sources like the wire services may mean that members of this community have an understanding of how news works, that is, they use their computer access to bypass local sources to get straight to *the* source, say, the Associated Press.

Second, and more importantly, community members use news sources to provide a foundation for their own arguments and opinions expressed within the discourse in the news group. Consequently, the most useful sources are the ones that seem most unbiased, such as the wire services themselves (since those sources most often feature stories filed directly by reporters in the field). Jensen argues that American social thought is "concerned about 'modern' public opinion being formed by the mass media, [deemed to be] an untrustworthy, self-serving source" (1991, p. 77). In this instance, it is individuals who may be using the media in a self- serving fashion to support and elevate their own opinions.

One might as well have expected to find news sources from areas where there is a substantial population of Yugoslav immigrants, as there is in Germany, or in U.S. cities like Cleveland, Pittsburgh, and Chicago. Nothing was found in this study to support such an expectation. An immigrant press, or at least one sensitive to immigrants in its area, seems unimportant to this electronic community, and yet the immigrant press is claimed to have "established more personal, helpful ties with (its) communities than did the majority press" (Reed, 1990, p. 77). What happened to such ties in this newsgroup?

Conclusion

This study raises several questions for future research: What are the rhetorical dimensions of media use in electronic communities? How might our understanding of readers and communities be affected by new patterns of media use in electronic communities? Future research should also employ readership surveys in an attempt to understand readership patterns and to better collect demographic information.

What is particularly interesting about these findings is that they run counter to claims that the media of communication eviscerate history. Clifford Christians notes that Jacques Ellul wrote:

> ...the unrelenting flow of news inebriates human memory, a loss Ellul laments...."There is no politics where there is no grasp of the past, where there is no continuity, where there is no analysis of errors or capacity to understand the present through that analysis and in that continuity." Man aids in that evaporation and consequent weakening of his political order by driving events into oblivion, that is, actively forgetting for the sake of maintaining sanity (Christians, 1976, p. 13).

Those posting to soc.culture.yugoslavia are tinged with a deep sense of continuity with past Usenet exchanges, and postings often included quotes and replies several messages back in a thread. Though one can filter messages on particular topics or from particular senders using "kill files" (MacKinnon, 1995), message threads can continue for weeks, months, even years.

One of the consequences of the externalization of memory (Ong, 1982) in such a public (and print-based) fashion as this is that one's words do not evaporate. As Aycock and Buchignani note:

> Interpersonal discourses confer upon the individuals who engage in them an immediate sense of authorship and authority.... Print-based discourses delimit texts that are forever fixed in place and identified with a specified author or authors.... Computer-based discourses partakes of some of the characteristics of interpersonal and print-based discourses... (1995, pp. 223-224).

Like Aycock and Buchignani, who found some evidence of authority being questioned, critical readership is evident among those who posted to soc.culture.yugoslavia. However, such critical readership is tempered by authorship that is often uncritical, and it is that tension between readership and authorship in soc.culture.yugoslavia that fuels both the need for information and, ultimately, discourse within the newsgroup.

Survey of Usenet NEWS Users

This study is being conducted by Steve Jones, assistant professor of communication at the University of Tulsa. It is intended to create an understanding of media use in electronic communities. The study is focusing on Usenet newsgroups with heavy message traffic related to the war in the former Yugoslavia as those newsgroups exhibit a high rate of media-related content.

The information disclosed in this survey will remain confidential and will be used for research purposes only by Steve Jones, Faculty of Communication, University of Tulsa, Tulsa, OK 74104 (Bitnet SJONES@TULSA, Internet COMM_SJ@VAX1.UTULSA.EDU). If you wish to receive a general summary of the study please send e-mail to the author's address.

Please respond to this survey in any of the following three ways:
1. Return it via e-mail.
2. Print it out and return it via snailmail.
3. Send e-mail requesting a hard copy along with your snailmail address.

Replies to the survey signify your consent to participate in this study. Thank you very much for the time and effort taken to fill out this questionnaire.

Please mark the correct answer for yourself:

1. Most recent academic degree:
   Ph.D.
   Master's
   Bachelor's
   High School or GED

2. Sex
   Male
   Female

3. Ethnic Data
   White (not of Hispanic origin)
   Black or African-American
   Asian or Pacific Islander
   American Indian or Alaskan Native
   Hispanic

Are you affiliated with an academic institution? If not, please skip to question 7.

4. Academic Rank:
   Undergraduate Student
   Graduate Student
   Instructor
   Assistant Professor
   Associate Professor
   Professor

5. Academic Department/Unit:

6. Institution Type

4-year
University
Public
 2-year
College
Private

7. Your age

8. Occupation

9. How much time (in hours) do you spend a week reading any Usenet newsgroups?

10. How much time (in hours) do you spend a week reading Usenet newsgroups for information on the war in Yugoslavia?

11. From question 10, which newsgroups have the information you prefer to read? Why do you prefer these?

Rate the following statements about the newsgroup. Please use this scale to rate your opinion:

1 = Strongly Agree
2 = Agree
3 = No Opinion
4 = Disagree
5 = Strongly Disagree

12. I believe the newsgroups I read contain objective opinions.

13. I find that in the newsgroups all sides of the conflict are represented.

14. Everyone who posts messages to newsgroups is biased.

15. What is your overall opinion of the objectivity of those newsgroups?

16. What other sources of information do you use to learn about the situation in the former Yugoslavia?

Continuing to use the same scale, give your opinion of the following statements:

17. Television news coverage of the war in former Yugoslavia is better than other media coverage.

18. Newspapers provide more accurate coverage of the war.

19. American newspapers provide the least information about the war.

20. Please rank the following news sources in order of the importance they hold to you for providing news about the former Yugoslavia. Use the following scale:

1 = very important
2 = important
3 = somewhat important
4 = not important
5 = I do not use this source

ABC-TV
Associated Press

BBC
CBC
CBS-TV
Chicago *Sun-Times*
Chicago *Tribune*
CNN
Danas
London *Times*
Los Angeles *Times*
NBC-TV
Newsweek
New York *Times*
NPR
Politika
Reuters
Time
United Press International
U.S. News & World Report
USA Today
Vreme News Digest
Wall St. Journal

21. What is your overall opinion about the objectivity of media coverage of the war in the former Yugoslavia?

22. Do you use electronic networks like the Internet to retrieve information from any of the above-listed news sources? If yes, please list the names of the ones you use.

23. Please rank the same news sources in order of the objectivity you believe they show when providing news about the former Yugoslavia. Please use the following scale:

1 = very objective
2 = objective
3 = somewhat objective
4 = not objective
5 = I do not use this source

ABC-TV
Associated Press
BBC
CBC
CBS-TV
Chicago *Sun-Times*
Chicago *Tribune*
CNN
Danas
London *Times*
Los Angeles *Times*

NBC-TV
Newsweek
New York *Times*
NPR
Politika
Reuters
Time
United Press International
U.S. News & World Report
USA Today
Vreme News Digest
Wall St. Journal

24. Do you find it useful when information from newspapers, TV and radio is posted to a newsgroup? Why or why not?

For the following please use this scale to rate your opinion:

1 = Strongly Agree
2 = Agree
3 = No Opinion
4 = Disagree
5 = Strongly Disagree

25. I find replies to messages I post on newsgroups infuriating.

26. My interactions on newsgroups are satisfying.

27. I find Usenet newsgroups informative.

28. Overall, what I read on newsgroups makes me angry.

29. I find it frustrating that I am unable to communicate with others on the newsgroup face-to-face.

30. I only read newsgroups. I never post messages.

31. The Usenet newsgroups I participate on are fun.

32. I feel flattered when there are responses to my postings.

33. I have become friends with people I met on newsgroups.

34. If it were not for these newsgroups I would know very little about events in the former Yugoslavia.

35. It bothers me when no one responds to a posting I make.

36. Reading these newgroups helps me make sense of events in the former Yugoslavia.

37. Please write any additional comments or observations about Usenet, newsgroups, media coverage of the war in Yugoslavia, etc.

THANK YOU VERY MUCH FOR YOUR PARTICIPATION!

Acknowledgements

I am greatly indebted to Professor Joli Jensen and Professor Joseph Schmitz in the Faculty of Communication at the University of Tulsa for their valuable suggestions and insights.

Note

1. Respondents to the initial questionnaire and interviewees were promised confidentiality and anonymity. Full-text responses are available from the author.

CHAPTER SIX

From Terminal Ineptitude to Virtual Sociopathy

How Conduct Is Regulated on Usenet

Christine B. Smith, Margaret L. McLaughlin, and Kerry K. Osborne

U senet began in the late 1970s as a university-based network of computers linking researchers working in UNIX. Although initiated primarily for the exchange of research and computing resources, Usenet soon became a forum for electronic discussions, on topics ranging from hobbies to current events, among those with computer access at many universities (Miller, 1994). By the late 1980s, Usenet store-and-forward conventions were firmly established and much of its traffic was carried on the Internet, making Usenet discussions, or "newsgroups" as they are called, accessible to government workers as well as the educational community (Hardy, 1993). Eventually, as more and more businesses availed themselves of Internet access, a vast segment of the global corporate workforce joined in the ongoing discussions. Today, millions of active newsgroup users, their numbers augmented by commercial Internet access providers like America Online, Compuserve, and a host of smaller proprietary access providers, participate in over 13,000 topic-oriented local, regional, national, and global newsgroups (Liszt Directory, 1996). Because Usenet news is available in read-only mode in libraries, airports, and other public spaces, as many as 20 million users may participate non-interactively. Users who habitually read newsgroups of interest without contributing to the discussion are commonly called "lurkers" (Adams, 1994; Reid, 1994).

For a small but growing minority of users, however, Usenet has provided a medium which facilitates communication among widely dispersed members of groups and teams. Furthermore, Usenet promotes the development of new relationships by affording immediate access to thousands of others with similar interests and spheres of expertise (McLaughlin, Osborne, and Smith, 1995).

Usenet remains the primary vehicle for exchange of information and resources among computer aficionados, but it also attracts those with more ar-

cane and mundane interests. Netters with diverse sexual tastes tease and titil-
late (Penkoff, 1996). Virtual friends celebrate and console their way through
"real-life" events while bemoaning the fates of their favorite soap-opera
characters (Baym, 1992; 1995). Amateur artists distribute and solicit comments on their creations (for example, alt.binaries.pictures.fine-art.graphics;
alt.ascii.art). Parents and official agencies try to locate missing children
(alt.missing.kids). And, long before current box office hits appear in video
stores, they are carved into brief sound bites, stills, and shorts and are posted
to the "net" for consumption by movie and multimedia buffs (e.g., alt.toons;
comp.multimedia).

Some of the conventions of interactive Usenet participation, i.e., posting
and responding to as well as reading newsgroup articles, are dictated by the
newsreading software. More sophisticated software enables users to organize
newsgroup articles (posts) by size, sender, date, or "threads" (specific discussion topics which are indexed by the word or phrase appearing in the subject
heading of the article) (Krol, 1992). Follow-up postings to earlier articles,
generated with a reply function or its equivalent while reading a particular
article, appear with the same header preceded by "Re:" and may be cross-
posted to several different newsgroups. Readers wishing to follow a specific
thread of discussion may easily do so by scanning the indexed headers and
retrieving the texts of only those articles they wish to see.

Other Usenet conventions, such as encrypting sensitive or offensive information or otherwise flagging material with a subject pointer (an acronym,
word, or phrase which conveys the nature or content of the post), are newsgroup specific and have evolved as communication rules for posters (Baym,
1995; McLaughlin et al., 1995). Such conventions are usually propagated
regularly for the benefit of new readers in informative postings known as
FAQs, a well-known and ubiquitous acronym for "frequently asked questions" (Emily Postnews Answers Your Questions on Netiquette. news.an-
nounce.newusers and news.answers). FAQs are usually generated by volunteers, newsgroup regulars who tire of seeing the same old questions and as a
result begin to post Socratic dialogues of recurring questions and answers
(Hahn and Stout, 1994). So widespread is the FAQ phenomenon that readers
of more esoteric newsgroups have created tongue-in-cheek FAQs which are
more on the order of inside jokes than they are informative. Nonetheless, this
type of FAQ is still posted more or less regularly (see, for example, FAQs for
alt.alien.vampire.flonk.flonk.flonk; alt.buddha.short.fat.guy; alt.angst;
alt.devilbunnies; and alt.peeves). For many newsgroups, however, FAQs
have become indispensable forms of information distribution and a means of
archiving the history and evolution of a particular newsgroup. Maintenance,
distribution, and updating of FAQs are important functions which are not undertaken lightly. FAQ maintainer Mark Moraes (news.announce.newusers,
etc.) notes that while most members of the public recognize and appreciate

the effort and long hours that go into "a service they have come to expect," others sometimes forget that such services as FAQ maintenance, newsgroup moderation, and vote-taking are rendered by volunteers: "One of the necessary qualifications for a volunteer on Usenet has always been the ability to ignore the peanut gallery" (personal communication, October 25, 1994; quoted from an article posted to alt.config, alt.config.news, alt.config.misc, and alt.fan.joel-furr, September 9, 1994).

In addition to newsgroup-specific standards of conduct, overarching Usenet standards, collectively known as "netiquette," guide proper interaction (Von Rospach, 1993; Shea, 1994; Spafford, 1993). For example, one is expected to quote just enough of a preceding post to enable readers to follow one's commentary. However, follow-on posters frequently include the entire thread, consisting of not only the original post, but subsequent comments made by other posters as well. The enormous bandwidth-wasting article that results may signify defiance or ignorance of netiquette, but in many cases it merely signifies technological deficiency in using the newsreader editor.

Netiquette and other standards of communicative practices have developed so that newsgroup participants can digest an immense quantity of information as quickly, efficiently, and economically as possible. For example, a feature of most newsreading software is the ability to ignore unwanted posts, either those from designated authors or with designated subject headings, consigning them to a kill file. This reduces substantially the number of articles one is exposed to in a given newsgroup, an important feature for time-and/or money-conscious readers who pay for their online time directly or indirectly with associated costs for transport and storage of Usenet messages. In the newsgroup rec.arts.tv.soaps.abc, for example, posters are strongly encouraged to use abbreviated forms of the soap names in the headers so that readers not interested in discussion about specific soaps may filter out those articles (Baym, 1995).

Technological proficiency, demonstrated knowledge of the FAQ, and conformity to newsgroup practices are among the conditions of acceptance in many well-established newsgroups. Failure to observe net and newsgroup standards is quite common, however, and may range from "relatively innocuous errors in the use of newsreading software to actions characterized as 'net terrorism'" (McLaughlin et al., 1995, p.95). Whether such behavior is caused by error or choice, it often provokes comment from other users. Reprimands are rampant, ranging from private (emailed) admonitions to public censure across several newsgroups to crusading efforts to deprive offenders of their net access.

While we can effectively gauge the nature and extent of corrective episodes conducted publicly in newsgroup discussions, it is important to note that an indeterminate number of such episodes may occur privately, either wholly or in part, via e-mail. For example, when a poster is publicly excoriated for offensive behavior, he or she may choose to respond to detractors privately and individually rather than encourage further communal discussion with a public response. Presumably, those who take offense at the behavior of others may exercise the same restraint and voice their concerns directly to offenders in e-mail messages.

Nevertheless, conduct-correcting episodes which occur in the public arena are numerous enough to warrant scrutiny. In the study of recurring discursive practices in Usenet, we gain a better understanding of emergent standards of behavior and communal responses to violations of those standards.

Tsk, Tsk! Taking Transgressors to Task on Usenet

McLaughlin et al. (1995) analyzed postings from five popular newsgroups and, using the concept of a reproach as defined in the literature on accounts and explanations (Cody and McLaughlin, 1990a; Cody and Braaten, 1992; McLaughlin, Cody, and Read, 1992; Schonbach, 1990), generated a taxonomy of reproachable conduct on Usenet. Offending posts, those which presented behavior sufficiently in violation of normative expectations to prompt comment and spark remedial discussion and debate, were analyzed for type of offense(s). Seven preliminary categories resulted (adapted from McLaughlin et al., 1995):

1. *Incorrect/Novice Use of Technology:* e.g., editing and formatting errors, multiple postings or signatures, failing to use follow-on option

2. *Bandwidth piggery:* e.g., excessively long article or signature, quoted material longer than comment, indiscriminate cross-posting, asking a frequently answered question

3. *Violation of Usenet Conventions:* e.g., incorrect or missing subject headers, failing to encrypt offensive material, posting to an inappropriate newsgroup or otherwise demonstrating lack of regular reading

4. *Violation of Newsgroup Conventions:* e.g., failing to use spoiler warnings, lack of familiarity with and failure to use appropriate subject headers or abbreviations, failing to conform to group spirit or style and group traditions regarding appropriate topics

5. *Ethical Violations:* e.g., posting private e-mail or personal information about others without permission, misattributions or misquoting of sources, harassment of individual posters

6. *Inappropriate Language:* e.g., flaming (personal attacks, ridicule), hostile or coarse language, linguistic affectations which distract or detract from message content

7. *Factual Errors:* e.g., spelling and grammatical errors, mistakes with respect to names, dates, places, and events, errors in summarizing others' posts.

Some offenses are likely seen as more egregious than others, and it is equally possible that what one newsgroup condemns, another condones. For example, while flaming (directing a particularly vindictive or hostile post at another user) is perfectly acceptable on some newsgroups (e.g., alt.fan.war-lords, alt.flame, and alt.irc), vicious verbal attacks invite censure on many socially-oriented newsgroups.

In this chapter, we explore further the nature of offensive conduct and its treatment on Usenet. Specifically, we examine the frequency, form, and tone of reproaches and, when available, offenders' subsequent accounts.

The typical remedial episode consists of four components: the failure event, a reproach, an account, and an evaluation of that account (i.e., honoring it or rejecting it) (Cody and McLaughlin, 1990a; Cody and Braaten, 1992; McLaughlin, Cody, and Read, 1992; Schonbach, 1990). Reproaches may be explicit or implicit, depending on the situational dynamics or communication style of the reproacher. Reproaches may range in harshness or severity from a simple "What happened?" to a tirade laced with profanity and attacks on the offender's self-esteem (Schonbach, 1990). In some contexts, reproaches may be wholly unnecessary, for instance, in traffic court, where procedural rules include the expectation that defendants will offer accounts for their traffic violations (Cody and McLaughlin, 1988). Two of the more common forms of accounts offered are excuses and justifications (Scott and Lyman, 1968). Other forms include apologies, concessions, and denials (Schlenker, 1980; Schonbach, 1990). Apologies and excuses are generally perceived as more mitigating, i.e., more likely to result in an account being honored, whereas justifications and denials are usually deemed more aggravating and could escalate conflict (Cody and McLaughlin, 1990b). Concessions, depending on the extent of apology included and/or restitution offered, may be mitigating or aggravating (Schonbach, 1990).

It is reasonable to wonder if severe reproach forms result in similarly fierce accounts or, as may often be the case with new or infrequent posters, a tendency to eschew response. Little research has been done on the relationship between forms of reproach and subsequent accounts; however, a review of the literature on account episodes in face-to-face settings (Cody and Braaten, 1992) suggests at least one possible relationship in this medium: in the case of particularly aggravating reproaches the form and tone of a reproach influence the form and tone of a corresponding account. For example, a reproach that is rudely phrased and targeted at the offender's self-esteem may be more likely to result in a defensive rather than apologetic account. Also, humorous or sarcastic reproaches may elicit similar responses in an unusually free-wheeling environment which prizes wit more than it does behavioral conformity or social niceties (Coates, 1993). And, as suggested above, the form and tone of reproaches may be a factor in whether an offender responds publicly by offering an account to the newsgroup at large.

Somewhat more is known about the influence of gender on remedial episodes. Women, for example, tend to offer fuller apologies than do men and engage in more relational repair work with accounts (Gonzales, Pederson, Manning, and Wetter, 1990; Schonbach, 1990). Pasting this hypothesis to the medium of Usenet is problematic, however. Not only do men have greater access to technology (Balka, 1993; Truong, 1993), their dominant posting behaviors, even on newsgroups specifically oriented to women's discussion (Kramarae and Taylor, 1992), may affect both the level of women's participation and women's posting behaviors. Gender study in electronic media is therefore a task of increasing complexity, but because researchers have begun to take note of an inequity of female participation on the internet (Ebben and Kramarae, 1993; Kramarae and Taylor, 1992; Herring, 1993; Shade, 1993), we make a tentative survey of gender differences as they pertain to conduct-correcting episodes on Usenet.

Method

As a preliminary exploration of reproach characteristics and account sequences in Usenet, we return to our earlier data, a 3.09 Mb corpus of conduct-correcting episodes which constitutes roughly 15 percent of all postings to five popular newsgroups —comp.sys.ibm.pc.games, rec.sport.hockey, soc.motss (members of the same sex), soc.singles, and rec.arts.tv.soaps.abc —over a three-week period (see McLaughlin et al., 1995 for a detailed description of sampling procedures). Ten offenders were randomly selected from each of the five newsgroups. All posted messages which followed up an offender's article with corrective comments were saved for analysis. Each corrective message was considered a reproach episode for the purposes of defining cases. The original offending article was also analyzed in all but one episode and, in this case, a sufficient amount of the offending post was quoted by reproachers to warrant including the case. If the offender posted a response to a reproach during the data collection period, that message was retained as part of the episode data. Finally, as McLaughlin et al.'s (1995) data suggest, reproachers themselves are occasionally taken to task for bullying newcomers, flaming, or nit-picking. If a follow-on poster (excepting the offender) reproached another reproacher, a new case was defined and coded as a reproach episode. Two coders each rated two of the newsgroup samples and both coders rated the remaining newsgroup message corpus independently. A satisfactory level (Nunnally, 1978) of interrater agreement was obtained (Scott's pi = 80%; $N = 56$ reproach episodes) on both categorical and scale variables.

Gender of reproachers and offenders was coded where information was available and reasonably unambiguous. The number of messages posted by each individual during the data collection period was also recorded. Reproaches were first analyzed for nature of offense(s) using McLaughlin et al.'s (1995) taxonomy of reproachable conduct on Usenet. As posters are frequently rebuked for more than one offense, a given case may present one or more of the following categories: technological ineptitude, bandwidth waste, violation of Usenet norms, violation of newsgroup norms, ethical transgressions, language faults, and factual errors. Reproach messages were then rated on the magnitude of each of eight characteristics (see below), which were then reformulated into the following four bi-dimensional properties:

1. Affect

- *Friendly:* The reproacher treats the offender in a cordial or congenial manner
- *Hostile:* Obvious belligerence toward the poster; may or may not entail the use of profanity

2. Intent

- *Helpful:* The reproacher offers correct information, aid, or politely informs offender of the applicable "netiquette" rule with the obvious aim of preventing repeat offenses
- *Sarcastic:* Implicit or explicit derision or ridicule; may be condescending and the reproach implicit; intent is to demean

3. Style

- *Witty:* An obvious attempt to be witty or funny without sarcasm; reproach may be implicit
- *Factual:* A simple statement of offending behavior

4. Reproach Orientation

- *Directed at Behavior:* Reproach directed at behavior rather than the person
- *Directed at Person:* Reproach directed at the person more than behavior

Accounts were rated on identical attribute scales. Additionally, accounts were rated (1 = not at all characteristic; 5 = extremely characteristic) on the following properties offered by Cody and McLaughlin and their colleagues (see, for example, Braaten, Cody, and Bell, 1990; Cody and McLaughlin, 1988; McLaughlin, Cody, and O'Hair, 1983):

- *Apologetic:* ranging from no apology offered to sincere and explicit "I'm sorry"
- *Conciliatory:* Admitting error or wrongdoing with or without apology
- *Excusatory:* Offering extenuating circumstances for behavior; meant to mitigate culpability
- *Justificatory:* Offering "good reasons" for behavior; meant to absolve or exonerate
- *Denial:* Disavowal of wrongdoing; may question posters' right to reproach

OFFENSE	NEWSGROUP					
	pcgames	motss	singles	hockey	soaps	Total
TECH	-	1	3	-	-	4
BAND	3	-	-	-	1	4
NETNORM	4	2	5	1	3	15
GRPNORM	4	2	5	20	9	40
ETHICS	-	1	2	1	1	5
LANG	1	9	2	21	3	36
ERRORS	2	7	4	8	3	24
Total	14	22	21	51	20	128

Table 1. Frequency of offense type by newsgroup.

Results

Only a fraction of offenders responded publicly to their reproachers during the data collection period (n = 13, 25%) and, of these, only four accounts were publicly evaluated in newsgroup discussion. Given the small number of complete traditional corrective sequences (i.e., failure event, reproach, account, evaluation (Cody and Braaten, 1992)), data analysis was largely confined to reproach characteristics and descriptive statistics for the overall sample and each of the five newsgroups.

The overall sample yielded 83 reproach episodes in which 52 posters were chastised by 70 other posters for a total of 128 offenses (poster $N = 116$; 6 reproachers were in turn reproached for their offensive reprimands, thus increasing the number of offenders). One person rebuked another for four different infractions, and several people were reproached for two or three offenses. All of McLaughlin et al.'s (1995) reproachable conduct categories were represented; however, not all categories were present in every newsgroup. Conduct data is summarized in table 1.

More than 75 percent of poster transgressions fell into three of the seven offense types: violation of newsgroup norms, which includes failure to demonstrate knowledge of FAQs or undermining the communal spirit of the newsgroup ($N = 40$; 31%); language, which is associated with flaming ($N = 36$; 28%); and errors, which may involve spelling and grammar as well as facts ($N = 24$; 19%). Participants in the newsgroup rec.sport.hockey were the most active reproachers, accounting for roughly 40 percent of both total offenses and total reproach episodes. Failure to conform to newsgroup norms and flaming were the source of most of the reproach episodes. The next section reports findings of a discriminant analysis which examined the nature of reproaches levied against errors, imprudent language, and violations of group norms.

Variable	Wilks' Lambda	F	Significance
AFFECT	.78765	6.291	.0008
INTENT	.68090	10.93	.0000
STYLE	.74904	7.818	.0001
REPOR	.77785	6.664	.0005

Table 2. Univariate test results.

Wilks' Lambda (U-statistic) and univariate F-ratio with 3 and 70 degrees of freedom.

Discriminant Analysis

A discriminant function analysis was conducted in order to determine if reproaches differed in tenor among the three most common offenses. Because several reproach episodes involved recriminations against offenders for discursive improprieties along with violation of group norms, a fourth classification reflecting these dual offense incidents (language + groupnorms) was included in the analysis. To test the hypothesis that different offense types elicit reproaches significantly different in tone and form, a stepwise discriminant method was used in which the dependent measures were affect, intent, style, and reproach orientation. Nine of the 83 reproach episodes did not involve any of the three major offense types and were consequently dropped from the analysis.

The Wilks' lambda criterion was used for the discriminant function analysis, with values of F-to-enter and F-to-remove set to default (1.0). With the addition of a dual offense category in the grouping variable, prior probabilities were set to .25. The four groups differed significantly on each of the reproach variables when considered separately: affect $F(3, 70) = 6.29$, $p = .000$; intent $F(3, 70) = 10.93$, $p = .000$; style $F(3, 70) = 7.82$, $p = .000$; reproach orientation $F(3, 70) = 6.66$, $p = .000$. Results of the univariate tests are reported in table 2.

Offense types differed significantly along all three linear combinations of the discriminating variables. The first function, which accounted for 63 percent of the variation in the discriminant space, was significant at $p < .0000$, Wilks' lambda = .4773, Chi-square = 51.03. A second function was obtained which accounted for 24 percent of the variance, and was significant at $p = .002$, Wilks' = .7420, Chi-square = 20.59. The third function accounted for the remainder of the variance (12%): Wilks' = .8991, Chi-square = 7.34, $p = .025$. The Box's M test for equality of the group covariance matrices indicated no significant differences ($M = 36.20$, $F(30, 8162) = 1.07$, $p = .3649$).

When reclassification of cases into groups is based on more than one function, the values of each case on all functions must be considered simultane-

Standardized canonical discriminant function coefficients			
	FUNC 1	FUNC 2	FUNC 3
AFFECT	.23260	1.27466	.50790
INTENT	.54085	-.81886	-.68315
STYLE	.50194	.52841	-.34828
REPOR	-.01984	-.67498	.97444
Functions evaluated at group means (group centroids)			
Group	FUNC 1	FUNC 2	FUNC 3
1 (group norms)	.03016	-.72741	-.16365
2 (language)	.88814	.50377	-.50421
3 (errors)	-.95827	.25798	.00543
4 (norms + language)	.61936	.08336	.47524

Table 3. Discriminant coefficients and group centroids.

ously (Norusis, 1993). The first function discriminated among reproaches moderately high in style and intent, low in affect, and very low in reproach orientation scores. The second function further separated those reproaches scoring very low in orientation and intent from those extremely high in affect and moderately high in style. The final function discriminated between reproaches on the basis of moderate-to-high affect and orientation scores and very low scores on style and intent. The standardized coefficients and group centroids are depicted in table 3.

As can be seen in table 3, groups 2 and 3 were maximally discriminated by the first function (+.88 versus -.95). Those reproached for language and errors were likely to differ on style, intent, and orientation of reproaches (e.g., errors eliciting factual, helpful, behavior-oriented reproaches vs. the more sarcastic and person-oriented reproaches against "flaming"). Function 2 further distinguished those reproached for language from those reproached for violations of group norms (+.50 vs. -.72); here, affect, intent, and reproach orientation were likely to differ (+1.27, -.82, and -.67, respectively). Function three served to further distinguish those reproached for group norm infractions or language improprieties from those who were reproached for both (-.16, -.50, and +.47, respectively). Not surprisingly, perhaps, these reproaches differed in orientation and intent (e.g., somewhat more obviously directed at the person or the behavior, and more obviously sarcastic or helpful).

Table 4 indicates that the reclassification of groups based on the three functions was moderately successful. Slightly over half (54%) of the cases were correctly classified. Groups reproached for either language only or errors only were most successfully classified (66% each). The lower hit rates

		Predicted group membership			
Actual group	No of cases	1	2	3	4
Group 1	19	8	3	5	3
GROUPNORMS		42.1%	15.8%	26.3%	15.8%
Group 2	12	2	8	1	1
LANGUAGE		16.7%	66.7%	8.3%	8.3%
Group 3	24	2	3	16	3
ERRORS		8.3%	12.5%	66.7%	12.5%
Group 4	19	4	4	3	8
NORMLANG		21.1%	21.1%	15.8%	42.1%
Ungrouped cases	9	0	3	3	3
		0%	33.3%	33.3%	33.3%
Percent of "grouped" cases correctly classified: 54.05%					

Table 4. Classification results.

of groupnorm violators and double offenders (42%) probably reflects a tendency to view language improprieties as violations of group expectations for normative behavior in some of the newsgroups we studied. Analysis of differences in reproach characteristics across the newsgroups will be reported later in this chapter. The next section reports differences in posting patterns between reproachers and offenders.

Posting Patterns of Reproachers and Offenders

Reproachers were somewhat more prolific than offenders, averaging 22.5 (SD 30.2) messages to offenders' 17.9 (SD 24.7), but this difference was not significant: $t(118) = -.91$ ($p = .18$). One-time posters accounted for 25 percent of offenders, while only 7 percent of reproachers posted once during the data collection period. Furthermore, those who responded publicly to their reproachers appeared to have a much higher rate of posting than those who failed to respond publicly during the data collection period (M = 27.15, SD 36.6 and M = 14.87, SD 18.9, respectively). However, given the lower power associated with such few responses and the broad range of posting frequency by offenders, it is not surprising that the difference failed to reach significance, $F(1,50) = 2.47$ ($p = .12$). With the exception of rec.sport.hockey, reproachers posted more often than offenders in each newsgroup. The newsgroup soc.singles was by far the most prolific in our sample; both reproachers and offenders had the highest mean number of messages (67.8, SD 55.56 and 35.6, SD 45.58, respectively). In sum, newsgroups differed significantly in frequency of posting by both offenders, $F(4,47) = 2.76$ ($p = .038$), and reproachers, $F(4,65) = 8.05$ ($p = .000$).

Property	Newsgroup					F
	pcgames	motss	singles	hockey	soaps	
Affect						4.99***
Mean	1.45	3.23	2.68	3.06	2.29	
SD	.79	1.49	1.15	1.31	.64	
Intent						4.00***
Mean	1.95	3.40	3.81	3.59	3.07	
SD	1.35	1.42	.98	1.44	.80	
Style						1.76
Mean	1.64	2.80	3.04	2.56	2.61	
SD	1.14	1.67	1.08	1.15	1.69	
Orientation						3.35**
Mean	1.41	2.73	2.81	3.16	2.25	
SD	1.20	1.49	1.55	1.48	1.35	
N=83	11	15	11	32	14	
Note: p < .05; ** p < 01; *** p < .001						

Table 5. Reproach characteristics by newsgroup.

Reproach Characteristics

Reproach message characteristics were examined according to their effects on offenders' responses (again, a very small sample, $N = 13$) and for characteristic trends and differences across groups. Newsgroups differed significantly on affect, intent, and reproach orientation, but not on style of reproach. As can be seen in table 5, pcgamers were friendliest, while motss and hockey vied for the title of "most hostile." Hostile reproaches were somewhat more likely to prompt public responses from offenders, but not significantly so. Reproaches aimed at those who publicly responded did not differ significantly in affect orientation from those who failed to respond.

Although groups differed similarly with intent to help or demean offenders—pcgamers were considerably more helpful toward offenders while singles more frequently injected their reproaches with sarcasm—degree of helpfulness versus sarcasm was not a significant factor in whether an offender offered a public account.

Newsgroups did not differ significantly on style; witty and factual reproaches were equally prevalent across groups, although pcgamers tended to use a more factual approach. Witty reproaches prompted fewer offender rejoinders; however, this tendency was not statistically significant. Not surprisingly, perhaps, posters from the three newsgroups which may be construed as more social—soc.motss, soc.singles, and rec.arts.tv.soaps—displayed somewhat more humor and wit. When humor/wit is rated as a unidimensional attribute, significant differences emerge among newsgroups in terms of reproach humor and/or wittiness, $F(4,78) = 2.56$ ($p = .04$).

Reproach orientation focused on the extent to which reprimands targeted offenders' behavior or constituted personal attacks on the offenders themselves. Hockey enthusiasts resorted to more ad hominem reproaches than did other newsgroups, while pcgamers were decidedly behavior-oriented. The newsgroups in our sample differed significantly on the tendency to condemn the person, $F(4,78) = 3.35$ ($p = .0138$). Furthermore, of all the reproach characteristics rated in our sample, person-directedness, as a unidimensional attribute of reproach messages, was the only property which had a significant effect on offender responses, $F(2,80) = 5.16$ ($p = .007$). Reproaches that prompted response were more person-directed than the reproaches that went unanswered.

For example, the following post violated soc.singles norms regarding personal ads:

>Hi, I'm a 23 year old graduate student and would like to
>communicate with any females on this news net.
>————————————(Posted for a non-net friend)————————————

A witty, but person-directed reprimand resulted:

Well, Howdy! Finally, a request for female that doesn't specify species—you wouldn't believe how many people on this net want a woman, which of course means a person.
giggle

My name is Susa, and I'm a five-year-old Lemur in the Philly Zoo. My measurements are 12-12-12, which is considered quite sexy for a lemur *giggle* we all fail the pencil test *giggle*

My hobbies include running around, climbing trees, and picking lice; I hope you have a nice thick head of hair!

I only write to stupid people who post personals on soc.singles; the other ones are too smart for me—we lemurs may be very_cuddly *giggle* but we tend to be on the low end of the smarts scale. I know that with that post, you'll be really_dumb for a human, and perfect for me! *giggle*

P. Smith

To which the hapless "friend of a non-net person" responded:

In reference to my posting a few hours ago...I have just discovered that this is the wrong news group! Thanks to so many people, <postername> among others, so if you'll all quit sending me more messages, I move on. OK? But those who seem to have nothing better to do <postername> feel free to do whatever you want!

Several people wrote in support of offenders. Four offenders were defended once; two offenders were supported by two or more people. Six reproachers were in turn reproached by other posters, usually for flaming or nit-picking. In one episode, a poster requested strategic information about a popular computer game and was accused (rather subtlely) of software piracy:

>It should be in the book that comes with the game!
(Unless you have a pirated copy.)

In defense of the original offender, another poster recalled that the manual was missing from his legitimately purchased copy of the same game:

[snip...]
So, <postername>, next time don't be too quick to shout
PIRATE! There may be a perfectly reasonable explanation.

Of public responses to reproachers ($N = 13$), the wittiest rejoinders were from soap fans, followed by accounts offered in motss; however, these differences were not significant. The hypothesis suggested by Cody and Braaten (1992) that form and tone of reproach influence form and tone of corresponding accounts was in part supported. Specifically, as suggested by Coates (1993), humorous or witty reproaches were strongly correlated with humorous or witty accounts ($r = .86$; $p < .001$). Form of account, i.e., apology, concession, excuse, justification, and denial, was not significantly correlated with reproach characteristics.

Gender Democracy in a Male Domain?

In keeping with the popular net wisdom that males greatly outnumber females in this medium, the posters in our sample were predominantly male (78% of posters whose gender was clearly established; $N = 109$). Furthermore, 70 percent of the reproaches were targeted at males, 32.7 percent at females; and 4.1 percent were targeted at individuals whose gender was indiscernible from information available. Males accounted for two thirds of the 52 individuals reproached ($N = 33$), females 31 percent ($N = 16$). The remaining 6 percent were those of unknown gender ($N = 3$). Females comprised an even smaller proportion of those issuing reprimands (13%); however, female reproachers were more prolific than female offenders (mean number of messages = 38.22 and 16.69). In fact, female reproachers outposted all others, but not significantly so. Same-sex reproaches were most common (71%); females reproached females 7 times while males reproached each other 52 times. Cross-gender reproaches occurred 20 percent of the time; men reproached women more frequently than women reproached men. Table 6 shows gender distributions across newsgroups.

One might expect women to be more temperate in the tone of their reproaches. Such was not the case. Female reproachers were no more friendly and helpful, or less hostile, than were males. Neither was wit the province of any particular gender. When rated unidimensionally, however, sarcasm $F(2,67) = 3.42$ ($p = .038$) and person-directedness $F(2,67) = 5.32$ ($p = .007$) were significantly more characteristic of reproaches from males and those of unknown gender.

Recall that only 13 people offered accounts for their conduct. Of these, 10

| | Newsgroup | | | | | |
	pcgames	motss	singles	hockey	soap	TOTAL
OFFENDERS						
Male	6	8	5	13	1	33
Female	-	2	4	1	9	16
Unknown	3	-	-	-	-	3
TOTAL	9	10	9	14	10	52
REPROACHERS						
Male	10	12	5	27	3	57
Female	-	-	2	1	6	9
Unknown	1	-	1	-	2	4
TOTAL	11	12	8	28	11	70

Note: 6 reproachers were also coded as offenders when subsequently reproached for the nature of their reprimands; 1 of these was female; 5 were male. Gender totals for the sample are male = 85, females = 24, unknown = 7

Table 5. Reproach characteristics by newsgroup.

were male and 3 were female. The between group differences for type of account—apology, conciliation, excuse, justification, and denial—were not significant. Although women were less apologetic than men, they tended to offer more mitigating accounts (e.g., they conceded error, provided excuses, or attempted to justify their behavior while men more often denied wrongdoing). Men and women did not differ significantly on message characteristics of their accounts; however, male offenders tended to be somewhat more sarcastic $F(1,11) = 4.09$ ($p = .068$), while women exhibited more humor and wit.

Discussion

One of the unique aspects of remedial episodes in an asynchronous communication context like Usenet is the ease with which offenders can duck out of accounting for their behavior. Unlike face-to-face mode, in which conversational maxims (Bach and Harnish, 1979; Grice, 1975) dictate some response to even the most implicit reproach, Usenet participants frequently fail to respond to reproaches. Given the lack of reliable lurking statistics and the ease with which offenders can ignore their reproachers, it is difficult to assess why a particular reproach goes unanswered. Our data suggest that offenders targeted by reproachers are often such infrequent posters that the likelihood of their responding to reproaches is greatly reduced, and in fact, they might not see the reproach at all. It is also possible that first-time posters, unfamiliar with newsgroup practices, may fail to respond because they are put off by what they perceive as excessively rude or harsh reprimands. Many communicators in this medium have a propensity to display somewhat less inhibition than communicators in face-to-face interactions (McCormick and Mc-Cormick, 1992; Turner, 1990; Wilson, 1993), and the resulting lack of conversational niceties may shock or dismay the net neophyte.

Alternatively, as we discussed earlier in this chapter and as is evident in the offender's response to the "Susa the lemur" post, many of the discursive episodes originating in Usenet are continued via more private channels, such as e-mail. Still, those regular posters wishing to maintain a presence within the newsgroup community (MacKinnon, 1995; Rheingold, 1993) may be more likely to respond to reproaches with some accounting for their putative offenses. A positive relationship is indicated between active participation (as determined by frequency of posts) and the likelihood of publicly responding to a reproach. However, with the notable exception that person-directed reproaches prompted responses in our sample, our preliminary investigation remains inconclusive regarding factors affecting likelihood of response. Beyond a common-sense conclusion that people will fight for their image and honor, even among virtual strangers, a closer look at what affects likelihood of response is warranted given our findings of higher numbers of posts by account-givers and the tendency for ad hominem reproaches and hostility to prompt response. One distinct possibility meriting further study is potential interactive effects between degree of participation and reproach characteristics. Also, it may be the case that net-newbies and frequent posters are distinct populations with regard to factors influencing likelihood of response.

The relationship between reproach characteristics and the nature of corresponding accounts may be one of the more promising areas of research in this medium. We saw a distinct tendency for humorous and/or witty reproaches to inhibit likelihood of response on the one hand, but on the other hand, when an account was offered, it was likely to match the reproach in humor and wit. A methodological concern is ensuring an adequate number of complete account sequences for comparative analysis. Our data collection period was three weeks, and this yielded a huge data corpus, but as our sample is a relatively small proportion of the total data corpus, our results should be viewed as preliminary and interpreted with caution.

The discriminant analysis supported a tentative conclusion that different offense types tend to elicit reproaches which vary in form and tone. Also, there is sufficient evidence to suggest that reproaches for multiple offenses, particularly those associated with each other like language improprieties and group norm violations, reflect even less tolerance of offenders' behavior than do reproaches aimed at a single offense. However, these observations are tentative precisely because flaming and other language improprieties were negatively associated with normative behavior in most of the newsgroups we studied. Future studies should strive to examine newsgroups from the standpoint of their similarities and differences in overall descriptive variables such as mission (e.g., social vs. informative), style (e.g., freewheeling or straight-forward), and spirit (e.g., degree of communality; tolerance). Further study is recommended in the area of functionally describing and distinguishing news-groups.

The tenor and frequency of reproaches varied according to type of offense and individual newsgroup, supporting the thesis that norm violations are dif-ferentially treated in Usenet. Newsgroup participants appear to be less toler-ant of those who violate group standards and practices, particularly when it comes to potentially undermining the communal spirit of the group (McLaughlin et al., 1995), and, with the exception of errors, somewhat more forgiving of other offenses. Of particular interest is the finding that, while the reproaches of soc.singles posters were notably more sarcastic than other re-proaches, this was evidently not cause for concern among the newsgroup at large (none of soc.singles reproachers were reprimanded and only two re-proaches targeted language in soc.singles). The high incidence of reproaches stemming from poster errors perhaps underscores the original mission of Usenet. Despite the fact that much of the traffic on Usenet is demonstrably social in spirit, Usenet is still a medium for exchange of information, and even when expressing an opinion, one needs to adhere to Grice's (1975) quality maxim of truthfulness.

Flaming or similarly antisocial behavior was not well tolerated in any of the newsgroups we studied, but this, too, should be interpreted with caution. Incidences of flaming were not equal across the five groups. One possible ap-proach for future analyses would be to analyze the same number of flaming incidences across newsgroups for quantitative and qualitative differences in corresponding remedial episodes.

The gender analysis in this study strengthens a growing concern regarding unequal representation of women on the net. While female participation in Usenet is probably increasing along with the overall growth in usage, our study does not indicate female participation in Usenet is catching up to that of males. Reports of men's participation on the newsgroup soc.women, for example, have ranged from 63 percent (Balka, 1993) to approximately 80 percent (Shade, 1993; We, 1993). Furthermore, Kramarae and Taylor (1992) observed that on some days, only men posted to soc.women. Our study also examined a "women's" newsgroup (rec.arts.tv.soaps—r.a.t.s.—is traditional-ly viewed as appealing primarily to women) as well as two newsgroups geared towards socializing among and between the sexes (soc.motss, soc.sin-gles). While the newsgroup r.a.t.s. was indeed dominated by women in our sample (78% women), the gender distribution of those posting to motss and singles was more in line with recent findings in other studies.

It has been noted that women have less access to computing technology (Balka, 1993; Truong, 1993). Kramarae and Taylor (1992) have voiced a concern that men's dominating posting behaviors, such as sending more messages, introducing more new topics, and disagreeing with others more frequently, may inhibit women's participation. Our findings did nothing to dispel Kramarae and Taylor's concern; however, some encouraging trends may be seen in our sample. For example, we found that female reproachers were slightly more prolific than any other group of posters, perhaps indicating a somewhat stronger voice among women who participate frequently. Also, the percentage of female offenders (31%) is highly disproportionate to the estimated percentage (10-15%) of women's presence in network traffic (Shade, 1993). But this latter finding raises yet another concern: the higher proportion of male to female cross-gender reproaches suggests that additional study is needed regarding the treatment of women by men in newsgroup conversations. The biological divide in virtual spaces seems very real in Usenet and deserves ample study from multidisciplinary perspectives.

CHAPTER SEVEN

Investigation of Relcom Network Users

Alexander E. Voiskounsky

The idea of a planned research project to be conducted with global network users in Russia might have seemed unthinkable a few years ago, when a community of regular network users was entirely missing. In 1984, the author had the first chance to observe a global computer conference and to fulfill pilot research in the field. The computer conference on *Bioconversion of Lignocellulosics for Fuel, Fodder, and Food* (Balson, 1985) was held on a year-long basis under the auspices of the UNESCO and the UNEP. During the entire year there was only one Russian participant. But in the final session it was intended to practice a Delphilike formal procedure in order to elaborate the whole range of expert solutions. A dozen experts from the former Soviet Union were thus invited to participate in a three-day session.

The procedure was unusual as the participants had to gather in Moscow to discuss the printed versions of expert forms and, after that, Klyosov, the moderator, used the network to pass the marks and the opinions expressed by the participants to the computer conference organizers. For many years it was impossible to realize the expressed interest in conducting experimental research on global computer network users. Opportunities for such research were restricted to local area networks only. It was an extremely tiresome task for the moderator to get permission to participate in the computer conference. It was even more difficult to be allowed to form the expert group. If not for the auspices of the United Nations, the initiative would have failed. Free online information exchange via global computer networks obviously seemed contradictory to the restrictive rules of the closed totalitarian society in which citizens were not permitted to be involved in computer telecommunications.

The pilot research was restricted to observing the procedures of the expression and exchange of opinions, to interviewing the participants, and to analyzing the printed listings of the year-long computer-mediated professional communications.[1] The theme of the research was concerned mostly with speech peculiarities of information exchange via the computer (Voiskounsky, 1992).

Relcom Network

The dominant network in Russia is Relcom. From the beginning, Relcom (which means *reliable communications*) was a nongovernment enterprise, developed by a group of Unix computer programmers. For the sake of close and efficient collaboration, small dispersed teams of computer programmers started to communicate via computers and telecommunications links. While using this kind of purely professional communication the programmers realized that the new telecommunication service might be expanded beyond the various teams of originators. This enterprise was the beginning of commercial networking in the former USSR.

Having no government support, Relcom struggled for survival. Quite a difficult task was to contact the monopolistic Ministry of Communications to rent the communications links. The real victory was the start of world-wide networking. As Press (1991) expresses it, Relcom "established a link to EU-net through Helsinki, Finland, on August 22, 1990, thereby connecting the Soviet Union to the rest of the world."

Unlike some other telecommunications enterprises, Relcom offered services for Russian roubles (i.e. noncurrency) and for rather low costs. The strategy chosen was to expand quickly in order to gain the critical mass of users to survive even if legislation changed and/or taxes increased dramatically. As there was no precedent of computer networking in the former Soviet Union, and not the slightest understanding of that type of service, it was necessary to advertise. To win additional support some influential institutions were connected for free, including new banks, stock exchange companies, newspapers' editorials and publishers, industrial and cultural associations, and so forth. More important and, in many aspects, less prestigious was the constant activity resulting in the promotion of new computer communication centers serving as network nodes. Emerging outside Moscow, they strengthened Relcom and gave the critical mass needed. As a result, it became evident that Relcom would not be prohibited.

It was neither prohibited nor censured, even during the August 1991 coup when the President was arrested and the junta suppressed and/or censured in most media. In fact Relcom users exchanged both news and personal comments about the opposition to the junta defenders in a free manner (for more details see the Appendix in Press, 1991). Further, it is known that a certain officer inside the Ministry of Defense was able to e-mail a message explaining that he had been given an order to destroy documents of a recent coup when it became evident that the coup had failed. Hearing about the message, someone contacted the President, and Chief Commander Gorbachev consequently ordered the democratically-minded officer to stop destroying the documents. Thus Relcom gained a good reputation and, after the coup, most information agencies, newspaper editors, and magazine/journal publishers initiated their connections to Relcom.

The last two or three years prior to the disbandment of USSR in 1991 might be characterized as a period of rapid computerization. Relcom enjoyed a period of rapid expansion during this period for two reasons. First, in a short period of time, the number of desktop PCs grew rapidly and computers became accessible (though not as numerous and as reachable as compared to more developed states). Second, the mail service and telephone connections were suffering an unprecedented shortage and unreliability. This latter factor is ambiguous. On the one hand, a great need is expressed to gain fast and safe connections and, on the other hand, computer networking is extremely dependent on reliable communications. The telecommunications sphere is rapidly expanding in Russia, and the highly respectable Western/Eastern investors have come to operate here. Thus computer networking service gained its attraction among users due to the rapid transmission of messages, due to being rather reliable and inexpensive, and due to the fact that computers became available (as it should be on the eve of stepping into an information society). It was therefore extraordinarily important that Relcom give access to the Internet and Usenet. Computer networking is understood to be the cheapest possible way, compared to mail services, fax, telegraph, or phone switching, to communicate abroad.

Based on a highly primitive communications system, Relcom has inherited most of its disadvantages, the most serious being insufficient reliability and long traffic delays. Efforts to improve reliability and hasten the message exchange process never stop. Despite serious and crucial technical problems, Relcom has survived. In 1994, it operated in more than 100 cities in Russia (and in the former USSR), and reported the greatest number of users, approximately 200,000 (McHenry, 1994). The latter fact is important to an investigation of global computer network users.

Characteristics of Relcom Users

The community of Relcom users is actually a specific sample of Russian (and ex-USSR) citizens. The community represents an active and intellectual (or educated) section of the population so an investigation of this sample is both provocative and important.

It so happened that Relcom became a highly polyfunctional computer network. This is indicative of the peculiar economic and political situation in the former Soviet Union: cultural and industrial connections among neighboring regions and republics (now independent or in the process of gaining independence) were suddenly aborted. The system of materials and goods exchange needed to be restored or formed anew. The information exchange system needed to be created as well, and it needed to be convenient and available both to the older economic residents (e.g. factories, collective farms, financial and trading companies) and to the newest economic structures (e.g. cooperatives, farmers, private trading firms). As almost all economic partners were equipped with a phone and a computer, many of them preferred the relatively cheap and rapid means of exchanging information offered by the forming computer networking infrastructure, and Relcom was the largest network. Thus Relcom, as well as most of the other networks, took on a role as an intermediary in trading.

Strange as it may seem, although initiated as a media for the professional communication of computer programmers, Relcom gained dozens of purely trading teleconferences (i.e. newsgroups). They are as diverse as a catalog of goods and supplies can be expected to be. The subscribers to commercial teleconferences pay more than the other users, which gives Relcom the chance to survive. At the same time Relcom also remains a means for computer programmers to communicate—its first and primary functional role—and promotes the professional communication of researchers and educators. RELARN Association (financed mostly by government sources) provides important financial support for educational institutions to establish connections and participate in computer networking. And, as mentioned above, among the subscribers are representatives of news and information agencies. Thus it is usually concluded that the users of the polyfunctional Relcom—educators/researchers, trading/financial elite, journalists, and computer programmers—represent the active and/or intellectual population of the ex-USSR.

Aims and Methodology

The aim of this research was to initiate a type of sociological and psychological monitoring: to identify the processes that influence network users, to monitor them, and to offer support. Thus one of the goals of the research was to explore acceptable areas for that kind of monitoring service and to determine which functions of the monitoring service might be approved by the respondents. Another and no less important goal was to gain some knowledge of Relcom users, including their interests, attitudes, devotion to computer-mediated communication, need for remote database access, satisfaction with the partners, with the teleconferencing system, and with the kind of hardware and software used, the users' competence and the sources of competence, and their willingness to deliver and/or acquire expert knowledge. This kind of knowledge was intended to form the basis of the monitoring service.

The research was conducted by a special interest group, formed in 1992, consisting of faculty members of the Psychology Department, Moscow University and headed by the author. The first tasks were to develop a questionnaire which would be e-mailed to a sample of network users or presented to selected teleconferences, and to collect and process responses. To develop the questionnaire it was considered essential to observe the processes of message exchange in teleconferences. The best way to observe this process was to subscribe to the teleconferences, to read the messages, and to take part in the discussions when it was appropriate (that is, when the discussed themes were close to the competence of the researchers). Thus the participant observation was considered to be an important principle of the research methodology. The problems raised in the discussions were to facilitate the process of questionnaire elaboration.

It was important to develop a questionnaire consisting of closed questions. To formulate the questions with an adequate menu of answers, it was necessary to conduct face-to-face interviews, consultations, and pilot surveys—both paper-and-pencil and via the network. In the latter case it was sufficient to address the questionnaire items to the small samples of respondents. The samples might be constructed, for example, either of network users who were selected by chance or of network users who expressed their willingness to collaborate with the researchers. During pilot surveys, special messages were sent to respondents asking them to disclose their motivations for the choice of the answers.

Finally, two types of surveys were devised:

Local surveys: short, specialized and, in most cases, monothematic questionnaires sent directly to samples of network users. The samples were constructed according to respondents' age, profession, and experience in network usage.

Global or universal surveys: questionnaires containing more questions (the largest instrument contained 27 questions), multithematic, and nonspecialized (i.e. universal). These surveys were to be sent to teleconferences, not e-mailed to any of the potential respondents personally. This way of administering surveys was necessary as Relcom is a commercial network, and users pay for each message received and sent. The universal survey was intended to limit the community of would-be respondents to those who subscribe to the teleconferences. Those who did not subscribe were assumed to be too passive to take part in group discussions, and thus were only able to participate in global surveys by chance (e.g. hearing of the survey from a colleague).

After developing the methodology for obtaining data via computer networks, several local and global surveys were carried out. The preliminary results were published elsewhere (Arestova et al., 1993).

Experimental Results

The results of the global survey conducted in 1993 are given in the following sections. The number of responses to the questionnaires distributed via Relcom network teleconferences was 305.

Geographic Dispersion

The first result to be noted is the wide geographic dispersion of the respondents. Responses were received from all geographical regions in Russia—Central, Northern, and Southern Russia (European part of the state), the Urals, Western and Central Siberia, and the Far East. As well, responses came from almost all the states that formed the former USSR: the Baltic states (Latvia, Estonia, and Lithuania), the Ukraine (Central, Western, and Southern Ukraine), Belorussia, Moldovia, the Central Asia states (including Kazakhstan), and the Caucasus states. Fewer responses than in the past were received from Georgia, probably because this state was engaged in combat actions at the time of the survey. Responses were also received from Azerbaijan and Armenia which were in conflict with each other due to the Karabakh autonomy problem.

As the sample was not formed before the survey, the geographic dispersion of the respondents corresponds in a way to the "density" of Relcom nodes in different regions. To support this conclusion, let us mention that, as expected, over one third of respondents were from greater Moscow, and St Petersburg. These two cities are known to be the most advanced in the fields of informatics and computer networking. Another expected result was that the respondents were from well-known research centers located outside of large cities and towns. An unexpected result was responses from a research center which was secret before; for the first time, perhaps, researchers from this center were freely connected to the network and had the opportunity to participate in such a survey.

Age of Respondents

To characterize the respondents, let us note first they are rather young: more than half are in the age range of 21 to 25 years, and more than three fourths are between 21 and 35. The distribution of respondents according to their age is shown at the figure 1.

The results correspond to observations made while interviewing network users and reading the messages exchanged in teleconferences. The users are mostly young, and the topics of their messages rarely include problem areas associated with older people (e.g. pensions, illnesses and the like). Younger people are generally assumed to be the most active; therefore, the answers given by the respondents seem to correspond to at-

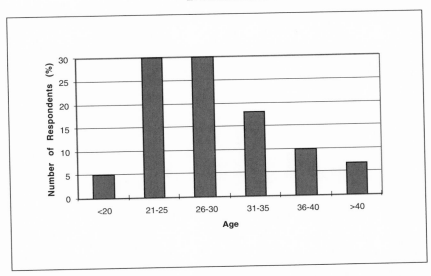

Figure 1. Age of respondents.

titudes characteristic of the most active sector of post-Soviet citizens.

Experience in Network Usage

The respondents are not only relatively young, they are also new users. About two thirds of respondents had joined the network community a year or less prior to the survey (figure 2).

It can be observed that long-term users are not numerous. Only 5% of the respondents joined the network over two years before the survey; 3% said they had been connected to Relcom from the moment the network was initiated. These data are highly characteristic, as networking itself was an extremely new way of communicating in the former Soviet Union. Another result worth mentioning is the approximate acceleration rate of the number of Relcom users. During the six months before the survey was administered, the community of users was increasing rapidly and proportionally—the increase was approximately 20% every three months. During the lag time from 6 to 24 months before the survey, the number of users grew 13-23% every six months. These figures indicate that the network has good prospects for further extension and enlargement.

Competence in Computer Networking

Being mostly new users, the respondents were interested in gaining more

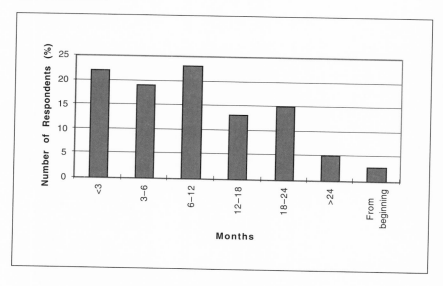

*Figure 2. Time when respondents switched to the network
(given in months prior to the survey).*

competence in computer networking. Of the total number of respondents, 42% noted it would be useful for them to participate in special workshops in order to enhance their knowledge of how network facilities might be used more effectively. Only 14% of respondents deny the usefulness of that kind of workshop. One fourth of respondents considered workshops would be useful for beginners and new users, but not for themselves. No definite opinion was expressed by 17% of respondents on the problem of usefulness of workshops. As expected, the newest users (those connected less than three months before the survey) are the most interested in participating in a workshop. Of the newcomers, 30% expressed their willingness to acquire more competence in computer networking and 31% were subscribed to a special teleconference for new users. In the whole sample of respondents, the proportion who were subscribed to this teleconference was lower (22%).

Thus the newcomers had more expressed cognitive interests than qualified users. The former had problems acquiring competency in network usage. The problems grew partly from the fact that those who lack expertise in computer programming have difficulties in understanding the descriptions of network services and facilities. The descriptions are indeed too concise and specialized to be understood easily by users with low levels of skills in computers and informatics. This obvious drawback is because the initiators of Relcom and its administration pay too little attention to the problems that newcomers face.

Respondents' options	%
Subscription to professional teleconferences and newsgroups	63
Search for contact persons	57
International correspondence	53
Commerce and business (business agreements and offers; updated information on demand/supply rates, etc.)	50
Establishment of interpersonal contacts	48
Remote access to archives and databases	44
Fun, recreation, chatting	31
Research data exchange	26
Preparation of joint publications	17
Administrative and managerial work	15
Subscription to actual information from news agencies	7

Table 1. Motivation for network usage.

The special cognitive interests of the most qualified users are not touched in the survey reported because, in 1993, there were few users equipped and experienced enough to connect to Archie or Gopher, to use telnet, or navigate the WWW; the more skilled users were partly outside Relcom, since at that time Relcom operated the more inexpensive services based on UUCP/TP switching.

Motivations for Network Usage

As might be expected, new users were less satisfied with Relcom usage than the more experienced respondents, but the difference in satisfaction (measured on a Likert scale) is not great. There was almost a complete absence (4% only) of extremes—both positive and negative. It could be interpreted, therefore, that the community of Relcom users possesses certain integrity and balance in the evaluation of computer networking services.

A list of possible motivations and purposes for using Relcom, defined in the pilot research, was presented to respondents and users were asked to choose the most relevant ones. The most frequently chosen option was the possibility of subscribing to professional teleconferences and newsgroups (63%) (table 1).

There are some slight differences in the comparison of preferred ways in which newcomers and qualified network users use the network. The inexperienced users, for example, favor more highly the opportunity to search for new partners and contact persons, and to maintain electronic correspondence with their partners from abroad. The experienced users chose more often than their inexperienced colleagues the options for chatting and having fun, for managerial and administrative work, and for remote access to databases and archives. The differences in ratings between the experienced and inexperienced network users are very slight—less than 4%. An important feature is the order of the chosen options, which is the same for the each sample.

Network Usage, Occupation, and Orientation

The claimed preferences for Relcom usage do not correspond to the respondents' occupations. Over half of the respondents reported that their main occupation is either professional or amateur computer programming. That is, they claim they are not so-called end users, but consider themselves professionals in computer programming and/or computer applications. The applications spheres mentioned included mathematical modeling and applied software for telecommunications management. Most respondents noted they have several occupations. This is characteristic for present-day Russia (as well as other ex-USSR states)—the more active and the younger population seek more than one job. As a rule, one salary is not enough income to live well. The other occupations reported by respondents include: teaching in colleges or universities; research in science and, to a lesser degree, in the humanities fields; management and administration; books, magazines and newspapers publishing; trading, marketing, commerce and financing; learning in colleges, and consulting.

Thus the responses to the questionnaire item related to chief occupations are somewhat misleading as the sample seems to be biased towards computer programming and applications specialists. In many cases these data disagree with some other options of the same respondents; for example, teleconferences to which they claim to be subscribed, preferred ways of using the network, and so forth. It might be concluded that the Relcom users who represent biomedical or engineering/construction institutions, editorials or banks, trading companies or industrial manufacturers, prefer, for some reason, to present themselves as regular network users and computer applications professionals. Computer networking certainly is a very important part of the respondents' professional occupation, but the primary occupation is usually close to their formal education.

The general conclusion to be drawn is that the survey medium influences some of the respondents' reactions, and that the responses to the questionnaire item on the chief occupation should not be considered relevant. Much more accurate would be to define orientations, not occupation. The orientations might be derived from several sets of data, i.e. the responses given to several questionnaire items. Applied to the computer networking field, the orientation depends on: (1) subscription to teleconferences and/or newsgroups of a certain content; (2) claimed preferences for using Relcom; and (3) expressed interest in databases of a certain content. The reported chief occupation might therefore be considered an auxiliary piece of data. It should be stressed, however, that the orientations are not to be taken as the sole mode of network usage, which is always a mixture.

There are several orientations to be noted, some quite obvious: the computer programming orientation; the commercial/financial orientation, and the research/educational orientation. Clearly, the *computer programming orientation* means that the respondents: (1) consider themselves computer programmers, (2) subscribe to teleconferences dealing with software production, and (3) use more than one operating system. The *commercial/financial/trading orientation* means that the respondents: (1) give trading and commerce as their chief occupation (often in combination with computer programming, which may mean that the respondents are engaged in commerce in the computer hardware/software/telecommunications field), (2) subscribe to certain commercial teleconferences, and (3) report they have found new commercial partners and/or offers via computer networking, and (4) are interested mostly in commercial databases. The *research/educational orientation* means that the respondents: (1) report that their occupation is in research/education institutions, (2) subscribe to Internet sci.newsgroups, (3) use Relcom primarily for research data exchange with colleagues or for writing/editing joint articles with colleagues, and (4) are greatly interested in gaining access to certain remote databases (factual, bibliographical, archives of research data processing methods, or needed software).

The communicative orientation was not displayed in the pilot research, so it should be considered as quite a new one. The respondents oriented in this way report that they are: fond of chatting via the network; interested in recreational or hobby databases; subscribe to the mostly "talkative" teleconferences (relcom.penpals or relcom.talk, and the like); finding new communicative partners for personal communication; and satisfied with the way they use Relcom. With all these activities those who are marked as having communicative orientation differ from those whose chief orientation is of different kind. That is, to consider the sample itself, about half of the respondents use Relcom for personal communication; over half of them use it for initiating new personal contacts; about one third of them use the network for recreation; and some of them expressed interest in any kind of entertainments database. In other words, the activities mentioned are rather popular among the Relcom users.

It is quite possible nevertheless to select a group of those users for whom the communicative orientation is especially characteristic. Communicatively oriented respondents are highly uniform. To present them as a uniform group of respondents we need to choose a special item in the questionnaire and to select those who give definite responses to this item. Then we need to determine the responses of the members of the selected group to other questionnaire items relevant to the communicative orientation. We chose as the selected group, therefore, those respondents who claimed that they use the network primarily for personal communications. Table 2 shows the difference between the members of the group mentioned and the whole sample.

From table 2 it is evident that 70% of those who use the network for personal communication use it as well for initiating new contacts (13% more

Positive response on selected questionnaire items	Respondents who use network for personal communication (%)	Respondents of whole sample (%)
Initiate new contacts	70	57
Recreate and distract	45	31
Subscribe to humor and hobby teleconferences	51	41
Found new partners	40	24
Failed to find new partners	17	28

Table 2. Communicatively oriented respondents vs general sample members.

than in the general sample); 45% use it for both personal communication and recreation (14% more than general sample); 51% subscribe to humour and hobby teleconference (10% more than general sample); 40% claim to acquire new communicative partners via the network (16% more than general sample); 17% failed to get new partners (11% less than general sample). Thus the data presented make it quite evident that the communicative orientation might be characterized as more intensive initiation of new personal contacts and much better results from this kind of initiation compared to the general sample of respondents, and greater interest displayed in humorous and recreational use of the network. It should be noted that in the pilot investigations carried out earlier, the purely communicative orientation was not selected and described. The extraction of the communicative orientation is an awaited result of the current research. One might maintain now that the Relcom network is a purely communicative medium, as it should be.

Network Monitoring Service

To establish any kind of network monitoring service, one should first define its possible purposes. This was done during the pilot research, and the list of potential ways of network monitoring service operation was presented to the users (table 3). They could choose several options, or none. The resulting list includes the items determined. Obviously the practical establishment of a network monitoring service needs special support and to apply for such support one should determine first whether the potential users of a new service consider it worthy and useful.

As can be seen from table 3, most options have considerable support from respondents. The strongest support is given to performing the surveys of users. For that reason, continuation of the administration of surveys is being considered, each time changing the previously used questionnaire and devising new ones. This is thought to serve as a means of adaptation of network users to the possibility of advancing some equivalent of the monitoring ser-

	Users' choice
Aims of network monitoring service	
Administer surveys of users	73%
Participate in network advertizing and marketing, search for new network services	59%
Fulfill psychological and ergonomical expertize of the existing and new human-computer interfaces	48%
Manuals and/or handbooks for network users	44%
Participate in newcomers' training	40%
Intermediate in possible conflicts (financial, managerial, ethical, etc.) resolution and forecasting	36%
Consult the netters in applied psychology and sociology	34%
Moderate a new specialized teleconference on psychology and/or sociology	31%
Participate in the network staff employment policy	22%
Work out and administer the individual and/or group psychotherapy techniques in order to help relax the network staff officials	17%

Table 3. Possible directions of a social monitoring service and users' ratings

Network monitoring service:	Respondents' rates (%)
Is it really needed	45
Will it be needed in the future	14
No need at all	4
No definite answer	37

Table 4. Users' rates of the necessity of a social monitoring service.

vice (with a reduced list of purposes). After all, the decision to introduce a new kind of service must be based on subsequent questioning of the users. In the 1993 survey, besides marking the chosen option, respondents were asked whether they think there is a need for the network monitoring service.

Table 4 shows that the respondents expressed support of the worthiness of administering surveys: 45% considered the network monitoring service is really needed; only 4% considered there is no need. More than two thirds of the respondents gave no definite answer to the question. They might have a need to adapt to the advancement of the network monitoring service. The adaptation process needs considerable time and some preparatory activity of the research group members to plan the subsequent research work.

Conclusions

The research was intended to commence a series of surveys constituting part of a social monitoring service in a computer networking field. Although responses of the Relcom network users on the necessity of this kind of monitoring service differed a lot, the option of administering surveys of users proved to be the most favored by network users as the aim of projected monitoring service.

Thus one of the research aims was to find out network users' attitudes towards the surveying procedure. It was evident from the data that attitudes were mostly positive. Other aims included refining the research instrument, and achieving new data to characterize the network users, or regular Relcom users. The data gained included age and geographic dispersion of respondents, their experience and competence in computer networking, their professional occupation and orientations in computer telecommunications, and motivations for network usage. It is important to note that an inherent communicative orientation in computer networking was displayed and determined.

The questionnaire that was developed and used in the research proved to be reliable and informative. To conduct further research projects, the research instrument needs to be modified as computer networking, as a specific area of social activity, is very mobile and dynamic, and its development is accelerating. As psychological changes usually follow technological ones, the nearing transition to modern information technologies would necessitate updating previously used questionnaires. Thus the need to keep modifying research instruments seems to be the most desired symptom of the evolution of computer networking in Russia and in the former Soviet Union.

Acknowledgements

The financial support to carry out the research was given by the Russian Foundation for Basic Research. The author appreciates technical assistance and consultations from the Russian Institute for Public Networks (RIPN). The RIPN is the institution that carries out the administration of the RE-LARN Association, which is enlisting state educational and research institutions for computer networking in Russia, and supports investigations in the field.

Note

1. Content analysis was not done, as some of the listings were missing.

CHAPTER EIGHT

Practicing Safe Computing

Why People Engage in Risky Computer-mediated Communication

Diane F. Witmer

I wanna feel your viscosity, honey,
Melt my rheological mind;
Let your female forcefield vortex
Deform my male spacetime.
— Nick Herbert,

*Does She do the Vulcan Mind
Meld on the First Date?*

ybersex, computer dating, and net sex are prevalent buzzwords in popular press and daytime talk shows. As the tongue-in-cheek excerpt above suggests, computer users are enthusiastically exploring "safer sex" alternatives. Exchanges of pornographic pictures, x-rated e-mail, and computer chats that are nothing less than sexual encounters are wildly popular, and magazines such as Boardwatch run numerous ads for sexually explicit bulletin boards (BBSs).

Every day, millions of people around the world inhabit cyberspace, participating in research, scholarly discourse, social interaction, politics, hobbies, and explicit sexual fantasies. Whether the electronic exchanges occur within organizations or around the globe, the touch of a button sends a message to its recipient in a matter of minutes, and often, within seconds. The same technology that provides these marvels creates new challenges for the user, and a variety of ways in which embarrassment or even disaster can occur as the result of a mere keystroke. Knowing this, why would a user engage in computer-mediated communication (CMC) that creates personal or professional risk? The study described in this chapter asks computer users who participate in potentially embarrassing CMC how risky they perceive their communications to be, and why they feel secure enough to engage in those actions. First, this chapter provides basic definitions and contextualizes various forms of CMC as non-private media. It then reports a study that focuses on Usenet newsgroups. Finally, this chapter discusses the implications of the findings as they may relate to the broader context of CMC.

From Fliers to Fiber Optices:
Communicating in the Computer Age

Once upon a time, people posted important messages on trees and church doors, and letters were delivered by hand. Today, people still post messages on kiosks and bulletin boards in supermarkets, employee lounges, and convention centers, and letters are delivered by postal or courier services. With the advent of the personal computer (PC), new methods appeared for these age-old forms of communication—the electronic BBS and e-mail.

The symbolic nature of electronic communication is well recognized (e.g., Short, Williams, and Christie, 1976; Sitkin, Sutcliffe, and Barrios-Choplin, 1989). Although World Wide Web hypertext capabilities are expanding the breadth of symbolic exchange, much CMC is still limited, which constrains the discourse in ways unique to the medium. CMC systems often support only a low-end ASCII character set. This means the communicator is restricted to American upper and lower case letters and numerals, and some commonly-used mathematical and punctuation symbols (e.g., "$," "%," "()," "+," etc., omitting umlauts and other European characters). Therefore, the sender and receiver must rely on a fairly narrow set of predetermined symbols with which they endeavor to create and share meaning.

In CMC, the medium is the message, not in the McLuhan sense, but in a structurationist sense (e.g., Contractor and Eisenberg, 1990; Fulk, Schmitz, and Schwartz, 1992; Giddens, 1976; Poole and DeSanctis, 1989; Poole and McPhee, 1983; Riley, 1983). The medium's symbolic meaning becomes both a product of and a constraint upon the communication process, as illustrated by the emergence of an infant e-mail etiquette," (see Shapiro and Anderson, 1985) complete with symbols and conventions that, while continually evolving, are largely accepted system-wide, and often inter-system. Abrasive, even abusive electronic communication is common enough to have been dubbed "flaming," a term unique to the medium.

Although electronic groups may consist of unseen members who do not occupy shared physical space and who interact asynchronously, Finholt and Sproull (1990) report that they tend to behave like social groups. Furthermore, communicators develop social alliances, and heavy users actually tend to form new friendships via computer-mediated means (e.g., Hellerstein,

1985). In some cases, the interpersonal behaviors are of a nature usually reserved for intimate encounters (e.g., Furniss, 1993), both on bulletin boards and in private e-mail.

While public bulletin boards typically are read by groups of people who share similar interests, e-mail can be used to communicate one-to-one or one-to-many. Person-to-person, "private" e-mail is the computerized equivalent of correspondence in the federal postal system (colloquially known as "snail mail" in high-tech circles). The e-mail user composes a message and sends it via a computer network to a recipient or several recipients at other locations. But unlike the postal system, or the telephone system, for that matter, the law does not fully protect privacy of e-mail. User accounts are protected under the Electronic Communications Privacy Act (ECPA) of 1986, which amends the federal wiretap law and makes accessing stored electronic messages by breaking into an electronic system or exceeding authorized access a criminal offense (Hernandez, 1987). But a manager, investigator, or system administrator (sysop) with global access to the computer system (God powers) is capable of monitoring any electronic message. Furthermore, recipients can and do forward e-mail with the touch of a button to other users, and the messages may be captured and archived on computer disks without the knowledge of the original author. It is the naive user who ignores the reality that somehow, somewhere, someone can read and preserve privately posted messages.

E-mail privacy can be compromised in other ways, too, if a user is unwise or careless. Krol (1992) lists four ways in which computer security is compromised, in descending order of likelihood: (1) choosing bad passwords; (2) importing corrupt software by valid users; (3) entering through misconfigured software; and (4) entering through an operating system security flaw. He cautions the user to remember that computers, not people, crack passwords, and most of those attempts are based on words from the dictionary. Indeed, some systems will not permit users to use dictionary words as passwords. But some universities use Social Security numbers for user passwords, making e-mail security more of an illusion than a reality.

Various systems impose different balances of privacy and censorship. Some systems have a reputation for maintaining correspondent privacy. Other systems, ostensibly valuing standards over privacy, go so far as to censor "private" messages. The widely-used Prodigy network, for example, has been under fire for maintaining a policy of censorship (Lewis, 1990, p. F8). For some commercial subscription services, of course, these decisions probably are economically based, because users often are charged for connect time. Sending and receiving heavy graphics or "chatting" (described later in this paper) keeps the user online. But no matter how computer services remain fiscally viable, the issue of privacy is problematic for all systems. Indeed, "system administrators seeking to deliver misaddressed electronic mail can hardly avoid reading the messages" (Turner, 1991, p. A13). Miller (1992, p. p8F N) suggests that employees should "assume [e-mail security] … doesn't exist." In other words, the term "e-mail privacy" is an oxymoron.

Privacy problems also arise on the systems known as electronic bulletin board services (BBSs). Typically operated privately, these bulletin boards post messages that are the electronic counterparts to those pinned on physical bulletin boards. The messages are readable for all who care to call the service and log onto the system. Some systems permit "private" messages on the bulletin boards, which makes them invisible to the casual reader, but readable to the intended recipient (and the sysops). One might say they are posted on the bulletin board in electronic envelopes, which, although sealed, are by no means secure. Clearly, the security of both forms of electronic communication is questionable, particularly if not encrypted—and most e-mail messages are not.

Somewhere between one-to-one e-mail and BBSs lie e-mail subscription lists and newsgroups. These proliferate on the Internet, a huge, international, amorphous network of networks. Any user with Internet access can subscribe to various lists, and read and post messages to the newsgroups supported by the local system. Rather than dialing to the individual lists, as with a BBS, these messages are available via the user's regular e-mail account. Some newsgroups, particularly those dealing with explicit sexual topics, have host servers that create pseudonyms for anonymous postings, if the users wish. Of course, this anonymity, like all e-mail anonymity, is only as secure as the system itself. In other words, it isn't.

Beyond asynchronous e-mail, newsgroup, and bulletin board capabilities, many computer networks and systems support synchronous ("real time") computer conferencing. Typically, computer conferencing is open to anyone who logs on and enters the command to enter a "chat." Often, however, users also can create "private" conferences, accessible to other users only by invitation. The Internet relay chat (IRC) supports conferences, both private and public—a number with adult or pornographic themes.

Rights and Responsibilities: Thorny Questions for Sysops & Users

Where does system responsibility end and user right to privacy begin? Kahn (1989) describes the all-too-common phenomenon of a computer user dialing up a local BBS, logging in with her secret password, and being "deluged with lewd electronic mail from complete strangers and hostile messages from persons with whom she believed she was on friendly terms" (p. 1). The BBS user eventually realizes she is the victim of a computer "hacker" or "phreaker;" her password was pirated, and someone has been electronically impersonating her. Recently, a similar incident occurred on a university BBS. A regular user's password was discovered by a hostile hacker, who logged on several times a day, leaving violent, racist and sexist, public and private messages. It was several days before other BBS users alerted the sysop, who deleted the phreaker's bogus account from the system and contacted the individual who was being impersonated.

Let's assume our local BBS user is enraged by the public humiliation of the offensive public messages. Is he justified in suing the sysop and/or the owner of the BBS for defamation? Most BBSs, the university BBS included, are run at a loss by volunteers (Riddle, 1990). Must the sysop monitor all messages and be responsible for those in poor taste or of a defaming nature? High volume boards make message-by-message monitoring nearly impossible.

Many organizations, including academic institutions, are struggling with issues of balance between system security and system standards vs. freedom of speech and privacy. This problem is made thornier by the popularity of e-mail lists, often with huge memberships, that are devoted to adult topics. On the Internet, for example, four of the fifteen most popular newsgroups focus on sexual topics, including erotic arts, stories, and bondage (Reid, 1993). Turner (1991, p. A13) notes that in local, university-owned systems, "The kinds of messages once limited to lavatory walls are now causing problems on campus computer networks—for reasons that may have as much to do with technology as with moral standards."

In addition to security compromises, much of what feels like a private interaction between user and computer is, in fact, very public on many computer systems. UNIX systems, for example, support a command that allows users to determine who else is on the system at a given moment. The IRC, often accessed under pseudonyms or handles, permits callers to determine the real electronic mailing addresses of other users. It is even possible to obtain information about users after they have left the system, and falsifying one's true mailing information can lead to access denial. Many private BBSs make available lists of recent callers and the times they called. Some even list, in terms of bytes, how much a caller has posted to the system.

Privacy difficulties arise from user error, as well as from external monitoring. The user always is a mere keystroke away from disaster, and can send a message to the wrong party, or even to large groups of people, with a single typographical slip-up:

> One job-seeker mistakenly sent his resume and a letter to a 1,000-person mailing list rather than to the hiring manager, [inadvertently] divulging salary demands and why he wanted the job (Keubelbeck, 1991, p. E2).

Anyone using CMC undoubtedly is aware of the flurries of media attention paid to the issue of security and privacy in electronic mail systems (e.g.,

Anderson, Johnson, Gotterbarn, and Perolle, 1993; Keppel, 1990; Moore, 1992). Organizations and individual users alike are discovering the complexities of communicating in a new medium. Horror stories abound (e.g., Lewis, 1990; Solomon, 1990; Keubelbeck, 1991). For example:

> Bonita B. Bourke and Rhonda L. Hall sued Nissan Motor Corporation of USA in Carson, CA. They alleged that their manager "electronically eavesdropped" on their e-mail and that they were fired after filing a grievance over it (White, 1991, p. D3).

> Epson America was slapped with two lawsuits for invasion of privacy. One was filed by a former e-mail manager who alleged she was fired for trying to stop company managers from reading e-mail messages between employees (Burke, 1990, p. 124; Keubelbeck, 1991, p. E2).

> Lotus Development Corporation canceled its development of the software package, "Lotus Marketplace," a market research and direct marketing package that included an electronic database, due to mounting concern that it placed excessive power in the hands of small businesses, creating invasions of privacy. (Francese, 1991; Miller, 1991, p. B1).

> In the wake of the infamous Rodney King beating, a number of Los Angeles Police officers experienced, first-hand, the archival nature of electronic communication. In the process of investigating the incident, Christopher Commission studied squad car messages and characterized approximately 700 of them as improper and "apparently racist or sexist" (Keubelbeck, 1991, p. E2).

Michael F. Cavanagh, executive director of the Electronic Mail Association in Arlington, VA, sees the problem as one of balance, and suggests that "the juxtaposition of that LAPD situation and the public's right to know what was on the tapes with the issue of how to have a secure workplace illustrates how complex the issue is" (Keubelbeck, 1991, p. E2).

The corporate sector toes a similar fine line between electronic supervision of employees and invasion of their rights. Miller (1992) notes that although it's against the law for organizations to monitor employee telephone conversations, even on a company-owned phone, the regulations concerning e-mail are less clear. A case that may change this is reported by Kapor (1992) and Ratcliffe (1992) concerning Borland International, Inc. and Symantec Corporation. Eugene Wang, a Borland employee, left the company and and joined Symantec. Borland claims to have found memos in Wang's MCI mail to Symantec—memos written prior to Wang's departure that include Borland proprietary information. When Borland executives turned over Wang's mail messages to local police, the messages were used to obtain search warrants to enter Wang's home and that of Gordon Eubanks, the Symantec chief executive officer. Ratcliffe (1992) speculates that Wang and Eubanks would argue violation of the ECPA, although Borland indicates that as owner of the account, the search was legal. Kapor points out that although current law protects messages while they are in transmission over public services, this case may help define the degree to which employers can search employees' stored e-mail messages. Organizations argue that the mailbox is company property and it is not uncommon practice for employees' mail to be read.

Gender issues, too, are emergent in organizational CMC. One case study that appears in *Harvard Business Review* raises the issue of an employee being sexually harassed by a superior. The dilemma: if a manager discovers evidence of such harassment in the employee's electronic mailbox, at what point does justice lie between reporting the incident and protecting the employee's right to privacy (Niven, Wang, Rowe, Taga, Vladeck, and Garron, 1992)?

System administrators and owners of academic systems join private and corporate sectors in walking an ethical and legal tightrope. Apparently valuing intellectual freedom and the right to free expression, they still have to weigh security with freedom:

> System security takes priority over privacy at most [scholarly] institutions, although most colleges and university [sic] do not compromise privacy lightly. Most require system administrators to check with university officials—often up to the level of a vice-president or provost—before reading a user's account. (Turner, 1991, p. A13).

As technological advances continue, the legal, ethical, moral, and technological issues intensify.

Desperately Seeking Solutions

A number of authors are grappling with legal and ethical solutions for privacy issues in CMC. Anderson, et al. (1993) describe nine case studies for applying the Code of Ethics of the Association for Computing Machinery (ACM) in practice. Included in the Code are stipulations requiring that unauthorized or inappropriate access to data be prevented, and that organization leaders should determine if systems are adequate to protect privacy. In response to consumer concerns, software developers are designing programs to keep e-mail private, for example. "privacy enhanced mail" and "pretty good privacy" (Wallich, 1993). One proposed solution in dealing with electronic evidence of sexual harassment involves coaching the employee in handling the situation (Niven, Wang, Rowe, Taga, Vladeck, and Garron, 1992). But employees still have a right to know that their electronic correspondence may be monitored. Loebl (1992) suggests that employers can deal, at least in part, with employees' privacy issues by including an addendum of the organization's policy on privacy and computer security in the employee manual. BBSs, of course, walk similar ethical tightropes.

Riddle (1990) attempts to sort out the legal responsibilities and rights of BBS administrators. He considers four key areas: (1) what, if any, role might electronic bulletin boards play as press, in terms of First Amendment rights; (2) what decision rules might apply to system operators concerning their liability for defamation when defaming material is posted by users; (3) other liability for message content; and (4) how search and seizure may or may not apply to electronic bulletin board services. Since state laws vary, though, the issues for bulletin board services remain problematic. The laws clearly are lagging far behind the technology. Some BBSs post a login message that informs users that their participation is not private. One message, which appears at logon to the Blazin' Bytes BBS in Southern California, reflects administrative concern and typifies disclaimers seen on BBS systems. It appears here with permission of the BBS sysop/owner:

> Pursuant to Title 18, Section 2516 of the US Code, known as the Electronic Communications Act of 1986, notice is hereby given that THIS SYSTEM CONTAINS NO *PRIVATE* MAIL, E-MAIL, POSTS, or MESSAGES WHATSOEVER.
>
> All messages, whether listed as *private* OR public can and may be read by the Sysop, or the Sysop's designated agent(s).1

Solutions to ethical problems, too, are slippery. Researchers, apart from legal considerations, are wrestling with the ethics and moral responsibilities of online research (e.g., Jones, 1994), and methods of drawing text samples from public bulletin boards and mailing lists (e.g., ProjectH, 1992a; ProjectH, 1992b). One solution is to draw samples that e-mail recipients forward to the researcher, although the original sender may be unaware that the document is so used (e.g., Wambach, 1991). Although disguising identifiers may prevent recognition of the author, this approach does not address the question of intellectual propriety or informed consent. Another solution (e.g., McCormick and McCormick, 1992) triangulates methods with logon warnings that CMC can be read by other parties as well as deleting all identifiers from the text. To date, however, ethical approaches are as varied as the number of researchers, and the discourse as diverse as computer users.

Research Questions

The review of literature suggests that many privacy issues stem from the fact that the content of messages is of a personal or embarrassing nature for the writer. But clearly, the computer is not a secure medium for private communication. And equally clearly, users who do not practice "safe e-mail" are at risk of embarrassment or professional disaster. As the use of electronic mail increasingly replaces other channels of communication such as surface mail, telephone, and in-person meetings (Schaefermeyer and Sewell, 1988), resolution of these concerns becomes more critical. This speaks to the issue of caution (or lack of it) exercised by cyberspace inhabitants. The question is whether these caution levels relate to user perceptions of privacy, and what makes them feel secure enough to engage in intimate virtual activities in the midst of online strangers. Why would users knowingly expose themselves to embarrassment, professional hazards, or even legal action by writing e-mail messages of a personal or compromising nature?

Unguarded or cautionless communicative behavior in cyberspace may become (if it hasn't already) profoundly embedded in the network, thus becoming part of the structure, constraining it, producing it, and recreating it as it creates the discourse. Do users lull themselves into a false sense of electronic security? Do risky CMC behaviors take place in spite of user awareness that privacy is virtually nonexistent? These considerations lead to two research questions:

- RQ1: To what extent do users who engage in risky forms of CMC perceive the medium to be private?
- RQ2: How users who engage in risky forms of CMC come to feel secure enough to do so?

Method

This study is an online survey of users who engage in risky CMC via the Internet. The literature indicates that, although still relatively new as a data-gathering tool, researchers are beginning to use CMC for online research and analysis (e.g., Allen, 1987; Guthertz and Field, 1989; Huff and Rosenberg, 1988; Kaplan, 1991; Rafaeli and Tractinsky, 1989; Rafaeli and Tractinsky, 1991; Rice, Sell, and Hadley, 1990; Vasu, 1990). Thus, the method is both appropriate for the medium under study and follows research precedents. Because it supports newsgroups of a sexually explicit nature that could be personally or professionally embarrassing or compromising to participants, Usenet offers an excellent arena for surveying individuals who engage in risky CMC. While the e-mail that is posted to newsgroups is intended for public reading, rather than as a private exchange with another individual, the potential of embarrassment exists, and is demonstrated in the widespread use of anonymous servers that mask participants' identities. Thus, despite their public nature, sexually explicit groups pose an element of "risk" for participants, and they constitute the venue for this study.

All of the data was gathered via questionnaires sent to individuals whose mailing addresses were readily available to anyone with Internet access as return addresses in publicly posted, unmoderated newsgroup messages. The study surveyed authors of messages appearing in seven "alternative" unmoderated newsgroups that addressed sexually explicit (and potentially personally or professionally risky) topics: alt.sex, alt.sex.bestiality, alt.sex.bondage, alt.sex.fetish.fa, alt.sex.wanted, alt.sex.wizards, and rec.arts.bodyart.

Each respondent was contacted individually, by private e-mail. An explanation of the nature of the research appeared at the top of each questionnaire and offered results to anyone interested. In order to protect the identities of respondents, all questionnaires were sent to individuals via an anonymous server. The server stripped all identifying information in the headers of outgoing and incoming messages, and assigned anonymous numbers for addresses. Since an active effort was required to respond, all participation was entirely voluntary.

Survey Instrument

Risky CMC appears similar to that of other high-risk behaviors in health or safety practices. Thus, questionnaire items were drawn from the literature that addressed such risky behavior. Numerous studies show that, despite the risk of AIDS, individuals engage in risky sexual behaviors, and scholars cite a variety of underlying factors, including risk-taking (Sherr, Strong, and Goldmeier, 1990), sensation seeking (Horvath and Zuckerman, 1993), social or sexual anxiety (Hobfoll, Gayle, Gruber, and Levine, 1990), social responsibility (Baldwin and Baldwin, 1988), gender (e.g., Goldman and Harlow, 1993; Ford and Norris, 1993), and low self-concept (Perkel, Strebel and Jourbet, 1991). Other studies concerning risk and seat belt usage consider gender differences (Tipton, Camp, and Hsu, 1990), and habits and attitudes (Mittal, 1988). Jonah (1990) reports that age is a factor, and that drivers under 24 years old not only engage in risky driving, but in other risky behaviors as well. This last factor may be of particular interest, as high-tech, computer-savvy young adults are attracted to cyberspace. The survey instrument asks users a total of 32 questions about these factors and about their perceptions of system security and their own technical skills, to determine how or if they feel secure in their risky CMC (see Appendix).

An analysis of variance (ANOVA) was used to determine if there were differences between men and women in their perceptions of newsgroup participation. A standard multiple regression was performed between dependent variables (DVs) identified through factor analysis, and age and length of newsgroup participation as the independent variables (IVs).

Results

Questionnaires were sent to private e-mail addresses collected from recent postings to the seven targeted newsgroups. All addresses were sorted alphabetically in order to discard any duplicates. Of the 238 survey instruments sent, 38 were returned because the addresses were invalid, the recipient's site did not accept the user name or address, or other electronic routing problems prevented delivery. Fifty-two respondents representing all seven newsgroups returned questionnaires. This 26 percent response rate may be deceptively low, however, since the technical problems of posting through the anonymous server might have created undetected delivery problems. Most participants responded through the anonymous server, although two opted to answer via direct e-mail. Headers and other potentially identifying information were stripped manually from these questionnaires.

As might be expected, considering the sensitivity of the context in which participants were contacted, the questionnaire elicited a variety of reactions, which ranged from "Who the hell *are* you?" to offers of more information on groups that engage in bestiality or bondage within a specific geographic area. Several people expressed awareness that they received bogus surveys where the senders were simply out to "get their jollies." Some of these responded based on the information in the questionnaire, but others requested further information. To avoid biased responses, a general description of the study was sent to these individuals that did not include specific research questions nor reference to "risky" behaviors. A log was maintained of all respondents who wished to receive results of the survey.

As anticipated, respondents were relatively young, ranging in age from 19 to 42 years, with most (60.8 percent) being 27 years or younger. The majority (78.8 percent) were male and most (73.1 percent) considered their computer skills above average or expert. Seventy-five percent of the respondents had been involved in their newsgroups for two years or less, and the longest tenure on a newsgroup was 6-1/2 years. Most (86.5 percent) did not use an anonymous server, although this seemed to vary with the individual and the list. One person, for example, did not use an anonymous server to post to the newsgroup, but did use a pseudonym. Another respondent was not anonymous on the alt.sex.* newsgroup but chose anonymous posting on another alternative list where he perceived higher risk.

The reason most often expressed for participating in the newsgroups was to exchange ideas (44.2 percent). An additional 21.2 percent indicated they participated out of curiosity and 11.5 percent said they did so to kill time. Only 7.7 percent of the respondents indicated they participated in their newsgroups to meet social needs, and one individual indicated it was for a thrill. Additional reasons varied widely, from frivolous to ponderous. One respondent wrote:

Sexuality and religion are two of the topics which have caused much of histories [sic] bloodshed. It's an important issue, and I like to contribute to it. I also followed net.sex (before alt.sex existed) when I was 15, and it helped me a lot with accepting my sexuality. I'd like to give something back to the net by means of contributing to it.

Another participant indicated a sense of community, saying that he participated:

to associate with people who share the same sexual preference as myself. To give me a peer group. To answer honestly and frankly any questions and concerns on the subject.

Still another respondent wrote that participation was partly:"to be amused by the general silliness."

An exploratory factor analysis was performed on 25 questionnaire items drawn from literature on risky behaviors and computer privacy. The scree test indicated a five-factor solution, which accounted for 54.8 percent of the variance. The five factors were extracted using varimax rotation, with a cutoff of .45. Factor loadings appear in table 1.

Six of the variables failed to load on any factor, which reflected heterogeneity of the items on the questionnaire. Two factors were discarded because they were not internally reliable, as reflected by Cronbach's coefficient alpha of .53 and .50. The three factors that were retained were internally consistent and well-defined by the variables, with alpha values ranging from .70 to .87.

The four variables that loaded on the first factor were respondent agreement with posts on the newsgroup, closeness of relationships formed with other members of the newsgroup, and degree to which the respondent felt stimulated by computer-mediated discussions and face-to-face discussions of the newsgroup subject. This factor generally addressed social needs that respondents might seek to meet through participation in the newsgroup. The second factor included seven variables: levels of anxiety in face-to-face discussions or computer-mediated discussions of the newsgroup topics, perceived likelihood that a hacker might access the respondent's e-mail account, perceived risk of participation in the newsgroup, importance of system privacy, likelihood that the respondent's professional life might be helped or hurt if participation in the newsgroup were made public, and general feeling of security. These variables broadly addressed the respondent's perception of security in participating in the newsgroup. The third factor consisted of three variables: perceived likelihood that people other than those addressed or the sysop might read or repost messages, and perceived privacy of the medium. This factor was labeled "privacy."

A 2 (gender) x 3 (social needs, security, privacy) ANOVA indicated no significant differences between men and women in their perceptions of newsgroup participation. A standard multiple regression was performed between

Variables	Factor 1 Social needs alpha=.865	Factor 2 Feeling of security alpha=.709	Factor 3 Social responsibility alpha=.527	Factor 4 System privacy alpha=.702	Factor 5 Personal competence alpha=.504
Agrees with posts on newsgroup	.71179				
Closeness of relationships with newsgroup members	.72545				
Stimulated by topic in CMC	.79675				
Stimulated by topic in face-to-face	.73517				
Anxiety discussing topic in CMC		.68576			
Anxiety discussing topic face-to-face		.49981			
Perceived likelihood of hacker accessing account		.51953			
Perceived risk of newsgroup participation		.76056			
Importance of privacy		.51819			
Discovery can help professional life		.47813			
Feeling of security		.68393			
CMC requires social responsibility			.82815		
Face-to-face discussions require social responsibility			.80575		
Likelihood that others read posts				.75548	
Perception of CMC privacy				.68673	
Likelihood that sysop reads posts				.80617	
Likelihood of accidental postings					.65380
Technical proficiency					.63116
Self-esteem in area of newsgroup topic					.71982
Likelihood of being embarrassed					
Likelihood that someone will access personal data					
Discovery can help personal life					
Importance of system reliability					
Desensitization to risk over time					
Technical reliability of system					

Table 1. Factor loadings .45 or more.

social needs, security, and privacy as the DVs, and age and length of newsgroup participation as the IVs. Only the regression on length of newsgroup participation approached significance, $F(3,43)=2.68$, $p=.059$, predicting 16 percent of the variability in the three factors (Adjusted R2=.10). Length of newsgroup contributed significantly only to the prediction of social needs (beta=.346, $p=.019$).

Discussion

The first research question asked the extent to which users who engage in risky forms of CMC perceived the medium to be private. The responses to this survey were equivocal on the three variables that comprised privacy as extracted from the factor analysis. In general, survey participants seem neutral or undecided about the privacy of computer-mediated forms of communication. Respondents were evenly divided between the likelihood or unlikelihood of unintended others reading or reposting their messages and only 25% believed it was likely or extremely likely that the sysop might read their messages. Nearly half (47%) believed the medium to be private. Another 17.6% had no opinion on the privacy of CMC. The rest of the sample, only 35.3%, perceived CMC to be public or extremely public. This finding is surprising, since all the users surveyed were selected as a result of posting to public newsgroups, and their posts can be read by anyone with Internet access (if the newsgroup isn't censored at the local site).

The data suggest a clearer answer to the second research question concerning how users who engage in risky forms of CMC feel secure enough to do so. Most respondents (57.7%) considered privacy unimportant or extremely unimportant, and another 25% were neutral concerning the importance of privacy. These data suggest that privacy is not a serious issue for respondents who post on the lists. One respondent, for example, indicated that the activities in which he engaged were "no secret." None believed their activities on the newsgroup might harm their careers, and they generally felt secure across all other variables comprising security (means ranged from 3.5 to 4.2). In addition, 73.1% considered their proficiency levels above average or expert. Thus, respondents tended to feel personally and technically secure in their CMC, and felt that they had little or nothing to lose if their activities were discovered by unintended others. This, then, indicates that the perceived risk is low among users who engage in risky CMC on these newsgroups.

This study serves as a beginning to answering the question of how users come to feel secure in engaging in risky CMC. The small sample size limits generalizability to all system users, as does the narrowly-defined frame from which the sample was drawn. It does, however, provide a sense of the relatively low importance of system security for individuals who engage in risky CMC, and a general confidence in their own expertise. The publicly disclosive behavior may be magnified as a result of the relative youth of the respondents. A larger sample with a wider range of ages might indicate more conservative attitudes in older respondents. Future studies should include other sample populations to determine if risk is perceived differently between groups who engage in self-disclosive behaviors via CMC.

Additional studies should address similar issues in private e-mail. The review of the literature indicates that users send "private" messages that can and do have devastating effects when seen by unintended eyes. Future studies might address the extent to which users of e-mail (via the Internet, local area network, or BBS) perceive risk and to what extent they equivocate in their e-mail messages. An interesting point of comparison might include the use of equivocal language in other forms of written discourse. These and other questions concerning the ways in which users present their identities to an electronic world are intriguing scholars around the world. Certainly, the question of virtual intimacy and sexuality is of increasing interest as it makes newspaper headlines (e.g., Burgess, 1993; Schwarz, 1993) and talk shows. The information highway is here, and becoming more crowded every day. It is opening new doors to a mediated human interaction that transcends time and space, and is perceived to offer a relatively safe sexual outlet in this age of AIDS and fear.

The Questionnaire

The following questionnaire is designed to gather data concerning user perceptions of system security in relation to their computer-mediated communication (CMC). You are receiving it because your e-mail address recently appeared on the alt.sex newsgroup. Your participation is strictly voluntary, and will give you an opportunity to gain some insights to your own perceptions of computer systems and how you use them.

If you would like to participate in this study, please take a moment to answer the 32 multiple-choice questions below, as they apply to your participation in the newsgroup. Please note that this questionnaire has my anonymous return address, an45249@anon.penet.fi. When you return the survey, please be sure to use your automatic reply, or send it to the anonymous address. This will guarantee that all responses remain anonymous, and that your individual privacy is protected. PLEASE BE SURE TO SEND YOUR RESPONSE THROUGH THE ANONYMOUS SERVER. If you have any questions or concerns, feel free to e-mail me at Witmer@rcf.usc.edu.

Thanks in advance for your participation.

For each item, please type an "X" by the ONE letter that MOST CLOSELY reflects your attitude or experience.

1. How long have you participated in this newsgroup? Please type the approximate number of months on the next line:

2. Why do you participate in alt.sex? (Please mark only one item.)
   a. To meet social needs
   b. For curiosity
   c. For research purposes
   d. To exchange ideas on the topic
   e. To kill time
   f. For the thrill
   g. Other (please specify):

3. How proficient do you consider yourself in using this form of communication? (e.g., comfort with software and system commands; keyboard skills, etc.)?
   a. Expert
   b. Above average
   c. Average
   d. Below average
   e. Novice

4. How do you rate the likelihood that a sysop on this system might read and/or repost messages sent to or from you?
   a. Extremely likely
   b. Likely
   c. No opinion
   d. Unlikely
   e. Extremely unlikely

5. How do you rate the likelihood that someone else on this system might read and/or repost messages sent to or from you?
   a. Extremely likely
   b. Likely
   c. No opinion
   d. Unlikely
   e. Extremely unlikely

6. How do you rate the likelihood that you might accidentally post a message to a person or persons other than you intend?
   a. Extremely likely
   b. Likely
   c. No opinion
   d. Unlikely
   e. Extremely unlikely

7. How do you rate the likelihood that a hacker or phreaker might access your account or e-mail?
   a. Extremely likely
   b. Likely
   c. No opinion

d. Unlikely

e. Extremely unlikely

8. How do you rate the likelihood that someone might obtain personal information about you through this computer system?

a. Extremely likely

b. Likely

c. No opinion

d. Unlikely

e. Extremely unlikely

9. Do you consider your communication in this medium to be technically reliable (e.g., free of system or software errors that might compromise reliability of your posts reaching ONLY your targeted destination)?

a. Extremely reliable

b. Fairly reliable

c. Neither reliable nor unreliable

d. Fairly unreliable

e. Extremely reliable

10. As it relates to your participation in alt.sex, how important is reliability to you?

a. Extremely important

b. Fairly important

c. Neutral

d. Fairly unimportant

e. Extremely unimportant

11. Do you consider your communication in this medium to be private? (e.g., posts via an anonymous server completely protect your anonymity; what you post will not appear in another newsgroup without your permission; you are not likely to misdirect your posts; the sysops are ethical; hackers and phreakers are unlikely to break in, etc.)?

a. Extremely private

b. Fairly private

c. Neither private nor public

d. Fairly public

e. Extremely public

12. As it relates to your participation in alt.sex, how important is privacy to you?

a. Extremely important

b. Fairly important

c. Neutral

d. Fairly unimportant

e. Extremely unimportant

13. Would your personal life be helped or compromised if your participation in alt.sex became known outside the newsgroup?

a. It would definitely help my personal life.

b. It might help my personal life.

c. It would no have no impact on my personal life.

d. It might hurt my personal life.

e. It would definitely hurt my personal life.

14. Would your professional life be helped or compromised if your participation in alt.sex became known outside the newsgroup?

a. It would definitely help my career.

b. It might help my career.

c. It would no have no impact on my career.

d. It might hurt my career.

e. It would definitely hurt my career.

15. Overall, how secure do you feel about your participation in alt.sex?

a. Extremely secure

b. Fairly secure

c. Neither secure nor insecure

d. Fairly insecure

e. Extremely insecure

16. Do you consider your participation in personally or professionally risky?

a. Extremely risky

b. Fairly risky

c. Neither risky nor safe

d. Fairly safe

e. Extremely save

17. Do you feel anxious discussing the topics found on alt.sex in the electronic environment?

a. Extremely anxious

b. Fairly anxious

c. Neither anxious nor secure

d. Fairly secure

e. Extremely secure

18. Do you feel anxious discussing the topics found on alt.sex in face-to-face settings?

a. Extremely anxious

b. Fairly anxious

c. Neither anxious nor secure

d. Fairly secure

e. Extremely secure

19. Do you feel stimulated by the topics discussed on alt.sex in the electronic environment?

a. Extremely stimulated

b. Fairly stimulated

c. Neutral

d. Fairly unresponsive

e. Extremely unresponsive

20. Do you feel stimulated discussing the topics discussed on alt.sex in face-to-face settings?

a. Extremely stimulated
b. Fairly stimulated
c. Neutral
d. Fairly unresponsive
e. Extremely unresponsive

21. Do you feel that participating in discussions on alt.sex requires you to act socially responsible?
a. Extreme responsibility
b. Fair responsibility
c. Some responsibility
d. Little responsibility
e. No responsibility

22. Do you feel that participating in discussions about alt.sex in face-to-face requires you to act socially responsible?
a. Extreme responsibility
b. Fair responsibility
c. Some responsibility
d. Little responsibility
e. No responsibility

23. Do you know of any instances where people have been personally or professionally embarrassed through electronic activities?
a. Yes
b. No

24. Which of the following statements most closely reflects how you feel about the possibility of your ever being personally or professionally embarrassed through electronic activities?
a. It'll never happen to me.
b. It's not likely to happen to me.
c. I don't think about it and have no feelings.
d. It's likely to happen to me.
e. It's a sure thing that it'll happen to me.

25. Does participating in alt.sex feel more risky to you than when you first started participating in it or other groups like it?
a. Much more risky
b. More risky
c. No different
d. Less risky
e. Much less risky

26. How do you see your relationship to the other members of alt.sex ?
a. They are close friends.
b. They are casual friends.
c. They are regular acquaintances.
d. They are casual acquaintances.
e. I don't have a relationship with them.

27. What do you think of the things that other members of alt.sex post?

    a. I agree with all of it.

    b. I agree with most of it.

    c. I don't think about it one way or the other.

    d. I disagree with most of it.

    e. I disagree with all of it.

28. How do you feel about yourself in the areas typically discussed in alt.sex?

    a. Terrific

    b. Okay

    c. Neutral

    d. Not too good

    e. Lousy

29. Do you post messages through an anonymous server?

    a. Yes

    b. No

30. If you are posting anonymously, are you concerned that your identity will be traced?

    a. Extremely concerned

    b. Quite concerned

    c. Concerned

    d. A little concerned

    e. Not concerned at all

31. What is your gender?

    a. Male

    b. Female

32. What is your age?

That's it! Thanks again for participating in this survey. If you wish to see a copy of the results, please let me know. I'll be happy to e-mail them to you as soon as they're completed.

CHAPTER NINE

The Social Construction of Rape in Virtual Reality

Richard C. MacKinnon

The incident known as the first widely publicized rape in cyberspace occurred in the virtual place or MUD called LambdaMOO. In front of witnesses, the alleged rapist, Mr Bungle, sexually assaulted several persons until he was captured (Dibble, 1993). This chapter analyzes rape as a social construction and, using the "Bungle Affair" as a case study, recommends a course of action for reducing or eliminating instances of rape in virtual reality.

While the act of rape is almost universally condemned, the conception of rape is far less universally agreed upon. The event described as rape varies from one culture to another. Indeed, the socio-historical and cross-cultural analysis to follow reveals that the concept of rape is embedded in the habits, folkways, mores, and laws of a given society. Despite this variation, common origins, similar original conditions, and shared development contribute to similarities found throughout the sample.

The development of computer-mediated communication (CMC) has led to the phenomenon of a virtual reality peopled by networked users interacting within developing virtual societies replete with habits, folkways, mores, and laws of their own. The concept of rape is currently being addressed by participants in virtual reality and adapted so that the virtual act of rape is recognizable as such and condemnable within their virtual society. This iteration of the social construction of rape is thought laudable by most, but I argue that it is seriously misguided in the end.

The fact that virtual reality is nonphysical in character provides theoreticians with the opportunity to reanalyze rape as a mutable social construction. They may therefore be able to avoid nonconsciously importing the unmodified phenomenon into virtual reality. The rape construction in this chapter is proposed to alleviate the pain, stigmatization, and victimization typically attendant with the competing constructions.

The problem addressed in this chapter is encompassed by the questions:

What is rape in virtual reality and why is this a problem? The solution is based upon the historical mutability of real life rape constructions, the identification of an unnecessarily destructive rape construction in virtual reality, and the suggestion of a reconstructed version in that realm. To this end, the argument begins with a discussion of the concept of virtual reality as a preface to examining the case of alleged rape in cyberspace. The literature on virtual communities and cyberspace is increasing at a phenomenal rate and thereby boasts a plethora of competing theories and analyses in search of a paradigm. This chapter attempts to identify the recurrent themes necessary for adequately addressing the rape issue.

The argument continues with a treatment of the concept of rape, an area of research with a long history of scholarship. The concept of rape is even more controversial than the competing conceptions of virtual reality, for its scholarship too is undergoing paradigmatic changes. It is, of course, beyond the scope of this chapter to undertake a complete socio-history of rape. Instead, I shall offer a general historical analysis by means of a selective cross-cultural analysis of rape. The findings will be contrasted with contemporary interpretations of rape in America, where rape is in fact less defined than is commonly believed. By this point, it should become clear that rape is not a discreet concept, nor does it enjoy universal consensus. Rather, it is a social construction steeped in and subject to the influence of the culture in which it is manifested.

The argument then turns to the prevailing theories of rape which are competing for influence in the social construction of the concept. While these theories postulate the causes of rape and suggest possible solutions, most of them acknowledge rape as a phenomenon resulting in part from the unequal status of women relative to men. Whereas the socio-history and cross-cultural analysis of rape identifies the nonconscious, social construction of rape, these theories are attempts to consciously construct or recreate the concept.

Feminist theorists seeking social parity for women have fostered a broadening of the concept of rape to include conceptions which do not necessarily involve penetration or even any physical contact. Such a broad conception makes it possible to import rape into virtual reality, for only such a broad conception of rape would be adaptable to a society in which no physical bodies exist for either assault or penetration.

While a broad conception of rape may achieve societal goals in real life, the nonconscious importation of the same broad conception into virtual reality results in unintended, unfortunate consequences for the members of virtual society. Indeed, to construct rape for virtual reality is to introduce the emotional, psychological, and sociological consequences correspondent to rape in real life. Given these serious ramifications, the social construction of rape should not be imported into virtual reality without rigorous, conscious construction.

Finally, the argument engages the social construction of rape in virtual reality by first considering the characteristics of virtual society which make its inhabitants prone to rape, such as anonymity and transience within the online population. However, the "bodylessness" of virtual reality participants forces theorists to further modify the already broad conception of rape so that it can be feasible in virtual reality. To do this, rape needs to be constructed so that it is an assault upon the consciousness or mind rather than the body. Further, the prosecution of this special virtual reality construction of rape necessarily must include the means for punishing the virtual rapist. Since the rapist, like the victim, lacks a body, the punishment is problematically directed to the mind as well (MacKinnon 1997). All of this creative construction begs the question of whether it is worth it. The answer to this question inspires the central argument of this chapter.

Virtual Reality

Cyberspace is a globally networked, computer-sustained, computer-accessed, and computer-generated, multidimensional, artificial, or "virtual" reality. In this reality, to which every computer is a window, seen or heard objects are neither physical nor, necessarily, representations of physical objects but are, rather, in form, character and action, made up of data, of pure information. (Benedikt, 1992).

There is no shortage of descriptions for virtual reality, for virtually everyone who is aware of the concept can come up with a metaphor. Yet among these, there are those which have become famous because of their imagery. Rheingold (1991) writes about a futuristic virtual reality in which one is required to wear "something like a body stocking, but with the intimate kind of snugness of a condom. [The inner surface is] embedded with a mesh of tiny tactile detectors coupled to vibrators ... hundreds of them per inch." Once donned, this special suit via the telephone network creates a "totally artificial visual representation of your own body and of your partner's.... Your partner(s) can move independently in the cyberspace and your representations are able to touch each other..." (p.346) and manipulate objects as if they were physically real.

Rheingold's description refers to "cyberspace," a term often interchanged with virtual reality. It presents problems for some scholars because virtual reality does not depend upon cyber or space. It depends upon shared "collections of common beliefs and practices" (Stone, 1991, p.85). William Gibson, the science fiction author and coiner of "cyberspace" says it is a "consensual hallucination." Indeed, the same definition has been applied to reality itself.

The primary difference then between the real and the virtually real is the interposition of some mediating and transforming agent or interface between the senses and the shared perception. Popularly, electronic gadgetry such as suits, gloves, and goggles are identified as the equipment necessary for such mediation, but fundamentally it is not the gadgets that mediate, but rather the computers to which they are attached. It is for this reason that some scholars have organized their research around the notion of computer-mediated communication (CMC). The sharing made possible through CMC creates a virtual reality for its participants, often without the need of unwieldy apparel.

Further, it appears that sophisticated technology is not a requirement for it can be argued that a newspaper's op/ed page can create a virtual community among its readers. To wit, Gibson remarks, "Cyberspace is where you are when you're talking on the telephone" (quoted in Kramarae, 1995, p.38). With commonly found computer equipment, CMC allows persons to experience "desktop" rather than "immersion" virtual reality. This usually takes place via electronic mail and computer conferencing. In the case of the Usenet conferencing network, the high level of interaction among its users creates a more permanent community transcending the fleeting sense of community found among the participants of a newspaper's op/ed page (MacKinnon, 1995, p.117). Evidently, notions of virtual reality and the communities formed within it have in common the themes of sharing and interactivity.

For the purposes of this chapter, the theory and argument addressing the problem of rape in the communities and societies arising from shared experiences in virtual reality are not dependent upon the most technologically sophisticated manifestation of the virtually real. In this way, they will have relevant application even as technology surpasses the currently imaginable. Thus, although the rape in the case study analyzed herein occurred in the cyberspace of a stylized, electronic, meeting room or "MUD," a generalized notion of virtual reality is used so that the treatment of virtual rape extends beyond the "MUD" to other virtual realities.

Virtual Rape: The Mr Bungle Case

The facts of the case as reported by Dibbell (1993) are that [a] Mr Bungle used a voodoo doll to [b] force legba, a person of indeterminate gender, to "sexually service him in a variety of ... ways" (line 118) whereupon Mr Bungle was forced to move to another room; however, because the victim(s) were still in range of the voodoo doll, he was able to [c] force legba into "unwanted liaisons with other individuals present in the room" (lines 124-125). Further, as his actions grew progressively violent, he [d] forced legba to "eat his/her own pubic hair (lines 127-128), and [e] forced Starsinger to "violate herself with a piece of kitchen cutlery" (lines 128-129). The assault ceased when Mr Bungle was "enveloped ... in a cage impermeable even to a voodoo doll's powers" (lines 134-135).

Aside from the fact that rape, with or without the use of a voodoo doll, was not explicitly prohibited in LambdaMOO at the time of the incident (Dibbell, 1993, lines 432-433), the question to be answered is "Did a rape occur?" The given in the problem is that the reality of the parties involved is mediated via the computer which hosts LambdaMOO, that the textual narrative generated by the mediation constitutes the reality of the parties, and that the parties influence the generation of the narrative by interacting with the host computer. Given this, when Mr Bungle directed the host computer to report that legba engaged in sexual activities, the resulting computer-mediated reality reflected this direction despite legba's objections.

While this may be a case of a failing in the design of the computer's software, most societies do not have the luxury of software to control sociopathy in their midst. Although there was no law proscribing rape, it was generally understood to be anti-social behavior and the members of LambdaMOO society had relied upon the traditional methods of social control to curtail it (MacKinnon 1997). Interestingly, the degree of social control needed in LambdaMOO had been a subject for debate. Characterized as an anarchist by Dibbell, legba is on record as saying "I tend to think that restrictive measures around here cause more trouble than they prevent" (Dibbell, 1993, lines 240-242). Since this case, an arbitration system has been setup in LambdaMOO so that individuals can bring suit against one another, the range of possible judgments notably including virtual death (Dibbell, 1993, lines 744-753).

Ostracism and social admonition are available and are generally effective means for enforcing community standards of behavior in virtual societies (Reid, 1995; MacKinnon, 1995). Further, legba did not employ the technological means in his/her self-defense. By instructing the computer to "gag" or mute Mr Bungle, legba could have excluded Bungle's actions from his/her reality. Despite the existence of these means of social control, the incident nevertheless occurred, forcing the members of LambdaMOO society to confront the meaning of Mr Bungle's actions and why his actions foiled the existing system for preventing or discouraging their occurrence.

The fact that LambdaMOO is a text-based virtual reality, not only must one ask if a rape had occurred, but also, was it a rape or simply an inert description of the act? If the latter, does anything really occur in LambdaMOO? Reid (1995) writes, "Users treat the worlds depicted by MUD programs as if they were real." By implication, the words and worlds from the words are not inert descriptions, but the users' perceptions of the virtually real set into motion by sheer willingness. Reid continues, "The illusion of reality lies not in the machinery itself but in the user's willingness to treat the manifestations of his or her imaginings as if they were real" (p. 165, 166). The issue of willingness demands attention, for legba and the others opted not to gag Mr

Bungle. This choice will be considered later, but Reid's observations do support the given that the members of LambdaMOO accepted the textual narration as their consensual hallucination or virtual reality. Therefore, Mr Bungle did force legba and others to engage in sexual activity against their will; however, is this act properly called rape?

Nowhere did Mr Bungle inject the word "rape" into the narrative. Only by interpretation can one infer from the acts committed that a rape had occurred. Further, even if Mr Bungle had explicitly raped legba and the others, one wonders if the concept of rape lacks meaning in the context of virtual reality. If Mr Bungle had directed the computer to narrate legba's fatal burst into flames, one presumes that legba and the witnesses would have rejected that perversion of reality as fraudulent. Even legba concedes, "Mostly voodoo dolls are amusing" (Dibbell, 1993, line 237) implying that they are commonly used to influence reality in non-sensical or ridiculous ways—ways that are interpreted with levity or rejected outright.

This process for interpreting, reconciling, and incorporating events into the consensual reality prompts questions regarding that interpretive process. How are sexual "services" and "unwanted liaisons" constructed into rape? Is it due to the elements of force or violence? Or unwillingness on the part of the victim? Must penetration or violation be literal (i.e., virtually real) such as in Starsinger's induced self-violation with a steak knife or can it be figurative as in legba's forced act of eating his/her own pubic hair? If figurative, exactly what of legba's was violated, his/her autonomy, privacy, or peace (of mind)? Does the construction of rape necessarily include acts of a sexual nature? If legba had been induced into biting his/her own nails, would the act have been rejected from the consensual reality as nonsensical, retained as "amusing," or constructed into rape? How operative is the gender or apparent gender of the parties involved? If the victims lacked the necessary anatomy, how would they have reconciled this with a reality narrated as "legba fondles Starsinger's pouch with his/her tentacle"? Would such an act have been rejected, retained, or constructed? These questions draw attention to the elements of force, autonomy of will, sexuality, and gender. Perhaps when the elements are present in combination, the socio-historical development of sexual deviation compels the parties involved to identify the combination as constitutive of rape.

Virtual reality presents its inhabitants with the opportunity to selectively ascribe meaning and signification to the events which transpire. That legba and the others chose, however willingly, to retain the incident in their shared reality underscores the need to examine the development of the social construction of rape and its ramifications for society. It is no trivial matter that while legba would have rejected fatal immolation, he/she chose (more importantly and accurately, did not consciously choose, but felt or was compelled) to ascribe rape to the actions imposed upon him/her. It is not the intention of this argument to under-appreciate legba's emotional duress, and it is hoped that the rigorous analysis of the construction of rape and the resulting deprivation or reassignment of meaning to that act will forestall undue suffering for others.

Social Construction and Rape

The concept of the social construction of reality is understood in the terms presented by Berger and Luckmann (1967) and Holzner (1972). Incorporated into postmodern methodology, it has drawn the criticism of those who would call the practice "invention theory." Harvey (1989) is concerned with political agendas and the "projects to shape space and encourage spatial practices." He believes that the results are "at best conserving and at worst downright reactionary in their implications" (p. 277). The concern that some theorists are inventing reality or creating it out of whole cloth reaffirms the necessity of grounding social construction in the conservative and incremental development of socio-historical conceptions. This is not to say that all social constructions are and should be the efforts of conscious conservation. It is saying that those who guide constructions ought to be mindful of the criticism; however, the vast majority of social constructions are unguided by theory, whether mindful or not. Most constructions developed or evolved "naturally," that is, according to and within the frameworks of their respective cultures with little or no intervention by theory. This dichotomy between natural or evolutionary construction and guided or conscious construction is sometimes referred to as the difference between social construction and social creation (cf. Edwards, 1973).

The goal of this chapter is to undertake a conscious construction of rape in virtual reality rather than import intact the construction as it exists in real life. To accomplish this goal, one must examine the social construction of rape in real life. Chayko (1993) writes "It is one of the tasks of sociologists to problematize 'what is real.' Rather than assume that the real world is 'out there' to be learned about and internalized, we recognize that there is no reality apart from what social actors make of it" (p.72). Given this perspective, it is possible to see how sociologists and anthropologists are able to view a great many instances of reality as socially constructed. Among these constructions are gender, sexuality, and rape.

But there are arguable limits as to how much is or can be constructed. Foucault (1990) pushes these limits farther than most when he contends that sex itself, that is, desire, the erotic, and the procreative urge, is subject to the forces of socialization. Malinowski (1932) has a more restrained view when he cautions, "the sexual impulse is never entirely free, neither can it be completely enslaved by social imperatives. The limits of freedom vary; but there is always a sphere within which it is determined by biological and psychological motives only and also a sphere in which the control of custom and convention is paramount" (p. 371). Malinowski identifies the tension in the nature-nurture interplay, but he seems to underestimate the influence of the social upon both the human psychology and biology.

Thus admonished and remaining cognizant of the evolutionary nature of unguided social construction, one proceeds to understand sexuality and rape in our (late twentieth century Western) culture by first identifying its origins in the cultures of others.

The Social History of Rape

To find the theoretical origins of precivil society, one should turn to the "state of nature" treatises of Hobbes, Locke, and Rousseau, but to find the "first rape" in the state of nature, perhaps one should turn to Brownmiller (1975). Given the subject matter, it is no surprise that her conception accords more with Hobbesian brutishness than the happier cooperatives found in the others' conceptions. Brownmiller writes that the "accident of biology," which provides the male of the species with both the penis and superior strength, leads men to no other end than to use them. The female, possessor of relatively less strength and the anatomical counterpart, must comply or flee from unwanted interlocking. She continues,

> In the violent landscape inhabited by primitive woman and man, some woman somewhere had a prescient vision of her right to her own integrity, and in my mind's eye I can picture her fighting like hell to preserve it. After a thunderbolt of recognition that this particular incarnation of hairy, two-legged hominid was not the Homo sapiens with whom she would like to freely join parts, it might have been she, and not some man, who picked up the first stone and hurled it. (p.14).

Recognizing the futility of the battle, the precursor to or first clause of the social contract might have been a woman's surrender of her freedom and integrity to a man so that he would protect her from the assaults of other men. This compact, according to Brownmiller, lays the foundation for marriage and the reduction of women to property. Indeed, while both Hobbes and Locke observe that men must submit to the Sovereign, women must first submit to other men. But unlike these theorists, Brownmiller does not gloss over the historical evidence supporting her thesis. In this regard, she has set herself apart.

Ethnographic support for Brownmiller's "first rape" and resulting feminine social contract is found throughout history and across western and nonwestern cultures. Common to these cultures are factors which contribute to the "nonpresence" of rape; that is, the social status of women relative to men eliminates or reduces the occurrence of rape in those cultures. Nonpresence is attributed in some cultures to the nonrecognition of forced intercourse as rape because of mitigating circumstances such as chastity and the marital status of the victim. The distinction between rape as a proscribed activity and as a punishable offense relates to the difficulty in proving that the act was perpetrated, and second, by a particular person. The relative social status of women is pertinent because the proof often depends upon the testimony of the victim, who belongs to a gender and/or class of people whose credibility does not weigh equally with that of her attacker. The issues of proof and credibility do not combine well when the penalty for rape may be severe and the woman may have something to gain from a false accusation. As a result, it is often the case that the attacker is acquitted or given a lesser sentence in light of the extenuating circumstances. Indeed, the issue of proof is so operative that in some cultures the punishment or some aspect of it is left to their deities.

A Cross-Cultural Analysis

In a study on the attitude towards rape and the frequency of its occurrence (Broude and Greene, 1976), the issues of presence versus nonpresence and punishability are addressed. Of 34 anthropologically representative societies for which there were meaningful data, rape is not present in 23.5%, rare or isolated in 35.3%, and common in 41.2%. In the same study, of 40 societies (the sample size change is due to the availability of data), 25% accept or ignore the occurrence of rape, 10% only ridicule the perpetrator when it does occur, 20% mildly disapprove or assess a token fine or punishment, and 45% strongly disapprove and mete out severe punishment such as severe whipping, exile, and death.

A comparative study of the sexual mores in 110 societies (Brown, 1952) illustrates the effect which marital status has on the construction of rape; that is, whether it is "present" as such, and if so, how severely it is punished. In 99% of the societies for which there were meaningful data, the perpetrator is punished for raping a married woman, while 95% punish for the rape of an unmarried woman (p.138). In other words, 4% fewer punish the perpetrator if his victim is unmarried. Further, on a 4-point scale, the severity of punishment for raping a married woman is 3.3, while the rating drops to 2.4 for an unmarried victim. Established by a panel of 17 anthropological experts, the higher rating in most societies corresponds to castration, whereas the lower is typified by ceremonial penance, lowered brideprice, or knifing. These figures prompt at least as many questions as they may answer. For example, why do the frequency of rape and the attitudes towards it vary from one society to another? While the answers are not provided in the study, the statistics suggest that rape as a construct varies from society to society.

These differences with regard to marital status may be explained by the understanding that a married woman is already the property of her husband, whereas an unmarried woman is not (Brownmiller, 1975; Tabori, 1971). Indeed, although an unmarried woman has not been consigned to her husband, in some societies her rape is considered a crime against her family in that it lowers her brideprice (Schwendinger and Schwendinger, 1983; Goldschmidt, 1976; Brownmiller, 1975; Tabori, 1971; Brown, 1952; Malinowski, 1932). The construction of women as property is an important perspective in understanding the relationship between the contemporary construction of men relative to that of women. Brownmiller writes, "...the price of woman's protection, by *some men* against an abuse by *others* was steep. ... The historic price ... was the imposition of chastity and monogamy. A crime committed against her body became a crime against the male estate" (Brownmiller, p.17, emphasis hers). Schwendinger and Schwendinger (1983) discover in the laws of ancient Rome that raptus was originally a violent form of theft that could apply to both property and persons. Given that ancient Rome had a whole segment of persons classified as property, the abduction and sexual molestation of a woman was constructed as theft from the person who had legal power over her (p.95). In medieval England, the even less criminal interpretation of "rape as trespass" was prevalent for at least a decade (Carter, 1985, p.39).

Another possible explanation for the variation among societies is the developing social status of women. Indeed, Ruggiero (1975) reports that in early Renaissance Venice, when the victims were of marrying age, rape was handled leniently because it was "perceived by the nobility in the context of normal admitted human passions" (p.23). On the other hand, where it has been shown that raping an unmarried woman is a less severe crime, Tabori's (1971) ethnographic survey reveals how in some societies forced intercourse is not considered rape at all. This partially explains why rape is nonpresent in some societies. He attributes this to the change in women's value and importance to men. As her value and importance increased, her demand increased. In the style reminiscent of Brownmiller's hypothetical first couple, he writes,

When primitive man earned his living by hunting and fishing, woman was just an appendage, more of a burden than a help. Man had to do all the heavy and dangerous work and did not like it. ...All this changed when our distant ancestors began to settle down. They discovered at one stage or another that if they put seeds into the earth something edible came up. And at this job women were remarkably good. They had more staying power and patience than the males. (pp. 29-30).

Tabori contends that, as a result, every tribe increased "its stock of women," and initially married from within. The effect of inbreeding, although carrying no moral stigma, "weakened the otherwise robust constitution of pre-historic men" (p.30). Exogamy or the need to mate outside one's gene pool forced men to eye the women in other men's tribes. According to the study which rates the severity of punishments, there are only two offenses more serious than rape of a married woman and incest is one of them (Brown, 1952, p.139). The imperative of exogamy provides the social justification for abduction and rape, explaining, in some cases, rape's nonpresence. Indeed, why would rape be perceived as a crime when it is motivated by biological necessity? This sets the scene for playing out the war in Brownmiller's modified Hobbesian state of nature. If played out to its conclusion, the competition for women would cease when warring tribes realized that each possessed something the other needed. Rather than continue to kill one another, men would learn to peacefully negotiate a woman's brideprice and then barter for her.

Bridecapture and brideprice are not limited to theoretical states of nature, for indeed, they are concepts manifested in some degree in almost every culture. From the Sebei of Uganda (Goldschmidt, 1976), to the Trobriand Islanders in North-Western Melanesia (Malinowski, 1932), to the Indians of North America (Tabori, 1971), one finds abduction and barter institutionalized. In this way, the act of rape, ritualized within an interpretive community, is constructed into marriage. The claim that marriage is institutionalized rape can be based on this construction, but to do so overstates the development of the construction in that it takes both marriage and rape out of their contexts. In other words, it is a criticism of one community's standard of interpretation by the standards of another. Even so, the sentiment does illustrate how rape varies in concept and that the variation is socio-historically and culturally dependent.

Additionally, the insubstantiability of rape further undermines its own existence. Owing to the status of women relative to men, the difficulty in prosecuting the accused increases rape's nonpresence and mitigates its punishment when it is present. Unless there are witnesses, proving that a woman has been raped and by a particular man is difficult. Although ethnographic studies show a consistently high rating for the severity of punishment, other data indicate that there is a normative gap between the severity of the crime and the actual punishment delivered. Carter's (1985) study of rape in medieval England suggests that the normative gap owes to the difficulty in proving the crime coupled with the severity of the punishment associated with it. He writes, "… local communities were hesitant to kill or mutilate a man for rape because the crime was so difficult to prove" (p.41. Note that the severity in punishment is consistent with Brown). Although medieval legal theorists clearly believed in strict measures such as blinding, dismemberment, and death, the severity of these punishments may have had an opposite effect on the carriage of justice. Carter observes from court records or eyre rolls that the "evidence shows that local communities only rarely imposed corporal punishment on convicted rapists" (p.41). Of course, this was because medieval courts were afraid of wrongly convicting the accused.

Although modern medical examinations are able to detect signs of forced intercourse and assist in identifying the perpetrator, much still depends, as it did then, upon the testimonies of the victim, the accused, and the witnesses. If the Melanesians (Malinowski, 1932) caught a rapist inflagrante, he was put to death, otherwise "he was exposed to the danger of sorcery rather than to that of direct violence" (p.387). This distinction is made in part because of the socio-historically inferior social status of women relative to men. The significant effect of this is that the victim's testimony is often deemed less credible than her attacker's. Ruggiero (1975) observes this in early Renaissance Venice, "... indeed the damaged property of a rape victim was not taken too seriously. ... Rape of an unmarried woman was and remains a hard crime to substantiate, especially in male-dominated societies" (p.21). Noting another consideration, Carter writes, "Though there is not sufficient evidence to prove it, I suspect that many thirteenth century English rape appeals were ruses by the appellor and her family to enter into marriage" (p.85). Combining this perception or misperception of women with the risk of wrongly punishing a man with death, mutilation, or dismemberment, the accused often enjoy more than the legal benefit of the doubt. As a result, punishment by public humiliation accompanied by meting out accident, disease, and death from natural causes (attributed to sorcery or divine intervention) is tantamount to no severe punishment at all.

The issue of presence versus nonpresence of rape in a society is pertinent in modern American society as well. Baron and Straus (1989) note that a problem with the Uniform Crime Reports (UCR) data is that a large percentage of rapes are not reported to the police. As with the anthropologically representative studies, it seems that it is "not at all unreasonable to suppose that women in states where the status of women is high will be likelier to report a rape than in states where women have comparatively low status" (p.28). While the status of a woman in contemporary American society is much higher than her counterparts in many other societies, it is clear that the basis for constructing rape, that is, upon her social status, still holds true. Indeed, one observes that in American society, the construction of rape is not as immutable a concept as one might expect. Legal definitions of the crime vary from state to state on issues such as female-only victims, male-only perpetrators, adult-only perpetrators, and exempt spousal victims (Ellis, 1989, p.2).

Thus far it has been shown that the social construction of rape in a given society depends largely on the social status of women. The status of women relative to men provides the context in which women can be regarded as victims of severely actually-punishable crimes. Also, it has been shown socio-historically and cross-culturally that this is apparent in geographically and temporally distant societies. A final aspect considered here of the socio-historical construction of rape is the element of social involvement, that is, the public nature of rape.

Carter writes that although we tend to think of rape as a "heinous deed committed in private, in dark, foreboding haunts," historically it has been a very public affair even if the act itself is executed in private. He observes, "… the repercussions almost always concern the community, no matter whether the community happens to be twentieth century American or thirteenth century England" (p.52). Carter's observations are supported in the research. In Brown's study (1952) of 110 societies, the severity of the punishment varies with the degree of social involvement. In 23 societies, the act of rape is interpreted as "affecting only the participants or members of their immediate families," 30 societies believe it also affected members outside of the immediate families of the participants, and 2 societies think the act affected the whole clan, tribe, or community. Accordingly, the severity of the punishments, increasing respectively, are 2.4, 3.2, and 3.9. In other words, depending on the society's perception of the publicness of rape, the punishment's severity increases from ridicule to castration to death (p.141).

By no means has this been a complete survey of the socio-historical and cultural development of the social construction of rape. It has been shown that, as an unguided construct, the perception of acts constitutive of rape is dependent upon the cultural context in which they occur. Cultural differences notwithstanding, the development of the construction across cultural and temporal boundaries has resulted in many similarities in the manifestation of the conception of rape. The benefit of the survey is the understanding that the unguided social construction of rape is mutable and tied to other mutable constructions such as men, women, and their relationships to one another. Given this mutability, we are positioned to re-evaluate the construction of rape in virtual reality, but first, it is important to review how theorists have re-evaluated and consciously constructed rape in real life contexts.

Guiding the Social Construction of Rape in Real Life

The prevailing contemporary theories of rape attempt to explain the underlying causes of rape and can be useful for consciously reconstructing or guiding the social construction of reality as it pertains to sex, gender, and status. These competing paradigms can be generally categorized into three perspectives or approaches: feminist, social learning, and evolutionary. The feminist approach can be found in the works of LeGrande (1973), Brownmiller (1975), Davis (1975), Clark and Lewis (1977), Rose (1977), Groth (1979),

Dworkin (1981), and Schwendinger and Schwendinger (1983). According to Ellis (1989), "the feminist theory considers rape to be the result of long and deep-rooted social traditions in which males have dominated nearly all important political and economic activities" (p.10).

The social learning model, found in the writings of Donnerstein (1985), Malamuth (1981, 1983, 1984), Zillmann (1984), Check (1985), and Lin (1985), suggests that aggressive sexual behavior is learned through repeated exposure to it. If "original society" can be viewed as the inculcation of aggression from the Hobbesian-Brownmiller state of nature, then social learning theory is one way of explaining how rape is learned, transmitted, and reinforced within and among cultures.

The third perspective, the evolutionary or sociobiological theory of rape, is advocated by Barash (1979), Symons (1979), Gibson, Linden, and Johnson (1980), Rhodes (1981), Konner (1982), Shields and Shields (1983), Thornhill and Thornhill (1983, 1987), Quinsey (1984), Crawford and Galdikas (1986), and Thiessen (1986). Sociobiologists propose that rape is the manifestation of differences between the sexes with regard to reproductive priorities. Based on the assumption that the transmission of one's genes to future generations is a natural priority, proponents of evolutionary theory contend that natural selection favors males who inseminate as many females as possible. Since the use of violence may be necessary to accomplish this goal, genetic carriage of violent tendencies reinforces those tendencies in subsequent generations.

There is much contention among and within these approaches. By identifying a cause of rape, whether it is reified socio-political domination, learned sexual aggression, or genetic proclivity, each approach implies an agenda for a solution. It is this implication which concerns Harvey (1989); that is, the danger in shaping a social construct to match the needs of an existing faction's agenda. Feminist theorists view rape as the construction of a "male's decision to behave toward women in a possessive, dominating, and demeaning manner" (Ellis, 1989, p.11), thus suggesting that rape is an act of power or a "pseudosexual act" rather than an act of erotic or biological desire. The solution agenda here focuses on the uneven power distribution between the sexes. This contrasts with the proponents of social learning theory who acknowledge the sexual aspect as a noteworthy manifestation of learned negative behavior towards women. Correspondingly, the solution agenda focuses on the influence of pornographic materials and other negative portrayals of women in the socially pervasive media. Generally speaking, the former theory minimizes the role of sex, whereas the latter attempts to "put sex back into rape." Although these approaches are steeped in the politicization of the women's movement, it is apparent that they are not diametrically opposed and one finds members of both camps in collaborative efforts.

With the exception of the somewhat deterministic evolutionary theory, the perspectives identify possible avenues for guiding the continuing social construction of rape. Among these possibilities is the reconstruction of women as the social, economic, and political equals of men. The transformation of women-as-property to women-as-propertied is an important reformulation of a social construction which has been transmitted across cultural boundaries for centuries. Such a radical reconception takes time to effect in light of the resistance to change. But time-consuming, incremental changes allow social construction theorists to guide and inform the "natural" construction of reality by reconceiving mutable constructions and identifying flexibility in interpretations previously held as rigid. In this way, the essentialist and limiting concept of "woman" is set into motion as an evolving construct of identity. In the same vein, the advent of virtual reality allows theorists to exploit the technology and mutability of rape to the advantage and disadvantage of its potential victims.

Evaluating the Social Contruction of Rape in Virtual Reality

With the understanding that rape is an historically mutable construct susceptible to both natural evolution and guidance, one turns now to the present iteration in the context of virtual reality. Legba and the others believe that the events which transpired constituted a rape. Against the backdrop of the development of rape as a concept, it is understandable how these virtual acts can be constructed into a rape. Indeed, a psychological model known as "attribution theory" exists to explain how the average person explains behavior and makes judgments (Bourque, 1989, p.77). Attribution theorists present test subjects with hypothetical scenarios and assess how and why the scenarios are interpreted or not interpreted as rape. This method is found in Goldschmidt's (1976) study of the Sebei. He notes that "most respondents do not imagine a sexual outcome to the scene of a man lurking in the bushes watching a woman come down the path" (p.205). Of course, this interpretation is culturally dependent.

So in the case of LambaMOO, when Mr Bungle used his voodoo doll to force legba into "unwanted liaisons" with other individuals, this force was interpreted as rape. It was the collective ascription of meaning and signification to the event; that is, the (non)decision on all the participants' parts to retain and incorporate Mr Bungle's actions into their consensual reality. The element of decision is qualified because no victim rationally decides to be raped, yet it seems that it is possible for a victim of an unsolicited assault to interpret the assault in more ways than one.

The foundation for that interpretation is the subject of attribution theory and unsurprisingly is firmly rooted in the socio-historical and cross-cultural construction of rape. For example, Bourque (1989) observes that attribution theorists' findings center on the issues of the victim's marital, sexual, and occupational status; the relative status of the perpetrator; the context of the rape (rape by a stranger is viewed as more serious than rape by an acquaintance) and the degree of force used; and the gender of the observer—women identify more strongly with the victim and men are more likely to identify with a male perpetrator (pp.77-95). These are the same issues in the cross-cultural analysis which determined the presence and non-presence of rape as well as the severity of its punishment. It was the operation of these issues that Dibbell captures when he writes,

> They say he raped them that night. They say he did it with a cunning little doll
> ... imbued with the power to make them do whatever he desired. They say that
> by manipulating the doll he forced them to have sex with him, and with each
> other, and to do horrible, brutal things to their own bodies. And although I
> wasn't there that night, I think I can assure you that what they say is true . . .
> (lines 19-25).

The problematic acceptance of voodoo aside, the attribution of rape ("They say he raped them") to virtual acts ("he forced them to have sex with him") occurred and Dibbell and many others not present concur.

While it is noteworthy that the "first rape" in cyberspace occurred, it was inevitable that rape would follow humankind into the next social dimension as it has followed humanity from the hurling of the first stone. What is less understood as noteworthy is the general acceptance of this inevitability. Indeed, the passive transmission of rape from culture to culture is so infectious that the denizens of cybersociety are quick to open the doors to their virtual living rooms and bring in their attacker. Recall Reid's (1995) observation that reality within a MUD is set into motion by the "user's willingness to treat the manifestations of his or her imaginings as if they were real" (p.165, 166). Given this "willingness" and the compelling rationale of rape's sordid past, one cannot blame them, especially when this new reality is possibly the perfect hunting ground for the virtual rapist. The irony is that in trying to make virtual reality a more realistic experience, these founding citizens may be eliminating the best aspects of virtual in order to make it more real.

A Climate for Rape

Viewed as an anarchy destined for governance (MacKinnon, 1995), virtual society is undergoing a process of social organization, disorganization, and reorganization (Carey citing Thomas and Znaniecki in Baron and Straus, 1989, p.127). This process of social organization is evident in virtual realities

(Reid, 1991; MacKinnon, 1995). MacKinnon attributes the disorganization to the fact that "users are unable to 'bring' with them [into virtual reality] their respective social structures because the limitations of [the medium] deconstruct their external world social structure" (p.114). Just as the separation of persons from their usual social structure manifests itself initially as disorganization in real life, so too does it manifest itself in LamdaMOO and other virtual realms.

The (dis)organization of virtual society's population is due to a mix of varying degrees of permanence. There are certainly enclaves of relatively isolated communities as well as huge, heterogeneous concentrations. Movement among these communities and the resulting irresponsibility or freedom from responsibility is easily identifiable in virtual reality society. Further, it is well-known that the current virtual realities are primarily designed and peopled by men (Kramarae, 1995). The relative rarity of virtual women in a predominantly male cybersociety has led to the documentation of great numbers of instances of sexual harassment, the present case notwithstanding.

Baron and Straus (1989) construct a social disorganization index to measure key elements of disorganization in American society. Among these is the percentage of the population moving from a different state or abroad, the ratio of tourists to residents, the percentage of the divorced in the population, the percentage of the female-headed families with children under age 18, the percentage of the population with no religious affiliation, and the ratio of nonfamilied male housekeepers (p.129). Obviously these elements are culturally dependent and some have no current analog in LambdaMOO, but others, such as transient and tourist populations, immigration, and "nonfamilied male housekeepers," have direct bearing.

> [A]ny weakening of stability and integration has an emancipating effect on character and allows in varying degrees the development of irresponsibility, unconventionality, and disorganization. Those whose lives involve a considerable amount of mobility and who thus are forced to spend a large proportion of their time among strangers are subject to this effect. They are not controlled by an organized society to the extent that settled peoples are and are thus free to express individuality to a greater extent. (Faris, p.110).

Certainly the extreme degree of mobility within virtual society subjects its inhabitants to this phenomenon.

Faris treats tourists as "temporary migrants" and Cohen and Taylor (1978) "suggest that people take vacations to escape from the scripted roles and routines of everyday life" (in Baron and Straus, p.132). Baron and Straus concede that research into the criminogenic character is scarce, but cite additional studies which note vacationers sometimes view themselves as being on a "moral holiday" which allows them to steal hotel property and participate in such activities as gambling, prostitution, fraud, and theft.

Finally, the element of "nonfamilied male housekeepers" is studied in order to measure social isolation among single men. Baron and Straus surmise from the research beginning with Durkheim in 1897 that the "social and psychological consequences of different household arrangements supports the conclusion that men living alone increases the likelihood of personal and social problems" (p.134).

In his study of rape in medieval England, Carter (1985) observes that "strangers to a county like Berkshire probably felt more confident about committing a crime like rape because their identities would not be known. To commit rape and quickly disappear would not have been difficult in thirteenth century Berkshire" (p.59). Nor is it so difficult in twentieth century virtual reality. Because of the high degree of anonymity, the issues relating to transience and displacement are exacerbated in a society where persons can choose permanent transience of identity and corresponding unaccountability.

Virtually Unaccountable

MacKinnon (1995) suggests that the "personation" of one's self, the authority of the resulting persona, and the consequences of its actions matter only if the existence of the persona matters to the computer user who created it. If the user desires to have a viable persona in virtual reality, then his or her persona must conform to the social structure governing its interactions with others. In discussing possible penalties for Mr Bungle's crimes, the members of LambdaMOO pondered the possibility of contacting his user's university administrators. Deciding that there is a difference between real life and virtual reality crimes, they rejected this option in favor of a virtual reality penalty. "He had committed a MOO crime, and his punishment, if any, would be meted out via the MOO" (Dibbell 1993, lines 555-557). This decision supports MacKinnon's theory and legba's position that sufficient means for social control in virtual society arise from within the society itself and that no external coercion (from real life) is necessary, but what about cases in which the persona does not matter? Indeed, MacKinnon's theory is premised on the utility for the user of the continued existence of his or her persona. An investigation into the problematics of the punishment of personae is reserved for another project, but for now, there is some evidence that the persona of Mr Bungle did not matter to the New York University (NYU) user who created him.

Many of the personae inhabiting LambdaMOO are permanent and semipermanent members of its virtual community. They have established for themselves relationships and reputations. Their existence matters to their respective users, and accordingly, they abide by the existing collection of norms, mores, and guidelines known as netiquette. Breach of netiquette takes its toll on their viability (Reid, 1992; MacKinnon, 1995) and serves as effective social control.

The intended permanence of Mr Bungle, however, is in doubt. First, there was his extremely antisocial behavior which would have undoubtedly drawn unwanted community criticism and threatened his virtual existence. Second, there is the remarkable similarity of the Mr Bungle persona to the imagery found in the lyrics and accompanying illustrations to the compact disc album entitled Mr Bungle (Mr Bungle, 1991). The LambdaMOO Bungle was self-described as a "fat oleaginous, Bisquick-faced clown dressed in cum-stained harlequin garb and girdled with a mistletoe-and-hemlock belt whose buckle wore the quaint inscription 'KISS ME UNDER THIS, BITCH!'" (Dibbell, 1993, lines 101-104, capitalization in the original). The album illustrations feature several clown faces with expressions ranging from grinning to grimacing and shouting. The song's lyrics evoke images of carnivals, happy faces, clowns, cotton candy, and children juxtaposed with explicit, graphic, sexual violence and misogyny. Indeed, Mr Bungle's misogynistic antics on LambdaMOO may have been inspired by the lyrics from this album.

Finally, there is his response when confronted by the members of his virtual community and asked for an explanation. He said, "I engaged in a bit of a psychological device that is called thought-polarization, the fact this is not real life simply added to heighten the affect (sic) of the device. It was purely a sequence of events with no consequence on my real life existence" (Dibbell 1993, lines 617- 620). This self-admission that his persona did not matter to him is tantamount to insanity. When utility to the user or a "stake" is absent, a persona lacks accountability for its actions and presents a tremendous social liability. The unmasking of Mr Bungle revealed to the people of LambdaMOO that they were dealing with a virtual psychopath. In much the same way that it is morally difficult to punish children and the mentally incompetent, so too was it difficult for LambdaMOO to continue the fevered prosecution of Mr Bungle. By being informed that they had all been involuntary participants in another user's fantasy circus, they realized that the seriousness with which they had perceived the situation was the springboard for putting the joke on themselves. Perhaps if someone had stumbled upon the album prior to the incident the ruse would have been discovered and Mr Bungle's actions would not have been interpreted as seriously nor incorporated into the consensual reality; rather, the actions might have been rejected as misappropriated song lyrics of questionable taste.

Perhaps the high degree of anonymity, mobility, and voluntary accountability among virtual citizens exposes them to possibly greater consequences of social disorganization than is experienced in real life. Given this, it is easy to understand how the participants attributed the serious interpretation of rape to Mr Bungle's actions. Unfortunately, they inadvertently brought into virtual reality a criminal phenomenon well-suited to thriving under the cur-

rent technologically-induced conditions. If Faris is correct, the process of social organization will lead to reorganization and virtual society will adapt to
the introduction and transmission of rape much as every other society has in
the past. But at what cost comes this inadvertent, nonconscious, importation
of rape from real life?

Bodylessness and the Technology to Rape

Real life constructions of rape conceive it as an assault upon the body. Legal-
istic and other definitions of rape tend to include elements of physical force,
fear and unwillingness. Admittedly phallocentric, most theorists agree that
the act must involve intercourse and that intercourse necessitates some sort
of penetration. There is less consensus on whether the penetration can be
other than vaginal with other than a penis (Bourque, 1989). This problema-
tizes the case in which a male is the victim. The recognition of male victims
of rape and female victims of less conventional forms of rape has driven the
construction towards less physical and more generalized notions of body and
self.

Kelly (1988) identifies a feminist-derived definition which incorporates
rape into one of many forms of sexual violence. Defining violence as "involving damage to the self," Kelly notes that the damage may be physical,
emotional, psychological, or material. With "violence" predicated as the result of "violation," the violation can be of the body, of the mind, or of trust
(p.39). This broad construction of rape was conceived to remedy a dire situation in real life where rape is increasingly understood to take many forms.

When constructed as violence against the mind, rape moves quite readily
from real life to the virtual realm of the "bodyless." Indeed, when constructed as a violation of the mind, the virtual reality-adaptation renders moot the
problematic issues of arbitrarily presented bodies and gender indeterminacy.
The violation cuts through the veils of representation and stabs at the core. In
this way, rape becomes an assault not against a persona, but against the person behind the persona. It is a virtual violation that passes back through the
interface and attacks the person where it is real. Seen in this way, one can begin to sympathize with the Seattle woman who presented the persona of legba. She confided to Dibbell that "posttraumatic (sic) tears were streaming
down her face"—evidence that virtual rape has real-life emotional consequences (Dibbell 1993, lines 252-255). It did not matter that her body was a
mere representation of her own creation and that her gender was non-female.
What mattered is that her persona mattered to her, but even more pressing
was the discovery that this new virulent form of rape can penetrate the interface and hurt the user. Whereas Ulrich (1992) touts virtual reality as the ulti-

mate form of safe sex, calling it the "emotional condom of the twenty-first century," the Bungle affair suggests that the virtual reality-adaptation of rape easily defeats that condom and then some.

Stone (1992) warns that "no matter how virtual the subject may become, there is always a body attached" (p.111). She is critical of the virtual reality research inspired by Gibson's writings. The trend, she contends, is to conceive of the body as "meat" destined to obsolescence as soon as "consciousness itself can be uploaded into the network" (p.113). MacKinnon (1995) observes that the association between the persona and user is conveniently but foolishly forgotten and Stone calls the forgetting of the body Cartesian trickery. "It is important to remember," she writes, "that virtual community originates in, and must return to, the physical. No refigured virtual body, no matter how beautiful, will slow the death of a cyberpunk with AIDS. Even in the age of the technosubject, life is lived through bodies" (p.113).

Bringing the Rapist In

Given these considerations, if rape is to be given its due in virtual reality, then it cannot be constructed as an assault against mere virtual representations. To exist in virtual reality, rape must move from the "physical" to the mental. It must shift from the realm of virtual reality bodies, arbitrary as they are, to the realm of the emotional and psychological self. Such a shift raises the issues of nonpresence, primarily, if rape is to exist in the mind, in whose mind must it exist to be present?

To answer this question, one can return to attribution theory and its breakdown of the perception of rape. In the case of virtual reality, rape exists in the minds of the victim (V), the perpetrator (P), and/or the witness-others (O), but in which mind must it exist to matter? To rephrase this question, if rape could only exist in one mind, in whose mind must it exist?

V-dependent rape implies that only the victim is aware of the violation. There are no witnesses and there is no locatable suspect. It is only the word of the victim which gives existence and immediacy to the crime. How does a society adjudicate such a charge? Historically, women victims have not been trusted to supply uncorroborated testimony when the consequences are severe. Suppose the victim attributes acts to rape more broadly than most members of society would. Can society convict on the victim's interpretation alone? Does V-dependent rape account for hypersensitive, insane, or mentally incompetent victims? Socio-cultural history suggests that, given the consequences, it cannot and will not. Finally what about the cases where the victim is not aware of the rape? Consider the scenarios where the victim is drugged or unconscious? If rape is V-dependent, such a rape cannot exist. Surely this example invalidates the case of V- dependency.

The case for P-dependent rape is that if anyone knows that a rape has occurred it must be the perpetrator. This implies that it does not matter if the victim is aware of the violation. She does not need to know that her doctor exploited her while she was under anesthesia or that her psychiatrist seduced her while she was under hypnosis. It does not require witnesses nor does it require exposure via a trial. All that matters is that one person, the perpetrator, have awareness of the crime. But if the victim and others never become aware, does the crime have saliency? What distinguishes P-dependent rape from the perpetrator's fantasies? P-dependent rape is also unacceptable as a construction because perpetrators do not generally prosecute themselves. Indeed, they would not be allowed even if they desired because criminal confessions must often be corroborated. In other words, P-dependent rape lacks salience in the extreme, and because it often requires corroboration, lacks independence.

By process of elimination, the remaining case must be the answer. O-dependency relies upon the public trial, that is, the public-other must decide if a rape has occurred. O-dependency best accommodates the cultural view of rape as a public-involving act. In O-dependent rape, it does not matter if rape exists in the minds of the victim or the perpetrator. The requirement is that it exists in the minds of the witnesses, the jurors, and/or the community. In this case, the others take into consideration the testimonies of the victim and the perpetrator. This conception is a reconciliation of the weaknesses in V-and P-dependent rape conceptions. In the end, the others alone must decide if a rape has occurred independent of whether they know for sure if it has. The trial is the most widely used heuristic for attributing rape in a society. Certainly not all trials resemble the American jurisprudential process, but they all involve elements of weighing evidence in the collective, public mind. In the case of Mr Bungle, the public mind was largely convinced of his guilt without hearing his testimony. Since the crime was committed in the "public eye" in front of many witnesses, it is doubtful that the victims' testimonies were necessary to arrive at their verdict.

And what of punishing the virtual rapist? If rape is a crime against the mind, what good does it do to punish the persona as did the members of LambaMOO? Even in light of his eventual execution, the sentence was handed down to Mr Bungle and not to the user presenting him. If Mr Bungle's attack penetrated the persona and impacted the woman in Seattle, then the punishment should impact the student in New York. It is ironic, that although the virtual reality-adaptation of rape has real effects, the LambdaMOO people decided that the effects were not as real nor as serious as real life rape. As much as it can be reasoned that virtual reality rape has real consequences, reason also led to the privileging of the body over the mind. Ultimately, the crime was comparably less serious than if Mr Bungle's user had physically raped the woman in Seattle. As a result, the student's virtual reality body was punished, not his own—the mind behind the crime.

But punishing a virtual rape with virtual penalties does not address recidivism by the user. Indeed, the NYU user reappeared in LambdaMOO with a new persona. If virtual rape has real consequences, this cannot be allowed to continue. If punishing the persona through internally-developed social controls is ineffective when the crime has real effects, does it seem reasonable that social controls with real effects are necessary? If so, perhaps the users of LambaMOO should have contacted the NYU administration after all.

Invoking external controls on virtual society requires consideration. Firstly, since MacKinnon (1995) argues that external controls are unnecessary to govern virtual society, is it not a step backwards to rely upon them rather than develop and exercise independent, internal controls? How will continued dependence on external controls influence the development of arguably independent societies in virtual reality? Which external government's view of free speech should regulate speech-as-action among international users of text-based virtual reality's? How will the speech-as-action/narrative-as-reality linkage fare in the context of external civil liberty claims of free speech? How about the external controls on pornographic, harassing, and other prohibited speech? Does Mr Bungle's user have the right to speak violently to the person presenting legba? Was legba's user at any time exposed to danger? Will these questions become moot when technology supplants text-as-action virtual reality's with text-less environments? The answers to these questions are contentious enough to consider a reassessment of rape as a crime of the mind. When viewed as a crime of the body, albeit virtually, jurisprudence can be developed internally by the inhabitants of virtual reality. The result is a local, current solution relatively free from the conundrum and political legacies of external-world decision-making processes.

In the end, it seems that the virtual reality-adaptation of rape, even though it is now a construction directed to the mind rather than the body, resembles very much its real life counterpart. The construction accounts for bodylessness, renders gender irrelevant, and captures the severe nature of the offense by penetrating the interface and directly assaulting the person behind the persona. The construction is so compelling that Dibbell writes, "it was hard for me to understand why real life society classifies real life rape alongside crimes against the person or property. Since rape can occur without physical pain or damage, I found myself reasoning, then it must be classified as a crime against the mind" (lines 824-828). But what does this construction of rape do for humanity? What has been gained by conceiving virtual rape in such a way that its virtuality is irrelevant? Why should the people of LambdaMOO set a precedent by reasoning into existence a construction of rape more virulent and harmful than they realize? Is not rape of the body serious enough that it should not be reconstructed when bodies are absent?

Dibbell's sentiments indicate that rather than learning from our mistakes in real life and correcting them in virtual reality, we are headed down the path of worsening our situation in real life by misapplying what we have learned in virtual reality. This is a failing of theorists to avail themselves of the opportunity which virtual reality presents to construct a conception of rape which is less virulent, less dangerous, and less meaningful than its real life counterpart. The goal should be to limit pain and victimization, not chart out ways in which it can grow.

Empowerment Through the Conscious Construction of Rape in Virtual Reality

Hilberman (1976) contends that the "ultimate elimination of rape demands a massive restructuring of social values to include a reconsideration of the relations between the sexes." Resonating with the feminist solution agenda, Hilberman believes rape will not be eliminated until sex roles are no longer defined by stereotypical expectations based on sex and power motives. Sanders (1980) claims that the prevention of rape is not about new types of physical arrangements, better street lighting, or monthly community meetings. He calls for a reconceptualization of the rapist. The rapist must be made to appear foolish and this can only be done in terms of what the rapist is in the context of his actions in society (p.143). Further, Sanders wants a reconstruction of the victim in which the victim is at least as dangerous as the perpetrator.

Such reconstructions are difficult to effect in real life, but are relatively trivial to implement in virtual reality. Already it was suggested that other circumstances could have cast Mr Bungle's actions in another light. Similar to the rejection of the nonsensical narrations (legba would have rejected a command to self-immolate), Sanders' call for reconceptualization does not demand much more than this. It is understood that legba and the others initially and responsively felt the violation resulting from Bungle's actions, but just as social learning theory explains the transmission of violence through repetitive exposure, the same process can transmit the absence of violence. The repetitive rejection of undesired elements from the consensual reality fosters an environment hostile to the inculcation of undesirable values. The process begins with conscious, determined reattribution and concludes with a reformulated concept. With respect to rape in virtual reality, a reoccurrence of Mr Bunglelike actions would need to be consciously interpreted as foolish, meaningless, nonsensical, and irrelevant. At first this will be difficult, but it will become easier with time.

The reattribution of undesired sexual acts may draw the criticism of those who believe that this course of action crosses the line between self-empowerment and holding the victims responsible for their own pain. Critics may suggest that this reconception fails to acknowledge the "window of pain between the moment the rape-text starts flowing and the moment a gag shuts it off" (Dibbel 1993, 463- 469). Whereas the critics are concerned with victims of rape shutting their eyes to it, this reconstruction does not permit the acts to be interpreted as rape in the first place. While the "window of pain" is initially unavoidable, the reification of the reattribution process gradually closes the window and eventually shuts it completely. Is it not better to engage upon a project which safeguards the self from the harms of virtual actions?

Is it not better to say, "You can't rape me. I don't have a body" than "I believe rape is an assault upon the mind, and so, even though I don't have a body, you can rape me anyway"? Although we cannot currently break the lifegiving mind-body link of which Stone speaks, we can build protective walls and make the mind impervious from virtual assaults. The interface which generates the persona and the virtual reality should be that barrier to harm, and in the lapse of technology, we must rely upon social construction to ensure it.

Summary

This chapter has sought to criticize the attribution of rape to the events described in the Bungle case. It does this not out of antipathy for the victims; quite the contrary. The current iteration of rape as constructed in LambdaMOO poses serious, real consequences for users of virtual reality and complex problems for virtual reality theoreticians who will be forced to reconcile the consequences with real life power structures. It is hoped that these reasons alone will subject the current construction of virtual reality rape to reassessment.

The task of reassessment implies the guided construction of rape rather than its nonconscious importation from real life. By way of a socio-historical and cross-cultural analysis, it has been established that rape has always been a social construction—one more mutable than commonly believed. Further, the current broadening trend in the real life social construction of rape is making its nonconscious importation into virtual reality relatively easy. Despite this ease, logically rape does not have to exist in virtual reality now; rationally it should not. The importation of real life rape into virtual reality poses complex questions and creates complex problems unnecessarily. It would better serve the interest of virtual society to reconceive rape so as to render it less harmful or even irrelevant.

Controversially, the same challenge is available to real life social constructionists as well. The history of sexuality reveals that anatomy is socially coded in such a way that some body parts are hypervalued relative to others. Assaults involving penis/anus/vagina are socially constructed differently from those involving finger/ear/nose. Accordingly, the victim of the former is constructed differently than the victim of the latter. Whereas after an assault, the latter experiences little if any social repercussions, the former is traumatized, segregated, and introduced into a process specially created to treat the would-be victim. In effect and irrationally so, the process is created to await and treat the persons which are created/destined to be its victims.

The lesson learned from virtual reality enables positive constructionists to shortcircuit this process by eliminating previously unconsidered causes of victimization. In other words, whereas most rape theorists focus upon evening the relationship between men and women by proscribing certain activities, an alternative construction considers the removal of the sex from sexual assault by decoding or recoding the anatomy. Because anatomical coding is commonly perceived as immutable, this solution generally is not considered. But in the case of rape, virtual reality has served as a useful tool for re-evaluating rape as a historically mutable construction capable of positive- or reconstruction. Accordingly, anatomical recoding can reduce a sexual assault to a physical assault, mercifully transforming the victim of a sexual assault into a nonvictimized victim of a physical assault. Granted that reconstructing the value of anatomy is a difficult undertaking, it is yet hoped that the examination of the social construction of rape has shown that social constructions are not as rigid as they seem. Indeed, it is not the constructions which are rigid, but the persons who promulgate them.

Acknowledgements

I would like to thank David Edwards, Ann Cvetkovich, Julian Dibbell, and Jon Lebkowsky for their comments and support during the revision process and Allucquere Stone and Fay Sudweeks for their patience. I extend my apologies to the scores of persons for whom I have ruined countless dates and parties with the discussion of rape. Most importantly, I wish to recognize and thank my housemate, friend, and colleague, Judd Jeansonne for hours of insightful, energetic, and motivating discussions culminating in this work.

CHAPTER TEN

Interactivity on the Nets

Sheizaf Rafaeli and Fay Sudweeks

A network is a net. In sports, a "net" is a barrier. Net is also that which remains after all deductions and adjustments are made. A third etymological derivation for net is a means of entrapment, surrounding and captivation. Among all interpretations of the *net* in *net*work this third meaning is, in our view, the most appropriate. This chapter is about the captivation (or engagement) of participatory communication on the *net*works. How are we trapped by group computer mediated communication (CMC)?

We begin with the observation that group CMC is a series of experiments in social integration and democratic participation. By some measures at least, the experiment works. Group CMC succeeds in attracting sustained exponential growth. People want to join, and when they do, many stay. But the success is, in some ways, paradoxical. We propose to examine how captivation occurs through interactivity. Interactivity is a variable quality of communication settings. It expresses the degree to which communication transcends reaction (Rafaeli, 1988). Following classical scholars such as Goffman (1959) and Parsons (1962), and more contemporary work such as Bretz (1982), Steinfield (1987), Rogers and Rafaeli (1985), Rafaeli (1984, 1988) and others, we believe that interactivity is a pivotal measure (and, perhaps, cause) of the social dynamics of group communication. Such interactivity is made possible, but not always exercised, by CMC. It is especially interesting, but hardly studied as-of-yet, in the context of large groups.

In accordance with theoretical and experimental predictions, we report on the nature and levels of interactivity in the ProjectH data—a content analysis of a representative, random sample of computer mediated discussions. We relate interactivity to several dimensions of interest: activity itself, type of list (voluntary/academic vs commercial), list climate, the emergence of leadership (the guru phenomenon), and others. We propose that interactivity is associated with those message qualities which invite people and make people gravitate to groups on the net. Thus, interactivity may be a mechanism through which netting occurs on the net.

Group CMC

Many people congregate on the nets. They spend much energy in the collaborative effort. Networks are centralized distribution mechanisms that are both democratic and anarchic. Computer-mediated groups can be viewed as an enigma in traditional, rational and economic terms. After all, the medium is owned by no one. The process is unmanaged in any traditional sense of motivation, profit, control or censorship. Joining and departing participants do so without so much as a required introduction or an agreed upon etiquette. The groups are of an undetermined size or constitution. The situation is neither the classical written nor traditionally spoken communication. Group CMC is neither mass media as we have grown to know it, nor interpersonal face-to-face. If we weigh numbers of participants and symmetry in participation, we find that this is the largest form of conversation, or the smallest form of mass communication—or something else altogether?

Computer mediated groups beg the questions: why do people make this investment and why does this social phenomenon happen? Is the allure of group CMC in its emulation of face-to-face interaction? We argue that interactivity is the mediating phenomenon. Interactivity may occur in face-to-face contexts, but is not mandatory. It may be present in CMC contexts as well. Here, too, not always. In any case, it is not the direct similarity to face-to-face that matters.

Networked group CMC is unprecedented, not even by face-to-face, in several ways. The technology allows for conversations held simultaneously or asynchronously by numbers heretofore considered unmanageable. Group CMC is about dozens or hundreds or thousands of people interacting. It is as much a social and group phenomenon as it is psychological and interpersonal. Turn-taking and interrupting are another case in point. Interrupting is easier to do in CMC than in face-to-face. At the same time, interruptions are less disruptive for the speaker. After all, group "members" are not really members in any officially sanctioned way. Are they ever really there? There is no "there" to be at. There is no "when" to be on. Group CMC longevity, not to mention functionality, is not fully understood (Rafaeli and LaRose, 1993). And yet, the growth of group CMC is astounding. At the time we collected the data reported here, network users numbered over 10 million worldwide and growth rates were estimated at 5% monthly. Both size and growth rates have since increased appreciably. Governments have been moved to declare national "information highway" emergencies and policies to deal with the onslaught of traffic. Where is everyone going, and why? If group CMC is not simply magnified face-to-face, how should we study computer mediated groups, and how can we account for the social, communication phenomenon they represent?

Interactivity

Interactivity is a process-related, variable characteristic of communication settings. Like face-to-face communication, computer-mediated communication has the capacity of enabling high interactivity. One postulated outcome of interactivity is engagement. Interactivity can lead to sociability. We therefore propose that the concept of interactivity is a likely candidate to help in explaining how groups, especially CMC groups, stick together. And it is interesting to examine interactivity on the nets.

Interactivity is not a characteristic of the medium. It is a process-related construct about communication. It is the extent to which messages in a sequence relate to each other, and especially the extent to which later messages recount the relatedness of earlier messages. Following Goffman (1967, 1981), Bretz (1983), McLaughlin (1984), Rogers (1986), Tannen (1989), Schegloff (1987, 1992) and others, we note that communication is mostly about and for the purpose of interaction. Interactivity places shared interpretive contexts in the primary role. Interactivity describes and prescribes the manner in which conversational interaction as an iterative process leads to jointly produced meaning. Interactivity merges speaking with listening, and it is a general enough concept to encompass both intimate, person-to-person, face-to-face communication and other forums and forms.

Logically, interactivity is indicated as a useful concept for mapping group CMC because it is (like group CMC itself) a hybrid construct. The concept of interactivity directs our focus to the intersection of the psychological and the sociological, the bridge between mass and interpersonal communication, the meeting of mediated and direct communication, and the paradox of written vs. spoken. Interactivity varies along a continuum (Rafaeli, 1988). At one end is declarative (one-way) communication (e.g. most radio and television). Reactive (two-way) communication is further down the road. In reactive communication, one side responds to the other side. Fully interactive communication requires that later messages in any sequence take into account not just messages that preceded them, but also the manner in which previous messages were reactive. In this manner interactivity forms a social reality (see figure 1).

Interactivity is the condition of communication in which simultaneous and continuous exchanges occur, and these exchanges carry a social, binding force. Brown and Yule (1983) and Zack (1993) summarize additional qualities of interactive communication: allowing for multiple types of cues, potential spontaneity, emergent progression of the content, the ability to interrupt or preempt, mutuality, and patterns of turn-taking. But our definition of interactivity goes beyond Schegloff's simultaneous exchange and Goffman's continuous feedback. We support Schudson's (1978) contention that face-to-face

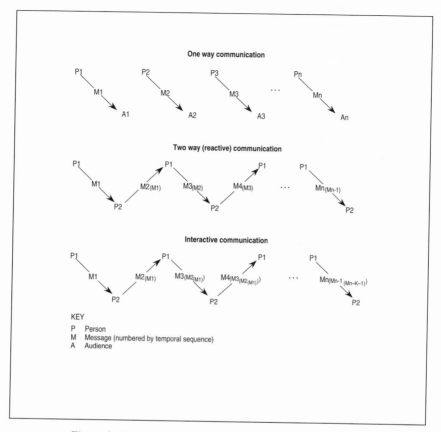

Figure 1. One-way, two-way, and interactive communication.

conversation cannot be used as the standard of comparison for group CMC. We argue that interactivity is a continuum, a variable, not just a condition, and we insist that most communication, face-to-face or not, falls short of full interactivity. The case of group CMC differs from conversation, if only for sheer size, and because interruptability and turn-taking take on different meanings.

What does interactivity do? Interactivity in communication settings is associated with the attitudinal dimensions of acceptance and satisfaction. But it is also related to performance quality, motivation, sense of fun, cognition, learning, openness, frankness and sociability (Rafaeli, 1988). Interactivity operates in a supplementation mode. Quasi-interactive (reactive) media can allow people to use the media as a substitute for sociability. The human need for interaction (Beniger, 1987), when satisfied, allows people to use interactive media to bolster their favorable disposition toward interacting with others. Interactivity can be shown to lead to more cooperation. What are the processes involved? We turn now to an examination of issues that arise from research on group CMC.

Experimental Evidence

Laboratory based, experimental work has uncovered a series of dysfunctional or problematic attributes of group CMC. Among the topics studied in the laboratory were flaming behaviors (McGuire, Kiesler and Siegel, 1987; Siegel, Dubrovsky, Kiesler and McGuire, 1986, Sproull and Kiesler, 1991), disinhibition and deindividuation (Hiltz and Johnson, 1989; Matheson and Zanna, 1988, 1990). Hiltz, Johnson and Turoff (1986) find CMC to be cold and unsociable when compared to face-to-face contexts. Somewhat more optimistic experimental work introduced findings on status levelling, consensus formation, group dynamics and brainstorming creativity and productivity (e.g. Dennis and Valacich, 1993; Dubrovsky, Kiesler and Sethna, 1991; Valacich et al., 1993; Osborn, 1953). Important as they may be, these concepts neither disprove nor explain either growth or the glue that keeps CMC groups together. The picture of group CMC painted by summing laboratory studies may be somewhat incomplete. The external validity of laboratory studies of group CMC is problematic for three reasons. (1) Most subjects in laboratory studies are an atypically captive audience. Experimental subjects (usually students fulfilling class requirements or paid) are not reflective of the group CMC environment. They are not voluntary participants who choose to participate. In any case, subjects' free coming and going (mostly coming) is not allowed, recorded or reported. (2) Groups studied in experiments tend to be small, usually a dozen participants or less. The real-life experience of group CMC is of a much larger group. (3) An almost natural inclination of experimental design is to contrast CMC with a face-to-face standard of comparison. As discussed earlier, this contrast may be misleading.

Survey Evidence About Group CMC

Many field studies of group CMC focus on the narrow bandwidth and cue deficiencies that typify CMC. Short, Williams and Christie (1976), Rice (1984), and Culnan and Markus (1987) use the term "social presence." Sproull and Kiesler (1991) refer to the "lack of social context cues." Trevino, Daft and Lengel (1990) mention "media richness." Taken together, these related terms suggest that CMC is best thought of as a task-related and/or problem-solving environment. In other words, much of the survey work on CMC hints at it not being a suitable context for social interaction. Others (e.g. Rice and Love, 1987) have uncovered actual emotional use of CMC, albeit often negative emotions. Self reports of CMC users are often in contradiction to the notion of media poverty; experienced CMC users rate CMC as richer than even face-to-face (Steinfield, 1986). Other field-based studies, mostly in organizational contexts, search for reasons people adopt or use CMC, frequently arriving at social influence or cultural construction explanations (e.g. Fulk, 1993; Schmitz and Fulk, 1991). Common to these studies is a focus on constructs such as social influence and critical mass. These are all external qualities, not internal to the communication setting. A focus on content has led some to study creative ways in which members of CMC groups seek to break the bandwidth barrier. The topic of nonverbal behavior on the net, for example, has been the subject of much study (e.g. Carey, 1980; Blackman and Clevenger, 1990).

Case studies of individual computer-mediated groups seem to be more upbeat and optimistic in their description of group CMC (c.f. Danowski and Edison-Swift, 1985). Finholt and Sproull (1990) observed CMC groups within an organization behaving like real social groups, despite the fact that their members shared no physical space, were invisible, and their interaction was asynchronous. Hahm and Bikson (1989) report on a field study among retired and employed individuals, in which group CMC resulted in increased interaction among members of the group. From the perspective of searching for the social glue, a description of the way in which computer-mediated groups come and hold together, it seems unlikely that either social presence or the use of emoticons is the answer. However, because they are case studies of single groups and often intraorganizational, these studies, too, do not offer a convincing driving force that would explain the cohesiveness, binding, netting force of group CMC. Group CMC is a sweeping enough social, volition-based phenomenon which deserves a social-level explanation.

Research Framework

Our hypotheses relate to: (1) the nature of messages; (2) the nature of interactive messages when compared to other messages; (3) the nature of interactivity on different networks; and (4) the nature of interactivity when comparing messages by the most active authors to the norm.

Generally, we support the concept that CMC conversations, as a whole, display similar characteristics as face-to-face conversations, in particular a preference for agreement. We expect the interactive messages subset of group CMC will surpass all messages on measures of agreement. In addition, interactive messages will be more opinionated, self-disclosing, humorous, and community oriented (using first-person plural). Networks will have different levels of interactivity, stemming from their differing structural arrangements. Authors who are more active (contribute more) will produce more interactive messages. Stated formally and specifically:

H1: The content of group CMC will demonstrate a preference for agreement

Group CMC is modeled on an extension of interpersonal conversations. As such, group CMC should contain a higher proportion of "agreeing" content than disagreeing content. McLaughlin (1984) summarizes how the conversational system has a built-in preference for accord among the conversants.

H2: If agreement is conversational, interactive messages are even more conversational, but also involving more than average

We expect interactive messages, within group CMC, to be even more agreeable than the norm for face-to-face, or other messages. And while interactive messages may be even more agreeable than average, they will also be more opinionated, humorous, self-disclosing, and community oriented. We interpret more opinionated and self-disclosing content as indications that groups have gotten beyond preliminary introductions (Duck, 1976). Sherblom (1990) has shown how the use of personal pronouns reflects the degree of involvement in organizations. Thus, we expect interactive messages to contain more first-person plural pronouns.

H3: Structural characteristics of networks affect their interactivity

Consider group CMC on the different networks. These differ in at least two ways: the manner in which messages are stored and disseminated, and whether group members pay to use the network. There should be differences in interactivity between voluntary nets and commercial nets. These differences are expected because there is a different implied social contract when one pays to participate. Compuserve special interest groups (SIGs) are managed by sysops who may exercise varying degrees of editorial intervention. And there will be a difference between groups that appear to the reader as a newsgroup (Usenet) and those that appear (to the reader/subscriber/member) as individual messages (Bitnet Listserv groups).

H4: Interactivity is related to individual activity and communication salience of participants

Consider the difference between those who write often and those who make only infrequent contributions. Messages by frequent (active) authors differ in the amount and nature of interactivity of their messages than infrequent authors. We expect frequent authors to produce more interactive messages.

Method

The data reported here are the result of a content analysis effort. A large international and interdisciplinary group of researchers carried out a content analysis of a representative, random sample of publicly available communication content in computer mediated discussion groups. The project had its inception and entire existence online. A complete description of the methodology is available in Rafaeli, Sudweeks, Konstan and Mabry (1994). Additionally, full copies of the data and message corpora, coding instruments, sampling and ethics policy statements are available online. See also Sudweeks and Rafaeli (1996) for a broader treatment of the group process and ethics issues. In this section we will provide a short account of sampling, coding and reliability practices.

Sampling

The sampling strategy aimed at obtaining a representative sample of message exchange over group CMC. Our goal was to address as broad a scope as possible. We needed to consider varying units of analysis: the single message, a thread, the group, and the network within which the group resided.

The sampling method chosen was of fixed-length message threads, at a given starting date, within randomly selected groups stratified to equal numbers by network type. Messages were selected over a restricted domain, in a single temporal sequence of 100 messages per each group. Equal numbers of groups were randomly selected from Bitnet, Usenet and CompuServe groups. Sampling was completely random, but common sense and the research purpose required exclusion of foreign language groups on local networks, announcement groups, help/support groups limited to specific products, test and control groups, groups whose contents are only excerpts of other groups selected by moderators, extremely low volume groups (lists with fewer than 25 messages and 3 authors during a selected test month). Some groups were excluded from the sample prior to random sampling where clearly inappropriate. Otherwise, lists meeting exclusion criteria were rejected after selection.

Corpora of messages were downloaded from three networks of group CMC: Internet's Usenet, Bitnet Listservs, and Compuserve SIGs. Populations of groups were compiled. Comprehensive lists of all groups were obtained from the appropriate servers on the respective networks, and the sample groups were screened and random-number sampled, resulting in group numbers as outlined in table 1.

The sampling period began on Monday 15 March 1993. Volunteer members shared the task of downloading, using several news servers in locations

	Bitnet	Usenet	Compuserve
Pre-filtered groups	3485	1868	337
Post-filtered groups	1907	986	94
Groups in completed sample	10	12	10
Duplicated groups	2	5	5
Messages in completed sample	1128	1694	1500

Table 1. Groups and messages sampled and coded.

around the world. Articles were collected according to the date and time of arrival at each news server. Including the post-sampling screening, 77 Bitnet lists, 39 Usenet newsgroups and 23 CompuServe SIGs were selected to get samples of 20 groups for each network. Due to coder attrition, the final database contains complete data for 40 lists (including 10 duplications), and partial data for 4 additional lists, totalling 4,322 messages.

Coding

A codebook containing 46 closed items was prepared and pretested by all coders. At first, the codebook was constructed in a brainstorming process, carried out publicly and online, with dozens of project members taking part. The codebook formation process involved several iterations and drafts. The rewriting of the codebook and pretests were repeated until we achieved average agreement percentages exceeding 90% on all items. The items included in the codebook are listed in figure 2.

Each batch of 100 messages downloaded from selected groups was prepared for coders. Computer programs were written to: (1) split files of 100 messages into individual files; (2) renumber, if necessary, in numeric alphabetical order; (3) precode the first six variables: CODERID, LISTID, MSGNUM, AUTHORID, MSGTIME and MSGDATE; (4) compile a cumulative database of authors across all lists; and (5) reassemble processed messages in one file.

After coding, data was exported as ASCII files and emailed to an account dedicated to data processing. Automatic verification and manipulation followed, including five stages: (1) check if incoming mail is data; (2) check for errors; (3) check for completeness; (4) manipulate the database into usable representation; and (5) status report to coder and coordinator.

Coders of each list completed a questionnaire to gather descriptive information about the coders, the technology used, impressions of the list, and problems experienced. Data from this questionnaire are not reported here.

No.	Variable	Brief description and comments
1	CODERID	Automatically supplied
2	LISTID	Automatically supplied
3	MSGNUM	Automatically supplied
4	AUTHORID	Automatically supplied
5	MSGTIME	Automatically supplied
6	MSGDATE	Automatically supplied
7	MSGLINES	Number of lines?
8	SUBJECT	Is it appropriate?
9	NOISE	Misdirected message?
10	FIRSTPER	Self disclosure?
11	OPINION	Does message contain an opinion?
12	FACT	Does message contain a fact?
13	APOLOGY	Does message contain an apology?
14	QUESTION	Does message contain a question/request?
15	ACTION	Does message contain a call for action?
16	CHALLENGE	Does message contain a Challenge/dare?
17	HUMOR	Does message contain attempts at humour?
18	METACOM	Does message contain metacommunication?
19	FORMAT	Is the message formatted appropriately?
20	STYLE1	Appropriate/excessive use capitalization?
21	STYLE2	Is there colloquial spelling?
22	NATURE	Overall rhetorical style
23	EMOTICON	Icon for emotion?
24	EMODEVICE	Device for emotion?
25	ARTICON	Art, other than emotion
26	GENDER1	Male/female?
27	GENDER2	How identify?
28	GENDER3	Gender cues?
29	GENDER4	Gender issues?
30	QUOTE1	From this list?
31	QUOTE2	From other CMC?
32	QUOTE3	From non-CMC?
33	DEPEND1	Reference to previous message or messages?
34	DEPEND2	Message number referenced?
35	DEPEND3	Is there reference to how previous messages related to even earlier msgs?
36	DEPEND4	Introduce new topic?
37	COALIT1	Does message contain agreement/disagreement with persons or ideas ON the list?
38	COALIT2	Does message contain use of first-person plural pronouns ("us", "we") about the group?
39	COALIT3	Directly address any persons on the list?
40	EXTCOAL	Does message contain agreement/disagreement with persons or ideas OFF the list?
41	FLAME1	What is the rhetorical tone?
42	FLAME2	Does message contain coarse language?
43	FLAME3	Does message attempt to avoid tension/calm?
44	STATUS	Is there mention of status of author?
45	SIGNAT1	Does mention contain any/stylized signature?
46	SIGNAT2	Does signature contain quotation?

Figure 2. Codebook items and short descriptions.

Reliability

Approximately one-third of the lists were double coded to establish repro-ducibility and reliability of coding. Of the 37 lists (batches of 100 messages) distributed to the research group members, 20 were single coded, 12 were double coded, and 5 were not coded. Of the 32 coded, 4 were unfinished, giving a final tally of 20 single coded and 10 double coded complete lists. The database(s), therefore, has a total of 4,322 messages from 30 fully-com-pleted lists, and 4 partially completed lists. Of these, 3,322 are unique mes-sages. In addition, there are 1,000 doubled-up codes.

It was important to maintain independence of coding, particularly those lists that were double coded. To eliminate a possible source of invalid (inflat-ed) reliability, coders were discouraged from discussing coding problems amongst themselves or within the group. Coder queries were directed, in-stead, to an advisory committee of twelve members. Each advisor, or oracle, fielded questions on a section of the codebook, responding in a non-directive manner.

The typical practice was for an enquiry to be posted to the advisory com-mittee, the specialist oracle—or the leader (the Commissioner of Oracles) if the appropriate oracle was not available—would post a recommended re-sponse, all oracles would comment on the response, and the Commissioner would summarize oracle recommendations and post the final recommenda-tion to the enquirer and/or the group.

Results

The database of messages and content-analysis values contains data about 4,322 messages. These messages represent three networks (Usenet, Bitnet, and Compuserve), 32 groups (lists), and the efforts of about 40 separate coders spread around the world.

The first reportable result was that the project was completed and a usable database was made available. Some evidence for the success of this group is in the measures of the reliability of coding between coders. In this chapter, we do not report on reliability of the data, other than saying that, on average, intercoder agreement exceeded 75% for the variables used in the following analysis, in the lists for which double codes were available. Reliability mea-sures in a project such as this are complicated, and should include coder-, list-, variable-, and network-focused orientations. We leave this analysis for another time.

Interactivity varied among groups from a high level of 40% in some groups, to absolutely no interactive messages in some groups. On average, just under 10% of the messages were coded as directly referring to how pre-vious messages related to others. We consider these 388 messages to be in-

	All Messages (N=4322)	Interactive (N=388)	Reactive (N=2269)
Contains agreement within list/group (COALIT1)	16.0	30.7[a]	19.6[d]
Contains disagreement within list/group (COALIT1)	12.0	21.1[a]	15.9[d]
Contains agreement with persons/statements external to the list (EXTCOAL)	9.5	17.5[a]	9.6[d]
Contains disagreement with persons/statements external to the list (EXTCOAL)	5.2	10.4[a]	5.7[d]
Primarily provide information (NATURE=1)	40.1	26.8[a]	41.9[d]
Contain a fact (FACT)	57.1	61.9	60.6
Primarily request information (NATURE=2)	14.6	8.5[a]	8.4[b]
Contain a question (QUESTION)	26.5	32.0[a]	21.5[d]
Primarily opinionated (NATURE=3)	18.7	24.0[a]	24.0[b]
Contain an opinion (OPINION)	50.0	67.7[a]	57.3[c]
Contain self-disclosure (FIRSTPER)	35.3	41.0[a]	36.8[d]
Attempting humor	20.8	27.1[a]	17.8[d]
Use of first-person plural (COALIT2)	9.3	24.5[a]	9.1[d]

Reactive messages are those coded as responding to one message. Interactive messages are those coded as containing references to the manner in which previous messages related to those preceding them.

Significance (Mann Whitney U Test):

[a]Interactive messages differ significantly (p<0.001) from noninteractive.

[b]Reactive messages differ significantly from noninteractive but not from interactive.

[c]Reactive messages differ significantly from interactive AND noninteractive.

[d]Reactive messages differ significantly from interactive but not from noninteractive.

Table 2. Messages content and nature:
All messages vs. interactive messages (percentages)

teractive messages. More than half the sample of messages (52.5%) were coded as referring to a single message that preceded them. These 2269 messages are considered "reactive." Table 2 compares characteristics of reactive, interactive and all messages in the sample.

Almost one third of the messages in the corpora quoted other messages verbatim (QUOTE1). Interactive messages were slightly longer than reactive messages. Reactive messages, in turn, were slightly longer than all other messages. The differences in length were not large.

Fully 57% of all messages (first column) contain statements of facts. More than a quarter of the messages contain a question or request. Examined in a different way, when coders classified the overall nature of each message, they found 40% of the messages to be primarily providing information, probably in response to the 14.6% of the messages that were predominantly re-

Interactivity:

	Usenet	Bitnet	Compuserve
messages coded as interactive	11%	3.8%	10.3%

Reactivity:

DEPEND1	Network type			Row Total
	Usenet	Bitnet	Compuserve	
Not at all	782	429	174	1385
	46.3	38.1	11.6	32.1
Yes, 1 message	664	554	1051	2269
	39.3	49.2	70.3	52.7
Yes, >1	147	59	82	288
	8.7	5.2	5.5	6.7
Yes, a sequence	96	83	187	366
	5.7	7.4	12.5	8.5
Column	1689	1125	1494	4308
Total	39.2	26.1	34.7	100.0

Table 3. Networks and interactivity level.

	Messages by most frequent contributors (≥10 msgs) (N=1021)	Messages by frequent contributors (4–9 msgs) (N=691)	Entire sample (N=4322)
Interactive messages	9.0	10.1	9.0
Reactive messages (responding to only one preceding message)	70.2*	60.5*	52.5
Reactive messages (responding to one or more preceding messages)	87.0*	81.3*	67.7
Significance: * connotes significantly different from rest of sample, using Mann Whitney U test			

*Table 4. Interactivity and reactivity in messages by
frequent contributors (percentages)*

quests for information. The other half of the message body was classified as "mixed" (22%), opinionated (18.7%), and persuasive (3.6%).

It appears that messages exchanged by participants in group CMC are predominantly factual, conversational, agreeable, and supportive. More than one in every five messages contained at least an attempt at humour. And more than a third of the messages contain personalizing content, in the form of a verbal self-disclosure, an admission or introduction. 9.3% of the entire corpora of messages use first-person plural pronouns. Messages were more likely to contain agreement than disagreement. This finding is repeated, using both measures of the expression of opinion about statements and persons within the list (16% over 12% agreement to disagreement) and opinions external to the list (9.5% to 5.2%).

Among interactive messages (reading across table 2), there is more statement of opinion in general, and specifically more expression of agreement. For example, interactive messages contain statements of agreement with persons or statements on the list twice as often as the general sample. Likewise, and even more interestingly, interactive messages are twice as likely as the general sample to contain statements of agreement. Using both the internal-to-the-list and the external measures, we find interactive messages to be even more agreeable than messages overall. These differences are statistically significant. Interactive messages contain more opinions, more self disclosure, and more than twice as much use of first-person plural pronouns.

Reactive messages resemble the general sample (and differ from interactive messages) in all these respects, with two exceptions: Reactive messages are as opinionated as interactive messages, and they tend, like interactive messages, to contain fewer requests for information. Interactive messages do not differ from others in how factual they are.

Table 3 displays the distribution of reactive and interactive messages by the three networks. Listserv mediated messages were significantly less interactive than either Usenet or Compuserve SIG messages. Compuserve SIG messages were least likely to contain no reference to previous messages.

Overall, 1,450 different authors contributed messages to the corpora content analyzed here. The most frequent contributor is responsible for 39 messages, however most frequent contributors had about a dozen messages. More than two thirds of the sample of messages were written by authors who appear in the sample only once or twice. Table 4 displays interactivity and reactivity of messages by frequent contributors. Messages by the most frequent contributors (10 or more messages per author), as well as those by frequent contributors (4 to 9 messages per author), are significantly more reactive than the norm. However, messages by frequent authors are not more likely to be interactive.

Discussion

Communication theory is based on a split in levels of analysis. Individual level motivations and the building blocks for social, interpersonal relationships reside in the minds of the relational partners. But the actual social actions and relations are transacted through observable behaviors, the exchanges of messages (Watzlawick, Beavin and Jackson, 1967; Cappella, 1987, Palmer, 1994). When we come to the new reality of group CMC there is yet another split. That which is communicated, the messages, is the fruit of an unknown proportion of the participating audience—only those who actively contribute. There is a silent portion of participants about whom we can only speculate. In a time when much is spoken of virtual reality, there may be a big irony here.

The most "real" part of the social phenomenon of communication is the text exchanged—more real even than the groups, people, and emotions involved. We follow this irony by focusing an empirical lens on the real artifacts of a new kind of communication. In a departure from previous perceptions, we believe the groups formed on the net are neither pseudo (Beniger, 1987), nor imagined (if that is what virtual means, e.g. Palmer, 1994). We believe the documented presence of interactivity in the behavior of these groups is both evidence for their reality, and a mechanism for their formation.

We are still far from a theory of interactivity. But these data may bring us slightly closer. The findings reported here do not prove the proposed definition of interactivity, or its role in group CMC, namely that interactivity leads to engagement. A typical lament of communication studies is of the paucity of data. This chapter is no exception to that practice. The data reported here are based on content analysis alone. There are no behavioral correlate measures available here. We are aware of the fact that lurkers, those who read but do not contribute, are just as much part of group CMC as the active authors. There is only little dynamic, time based information in these data, content-analysis alone are unidimensional and therefore too poor to capture the full model of interactivity. And the sample was, after all, collected within a limited time period. To study interactivity in all its gore or glory, we need (but may never really have) access to simultaneous, ongoing and longitudinal reliable measures of attitudes and behaviors, in addition to communication content.

However, the central claim of this chapter, that interactivity plays a role in creating the attraction of networks and in generating their growth patterns, has some support. The contribution here is an unprecedented, cross-sectional, representative account of group CMC. These data indicate a certain relationship between interactivity and captivating/engaging communication parameters as well as discrimination between varying levels of interactivity.

The results reported here support some of the hypotheses. While there is a propensity to agree displayed in all messages, this propensity is enhanced in interactive messages, along with (and maybe despite) the fact that interactive messages are more opinionated. Interactive messages are significantly more humorous, and more likely to contain self disclosure. Interactive messages are more than twice as likely to contain first-person plural pronouns in reference to members of the list, indicating that interactivity is associated with a sense of involvement and belonging. In addition, there are significant structural correlates of interactivity. The networks differ in the interactivity and reactivity of their messages.

The single unsupported hypothesis is the predicted association between frequency of contributions by the author and interactivity. Frequent authors write significantly more reactive messages, but are just as likely as all others to write interactive messages.

These data contain indirect validation of the construct of interactivity itself: (1) Not all networked content is interactive. Interactivity is a variable. In other words: messages, threads and groups can be more or less interactive. Group CMC is not necessarily interactive. In fact, it is more often humorous, playful or reactive. But it can be interactive. (2) The continuum leading from no interactivity through reactive messages, to fully interactive sequences received some substantiation. These data discriminate well (by nature of the messages, differences between networks, and the qualities of messages written by frequent contributors) between interactive, reactive and other messages. In other words: interactivity is a richer construct than a plain dichotomy; and, (3) several postulated behavioral correlates of interactivity were shown to covary with the interactivity of messages. In other words: it matters whether messages, threads or groups are interactive.

In summary, the interactivity construct is, at once, deceptively simple and profoundly (perhaps dangerously) predictive. The underlying hypotheses about interactivity suggest that less interactive uses of the net are not likely to see stable memberships. Individuals may come, but they will not tarry. While less interactive groups may be or become large, active or famous, they may be doomed to a rotating-door, shifting existence. In such groups there could be many who stop to visit, but few would be netted to stay because the content offerings are reactive at best. On the other hand, interactive groups are more likely to sustain their memberships, and yield other desired outcomes, such as symmetry in contributions, creativity and productivity, agreement, humour, and sense of belonging. Interactivity is related to longevity too. Therefore, it can turn from just a theoretical construct to practical use as well. Longevity of groups in this (stability) sense has obvious implications for the planning of nets, their management, and issues of ownership, pricing, and control.

Future work on interactivity can try to address the theoretical as well as the practical aspects. Will the speculations just outlined prove true? Is it possible to increase interactivity through structural interventions? Baseline measures of the content of public, large scale group CMC are now available. Longitudinal follow-ups, in which the comprehensive trend is measured, are obviously indicated.

Our data give rise to, but do not answer, a few curious questions. Does interactivity relate to group size? Is there a negative correlation between group size and interactivity? Is there an optimal size of group in the CMC context, analogous to the case in small groups? Does interactivity act the same in synchronous contexts?

Acknowledgments

ProjectH was made possible by ProjectH members. The full list of our membership with addresses and affiliations is available as part of the ProjectH technical report (cited below). ProjectH enjoyed the support of the following organizations and foundations: Comserve (vm.its.rpi.edu) sponsored the project and unwittingly endowed it with a name. Sponsorship is granted to research groups whose activities fall within the ambit of Comserve's aims to promote CMC-related research. The sponsorship includes a private hotline, listserv services and disk space for archiving logs. A grant from Compuserve provided access to archives and downloading time. The Recanati Fund provided funds for some computing resources and coordinating time. The network resources of the Key Centre of Design Computing, University of Sydney, Australia (arch.usyd.edu.au) was used extensively throughout the project: anonymous ftp site for archiving of ProjectH material (key documents, coding formats, database, papers related to the project), system aliases for distribution lists, an account for processing data, and disk space.

CHAPTER ELEVEN

"It Makes Sense"

Using an Autoassociative Neural Network to Explore Typicality in Computer-mediated Discussions

Michael R. Berthold, Fay Sudweeks,
Sid Newton, and Richard D. Coyne

As the global mesh of computer networks expands at an exponential rate, reaching into homes and organizations, and high-speed network highways provide a medium for communication and community formation on a scale that has never been feasible before, new mores are created. The virtual groups that were largely a phenomenon of education and scientific institutions are populating other domains and are changing communication practices and social structures.

The network is populated with people who invest varying amounts of time and energy in communicating on computer mediated discussion groups with other people they have mostly never met face-to-face. The groups that form vary along a continuum of communication interrelatedness. Why does this social phenomenon occur? More importantly, why do groups differ in communication styles?

Rafaeli and his coworkers (Rafaeli, 1986, 1988; Rogers and Rafaeli, 1985; Rafaeli and Sudweeks, 1997) argue that the variable that affects the interactive nature of messages, threads and groups is the theoretical construct of interactivity—the degree to which communication transcends reaction. Interactivity is a pivotal measure of the social dynamics of group communication.

In this chapter, we use a connectionist model to analyze and explore the features of messages that typically initiate or contribute to longer lasting threads. The data set comprises 3000 postings to 30 news groups classified on 46 variables or groups of features. In the context of categorization, each variable equates with a reference point or feature within some information setting. Our findings give further support to the construct of interactivity as a variable of communication settings.

A key component of human thought is our ability to identify distinct categories or classes of information, which imposes order on an otherwise amorphous, continuous mass of sensory input.

The classical view of categories is that they carve the world according to well-defined natural boundaries (Smith and Medin, 1981; Pulman, 1983). Categories are defined in terms of necessary and sufficient features: all members of a category share necessary features, therefore entities that have sufficient necessary features of a category are members of that category. This classical theory of categorization was established during the time of Aristotle and only recently has been questioned. Experimental evidence during the 1970s demonstrated that members of a category vary in typicality—in how good an example is of its category. Category boundaries are thus ill-defined, if they exist at all. What does exist are points of reference to which comparisons are made and which are combined in different ways depending on the particular context (Newton, 1992; Smith and Medin, 1981; Rosenman and Sudweeks, 1995). Rosch (1978), for example, claims that not all of the defining features of a category are necessary and that the more typical the example, the "better" the membership of the category. The most typical members are referred to as prototypes. One way of representing a prototype is through an actual instance of a member, referred to as an exemplar. There is considerable evidence to support the notion of an exemplar (Kahneman and Tversky, 1973; Collins and Loftus, 1975) but it remains extremely difficult to formulate its structure. How, for example, is the degree of correspondence (i.e. the similarity) between candidate and exemplar determined?

The most structural interpretation of similarity is based on features. The features are used to codify the known members, and act as a reference against which a decision about the membership of some candidate entity can be gauged. In its most trivial form, membership is determined on the basis of a candidate having a minimum threshold number of features in common with the category representation. Interestingly, the list of features that form the summary representation of a category (the prototype) are not necessarily realizable as an actual instance. There may be no member of the category which matches the prototype on every feature. Thus we have a notion of non-necessary, modal features.

The major limitation of the approach is that membership is determined on the basis of some critical sum of the weighted features. The best-known applications of this process are the "contrast" (Tversky, 1977) and "spreading activation" or "connectionist" (Collins and Loftus, 1975; Rumelhart and McClelland, 1986) models. In both cases, membership is determined on the basis of both similarity and dissimilarity. In the contrast model, ratings are summed statically; in the spreading activation model, weights are applied dynamically to coerce other features into play. Groups of features are formed, and these groups use their combined weights to force incompatible features out of consideration. In this sense, categories *emerge* over several iterations, and final groupings represent the summary features of an implied category (Coyne and Yokozawa, 1992). Categories are implied by the example entities used as input to the training part of the connectionist approach.

Statistical analyses, such as a Euclidean cluster analysis, provide techniques for identifying correlations between particular features in a given data set, which is a useful indication of where the aggregation (boundaries) within a data set might appear. This form of analysis is widely recognized as providing a static view of data (a snapshot of typical and atypical instances) as the clusterings are based entirely on pair-wise correlations. In human cognition, the clusterings are more dynamically created across all features synchronously. As features are drawn into particular groupings they form dynamic allegiances that can effectively overrule the original cohesion based on a simple pair-wise correlation. This dynamic clustering is the effect to be explored in this chapter.

The connectionist (or autoassociative neural network) approach (Rumelhart and McClelland, 1986; Hertz, Krogh and Palmer, 1991; Mehra and Wah, 1992) exploits a distributed description of each particular message (instance) as a pattern of activation across all features (nodes). A particular clustering of features (category) emerges as the network stabilizes on a particular pattern of activation. Each message is described in terms of features, such as relevance, time, tone and so on. The pattern of activation captures complex information about dependencies between combinations of features.

In identifying typicality in mediated discussions, a profile emerges of the features of messages that engage the attention of others, encourage participation, and predict the formation and/or maintenance of interactive communication settings.

The Data

The data set was created by ProjectH (Sudweeks and Rafaeli, 1996), a large group of researchers who collaboratively collected a representative sample of computer mediated discussions. More than a hundred people from fifteen countries used computer networks to plan, organize and implement a quantitative study of social and linguistic dynamics in public news groups and mailing lists. Batches of 100 messages were downloaded from randomly selected discussion groups on Usenet, Bitnet and Compuserve and coded on 46 variables (see Rafaeli et al (1993) for a detailed description of the methodology).

Preprocessing

UNIX scripts were used to precode each batch of 100 messages on mechanical variables (e.g. "coder-id," "list-id," and "author-id") and sent to coders to complete the remaining 40 variables. To accommodate a range of skills and technology, code forms were developed for different platforms. On completion, coders returned the full batch of coded messages for automatic processing. Each code form had an *awk* script to check syntax and to convert the data into a format suitable for most statistical packages. Other awk scripts checked field values for validity and consistency, and returned records with errors (e.g. missing values, values out of coding range, wrong message numbers, non-numeric codes). Error-free records were saved in a directory and the sender notified the number of records completed and outstanding. On completion of 100 error-free messages, the records were added to the database.

In all, 4,322 messages were coded of which 1,000 were double coded for reliability purposes, 2,000 were single coded, and 322 were partially coded batches. The partially coded batches were excluded, and one of each double coded list was chosen randomly resulting in a database of 3,000 messages.

Postprocessing

The database was converted to a form ready for processing by a neural network. First, the author-id, coder-id and message-id were deleted. Second, the date and time stamp were converted to two new entries, one indicating day of week and the other time of day (worktime, evening, night).

Third, three new entries were computed since the exploration of the nature of threads was a main focus of analysis:

- *Reference-depth:* how many references were found in a sequence before this message.
- *Reference-width:* how many references were found, which referred to this message.
- *Reference-height:* how many references were found in a sequence after this message.

These entries were extracted from the original database, but were not present in individual entries, because they refer to sequences of references.

The final list, now containing 51 entries per message was recoded to better suit a neural network by coding each of these entries individually. Because the original coding scheme has several options per entry (such as 4 different classifications for the number of lines of a message (<10, 10-25, 25-100 and >100) each entry was split into as many *features* as the entry had options. In the case of the number of message lines this led to four features, each of them having only two possible values: 1 (or ON), indicating the feature is present; or 0 (OFF), indicating the feature is absent. Note that each group of features, which resemble one entry in the original database, always has one option chosen—that is, each group of features is mutually exclusive. The re-coding resulted in 149 binary features in the new database. Table 10 lists all entries and how they are split into groups of features.

Autoassociative Neural Networks

Autoassociative neural networks (ANN) are special kinds of neural networks used to simulate (and explore) associative processes. Association in these types of neural networks is achieved through the interaction of a set of simple processing elements (called "units"), which are connected through "weighted connections." These connections can be positive (or "excitatory"), zero (which indicates no correlation between the connected units), or negative ("inhibitory"). The value of these connections is learned through the training process of the ANN. During training, patterns are presented to the network and the weights are gradually adjusted in a way that the final pattern of connectivity matches all patterns being presented. One complete presentation of all patterns with which the network is trained is called one "epoch." Usually a network requires many such epochs to perform satisfactorily. The weights can therefore be seen as a distributed representation of the data.

The interpretation of the units on the other hand can be manifold, for example they can represent aspects of things ("features") or they can symbolize certain actions or goals. Yet another possibility would be that single units represent an hypothesis about certain properties of a model.

In a more formal way an ANN can be defined by the following properties:

a set of n units, operating in parallel, each of them having an *activation rule a_i*, which leads to a *state of activation* $(a_1,...,a_n)$ resulting in an *output vector* $(o_1,...,o_i,...,o_n)$ using an *individual output function $o: = F_i(a_i)$)* for each of the units. These output-values are transferred using a set of *weighted connections* w_{ij} between units. And a *learning rule* is used to modify the weights w_{ij} to learn properties of specific *training examples*.

Figure 1 illustrates one unit of an ANN. In most cases the activation rule is nothing more than a weighted sum with an additional individual threshold θ_i:

$$a_i = \sum_{i=1}^{n} w_{i,j} o_j + \theta_i \tag{1}$$

The purpose of the output function is mainly to ensure that the output value stays in a predetermined range. Usually the so called step function

$$o_i^l(a_i) = \begin{cases} 1: a_i \geq 0 \\ 0: a_i < 0 \end{cases} \tag{2}$$

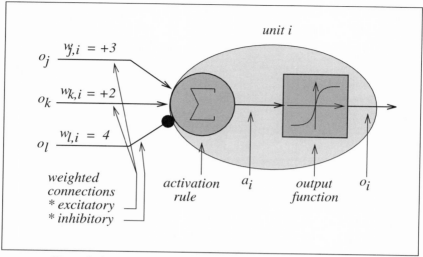

Figure 1. An example of one unit of an autoassociative neural net.

or a sigmoid is used (see figure 2 for a graph of both functions):

$$o_i^s(a_i) = \frac{1}{1 + e^{\beta a_i}}$$

(3)

The latter has the advantage of being differentiable which is a requirement for many learning algorithms since they compute the derivative of the error.

For the case of θ_i being 0 and the step activation function, the units will become active (or *fire*) if the sum of all excitatory stimuli is greater than the sum of all inhibitory stimuli. The threshold θ_i is only used to shift the zero point of the activation function. This threshold allows units to have an a priori excitatory or inhibitory state which has to be overcome by external influences.

Figure 3 shows an example of an ANN with three units. An additional pseudo-unit is used to model the threshold values. It has a constant value of +1 and is connected via weighted connections to the normal units. Note that we do not include weights with value zero, e.g. there is an arc between the threshold unit and unit 2, but since the value of the corresponding weight is zero it is not shown. The usual convention of drawing excitatory weights as arrows and inhibitory weights as lines ending in a point is used here.

To compute the state of activation of such a network, two methods were presented by Rumelhart and McClelland (1986). In the case of a *synchronous update*, the new activation value of all units is computed at once and then assigned to the outputs at the next point in time. Since this method can lead to oscillations in the output values, another method is often used, the *asyn-*

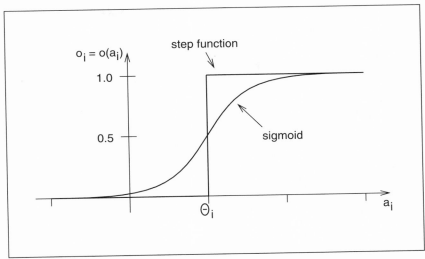

*Figure 2. The two most commonly used output function,
the step function and a sigmoid.*

chronous update (Hopfield, 1981), in which a unit's activation is updated and propagated to its output immediately. The order in which the units are updated is random every time. This method of computation usually avoids oscillations.

Of course, if this straightforward method of computing the state of activation for the network was used, one might get stuck in a local minima. Because the state the computation is started from is very important and the units updated first have a major influence on the final outcome, a stochastic way of updating activations is normally used. An additional parameter, called *temperature* (T) is introduced and is used to cool the system down over time. Instead of using the step function to compute the output of a specific unit a function is used that introduces an undeterministic behavior:

$$p_i = \frac{1}{1 + e^{\frac{\beta a_i}{T}}}$$

Figure 4 shows the probability distribution for two different settings of the parameter T. This equation computes the probability for unit i to fire (or have an output value of 1).

Using this technique an *annealing schedule* defines the cooling process. Usually it starts with a very high temperature where most activations are mainly chosen randomly and the temperature declines in an exponential manner until it reaches a point where the stochastic influence is almost nonexistent (the network *freezes*). The lower the temperature gets, the weaker the influence of the temperature gets, and the network behaves more and

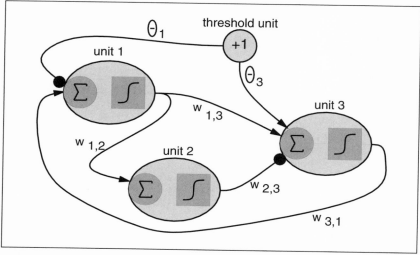

Figure 3. An example for an ANN.

Three units are connected to each other via excitatory (arrows) and inhibitory (lines ending in dots) connections. In addition a threshold unit with a constant value of +1 is shown. Note that connections with a zero-weight are not drawn.

more deterministically and the output of the units is more likely to be equal to the value computed by the step function. This methodology can be proven to provide an optimal solution under certain circumstances.

The "animals in one room" example illustrates the use of ANNs.

The "Animals In One Room" Problem

This is a famous computer-science problem. Assume there is a room with four possible inhabitants: dogs, cats, mice, and elephants:

- *Dogs.* Dogs chase cats (and since these are big dogs, they are stronger than cats too), don't care about mice and get stepped on by elephants.
- *Cats.* Cats kill mice and get chased by dogs, but they are too fast for the elephants.
- *Mice.* Mice frighten elephants and get killed by the cats, dogs just ignore them.
- *Elephants.* Elephants are frightened of mice and step on dogs, but not cats since they are too fast.

An appropriate network to model these facts would be one with four units, each representing the absence or presence of one the above species. Each of these units is connected to all of the other units with a weighted (uni-direc-

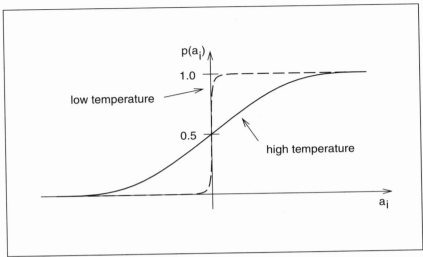

Figure 4. The probability distribution for a unit to fire,
depending on the activation value.

The influence of the temperature is illustrated, a low temperature leads to an almost deterministic behavior, at a high temperature the output is almost random for small activation values.

tional) connection, originating at one animal *(A)* and pointing to another animal *(B)*. If this weight is zero, animal *A* doesn't threaten animal *B*; on the other hand if the weight is negative (or inhibitory) animal *A* threatens (steps on, chases, kills) animal *B*. The case that the weight is positive (or excitatory) doesn't occur in this example, as this would resemble animal *A* liking animal *B*. In this example only threatening factors are considered. A positive weight could be used to model for example that the cat would actually like to be in a room with a mouse, but this would lead to a more complex network. Figure 5 shows the connections between the four units together with a threshold-unit.

The excitatory weight from the threshold unit (having a constant output of +1) is used to ensure that at least one animal will be present. Otherwise a trivial solution (no animal in the room) would be enough to satisfy all constraints of the network. The final matrix of interconnections is shown in table 1.

For larger networks this matrix is usually displayed graphically as shown in figure 6.

This network can now start to cool down in a random state and the asynchronous update of the units executed until the temperature reaches zero and the activations of the units reach a constant state (the network *settles*), i.e. the calculation of the activation value of each unit from the sum of all weighted

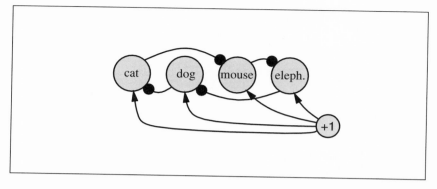

Figure 5. The animals in one room network.

Only connections with nonzero weights are shown, negative (inhibitory) weights are shown as lines ending in a point, arrows indicate a positive (excitatory) weight. The relationship between the different animals ("who threatens whom") is clearly shown. The excitatory weights originating at the threshold unit ensure the presence of at least one animal in the room.

from/to	cat	dog	mouse	elephant
cat	—	0	−1	0
dog	−1	—	0	0
mouse	0	0	—	−1
elephant	0	−1	0	—
bias	+0.5	+0.5	+0.5	+0.5

Table 1. The interconnection matrix for the dog-cat-mouse-elephant network.

incoming activations compared with the threshold value does not change the state of the network anymore. Several iterations are usually necessary to reach this final state. The network will always settle in a state which represents a room occupied by a combination of animals who won't threaten each other (for example elephants and cats, but no dogs and mice).

If one of the units is forced to be *on* (or having an output value of 1), the energy landscape of the network will change and the only states it will settle in will have this particular unit to be *on* as well. This forcing (or *clamping*) of units restricts the feature space of solutions to a sub-space and therefore eliminates unwanted solutions.

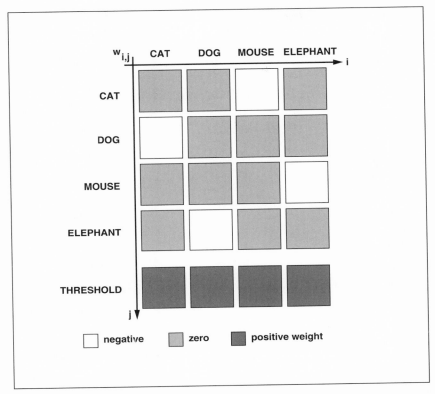

Figure 6. A graphical way of displaying the weights of the example network. This kind of diagram is often used for large weight-matrices.

The Hebbian Training Procedure

In the previous example the weights were assigned from common knowledge about the behavior of animals. Here we show how weights can be calculated automatically from examples. The Hebbian learning rule (Rumelhart and McClelland, 1986) trains the network through the presentation of examples and successive alterations of the weights.

The training examples are presented to the network one after the other, each unit is inspected and the weights leading to this unit (and therefore influencing its activation) are adjusted according to the following rules:

- When unit A and B are simultaneously excited (or correlated), increase the strength of the connection between them.
- When unit A and B are counter-correlated, decrease the strength of the connection between them.

This adjustment can be done by simply inspecting each of the units, comparing its activation and the activation of the units where the connection originates, and decreasing or increasing the weight accordingly.

In the previously used example one would use a database with several possible examples of animals in the room and use this to train the network. The network would pick up relationships between animals and adjust its weights accordingly. For example, since mouse and cat will never appear together weights connecting the corresponding units would only decrease (and thus become inhibitory), never increase.

For more complex tasks a more sophisticated training algorithm is used, but it is still based on the described method. It employs a stochastic component and also makes use of the thresholds. In the following section, a more advanced algorithm will be used.

Applying an ANN to 3,000 Messages

The network used for the experiments presented in this chapter, an autoassociative neural network, will be described in the following subsection.

The ANN

Because the data consisted of 149 features, each taking a value of either 0 or 1 after processing, the network has 149 binary units. This leads to 149*149=22,201 weights and 149 thresholds to adjust during training.

The idea of this type of network is to present each of the 3,000 training patterns to the network and adjust the weights in a way which stores the information contained in each of the patterns. Each unit is connected via a directed arc with each other unit and thus allowing them to have an excitatory (positive weight) or inhibitory (negative weight) influence on each other individually. The pattern of connectivity (or *weight matrix*) will be explored in the results section.

The annealing schedule for pattern completion started at a temperature of $T = 500$ and declined exponentially in 100 steps to its final value of $T = 0$. During each step 20 asynchronous updates of all units were performed.

Training a Network with Over 20,000 Weights

Training this neural network obviously requires millions of computations. In this case the network consists of 22,350 parameters (22,201 weights and 149 threshold values) to adjust and to update each of them 149 activations have to be computed, each of them requiring again 150 weighted summations.

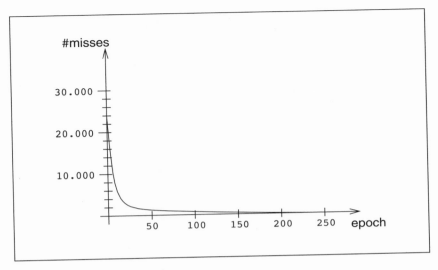

*Figure 7. The decreasing number of misses versus training time
is shown in this graph.*

After five days of training, when the error finally reached a plateau, training was stopped.

This has to be done for each of the 3,000 patterns in the database, which leads to a required computation of over 65 million weighted summations (or *connections*) plus roughly the same amount of compare- and update-operations per epoch. Almost 100 hours of CPU-time were spent before the error-rate of the network started to settle on a plateau (see figure 7) after five days.

Figure 8 shows a weight diagram. Each of the weights is presented as a small rectangle. Its color indicates the value of the corresponding weight: black means a negative value, grey equals zero and white indicates a positive weight.

Results Drawn from the Trained ANN

In this section, we will take a closer look at the weight matrix and its interpretation, and describe the creation of typical examples and typicality sets of features.

Interpreting the Weight Matrix

Looking at the weights (figure 8), one interesting property comes to mind. Using the 149*150 = 22,350 weights the network is able to recall the 3,000 messages almost perfectly. 3,000 * 149 = 447,000 *on/off*-informations (or

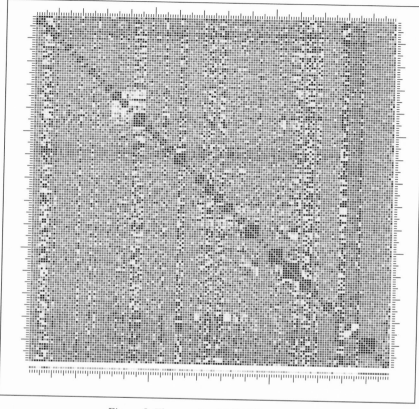

Figure 8. The matrix of 149*149 weights.

Dark grey means a negative value, lighter grey values indicate positive weights. The bottom row of points represents the threshold values of each unit.

bits) are stored in approximately 67,000 bits (each weight stores about 3 bits), a compression factor of close to one order of magnitude! In addition the access to common features of all messages is much easier using the neural network compared to a global search in the whole database.

A closer look at the weight matrix shown in figure 8 gives some interesting insights. Here only a few examples are listed.

The dark squares along the diagonal line show that all features of one group are mutually exclusive, only one of them can have the value 1 at a time. This results in strong inhibitory connections from one feature to all others in one group and can be seen as a block of black points along the diagonal with a size according to the number of features in this group.

Some excitatory connections (shown by white squares at the corresponding position): in column 1, corresponding with the feature MSGLINES-A (1-10 lines of original text, see also table 10) and row 13 (OPINION-A = no opinion is stated) an almost white square indicates a strong excitatory connection from unit 1 to unit 13. This leads to the conclusion that short messages (1) state no opinion (13). However this does not mean that short messages always state no opinion, but it is a property of the database the network picked up. It is still possible that other units inhibit unit 13 much stronger and therefore it is not always going to be active when unit 1 is active. Column 1, row 43: short messages (1) request information (43). Column 33, row 1: unformatted messages (33) are short (1). Another inhibitory connection (black square): if message contains artistic icon(s) (54, 55) it is *not* short (1).

Of course, those observations can only reveal relations between a few of the networks' units. To explore the dependencies between all of the 149 units, especially under certain conditions (usually modeled through clamped units), the network has to settle in a state with low energy. Clamping of units can be used to restrict the space the neural network is exploring to find a solution. In the case of the ProjectH-ANN this technique was used to define certain properties of a message and let the network determine which other features are correlated.

The creation of *typical examples* for specific features being *on*, will be discussed in the next subsection.

Creating Typical Examples

To create a typical example the feature(s) that are required to be present in the *feature set* are clamped and the network settles at the typical pattern. This worked well in the work described in Coyne and Yokozawa (1992) but in the case of the ProjectH-Network, there are several states the network can settle in, mainly due to the fact that the input data is not free from noise and not all of the units are going to be strongly correlated to other units (or correlated at all). This would be analogous to a very rough and elastic energy landscape. It is elastic because every move is going to change activations of states and those changes are again changing the energy landscape. Therefore the random update of the states will not always result in the same final state for the network. Instead one would expect the unaffected states to behave randomly and therefore the number of different states can be quite high.

But if the network is allowed to settle several times, each time starting from a different random starting state and using another random order for the asynchronous update, some features occur more frequently in the final states than others. Table 2 shows the frequency of 1's occurring for some features when feature 29 (message contains humour) was clamped.

The list in table 2 only contains a few of the 149 total features, but it illustrates quite well how some features are strongly correlated to the feature that

no	description	#1's
1	LINES-A: 1-10 lines of real msg	40%
2	LINES-B: 11-25 lines of real msg	50%
3	LINES C: 26-100 lines of real msg	10%
4	LINES D: >100 lines of real msg	0%
5	SUBJECT-A: no subject line	5%
6	SUBJECT B: subject line is appropriate	95%
7	SUBJECT C: subject line is inappropriate	0%
21	QUESTION-A: no question/request contained	70%
22	QUESTION-B: contains question/request	30%
28	HUMOR-A: no humor contained	0%
29	HUMOR-B: contains humour	100%
33	FORMAT-A: unformatted	25%
34	FORMAT-B: minimal formatted	35%
35	FORMAT-C: mostly formatted	35%
36	FORMAT-D: overformatted	5%
56	GENDER1-A: can't tell author gender	0%
57	GENDER1-B: female	20%
58	GENDER1-C: male	80%
112	FLAME2-A: no abusive language	100%
113	FLAME2-B: abusive language about content only	0%
114	FLAME2-C: abusive language about person	0%
115	FLAME2-D: abusive language about general others	0%
116	FLAME2-E: mixture	0%

*Table 2. The frequency of feature activations for feature no 29
(message contains humor) clamped.*

The columns show the number of the feature, its description and the frequency of *on*-activations.

was clamped and others are not correlated at all. For example, nonhumorous messages seem to be gender specific, since feature 58 (GENDER-C, male) is *on* 80% of the 20 experiments that were conducted. On the other hand, considering that almost 75% of all messages were written by males, the significance of this information might not be very high. Also, nonhumorous messages do not contain abusive language, as the strong response on feature

112 shows. Interesting is feature-group 33-36. Here none of the features has an exceptionally high occurrence. This leads to the assumption that a message containing humour does not depend on the formatting. This feature group seems to be not *significant* to feature 29.

This process can be done for all features separately or for combination of features clamped together. The result will be a list of features, each with an indication of how often the network settled in a state which had this particular state being *on*. This information can be used to produce typicality sets as shown in the next section.

Typicality Sets of Features

Because the primary focus of analysis is correlations between features, it is interesting to extract a set of typical features from the output of the ANN. An a priori specified threshold (Θ) can be used to choose features for this set. If every two members of the typicality set are required to have appeared at least 60% of all times together, the following computes Θ:

$$\Theta = 100\% - n(100\% - p) = (1 - n)100\% - np$$

with $n = 2$ and $p = 60\%$. This leads to a threshold Θ of 80%. If a higher likelihood for the appearance of features together (p) or a higher number of features occurring together (n) is desired, the threshold of selection (Θ) will increase.

The example from the previous section is again used to show its typicality set (see table 3). This table shows which features seem to be highly correlated with feature 29. But so far there is no information about the quality of the list. It could well be that one or even several of these features appear in almost every typicality set and are not well suited to distinguish between different message types. On the other hand a feature could most of the time just behave randomly and it was necessary to score the *sensitivity* of each feature.

Scoring Features and Sensitivity

Of course, some of the features in the typicality set might not be as interesting as others. Some features are typical for almost all messages and therefore will be *on* no matter which feature is clamped. A feature behaving like this is called *insensitive*. To distinguish between sensitive and insensitive features, the features have to be ranked or scored in a way that indicates the sensitivity of the feature to the clamping of other features. This information is hidden in the distribution of 1s over all typicality sets for single features (this leads to 149 typicality sets, one for each feature). For the further analysis the percentage of 1s in the case of a clamped feature was compressed into 5 classes:

no.	label	description
6	SUBJECT-B	subject line is appropriate
9	NOISE-B	regular msg
18	APOLOGY-A	no apology
26	CHALLENGE-A	no challenge/bet/dare
38	STYLE1-B	regular capitalization
53	ARTICON-A	no artistic icons
58	GENDER1-C	male
68	QUOTE1-A	no quoted text from this list
72	QUOTE2-A	no CMC text quoted from outside list
95	COALIT2-A	no first person plural
98	COALIT3-B	addresses other person
112	FLAME2-A	no abusive language
117	FLAME3-A	no intention to prevent/calm tension
120	STATUS-A	no identification of status
126	SIGNAT2-A	no ending quotation
145	EVENING	6pm–12am

Table 3. The typicality set for feature 29 (message contains humor).

$\oplus$ between 80% to 100% of 1s in one experiment
+ 60% to 80% of 1s in one experiment
• 40% to 60% of 1s in one experiment
– 20% to 40% of 1s in one experiment
Θ 0% to 20% 1s (or 100% to 80% 0s) in one experiment

Taking again the example where feature 29 is clamped, table 4 shows a few of those classifications.

Taking all 149 typicality sets it is easy to compute 5 global values for each feature, the frequency with which the feature was covered by that specific class over all experiments. Table 5 shows a few examples from the table of all features.

With these five numbers a number can be computed to measure what sensitivity of a feature really means. If for example the percentage of $\oplus$s for one feature is a perfect 100%, this specific feature is always *on*, but since it is never *off* it does not really help to *distinguish* between different classes of messages. It does however tell us about a typical message in the whole set database. On the other hand, a feature having 50% $\oplus$ and 50% Θ would be much better suited to group messages in the database, in fact this is the best case one could imagine. Somewhere in between are features with unbalanced

no.	description	#ls	class
1	LINES-A: 1-10 lines of real msg	40%	•
2	LINES-B: 11-25 lines of real msg	50%	•
3	LINES C: 26-100 lines of real msg	10%	Θ
4	LINES D: >100 lines of real msg	0%	Θ
21	QUESTION-A: no question/request contained	70%	+
22	QUESTION-B: contains question/request	30%	—
28	HUMOR-A: no humor contained	0%	Θ
29	HUMOR-B: contains humour	100%	$\oplus$
33	FORMAT-A: unformatted	25%	—
34	FORMAT-B: minimal formatted	35%	—
35	FORMAT-C: mostly formatted	35%	—
36	FORMAT-D: overformatted	5%	Θ
56	GENDER1-A: can't tell author gender	0%	Θ
57	GENDER1-B: female	20%	—
58	GENDER1-C: male	80%	$\oplus$

...

Table 4. The frequency of feature activations for feature 29 (message contains humour) clamped. The last column shows the classification.

percentages of $\oplus$ and Θ. To generate a unifying score for all features the following four heuristics were chosen:

1. A sensitive feature has at least one $\oplus$ (apart from the case where that feature was clamped) and one Θ.
2. A feature is more sensitive than another one if the number of $\oplus$ is better balanced to the number of Θ.
3. A smaller number of +, • and – indicates a sensitive feature.
4. An insensitive feature has either no Θ or no $\oplus$ and a high number of +, • and −.

These heuristics lead to the following way of computing the *sensitivity* s_i of a feature i:

$$
s_i = \begin{cases} \dfrac{(N(\oplus + N(\Theta)) * (\min\{N(\oplus), N(\Theta)\})}{\max\{N(\oplus), N(\Theta)\}} \\[2ex] \dfrac{N(\Theta) + N(\oplus)}{N(\text{—}) + N(\bullet) + N(+)} \end{cases} \quad \begin{array}{l} : N(\Theta) \neq 0 \wedge N(\oplus) \neq 0 \\[2ex] : N(\Theta) = 0 \vee N(\oplus) = 0 \end{array}
$$

with N(*) returning the frequency of the symbol passed as an argument. The

no.	label	description	Θ	—	•	+	⊕	score
28	HUMOR-A	no humor	1%	12%	32%	42%	12%	+1
29	HUMOR-B	contains humor	13%	42%	32%	11%	0%	−23
33	FORMAT-A	unformatted	53%	39%	6%	0%	0%	−66
34	FORMAT-B	minimal formatted	34%	49%	13%	2%	0%	−49
35	FORMAT-C	mostly formatted	17%	42%	30%	8%	0%	−28
36	FORMAT-D	overformatted	90%	9%	0%	0%	0%	−93
40	STYLE2-A	no colloquial spelling	4%	14%	22%	43%	16%	+5
41	STYLE2-B	contains colloquial spelling	17%	43%	22%	14%	2%	+2
56	GENDER1-A	can't tell	100%	0%	0%	0%	0%	−100
57	GENDER1-B	female	75%	22%	2%	0%	0%	−82
58	GENDER1-C	male	2%	0%	3%	38%	56%	+2

Table 5. A few examples of scored features.
For each feature the percentage of times it got classified as being in a specific class is shown and the final score resulting from these classifications is listed in the last column.

sensitivity-score $s_i \epsilon$ [−100, +100} and s_i =+100 in the best case, where both ⊕ and Θ occur 50% of all times (and therefore −, • and + occur not at all) and the worst case (s_i = −100) having no ⊕ or Θ but only —, • and +. Table 5 shows a few examples from the 149 features.

Table 5 shows how some features are not very sensitive towards the activations (caused by clamping) of others. A good example would be the format of the messages (FORMAT-A to FORMAT-D), all features have a negative sensitivity score because none of them appears in another typicality set besides its own. In contrast the STYLE2-entry has for both features positive scores. Looking at the table it becomes clear why. STYLE2-A appears in 5% of all typicality sets and is completely absent in 4% of all messages. Almost the same goes for STYLE2-B, it is absent for 17% and included in the typicality set for 2% of all cases. As expected, none of the features reached the perfect score of +100.

Typicality in CMC

The previous section described how typicality sets for single features can be generated by an autoassociative neural network. For an analysis of typicality in CMC, and especially an investigation of threads and their characteristics, some typicality sets are more interesting than others.

To analyze the nature of threads the comparison of a message which starts or continues a thread versus a message that ends a thread is interesting. Figure 9 shows a reference-tree to illustrate the used terms *reference-width*, *reference-height* and *reference-depth*.

The thread is the longest path from the top down into one of the branches in this tree. In the example this would be the path starting at A leading over B, E, G and K to L. Message E in this figure is being referenced directly by four messages (F, G, H and I) and results therefore in *reference-width* = 4, the same message E references a sequence of two messages (B and A), measured by *reference-depth* = 2 and is referenced by another sequence of three messages (G, K and L) leading to a *reference-height* of 3. Note that several of these messages could have been written by the same author. Different labels in this example only indicate different messages, not different authors.

To characterize a good versus. a bad message in the sense of participation in a thread the variable reference-width was used. A message is called good if it as at least referenced by one other message, it *participates* in a thread. In contrast a bad message is not referenced at all, it does not participate in a thread. Clamping the corresponding features (134, *no messages are referencing this message*; 135, *1-2 references to this message*) leads to two typicality sets for the two types of messages being investigated. They are shown in tables 6 and 7.

Interestingly the two typicality sets have several features in common. This is due to the fact that not every feature is sensitive to every other one. In addition some of the features have a low sensitivity-score meaning that they are not sensitive at all to other features. To create the final typical good and bad message, features appearing in both typicality sets will be deleted from both sets and features with a too low sensitivity score will be discarded too. This leads to tables 8 and 9 and finally enables us to extract some properties of the messages in the database:

- A good message has medium length (2) and an appropriate subject line (6).
- A statement of a fact (17) also enhances the chances of being followed-up.
- If during an already ongoing thread one introduces a completely new topic (87), the chances of getting a response are slim. This point seems to be a very strong one, regarding the high sensitivity score of that specific feature.
- Interesting also is that a message which does not reference seems likely not to be referenced. But the sensitivity score of this feature is reasonably low, which makes sense, otherwise threads would never start. But this dis-

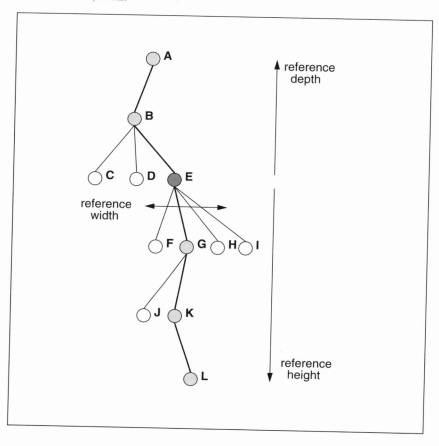

Figure 9. A reference-tree, illustrating the terminology.

A thread starts with message A and the last message participating is L. Message E is referenced by four messages (*the reference-width*), references itself a sequence of two message (*reference-depth*) and is referenced by a sequence of three messages (*reference-height*).

covery indicates that the start of a thread is not an easy task. Being followed-up when one already participates in a thread is much easier.

Conclusions

We have described an approach to use autoassociative neural networks to explore typicality in computer mediated discussions. We showed how to train

no.	feature description	sensitivity-score
2	11-25 lines of original text	1
6	subject line is appropriate	1
12	contains verbal self-disclosure	1
17	contains statement of a fact	1
21	no question/request	1
26	no challenge/bet/dare	1
38	regular capitalization	2
47	no emoticons	2
50	no punctuation device to express emotion	3
53	no artistic icons	1
58	male	2
60	identifies gender via name/signature	3
68	no quoted text from this list	2
72	no CMC text quoted from outside list	2
98	addresses other person	1
112	no abusive language	2
120	no identification of status	1
126	no ending quotation	1

Table 6. The typicality set of a referenced message.
Clamped feature: 135 (MSGWIDTH-B: 1-2 references to this message.

an ANN and how the final weight matrix can be used to extract relationships between variables. We then used the neural network to extract typicality sets for specified features and showed how messages which support threads (good messages) can be distinguished from those messages not participating in a thread (bad messages).

This approach can be used to act as a preprocessor for a more detailed statistical analysis, concentrating on the subsets of features already discovered by the neural network. The ANN would thus only be used to discover feature-groups that are correlated and further statistics would concentrate on the strength and statistical significance of those correlations.

In addition the approach presented here provides insights into the quality of the database. There are several blocks of features that are strongly correlated while other features are only loosely or not at all connected. In contrast to the example used by Coyne et al. (1993), noise from coder-errors as well as differences on opinionated variables (as described by Rafaeli and Sud-

no.	feature description	sensitivity-score
12	contains verbal self-disclosure	1
26	no challenge/bet/dare	1
28	no humour	1
38	regular capitalization	2
53	no artistic icons	1
68	no quoted text from this list	2
80	no previous msg referenced by this msg	4
87	new topic, no reference to previous discussion	18
95	no first person plural	1
112	no abusive language	2
117	no intention to prevent/calm tension	2
120	no identification of status	1
126	no ending quotation	1
128	no previous msg referenced by this msg	2
131	no references after this msg	9

Table 7. The typicality set of a nonreferenced message.
Clamped feature: 134 (MSGWIDTH-A: no references to this message).

weeks (1998) result in a database which is not as well structured as artificial ones.

The possibilities using an ANN are far from being exhausted and several features are well worth exploring: STYLE2, for example, which has both high sensitivity scores for all features of the group and a fairly unbalanced frequency distribution (see table 10 for a listing). This would be another way of exploring threads. But also an analysis about the quality of interactivity could be performed, by using feature-group DEPEND3, which describes the manner in which previous messages are referenced. Yet another example is GENDER3 which is also a feature group with a good distribution and high sensitivity-scores. GENDER3 codes the fact that gender-identification is an issue. The same approach can also be used to find features that are a typical for messages. Features with a very low sensitivity-score and a typical value of 0 have a strong negative correlation with almost every other feature. This would lead to an anti-message within a typicality set.

no.	feature description	sensitivity-score
2	11-25 lines of original text	1
6	subject line is appropriate	1
17	contains statement of a fact	1
21	no question/request	1
47	no emoticons	2
50	no punctuation device to express emotion	3
58	male	2
60	identifies gender via name/signature	3
68	no quoted text from this list	2
72	no CMC text quoted from outside list	2
98	addresses other person	1

Table 8. Typical distinguishing features of a referenced (or good) message.

no.	feature description	sensitivity-score
80	no previous msg referenced by this msg	4
87	new topic, no reference to previous discussion	18
95	no first person plural	1
131	no references after this msg	9

Table 9. Typical features of a nonreferenced (or bad) message.

Obviously only a very specific kind of neural network was used for this analysis—more architectures are being published every day. The ANN was chosen because the autoassociative structure supports the emergence of examples; if the main focus of analysis were on only a few variables, a feedforward architecture would also be feasible. An approach using feedforward neural networks would create a network to *classify* examples rather than create an environment for emerging examples. If a localized receptive field network (Moody and Darken, 1989) were used the prototypes represent typical

		deleted		
		recoded, see no. 52		
		deleted		
		deleted		
		recoded, see no. 51		
		recoded, see no. 50		
1	LINES-A	1-10 lines of original text	66.4%	-53%
2	LINES-B	11-25 lines of original text	22.2%	+1%
3	LINES-C	26-100 lines of original text	8.7%	-83%
4	LINES-D	>100 lines of original text	2.4%	-97%
5	SUBJECT-A	subject line is inappropriate	15.1%	-92%
6	SUBJECT-B	subject line is appropriate	81.8%	+1%
7	SUBJECT-C	no subject line	2.4%	-99%
8	NOISE-A	msg not intended for this list	5.6%	-76%
9	NOISE-B		89.4%	+2%
10	NOISE-C		4.8%	-100%
11	FIRSTPER-A	no verbal selfdisclosure	64.6%	-63%
12	FIRSTPER-B		35.1%	+1%
13	OPINION-A	no opinion is stated	50.9%	-36%
14	OPINION-B	opinion stated, not main item	30.2%	+1%
15	OPINION-C	opinion stated, is main item	18.5%	-70%
16	FACT-A	no statement of a fact	45.1%	-84%
17	FACT-B	contains statement of a fact	54.6%	+1%
18	APOLOGY-A	no apology	93.3%	+1%
19	APOLOGY-B	contains mild apology	4.5%	-99%
20	APOLOGY-C	contains clear apology	1.9%	-98%
21	QUESTION-A	no question/request	71.9%	+1%
22	QUESTION-B	contains question/request	27.8%	-66%
23	ACTION-A	no call for action	90.7%	-39%
24	ACTION-B	call for action, not main item	6.4%	+3%
25	ACTION-C	call for action, is main item	2.6%	-72%
26	CHALLENGE-A	no challenge/bet/dare	95.9%	+1%
27	CHALLENGE-B	contains challenge/bet/dare	3.8%	-82%
28	HUMOR-A	no humor	80.5%	+1%
29	HUMOR-B	contains humor	19.2%	-23%
30	METACOM-A	no metacommunication	85.2%	+1%
31	METACOM-B	metacommunication, not main item	8.6%	-91%
32	METACOM-C	metacommunication, is main item	5.9%	-74%
33	FORMAT-A	unformatted	13.3%	-66%
34	FORMAT-B	minimal formatted	64.5%	-49%
35	FORMAT-C	mostly formatted	19.6%	-28%
36	FORMAT-D	overformatted	2.2%	-93%
37	STYLE1-A	minimal or no capitalization	20.4%	-96%
38	STYLE1-B	regular capitalization	77.2%	+2%
39	STYLE1-C	mostly or all capitalization	2.0%	-100%
40	STYLE2-A	no colloquial spelling	89.0%	+5%
41	STYLE2-B	contains colloquial spelling	10.6%	+2%
42	NATURE-A	provides information	39.4%	+2%
43	NATURE-B	requests information	16.4%	-95%
44	NATURE-C	persuasive	3.5%	-89%
45	NATURE-D	opinionated	18.5%	-89%
46	NATURE-E	mixed style	21.1%	-71%

Table 10. The list of final features.

23	EMOTICON	47	EMOTICON-A	no emoticons	88.1%
		48	EMOTICON-B	contains 1 emoticon	8.6%
		49	EMOTICON-C	contains >1 emoticon	2.9%
24	EMODEVICE	50	EMODEVICE-A	no punct device to express emotion	88.0%
		51	EMODEVICE-B	contains 1 punctuation device	7.3%
		52	EMODEVICE-C	contains >1 punctuation device	4.4%
25	ARTICON	53	ARTICON-A	no artistic icons	94.9%
		54	ARTICON-B	contains 1 artistic icon	2.5%
		55	ARTICON-C	contains >1 artistic icon	2.2%
26	GENDER1	56	GENDER1-A	can't tell	13.6%
		57	GENDER1-B	female	14.3%
		58	GENDER1-C	male	71.9%
27	GENDER2	59	GENDER2-A	does not identify gender	19.4%
		60	GENDER2-B	identifies gender via name/signature	75.6%
		61	GENDER2-C	identifies gender directly	1.1%
		62	GENDER2-D	identifies gender indirectly	2.2%
		63	GENDER2-E	mixture	1.5%
28	GENDER3	64	GENDER3-A	no gender specific terms re others	79.1%
		65	GENDER3-B	gender specific terms regarding others	20.6%
29	GENDER4	66	GENDER4-A	no gender identification issue	94.8%
		67	GENDER4-B	gender identification is an issue	4.9%
30	QUOTE1	68	QUOTE1-A	no quoted text from this list	70.4%
		69	QUOTE1-B	1-10 lines of quoted text	22.2%
		70	QUOTE1-C	11-25 lines of quoted text	5.4%
		71	QUOTE1-D	>26 lines of quoted text	1.6%
31	QUOTE2	72	QUOTE2-A	no CMC text quoted from outside list	95.8%
		73	QUOTE2-B	1-10 lines of CMC text quoted	1.2%
		74	QUOTE2-C	11-25 lines of CMC text quoted	1.0%
		75	QUOTE2-D	>26 lines of CMC text quoted	1.6%
32	QUOTE3	76	QUOTE3-A	no non-CMC text quoted	92.5%
		77	QUOTE3-B	1-10 lines of non-CMC text quoted	3.9%
		78	QUOTE3-C	11-25 lines of non-CMC text quoted	1.8%
		79	QUOTE3-D	>26 lines of non-CMC text quoted	1.4%
33	DEPEND1	80	DEPEND1-A	no prev msg referenced by this msg	30.9%
		81	DEPEND1-B	1 previous msg referenced	52.0%
		82	DEPEND1-C	>1 previous msg referenced	5.9%
		83	DEPEND1-D	a sequence of msgs is referenced	10.7%
34	DEPEND2			recoded, see nos. 47-49	
35	DEPEND3	84	DEPEND3-A	no reference to manner of a prev ref	88.7%
		85	DEPEND3-B	reference to the manner of prev ref	11.0%
36	DEPEND4	86	DEPEND4-A	clearly part of an ongoing thread	69.2%
		87	DEPEND4-B	new topic, no ref to prev discussion	23.3%
		88	DEPEND4-C	new topic, ref to previous discussion	7.1%
37	COALIT1	89	COALIT1-A	strong agreement with previous msg	6.5%
		90	COALIT1-B	mild agreement	8.4%
		91	COALIT1-C	no indication, neural	67.3%
		92	COALIT1-D	both dis- and agreement	4.7%
		93	COALIT1-E	mild disagreement	8.5%
		94	COALIT1-F	strong disagreement	4.2%
38	COALIT2	95	COALIT2-A	no first person plural	89.9%
		96	COALIT2-B	contains first person plural	9.8%

Table 10. The list of final features (continued).

39	COALIT3	97	COALIT3-A	does not address other persons	64.2%	-67%
		98	COALIT3-B	addresses other person	35.5%	+1%
40	COALIT4	99	COALIT4-A	strong agreement (outside list)	6.2%	-14%
		100	COALIT4-B	mild agreement	3.7%	-97%
		101	COALIT4-C	no indication, neutral	81.8%	-80%
		102	COALIT4-D	both dis- and agreement	2.3%	-91%
		103	COALIT4-E	mild disagreement	3.0%	-92%
		104	COALIT4-F	strong disagreement	2.5%	-90%
41	FLAME1	105	FLAME1-A	neutral or no opinion	57.4%	-18%
		106	FLAME1-B	friendly opinion	27.1%	-35%
		107	FLAME1-C	diverging opinion	6.5%	-100%
		108	FLAME1-D	disagreeing	4.1%	-100%
		109	FLAME1-E	tension	2.2%	-91%
		110	FLAME1-F	antagonistic	1.6%	-97%
		111	FLAME1-G	hostile	0.6%	-100%
42	FLAME2	112	FLAME2-A	no abusive language	95.9%	+2%
		113	FLAME2-B	abusive language about content only	1.1%	-98%
		114	FLAME2-C	abusive language about person	0.9%	-97%
		115	FLAME2-D	abusive language about self/general	0.9%	-100%
		116	FLAME2-E	mixture	0.7%	-100%
43	FLAME3	117	FLAME3-A	no intention to prevent/calm tension	95.6%	+2%
		118	FLAME3-B	tries to prevent tension	1.8%	-99%
		119	FLAME3-C	tries to calm ongoing tension	2.2%	-88%
44	STATUS	120	STATUS-A	no identification of status	87.9%	+1%
		121	STATUS-B	status is identified	11.9%	-99%
45	SIGNAT1	122	SIGNAT1-A	no signature	29.1%	+2%
		123	SIGNAT1-B	simple signature	49.7%	-25%
		124	SIGNAT1-C	complex signature	15.6%	-98%
		125	SIGNAT1-D	artistic signature	5.3%	-99%
46	SIGNAT2	126	SIGNAT2-A	no ending quotation	87.5%	+1%
		127	SIGNAT2-B	contains ending quotation	12.0%	-95%
47	PREDMSG	128	PREDMSG-A	no prev msg referenced by this msg	32.7%	+2%
		129	PREDMSG-B	1-2 previous msgs referenced	44.5%	-92%
		130	PREDMSG-C	>2 previous msgs referenced	22.7%	-75%
48	SUCCMSG	131	SUCCMSG-A	no references after this msg	61.4%	+9%
		132	SUCCMSG-B	1-2 references after this msg	25.8%	-21%
		133	SUCCMSG-C	>2 references after this msg	12.7%	-93%
49	MSGWIDTH	134	MSGWIDTH-A	no msgs are referencing this msg	61.4%	+9%
		135	MSGWIDTH-B	1-2 msgs are referencing this msg	36.0%	+2%
		136	MSGWIDTH-C	>2 msgs are referencing this msg	2.5%	-91%
50	WEEKDAY	137	MONDAY		8.1%	-97%
		138	TUESDAY		9.7%	-97%
		139	WEDNESDAY		19.0%	-42%
		140	THURSDAY		19.7%	-75%
		141	FRIDAY		14.4%	-100%
		142	SATURDAY		13.9%	-96%
		143	SUNDAY		15.0%	-77%
51	WORKTIME	144	WORKTIME	8am-6pm	20.6%	-98%
		145	EVENING	6pm-12am	50.7%	+2%
		146	NIGHT	12am-8am	28.7%	-95%
52	LIST-ID	147	COMPUSERVE		30.0%	-79%
		148	BITNET		36.6%	+1%
		149	USENET		33.3%	+10%

Table 10. The List of Final Features (continued).

examples for each class and the radii and weights of those reference vectors are indicators for the value and generality of the example.

The approach we presented in this chapter is obviously capable of extracting a form of relationships between features, but the ANN-approach also helped to verify tentative hypotheses pertaining to computer-mediated communication as most results reported by the neural network did *make sense*.

Acknowledgement

This work was supported by a University of Sydney Research Grant (URG).

CHAPTER TWELVE

Modeling and Supporting Virtual Cooperative Interaction Through the World Wide Web

Lee Li-Jen Chen and Brian R. Gaines

The growth of the Internet has provided major new channels for the dissemination of knowledge. Increasing international connectivity has made the Internet accessible to special-interest communities world wide, and electronic mail and list servers now provide a major communications medium supporting discourse in these communities. Until recently, limitations on the presentation quality of on-line file formats restricted the publication capabilities of the Internet to rapid dissemination of files printable in paper form. However, advances in on-line presentation capabilities now allow high-quality typographic documents with embedded figures and hyperlinks to be created, distributed, and read on-line. Moreover, it has become possible to issue *active documents* containing animation and simulations and supporting user interaction with computer services through the document interface. The major part of this functionality has become accessible through the protocols of the World Wide Web, and the web itself is seen as a precursor to an *information highway* subsuming all existing communications media.

The development of the Internet has been very rapid, with little central planning. Despite its widespread use, there is little information about the social dynamics of Internet technologies. Many systems have been developed to cope with the information overload generated by direct access to the Internet. One common feature among the wide variety of indexing and search tools now available is the support they provide for selective attention and awareness in the communities using the net. It would be useful to analyze the design issues and principles involved in these tools in terms of the knowledge and discourse processes in the communities using these tools.

This chapter provides a model of the virtual cooperative interaction on the World Wide Web in terms of discourse and awareness and uses it to classify the types of support tools existing and required.

Computer-Mediated Communication (CMC)

It is tempting to consider the Internet as a new publication medium in which electronic documents emulate paper ones, and where the issues of basic human factors are those of indexing and information retrieval. This makes the vast existing literature on information retrieval, its techniques and human factors, relevant to the net. However, this addresses only one aspect of computer-mediated communication (CMC), neglecting its function of supporting discourse within communities. Much of the information retrieved from the net is generated as needed through discourse on list servers—the Internet is a mixed community of publications and intelligent human agents that both store knowledge and generate it on demand. When the information needed cannot be found through retrieval, then it may be requested through discourse, a phenomenon prophesied in the early days of timeshared computing:

> No company offering time-shared computer services has yet taken advantage of the communion possible between all users of the machine ... If fifty percent of the world's population are connected through terminals, then questions from one location may be answered not by access to an internal data-base but by routing them to users elsewhere—who better to answer a question on abstruse Chinese history than an abstruse Chinese historian. (Gaines, 1971)

The society of distributed intelligent agents that is the Internet community at large provides an "expert system" with a scope and scale well beyond that yet conceivable with computer-based systems alone. Computer-based discovery, indexing and retrieval systems have a major role to play in that community, but are only one aspect of Internet information systems.

Krol (1993) captures the essence of these considerations in Internet RFC1462, which replies to the question "What is the Internet" with three definitions:

1. a network of networks based on the TCP/IP protocols,

2. a community of people who use and develop those networks,

3. a collection of resources that can be reached from those networks.

These are complementary perspectives on the net in terms of its technological infrastructure, its communities of users, and their access to resources, respectively. Models of CMC must take into account all three perspectives: how agents interface to the network; how discourse occurs within communities; and how resources are discovered and accessed (Gaines and Chen, 1996).

In recent years we have witnessed new phenomena on the emerging net and novel social studies about them, for example, interactivity in CMC (Rafaeli, 1988; Rafaeli and Sudweeks, 1997); *flaming* (Mabry, 1997); theatrical performance on IRC (Danet, Ruedenberg and Rosenbaum-Tamari, 1997);

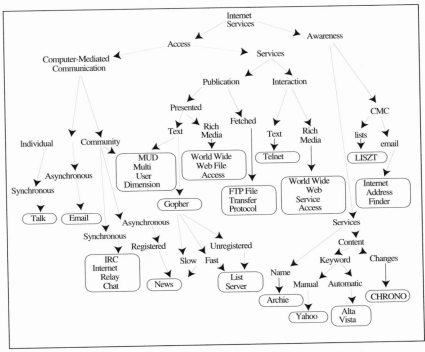

*Figure 1. Internet services in terms of dimensions of
computer-mediated communication.*

rhetorical dimensions and control structures on news group (Jones, 1997; Smith, McLaughlin and Osborne, 1997); and theoretical mirrored social constructs in MUD (MacKinnon, 1997). Those and many other engaging issues are covered in chapters throughout this book.

Dimensions of CMC

In examining the utility of the Internet and World Wide Web, it is useful to classify all the major services. They are classified by the significant distinctions that determine the relative utilities that characterize major net services in terms of their utility for CMC, access to services, or search (Gaines, Shaw and Chen, 1996).

Figure 1 is a concept map presenting the major services on the Internet in terms of a small set of fundamental distinctions:
- At the top level, the major Internet services are characterized in terms of their utility for access to resources or awareness of resources.

- Access is subclassified as to discourse, publications or services.
- Discourse is subclassified by whether it is agent-to-agent discourse or community discourse—synchronous with the agents conversing in real time or asynchronous with substantial time delays in responses.
- Asynchronous community discourse is subclassified by whether the channel is slow or fast, and whether the community is centrally registered or not.
- Publications are subclassified by whether they are just fetched or presented when fetched as text or rich media.
- Services are subclassified by whether they are text or rich media.
- Resource awareness is subclassified by whether it is by resource name or content; by keywords or by change in contents; by keywords generated manually or automatically.

The less well-known systems classified are: *Internet Address Finder,* which provides an index of e-mail addresses; LISZT, which assists users in searching for a list server by its name; and *CHRONO* (Chen, 1995), which indexes a World Wide Web site in reverse chronological order to provide automatic "what's new" pages. MUDs, multi-user dungeons/dimensions, are interesting because they provide a mix of services supporting both discourse and resource access. World Wide Web browsers such as Netscape are interesting because they provide a single tool that can access nearly all the services shown except talk and chat (Gaines, Chen and Shaw, 1997).

Cooperative Interactions and Communities on the Internet

The exponential growth of the World Wide Web and the growing availability of collaborative tools and services on the Internet have facilitated innovative knowledge creation and dissemination infrastructures. These infrastructures include electronic libraries, digital journals, resource discovery environments, distributed coauthoring systems, and virtual scientific communities. Collectively, the World Wide Web and Internet can be considered a large scale groupware for supporting special interest communities.

Large scale groupware differs not only in the quantity, but also in the quality of cooperative interaction (Dennis, Valacich and Nunamaker, 1990). The fundamental nature of interaction on the World Wide Web can be characterized as *virtual cooperative interaction.* The word "virtual" has two senses here: first, it denotes the notion of *virtual space,* i.e., cooperative interaction occuring in a nonphysical space that allows participants to be situated in geographically separate locations; second, it denotes that the *intent* to engage in cooperative interaction itself may not necessarily pre-exist or be conscious. Traditional notions of groupware focus on the first sense (telepresence in virtual space), but there is a need to extend the notion of cooperative interaction to encompass the latter sense of virtual cooperative interaction (Chen and Gaines, 1996a).

Frequently, information resource contribution and exchange on the World Wide Web involve cooperative interaction without preplanned coordination. In fact, participants on the World Wide Web may have no intent to cooperate in the first place. Quite often, a resource provider and a resource user are unaware of each other's existence until their first interaction. Nevertheless, the interactive process between them is still loosely cooperative in nature. It differs from traditional team-oriented cooperation where group tasks, goals, and purposes are usually well defined.

A classical *social exchange* model like the Interactional Matrix model (Kelly and Thibaut, 1978; Cook, 1987) cannot readily account for this unusual form of cooperation, where resource providers might not know the identity of their resource users but continue to contribute anyway. On the World Wide Web, the only feedback might be the frequency of accesses to the provider's information resources. What do providers gain in return for such a seemingly one-way cooperative interaction? Is it simply an expression of altruism? What are some possible motivations to contribute to the World Wide Web? In general, how would one ensure the continual contribution of an information provider? These questions can be answered more clearly in the context of *socioware*, which we define as computer-mediated environments for supporting community-wide processes that expedite virtual cooperative interactions. Information inquiry and response, dissemination of ideas, and social networking are examples of virtual cooperative interactions. USENET news groups and list servers are two prototypes of socioware that support dialogues within well-defined special-interest communities on the Internet.

The proliferation of personal home pages with cross-linkage of World Wide Web pages by people who share common interests has made the exploration process on the World Wide Web (i.e., net surfing) a *social experience*. Such a seemingly intrinsically rewarding experience can often be characterized as serendipitous, not necessarily task-oriented (as in traditional groupware).

Through home pages, individuals create their own *virtual persona* on the World Wide Web without any awareness of who their eventual audience might actually be (i.e. without *extensional awareness* of particular recipients). However they often have a sense of who the potential audience might be (i.e. with *intensional awareness* of the type of recipient). Sometimes individuals provide information resources as a by-product during some self-organization processes of their own knowledge. As observed earlier, this form of apparently cooperative behavior is prevalent on the World Wide Web.

In essence, the goal of socioware is to facilitate emergent prosocial behaviors for self-organized, virtual collaborative communities.

Conceptual Model of Virtual Cooperative Interaction

This section describes a detailed model for encompassing collaborative activities supported by traditional groupware and emergent socioware. The model analyzes the following five basic elements for virtual cooperative interactions in computer-mediated environments (CMEs):

1. Discourse patterns,

2. Time-dimension of virtual interactions,

3. Awareness hierarchy,

4. Motivations for cooperative behaviors,

5. Emergence and maintenance of virtual cooperative interaction.

Together these elements present three aspects (what, why, and how) of the conceptual model: (1) the descriptive aspect, comprised of the first three elements which characterize and classify virtual cooperative interactions; (2) the prescriptive aspect that provide motivational reasons for individuals to participate in virtual cooperative interactions; and (3) the operational aspect of how virtual cooperative interactions initiate and function.

Some Definitions

Before describing the conceptual model in detail, the definitions of some frequently used terms in the model are introduced in this subsection.

The term *social entrainment* refers to some endogenous biological and behavioral processes that are captured and modified in their phase and periodicity, by powerful (internal or external) cycles or pacer signals. The notion of entrainment contains two kind of synchrony: (1) The *mutual entrainment* of endogenous rhythms to one another; and (2) the *external entrainment* of such a rhythm by powerful external *signals* or *pacers* (McGrath, 1990).

When individuals participate in virtual cooperative interactions, depending on the nature of their present focus (e.g., discussing an idea or coreviewing a book), a natural cognitive processing time is involved in each activity. This processing time generates an endogenous rhythm within individual participants. This natural rhythm of interactions, in turn, creates *mutual entrainment* in sustaining continuation of virtual cooperative interactions. The processes of social entrainment are important in the time-dimension of virtual cooperative interaction.

A collaborative community can be seen as a group of individuals who provide resources to one other. The most significant dimension of the community is the *awareness* of who is providing a particular resource and who is using it (Chen and Gaines, 1997). Logically, resource awareness can be further distinguished as *extensional awareness* because the specific resource and provider are known. It is contrasted to *intensional awareness* in which only the characteristics of suitable resources or providers are known.

A Punctuated Discourse Model of CMCs

Recent developments on the Internet have been moving away from conversation and toward demonstration. This general trend is typified by the recent virtual explosion of voice, color, picture, and motion that seemingly overshadow plain ASCII traffic in ideas and emotions. Nevertheless the essence of the net remains categorically a medium for conversation (McLaughlin, 1984). Interactivity is one of the key qualities of discourse made possible by CMCs (Rafaeli, 1988; Rafaeli and Sudweeks, 1997). It remains a defining feature for conversations generally, and an especially curious one when the conversations are not held in physical proximity (Rafaeli, McLaughlin and Sudweeks, 1997). In this section, we propose an integrative model of discourse patterns that incorporates the current major innovations and services on the Internet.

Figure 1 presents a conventional model of Internet services in terms of their utility, but it does not provide an integrative model of the way in which they support communities. Such a model can be developed by noting what distinguishes discourse from publication. In discourse it is expected that the recipient will respond to the originator. Publication, however, is generally a one-way communication. However, on list servers some material is published by originators who expect no specific response, yet other materials are published where response is elicited or received.

One useful perspective for studying group CMC is interactivity. As noted previously (Rafaeli, 1988), there are at least three modes of communications on the net: one-way, two-way (reactive), and interactive (Rafaeli and Sudweeks, 1997). Hence CMC offers a very flexible medium that breaks down the conventions of other media. The following diagrams show the different characteristics of the main Internet services in terms of these issues.

Figure 2 shows e-mail discourse as a cycle of origination and response between a pair of agents communicating through a computer-mediated channel.

Figure 3 extends figure 2 to show list server discourse as a cycle of origination and response between agents that is shared with a community through a computer-mediated channel. The community involvement leads to more complex discourse patterns in that the originator may not direct the message to a particular recipient; there may be multiple responses to a message; and

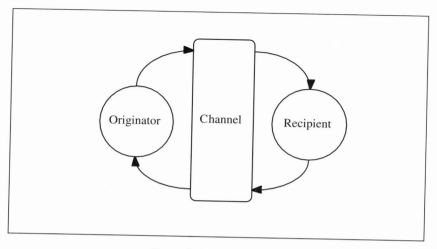

Figure 2. E-mail discourse.

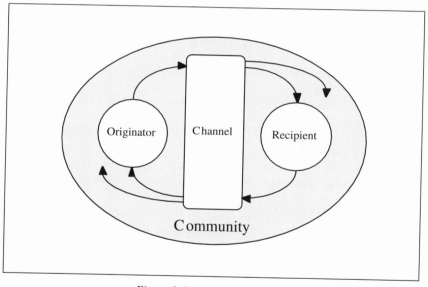

Figure 3. List server discourse.

the response from the recipient may itself trigger responses from others who did not originate the discourse. For a particular discourse sequence this leads to a natural division of the community into active participants who respond and passive participants who do not.

Figure 4 modifies figure 3 to show World Wide Web publication as an ac-

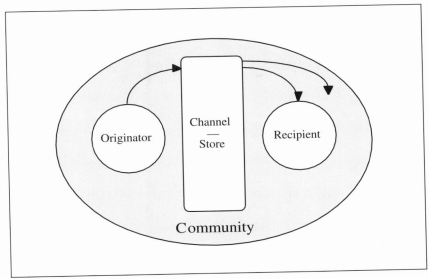

Figure 4. World Wide Web publication.

tivity in which the channel is buffered to act as a store also. The material published is available to a community and the originator is unlikely to target it to a particular recipient. Recipients are not expected to respond directly to the originator, but responses may occur through e-mail or list servers or through the publication of material linked to the original. Because the published material is not automatically distributed to a list, recipients have to actively search for and discover the material.

The common structure adopted for the diagrams is intended to draw attention to the commonalties between the services. List server discourse is usually archived and often converted to hypermail on the web. World Wide Web publications do trigger responses through other services or through links on the World Wide Web. A search on the web may not discover a specific item but rather a related item on a news group or list or by an author, and result in an request for information to the news group, list, or author. Individuals and communities use many of the available Internet services in an integrated way to support their knowledge processes.

Figure 5 subsumes figures 2 through 4 to provide an integrated model of Internet knowledge processes that capture all the issues discussed. It models the processes as discourse punctuated by the intervention of a store allowing an indefinite time delay between the emission of a message and its receipt. It introduces two major dimensions of analysis: the *times* for each step in a discourse cycle; and the *awareness* by originators of recipients and vice versa.

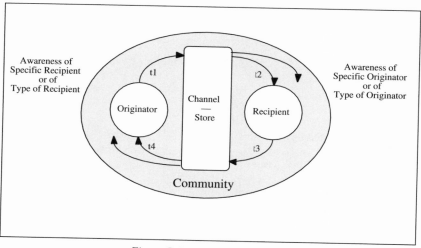

Figure 5. Punctuated discourse.

Time Structure of Punctuated Discourse

The four times shown in figure 5 are:

$t1$: the origination time—the time from a concept to its expression and availability

$t2$: the discovery time—the time from availability to receipt

$t3$: the response time—the time from receipt to expression and availability of a response

$t4$: the response discovery time—the time from response availability to receipt

Note that agent processing times and channel delays have been lumped. A study focusing on the impact of communication delays would want to consider them separately; otherwise there is no significant distinction—a general principle might be that communication delays should not be greater than agent processing times. Note also that the diagram is, to a large extent, symmetrical—the recipient becomes an originator when responding.

An important overall parameter is *time cycle:* the round-trip discourse time, $t1 + t2 + t3 + t4$. If this is small, (a few seconds or less) we talk in terms of synchronous communication. If it is large, (a few hours or more) we talk in terms of asynchronous communication. If it is infinite, (no response), we talk in terms of publication. However, this analysis shows that there is a continuous spectrum from synchronous through asynchronous to publication.

The discovery times $t2$ and $t4$ are very significant to publication-mode discourse. Attempts to reduce them have lead to a wide range of awareness-support tools that aid potential recipients in discovering relevant material and originators to make material easier to discover.

The Time Dimension in Virtual Cooperative Interaction

Awareness and coordination of cooperative interaction involve the processes of *social entrainment*. This subsection examines the relationship between the time cycle of virtual cooperative interactions and the relative strength of extensional and intensional awareness.

When two or more individuals participate in virtual cooperative interaction, they often take on the dual roles of originator and recipient in punctuated discourse. Gradually they become locked into *social entrainment* processes. Computer-mediated environments, such as news groups (Resnick et al, 1994) and shared drawing systems (Ishii and Kobayashi, 1992), provide specific external signals that set the pace for virtual cooperative interactions between participants. For example, the average *time cycle* for posting to a news group and receiving feedback is about one to a few days, whereas the partial time cycle ($t1+ t2$) for moving a mouse cursor in a real-time shared drawing system is approximately one to ten seconds. *External entrainment* occurs when the *actual* time cycle of a virtual interaction falls into the range of the *expected* time cycle anticipated by individual participants. When there is a wide discrepancy between the expected and the actual time cycle of interaction, participants often feel frustrated and decrease their desire to interact. For example, if cursor movements in a shared drawing system begin to take more than a few seconds to complete, the participants will tend to stop their interaction.

Continuation of virtual cooperative interaction can also break down when mutual and external entrainment processes are not synchronized with one another. When coreviewing a book, the natural time cycle for mutual entrainment is in days and weeks, since it often take that amount of time to read a book and absorb the material properly. It is unlikely that coreviewers will want to use Internet Relay Chat (Reid, 1991) to disseminate and exchange their reviews. Such a fast time cycle of interaction is not well suited for activities involving deep, reflective cognitive processes.

The relationship between the time cycle and the relative strength of *extensional/intensional awareness* in virtual cooperative interactions can be illustrated in a time-dimension diagram (figure 6). If the time cycle is relatively short, say in few seconds or minutes, we have an interaction that can be characterized as synchronous (real-time). If it is longer, we have interaction that is often described as asynchronous (delay-time). The key notion here is that the types of virtual cooperative interactions are differentiated on a temporal continuum rather than by discrete categories.

In intensionally oriented interactions, the level of intensional awareness is

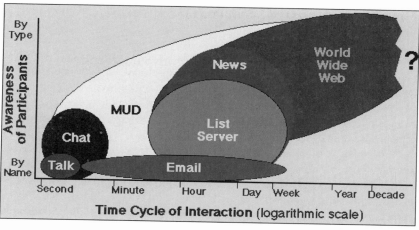

Figure 6. Time Dimension of Virtual Cooperative Interaction.

relatively high compared to extensional awareness, whereas in extensionally oriented interactions, extensional awareness predominates. Many groupware systems (e.g., coauthoring systems and shared workspace systems) have been designed to support collaborative teams in which interactions are between known group members. Therefore, in these CMEs, the virtual cooperative interactions focus on extensional awareness. In contrast, interactions in USENET news groups involve both extensional and intensional awareness of the targeted audience. For example, one can respond to a question from a specific individual (an extensionally oriented interaction) but do so publicly with the intention to address others who may have a similar question in mind (intensionally oriented interaction).

The time cycle in virtual cooperative interaction often varies according to cognitive processes involved in any given moment of an activity. For example, during a collaborative writing session (Neuwirth et al., 1994), when coauthors' focus is on correcting sentences or paragraphs, the time cycle involved is usually around a few minutes; when they focus on reviewing chapters, the time cycle involved shifts to hours. Therefore, coauthoring systems are classified in the range of time cycles from seconds to days, in addition to being extensional oriented.

The time dimension diagram of virtual cooperative interactions allows us to visualize CMEs in terms of an *interaction area* that they encompass as shown in figure 6. The area denotes the range of time cycle and the degree of intensional versus extensional awareness (Chen and Gaines, 1996a). In the figure, the question mark indicates that the World Wide Web has been operating for such a short period that any long-term estimates of its impact as a publication medium are speculative projections (Gaines, Chen, and Shaw, 1997).

Awareness Structure of Punctuated Discourse

A community can be regarded as a set of agents that provide resources to one other. The most significant dimension relating to the coordination of the community is that of the *awareness* of who is providing a particular resource and who is using it. In a tightly-coupled team, each person is usually aware of who will provide a particular resource and often when they will provide it. In logical terms, this can be termed *extensional awareness* because the specific resource and provider are known, as contrasted to *intensional awareness* in which only the characteristics of suitable resources or providers are known.

In a special interest community, resource providers usually do not have such extensional awareness of the resource users, and, if they do, can be regarded as forming teams operating within the community. Instead, resource providers usually have an *intensional awareness* of the resource users in terms of their characteristics as *types* of users within the community. The classification of users into types usually corresponds to social norms within the community, such as the ethical responsibilities in a professional community to communicate certain forms of information to appropriate members of the community. Resource users in a special-interest community may have an extensional awareness of particular resources or resource providers, or an intensional awareness of the types of resource providers likely to provide the resources they require. This asymmetry between providers and users characterizes a special-interest community. It also leads to differentiation of the community in terms of core members of whom many users are extensionally aware, and subcommunities specializing in particular forms of resources.

In the community of Internet users at large, there is little awareness of particular resources or providers and only a general awareness of the set of resources is available. Awareness of the characteristics of resources and providers is vague, corresponding to *weak intensional awareness*.

These distinctions are summarized in table 1. It is clear that the classification of awareness can lead to a richer taxonomy of communities than the defined three-way division. Analysis of awareness in such terms allows the structure of a community to be specified in operational terms, and in complex communities, there will be complex structures of awareness. The coarse divisions into subteams and subspecial-interest communities provides a way of reducing this complexity in modeling the community.

The differentiation of communities in terms of awareness draws attention to the significance of supporting various aspects of awareness in a CME system. *Resource awareness*—the awareness that specific resources exist—may be supported by various indexing and search procedures. However, there is also a need to support *chronological awareness*, the awareness that a resource has changed or come into existence (Chen and Gaines, 1997). Table 1

Locus of responsibility	Team	Special-Interest Community	Community at Large
Originator	*Extensional awareness of actual recipients.* Use email to notify. Use CHRONO to index.	*Intensional awareness of types of recipient.* Broadcast to list server. Establish HTML links. Use CHRONO to index.	*No awareness of recipients, or only weak intensional awareness of types of recipients.* Broadcast to news groups. Register in Yahoo. Initialize Alta Vista.
Recipient	*Extensional awareness of actual resources and originators.* Use email to inquire. Check CHRONO index.	*Extensional awareness of actual resources and originators, or intensional awareness of types of resources and originators.* Subscribe to list server. Follow HTML links. Check CHRONO index. Use WebWatch, Katipo or URL-Minder	*No awareness of resources or originators, or only weak intensional awareness of types of resources and originators.* Read news groups. Browse Yahoo. Search with Alta Vista. Search with MetaCrawler.

Table 1. Communities and tools distinguished in terms of awareness.

also shows how current tools for awareness support are classified within this framework.

CHRONO: Chronological Awareness Support Tools

CHRONO is an HTTP server-side system that generates chronological listings of World Wide Web pages that have been changed recently at specific sites. It provides a basic awareness support that lets visitors of a web site (e.g., members of a group, an organization, or other net surfers) see which web pages have been modified since their last visit. Currently, the CHRONO system is implemented on a UNIX platform and has been made widely available for use at other sites. As shown in figure 7, CHRONO presents to the visitors an HTML document that lists the site's web-page titles in reverse chronological order. This chronological listing of web pages also functions as a collection of hyperlinks to the listed pages.

This time-line dimension allows frequent visitors to a World Wide Web site immediate knowledge of what has changed since their latest visit. The changes they see may be pages in which they have particular prior interest, or it may be new pages that they have never seen before but will appeal to them. Hence this *chronological browsing* characteristic is analogous to a *spatial (subject-category) browsing* characteristic that library patrons often experience when looking for books on open bookshelves (i.e., accidentally finding [even more] relevant books near the books that they were looking for originally).

What is different here is that instead of finding relevant information by browsing the nearby subject-categories, users may now find relevant infor-

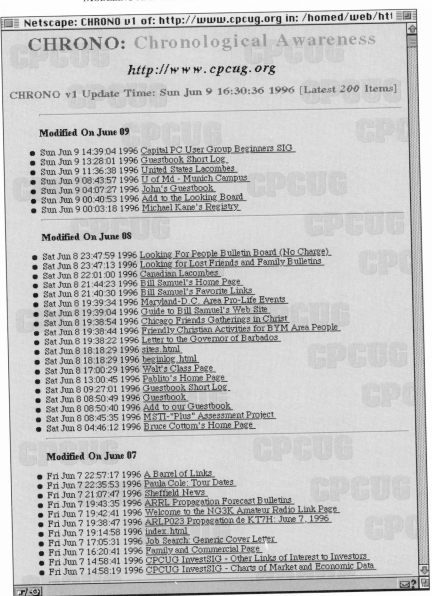

Figure 7. CHRONO in use at a PC user group site.

mation by browsing the recently modified or created web pages. Sometimes, conceptually related documents are created (or modified) around the same time: however their author(s) may not remember to update the HTML links to them. Unlike a manually updated *what's new* page, in which the users have to rely on the timely updates made by a webmaster (or by the document authors), CHRONO provides the time-line dimension to the users automatically, in a reliable, periodic fashion.

WebWatch (Specter, 1995), *Katipo* (Newberry, 1995), and *URL-Minder* (NetMind, 1995) are other chronological awareness tools that track changes in specified documents. WebWatch is a client-side chronological awareness system that keeps track of changes in selected web documents. When given an HTML document referencing URLs on the World Wide Web, it produces a filtered list that contains only those URLs that have been modified since a given time. Katipo is another client-side chronological awareness system built for Macintosh that shares many similar concepts with WebWatch. It reads through the global history file maintained by some World Wide Web browsers, checking for documents that have changed since the last time a user viewed them. It writes a report file (in HTML format) listing all such documents in a format that allows the user to visit the updated documents easily. URL-Minder is a centralized system that keeps track of resources on the World Wide Web, and sends registered users e-mail whenever their personally registered resources change. World Wide Web users can have the URL-Minder keep track of any World Wide Web resource accessible via HTTP. The resources can be anything—not just web pages that users personally maintain (Chen and Gaines, 1996b).

Each chronological awareness support system examined so far has various degrees of advantages and disadvantages. CHRONO has the advantages of: (1) simplicity of user interface; (2) support of accidental discovery where users need no extensional awareness of the newly created pages; and (3) server-side chronological awareness information on demand. It is nicely complemented by the efficiency of the targeting approach and customization capabilities of WebWatch and Katipo. Finally, URL-Minder uses e-mail as its notification channel. This feature is useful for users who use their e-mail systems more frequently than their World Wide Web browsers. Together as a whole, these chronological awareness support systems have covered a wide range of approaches in respect to major features of chronological awareness support (Chen and Gaines, 1996b).

Further Developments

The CHRONO research program is now measuring the structures and time constants of discourse on the Internet from empirical data. The rates of diffusion of information and the various knowledge acquisition paths and processes whereby individuals become aware of information on the net arecurrently being compiled and studied. List server archives are being analyzed to determine the fine structure of discourse and to track the trajectories of ideas.

CHRONO was issued in May 1996 and is now being used at a number of sites. META-CHRONO, a new program under development, will collect and collate information from multiple sites running CHRONO and provide awareness of activities being carried out on a distributed basis (Chen, 1996).

Motivations for Participation in Virtual Communities

This subsection examines the motivational dimension of virtual cooperative interaction. Here, a theory of *collective social exchange* attempts to explain the behaviors of participants in terms of exchange theory, effects of norms in virtual community, capacity of power, and social influence. These motivational explanations, together with *social learning theory* (in the next subsection), examine the fairness and reinforcement issues involved in virtual cooperative interactions.

When many individuals participate in a multitude of punctuated discourses (figure 5), a chain reaction occurs. The cumulative effect generated by this chain of inquiry-response-reaction-response-reaction (and so on) is an evolving topical thread that can become a part of *shared knowledge* among community members. Through automatic archival services such as Hypermail, or some individual efforts such as FAQs (frequently asked questions) and World Wide Web pages, the shared knowledge persists and grows. Why should individuals contribute to this pro-social process? How does the virtual community ensure that its participants will contribute to the growth of the knowledge pool?

First, why would individuals want to participate in virtual cooperative interactions? Generally, interpersonal behavior can be characterized as a *social exchange* between people, and these social exchanges typically involve both rewards and costs to participants. Generally, an individual will perform those actions that produce the greatest rewards for the least cost (Shaver, 1987). Therefore, according to this cost-benefit calculation, a perceived potential for reward must exist for individuals to participate and contribute in a cooperative relationship.

In contrast with *classical social exchange theories* (Cook, 1987) (e.g., Kelly and Thibaut's (1978) *Interactional Matrix* model), which emphasize dyadic interactions between individuals, *collective social exchange theory* focuses on interactions between individuals and their community. Conceptually, the Internet community is viewed from a *collective stance* (Gaines, 1994) as an entity with "whom" individual participants exchange information resources. This collective entity offers participants a valuable informational service, namely as *a pool of human knowledge* (Berners-Lee et al., 1994) in exchange for their contributions.

The *norm of reciprocity* is fundamental to social exchange and leads to contributing behavior. The reciprocity norm creates an obligation for repayment that must be satisfied if the interaction is to continue (Shaver, 1987). However, the way reciprocity operates in collective social exchange is more subtle than in conventional social exchange between individuals. Why should one reciprocate (through contribution) in a situation where social responsibility is relatively *diffused* among community members?

Positive *self-image* (Jones and Pittman, 1982) is one motivation for contributing to the Internet. In this case, an individual has internalized the norm of reciprocity and acts according to the principle of *equity theory*: that is, an individual will seek to maintain the ratio of rewards to costs at the same as that of relevant comparison persons (Walster, Walster and Berscheid, 1978). A sense of *guilt* would occur if individuals perceive they have not contributed enough to the community, and hence, they would want to reciprocate fairly.

Another more subtle motivation is that of contribution as an investment in *social power,* that is, the *capacity* of a person or group to affect the behavior of another person or group (Schopler, 1965). Contributions made by an individual may not only help others but also help that person to gain name recognition from his or her peers. The more one contributes publicly and receives recognition, the more one gains the capacity to influence others or the community as a whole. The added weight in recognizing who is first to contribute relevant information also motivates individuals to volunteer information resources more readily. The competition for priority in contribution has been well documented in Merton's studies on the reward system in scientific discovery (Merton, 1973).

The motivational dimension of the model illustrates the importance of *feedback loops* (Losada, Sanchez and Noble, 1990) in the reinforcement of virtual cooperative interactions. It provides a coherent explanation for the apparent altruistic behavior of information providers on the World Wide Web and Internet.

Reinforcement of Virtual Cooperative Interaction

One question raised earlier in the chapter is why people publish information resource to the World Wide Web in the first place. Usually resource providers might never know the identity of their resource users; nevertheless providers contribute even without any potential and apparent paybacks for their efforts. Two possible motivations described earlier for providing information resources on the web are: (1) to gain positive self-image; and (2) to gain name recognition. How does such a pro-social behavior initiate and continue?

The concern here is with the relationship between the *effect* of an individual's behavior in a *virtual cooperative community* and its impact on the individual's later behavior. This is the basis of *operant conditioning,* the learning process by which behavior is modified by the consequences of previous similar behavior (Ritzer, 1992). An individual emits some behavior. The community in which the behavior occurs in turn "acts" back in various ways. The reaction—positive, negative, or neutral—affects the individual's later behavior.

Social learning theory suggests that novel social behavior is first learned through imitation of actions taken by others who act as (social) models (Bandura and Walters, 1963). The reinforcement received by a model serves as information to the person about which behaviors are acceptable and appropriate for the circumstances. Once a novel action has been acquired through imitation, the probability of its continuation is dependent on the reinforcement it receives. *Vicarious reinforcement*, as well as direct reward or punishment, can play a part in social learning (Shaver, 1987).

On the World Wide Web, an individual's first successful encounter with a home page full of relevant information resources provides a positive role model for imitation. Subsequent positive net-surfing experiences will further increase the individual's exposure to other positive models. Once an individual internalizes the web culture, which encourages construction of a personal home page (and coincidentally also provides a virtual persona for self-image), that person's contribution to the web will be viewed as a pro-social behavior. The dynamic of *social exchange* then comes into play. If the costs (for example, the necessary skills and resources) of putting up information resources (such as research papers or hyperlinks to relevant web pages) are relatively low, the individual will contribute to the web. In addition, original intent to contribute to the World Wide Web community does not need to exist; using a home page to organize knowledge resources may only coincidentally contribute to the World Wide Web community (as an after thought or by-product). In this situation, the extensional audience is the individual, together with a vague sense of intensional awareness of other potential resource users.

How does reinforcement come into the picture? Frequently, one encounters home pages that have been constructed months or years ago without any revisions or new contributions. Their authors have neglected them and ceased to contribute. Once a novel behavior has been acquired, it needs to have *intermittent positive reinforcements* to sustain the behavior (Bandura and Walters, 1963). In order for reinforcement to take place, a feedback loop must exist. The round-trip cycle of virtual cooperative interaction provides an individual the necessary awareness of the *effectiveness of investment in social power,* which is crucial to reinforcing the behavior and leading to similar future actions.

An observable measurement of the effectiveness of social power on the World Wide Web is the relative popularity of web sites. The popularity of a home page can be inferred from its visitor frequency counter, commentaries in its public guest-book, awards given by reviewers of popular web sites, the number of other web pages linked to the page, etc. These gauges of popularity (which measure the relative power for social influence) provide direct reinforcements (either positive or negative) to an information provider. They also offer indirect vicarious reinforcements to other information providers by providing social models for comparisons.

Summary of the Conceptual Model

The past decade has seen the emergence of large scale collaborative activities on the Internet using e-mail, list servers, news groups, and the World Wide Web. There have also been developments of systems using some of these technologies to support smaller closely-coupled teams. In terms of the standard time and space taxonomy for CSCW, such uses of the Internet are generally virtual in space. They range from highly synchronous to highly asynchronous interactions. However, many of the major applications of the Internet raise new issues that are not adequately addressed by existing models and taxonomies of CSCW.

Small groups of individuals working together generally have well-defined roles and are mutually aware of roles, tasks, and activities. However, on an Internet list server, a discussion may be initiated with only a vague concept of other potential participants but with strong expectations that a collaborative activity will result. On the World Wide Web, material may be published with only a vague conception of potential users, yet that material may play an essential role in a collaborative activity in some community, possibility not involving the originator, and perhaps in a community of which the originator is not part. Such phenomena are common in various collaborative scientific communities conducting interdisciplinary research. Those loosely collaborative communities are moving their knowledge acquisition processes to the Internet. It would be interesting to know whether they can be modeled and supported using some extended CSCW frameworks (Chen and Gaines, 1997).

This chapter presented a conceptual model for virtual cooperative interaction that encompasses the collaborative knowledge acquisition activities of closely-coupled teams and those of the very diverse communities. It analyzed these activities in terms of the punctuated discourse processes, breaking down the cycles of action and response involved into a continuous temporal dimension. It analyzed them also in terms of awareness by originators of recipients and vice versa. The temporal dimension and awareness hierarchy enable the existing taxonomies and models of CSCW to be extended to encompass a very wide range of systems operating in both the short- and long-term and ranging from small teams to large communities. The model analyzes motivational aspects of virtual cooperative interactions. It gives rise to natural structural analyses of the activities, which allow the types of communities involved to be identified from their observed activities. It can also be used to categorize computer-mediated environments roughly into groupware and socioware (table 2).

The conceptual model presented in this chapter implies that for successful maintenance of continual virtual cooperative interactions, the following criteria must exist:

• Establishment of resource awareness for initial encounter

	Groupware	Socioware
Awareness	strong mutual extensional	weak mutual intensional
Time cycle of Interaction	short to medium (seconds to days)	medium to long (hours to years)
Motivation for Cooperation	individual social exchange	collective social exchange
Power Relations	well-defined roles as part of team definition	emergent roles from investment in social power capacity

Table 1. Groupware and socioware comparisons.

- Establishment of mutual awareness as a feedback loop for continual virtual cooperative interactions
- Compatibility between the expected and the actual time cycles of virtual cooperative interactions
- Properly situated expectation of fairness in terms of collective social exchange
- Accumulation of positive feedback for reinforcements in virtual cooperative interactions

The current model also identifies the types of socioware systems that are needed to expedite collaborative activities and provides a framework for classifying existing tools in use on the Internet. It focuses on participants' motivations and power relationships, which determine their social roles, goals, and expectations in virtual cooperative interactions. They are generally implicitly defined in groupware by the nature of group tasks (Mandviwalla and Olfman, 1994) and organizational structures (Kling, 1980). The chapter contributes to Internet research by drawing attention to significance in large-scale socioware like the World Wide Web where social and organizational structures are fluid and less well-defined. The conceptual model for virtual cooperative interaction expands the scope of groupware research. It provides a framework encompassing all forms of virtual knowledge acquisition processes from teams through organizational work groups to diffused, evolving communities (Chen and Gaines, 1997).

Conclusions

The purpose of the research reported in this chapter has been to develop a finer-grained conceptual model of the processes that support virtual cooperative interaction in Internet communities in order to support and improve those processes through new and better services. The model developed suggests three levels of analysis of services:

- *Message quality*: the improvement of the multimedia capabilities of the basic message channel. There have been continuous improvements from simple text to typography, images, movies, sounds, animations, simulations, and so forth.

- *Relationship modeling*: the incorporation of linkage information preserving discourse relationships. The hypertext links of the original web technology introduced this capability, and clickable maps extended it; there is scope for further extension based on greater understanding of the roles the links play in enabling people to grasp the argument forms of information on the web.

- *Awareness support*: the systematic reduction of the time ($t2$ and $t4$ in figure 5) for a potential recipient to become aware of relevant information. Manual and automatic indexing and various forms of search engines have made massive advances in coping with the information overload resulting from the growth of the web; however, there is scope for many different tools supporting the various ways in which people manage their awareness.

The key question to ask in developing new awareness support tools is "what is the starting point for a person seeking information? That is, what existing information is the basis for the search?" A support tool, then, is one that takes that existing information and uses it to present further information that is likely to be relevant. Such information may include relevant concepts, text, existing documents, people, sites, list servers, news groups, and so on. The support system may provide links to further examples of all of these based on content, categorization or linguistic or logical inference. The outcome of the search may be access to a document but it may also be e-mail to a person, a list, or a news group.

The net is a vehicle for discourse in which the goals of individual agents are supported through social knowledge processes, and support tool design needs to be based on increasingly refined models of those processes. Much of our current research is concerned with the empirical studies of discourse processes on the net through analysis of information diffusion, list server archives, and so on. We conjecture that tools that develop models of such processes and are made available to the participants may themselves result in improved usage of net resources.

Acknowledgments

Financial assistance for this work has been made available by the Natural Sciences and Engineering Research Council of Canada.

CHAPTER THIRTEEN

Guided Exploration of Virtual Worlds

Patrick Doyle and Barbara Hayes-Roth

The Wart did not know what Merlyn was talking about, but he liked him to talk. He did not like the grown-ups who talked down to him, but the ones who went on talking in their usual way, leaving him to leap along in their wake, jumping at meanings, guessing, clutching at known words, and chuckling at complicated jokes as they suddenly dawned. He had the glee of the porpoise then, pouring and leaping through strange seas.

"Shall we go out?" asked Merlyn. "I think it is about time we began lessons."

— T. H. White, *The Once and Future King*

As computers have become commonplace in homes and educational institutions, educators have searched for ways to use them in the learning process. The growth of Internet connectivity is fostering the creation of a range of interactive, multi-user educational environments. These environments are *virtual worlds* whose content and opportunities are limited only by the skill of their designers. Such worlds give each user the freedom to learn through exploration and experiment, placing them in situations and giving them abilities not to be had in the "real" world. In this way these worlds complement traditional didactic education. Our goal is to provide an interactive, intelligent agent as a guide to help users understand, navigate, and learn from these environments in an engaging and effective way.

Our specific interest is with children exploring entertaining virtual worlds that have an educational component. Several such worlds have already been built on the Internet, varying both in purpose and in scope. Some adapt the traditional lecture hall environment to an electronic setting, providing virtual classrooms complete with blackboards, projectors, and class meeting times. Many provide simulated analogs of real-world experiences, so that users can visit online museums or galleries, or play games with one another electronically. Others conjure unreal environments, such as a model of the human body that a user can walk through to see how it works from the inside. Since many of these environments can be extended by their users, some promote learning through the very process of building new instructional spaces, blurring the distinction between learning and teaching.

As part of the Virtual Theater project at Stanford, we are creating an intelligent agent as a guide, who will explore these places with children. The guide has its own personality and motivations; one of the central reasons for having such a creature is to give the children a friend with whom to explore. It can offer comments and conversation, suggest things to do or see, perform collaborative activities with the children, and actively explain what they are experiencing.

There are several appealing aspects to this research. It is an excellent testbed for research on intelligent agent design, computational models of personality, the creation of educational virtual worlds, and child development. It enhances the value of exploring experience-based learning environments, supporting the educational goals of these environments and the development of social skills. Finally, learning with a computer-controlled guide is a natural vehicle for examining social interaction as a paradigm for human-computer interaction.

Virtual Environments

As computers and computer networks become a part of daily life, interest is fast growing in "virtual environments" or "virtual worlds." These environments are computer-based, on-line representations of the real world or imagined worlds. They are software creations that allow one or more users to explore and act as if they were in some actual world. Their distinguishing characteristic is that they give a sense of *embodiment*, a sense of being in some place, rather than simply looking at information on a screen.

This sense can be conveyed in a variety of formats—text, graphics, or even sounds. Some environments, such as Internet Relay Chat (IRC), are no more than strings of words coming from many different speakers, an abstract space for people to talk. Others are rich graphical representations in which each user has an *avatar*, a character that gestures, makes actual sounds, and moves around buildings, scenery, and other characters. Although these advanced graphical worlds are becoming more commonplace, they often require considerable computational resources, and it will be some time before the average user's desktop machine can reproduce them with high fidelity, so most virtual worlds in use today are still text-based.

One important type of text-based virtual world is the multi-user dimension (MUD). MUDs first appeared in the late 1970s as recreational fantasy environments similar to the adventure games popular at the time (Bartle, 1980).

```
> look
On the Stage
   This is the large wooden stage of a small theater used for
improvisational experiments. The stage is bare but well-lit by
spotlights high above. The plush theater seats rise up all
around the stage into the darkness.

— There is one obvious exit: offstage.
William Shakespeare, the Bard of Avon.
A banana cream pie.
> examine spotlights
High above the stage, brilliant white spotlights illuminate
the actors.
> get pie
Ok.
> eat pie
It doesn't look very appetizing.
> say Hi, Will!
You exclaim: Hi, Will!
William Shakespeare says: A most amiable day to you, sir.
> smile shakespeare
You smile happily at William Shakespeare.
William Shakespeare bows with a flourish.
```

Figure 1. A Typical Interaction on a MUD.

These systems support many users simultaneously, allowing them to explore environments composed of rooms, objects, other people, and intelligent agents. Depending on the design of a particular system, themes vary from fantasy environments with dragons and wizards, to futuristic worlds with spaceships and aliens, to university settings complete with regular lectures and conferences.

Within a MUD, each user may pick up and manipulate objects, move from one location to another, interact with other beings or perform more complex actions such as playing games, sending electronic mail, or creating new objects. Figure 1 gives a typical example of interaction in a MUD. The user's commands appear in boldface.

In this example, the user's avatar is standing on the stage of a theater, together with William Shakespeare and a banana cream pie. (The opportunities for mischief are obvious.) By using a stylized English syntax, the user can examine the room, pick up and manipulate the pie, and talk with Shakespeare. Shakespeare is a very limited kind of agent that can recognize certain kinds of actions, such as saying hello or smiling, and react to them. Lacking sound and graphics, such worlds can still be compelling ones: text-based worlds, like books, allow the user to imagine the world, rather than forcing the user to accept a crudely-rendered approximation.

Our chosen environments for exploration are MUDs. Aside from the aforementioned reasons, they have several other compelling advantages when building an agent guide:

- *Text is easy to parse.* Compared to graphical worlds, in which the agent would have to use complex vision techniques to understand what is available and what is happening, MUDs communicate with simple and highly-structured text. This makes them ideal for agents that must reason about content.

- *It is easy to act in a text environment.* Rather than controlling the details of motion of a graphical avatar, which operates in a finely-grained environment, a text system restricts commands to such things as "go north" or "climb tree." This makes it easy for an agent to execute actions.

- *MUDs have generally-agreed syntax and semantics.* That is, many MUDs are currently operating for a wide variety of purposes, but almost all agree on the basic syntax of action and the meanings of actions such as "smile shakespeare." This means that our agent will require minimal reconfiguration as it goes from one system to another. It also means that there is a wide variety of example worlds from which to draw inspiration, and into which our guide might travel.

- *MUDs are extensible from within.* Most MUD architectures allow some or all of their users to reconfigure the world dynamically, by adding or removing objects, rooms, or living beings. This makes them ideal for adding information to direct the intelligent guide.

- *Educational research has already been done in MUD worlds.* From virtual classrooms to simulations of the first Mission to Mars, MUDs have been used in a variety of educational contexts. This gives us data about what kinds of educational resources do and do not work when translated into MUD worlds.

Of course, with the increasing popularity of graphical environments (and even graphical enhancements to text-based MUDs), we see no reason why our architecture cannot be adapted to more visually exciting interfaces. However, this would require a much more elaborate interface between the guide and the world, and this is peripheral to our research at best. For now, text-based communication is an excellent medium for testing.

Introducing the Guide: Goals and Motivations

Our guide is called Merlyn, after T. H. White's befuddled seer in *The Once and Future King* (White, 1958). In White's retelling of the Arthurian legends, Merlyn is a kindly but confused old wizard who, living life backward, is never entirely sure what will happen or what already has. Yet he is able to guide the young boy Wart, who will grow up to be King Arthur, through a series of lessons designed to prepare him to be a king. Wart learns through experience and, with the help of Merlyn's magic, he is transformed into a variety of creatures so that he can learn about their societies and governments — a fish, a bird, an ant, and others; Merlyn sends him to meet King Pellinore and the legendary Questing Beast; and after many adventures, Wart at last pulls the sword from the stone, demonstrating that he is the true King of England. Today's virtual environments can offer similarly varied, intriguing, and educational experiences to real children.

Merlyn is intended to be a playmate, a teacher, and a friend to exploring children. A potential problem with educational worlds is that, while the goal is to give children the freedom to explore, it is still desirable to emphasize gently the educational content. Part of Merlyn's job is to make it easier to understand that content through dialog and commentary, and to offer suggestions and assistance. By letting the children lead, Merlyn can be an active, friendly advocate of the educational environment's goals without forcing them down any particular path. There are four main tasks Merlyn performs to accomplish this.

1. Merlyn as a Friend

First, Merlyn is a friend to the children, a companion in visiting these new worlds. He is presented as a kindly old man, occasionally confused, sometimes wise, and invariably faithful. There is a growing interest in creating such *believable agents* for a variety of applications, ranging from educational guides to computer interfaces for everyday tasks, such as word processing or visiting sites on the World Wide Web. Past research, drawing on lessons from animated film (Thomas, 1981), computational drama theory (Bates, 1992), and improvisational theater (Hayes-Roth, et al., 1994), emphasizes the importance of emotion in building agents that present "the illusion of life" to the user (Thomas, 1981). Ordinary intelligent agents choose their actions based upon maximizing utility. Merlyn's actions are also influenced by constant personality traits, such as kindliness, as well as his transient moods, such as happiness or depression. The combination of these attributes creates an emotionally complex friend for the children.

The kinds of environments we are exploring lend themselves exceedingly well to treating Merlyn as a real being. Since he appears to the children through the same interface as everyone else, whether an animated graphic or a string of text messages on a screen, the natural tendency is to treat him as a living person. Past experiments in text worlds, such as Weizenbaum's (1966) famous psychotherapist ELIZA, could even fool users into thinking they were human, if only for a limited time. Julia, the infamous MUD robot (Foner, 1993; Mauldin, 1994), glibly carried on conversations with MUD users, and even when they discovered that she was a computer program, they continued to have feelings of friendship with her. These trials, along with the research of Nass (Nass et al., 1994; Nass et al., 1995) at Stanford, suggest that users have a natural tendency to treat agents as if they were human beings, and we want to exploit that tendency with Merlyn.

Making Merlyn a believable *friend*, rather than a handy computer reference, is a critical element of his success as a guide. Most of what Merlyn knows about an environment comes from information provided by its designers; and if Merlyn did no more than woodenly regurgitate that information he would serve no useful purpose. Children could simply interact with the environment directly, or be content to interact with one another. Instead, by giving him a personality and motivations, he can provide guidance and inspiration to the young explorers, making the process a social experience that is both more thought-provoking and challenging than it would be if there were no direction at all.

2. Merlyn as a Teacher

Merlyn's second task is to inform children about the environment. In this way, the facts encoded in the space can be absorbed and presented actively through his personality, rather than requiring the children to hunt for them. He can also tailor his presentations and the subjects he talks about to a child's level of understanding of the material, as well as the child's likes and dislikes. In order to do this, Merlyn scans the environment to learn what actions are currently available, what the consequences of those actions are, and what factual material is available and on what topics.

We are creating *annotated environments* that provide such data in a format meant specifically for intelligent agents, to enable those agents to organize and use that information directly instead of trying to extract all of the environment's meaning from the text provided to humans. People bring a large amount of common-sense knowledge with them to new places, and that knowledge means that many things can be left unexplained. Agents have no such knowledge base; as a result, the addition of explanatory information is critical for them to understand the environment. In this way guides, initially ignorant, can at once become limited experts in the domain. This allows the environment's designer to organize the data to suit the environment's educational goals, and it also provides a reasonable way to separate Merlyn's factual knowledge about the world from his mechanics.

As an example, suppose Merlyn is visiting an historical museum with a group of children. They are standing in a room exhibiting King John's signing of the Magna Carta. Merlyn, scanning the room, is told that *King John* and *Magna Carta* are important educational concepts, and he requests more data from the room on each. He can then offer to tell the children more about King John. If a child should ask him, Merlyn will relate what he has learned — perhaps biographical details on John's life, his ambitions for England, the prevalent social conditions leading to Magna Carta, and other related topics. The nature and complexity of the information would be up to the environment's creator, but it can be presented through Merlyn's friendly and decidedly idiosyncratic personality.

Merlyn has the ability to record the information he gleans from his explorations, so that the children can ask the same question at a later time or in a different place. Also, if Merlyn sees a relationship between old information and new (perhaps after a time they find an exhibit on Richard the Lion-Hearted that mentions King John) he can explicitly offer access to old information again.

3. Merlyn as a Guide

Merlyn's third task is to suggest activities to the children. By keeping a record of the places they have visited, the actions that are available, and the information contained there, he can offer these things to the children at appropriate times. Either when requested by the children or autonomously, Merlyn can make suggestions about fun or educational things to do. ("I believe we should visit the Barber of London to learn more about medieval medicine.")

Merlyn should be able to do simple user modeling by observing the things the children do and how they relate to what he understands about the world. If the children enjoy science instead of history, or playing games instead of doing experiments, then Merlyn can tailor his suggestions to those preferences. They can also be used to guide the children to interesting but as yet unexplored parts of the environment, particular parts the designers believe are important. The utility of such models depends on the size of the group with which Merlyn is interacting; it will be more effective in a one-on-one experience than with a large class, for example, but this is equally true of guides in the real world.

4. Merlyn as a Playmate

Finally, Merlyn can play with the children. "Play" is a loosely-defined term, ranging here from simple conversation to engaging in multi-player activities in these virtual worlds, such as playing chess or performing science experiments. Once again, Merlyn relies upon annotations in the environment to understand how to do these things, and his abilities are limited by the extent of the annotations and his ability to reason about them. However, we believe a well-annotated environment will give him enough instruction to make these behaviors interesting. The next section details how these annotations work.

Annotating Virtual Environments

In most MUD environments, it is possible to obtain certain basic information about objects, people, or locations through simple queries. Thus, even without additional information, Merlyn can determine where he can move given his current location, who else is present, and so on. However, this simple information is inadequate to allow Merlyn to fulfill his major functions as a guide. Without additional data about the content of an area, the types of activities available, and the meanings of those actions, he cannot intelligently choose activities that will be educational and relevant to the children's interests.

Our goal is to make Merlyn capable of operating in a variety of different MUD environments, so it would be ineffective to program him *a priori* with information about any specific one. There are some basic facts that hold in all MUDs (for example, what commands control speaking, moving, manipulating objects, and the like), but each virtual environment will have its own unique properties and features. We would like Merlyn to learn about these in the same way as a human would: through exploration.

To make this possible, we *annotate* these environments. In annotated worlds, Merlyn can directly query the environment about its content and possible actions he can choose to take. He does this as he travels. Merlyn can then store the data in his permanent memory for later use, subject to any updates that the environment will provide as it evolves.

By associating context-dependent data directly with the environment, we are increasing the burden on the world designers. However, they are better able to understand what the features of the environment are, and to provide that information to Merlyn. They are also able to update such information whenever the environment changes, something that cannot easily be done by requiring a human being to note any changes and then modify Merlyn's internal structure manually. Finally, in such a world any agent, and not just Merlyn, can learn through exploration.

There are four main kinds of information the environment should provide to passing agents. The first is a list of available actions in the current context, together with the semantics of those actions. So, for example, if Merlyn and the children are visiting an inventor's lab containing a time machine, the environment can inform Merlyn that the time machine is a transportation device, and pulling the big red lever is a transportation action. Thus he can suggest to the children that they take a little trip in the time machine, and even "understands" how to pull the lever to start it up. Other kinds of actions could include perception actions (looking through a telescope or examining a famous painting), communication actions (shouting down a wishing well), information actions (asking the librarian for help) or interaction actions. The last is broadly taken to mean activities Merlyn can perform with someone else, specifically the children he guides, such as game-playing.

The second kind of information is data about the content and meaning of the environment. Merlyn should be informed if he and the children are in a history museum that has exhibits on the Civil War, a classroom with a lecturer on advanced calculus, or a corner café with a chessboard. Knowing whether an environment is educational or entertaining, what kinds of things are to be found there, and what facts it can provide data on allows Merlyn to make suggestions about places to go to do different things, as well as allowing the users to ask Merlyn about places to go. "Merlyn, where can I learn about ancient Egyptian mathematical formulae?" might provoke the response "Well, I know where there is an exhibit on the Rhind Papyrus. Would you like to go there?" if Merlyn knows that the exhibit has to do with Egypt, history, and mathematics.

The third kind of information is actual facts about the environment itself, suitable for conveying to the children. Thus, if Merlyn has queried the environment and been told that it contains information on the Rhind Papyrus, he can ask about it specifically, and be given prepared text that he can offer to them.

This kind of information has a broad range of sophistication. In its simplest form, it consists of actual text about the subject that has been written by a human, so that Merlyn can absorb it and repeat it back to the children, either spontaneously or when he is asked about it. In such a case Merlyn does not really understand the details of what he is saying; he knows only that it relates to certain topic keywords the environment has given him.

More sophisticated versions might contain data about how complex the information is, or whether it relates to or relies upon other information in that location or in other locations. There might be, for example, a room full of medieval art, with a hierarchy of facts to notice that increases in subtlety and complexity. Merlyn can keep track of what the children have seen and asked about, and can tailor his responses to the level that they have already seen, so his dialog will be directed specifically to their level of understanding.

We can also imagine giving Merlyn the facts in a highly-structured Englishlike form, and allowing him to form them into sentences on his own. This is the most advanced form of parsing that he could perform, but it would allow him to provide dialog entirely in his own idiosyncratic way. We hope in the future to develop environments that are sophisticated enough to permit this.

All three of these types of information are meant for Merlyn to take and absorb into his permanent memory store, to be used later in deciding what actions to take or suggest to the children. The forth kind of information is meant for Merlyn, or any agent, to use in real time. This is contextual, situation-dependent advice provided by the environment about how to undertake certain kinds of actions within it.

Our principal example is again in game playing. We would like Merlyn to be able to play games with the children, though we also do not want to have to program him in advance with skills ranging from checkers to lawn bowling. Instead, we allow him to ask the environment how to begin a game, how he is doing, whether it is his turn to move, and what kind of a move to make. This sort of information is ideally part of its own environment, and is not the kind of data we want Merlyn to "learn" as it is not factual but procedural.

We could imagine an advanced agent that could ask the environment for the rules and suitable heuristics for game playing, and record these to perform its own processing, but this is considerably beyond our aims at this point. By allowing the world's designers to prepare such data, Merlyn can seamlessly appear to understand how to play games or have other multi-person interactions without needing such knowledge beforehand.

Merlyn is capable of operating in an environment that has no annotations in it simply by making the basic queries that any ordinary user might make. However, by annotating the environment we can reasonably easily provide him with a variety of information for guiding his actions, communicating facts and suggestions to the children, and performing complex actions in the environment that seem to require intelligence. The issue of annotation is a sophisticated one in its own right, though we are concentrating on it only to the extent needed to make Merlyn seem fundamentally believable and life-like to the children he guides.

Merlyn's Abilities

Merlyn is intended to operate in the virtual environment across an ordinary connection from the Virtual Theater system. To the MUD, he is just another character controlled from a remote location. However, his Virtual Theater "brain" gives him a variety of abilities to explore, to learn, and to adapt to his environment and the children he guides.

The basic traits that Merlyn takes from the Virtual Theater architecture are his personality, his moods, and his ability to evaluate and decide upon appropriate actions in context. Context is created by the personality, mood, user requests, and environment. However, unlike ordinary Virtual Theater agents, Merlyn has several additional features designed to make him flexible in an unknown environment, and specifically to help him interact with users.

First, Merlyn can scan the environment. That is, he can ask the environment to provide him with a list of annotations to guide him. If the MUD provides additional hooks to provide ontological knowledge of the environment to an agent, our intention is for him to use them as well. (Indeed, in our experiments we plan on incorporating such knowledge in a testing environment.)

Merlyn incorporates these actions into an action tree structure. Whenever a new action is discovered, it is added to the structure. He associates with new actions their locations and, when possible, their meanings. Data about features of the environment (e.g., a map of the Forest Sauvage, facts about military organization in ant hives, and the like) are stored in a keyword database for later retrieval and presentation to the children.

In addition to storing information about the environment, Merlyn also records the actions of the children as he perceives them. In this way he has an expanding database about what the children have done, and can extrapolate from it to suggest repeating old activities or trying new ones he has learned about that have similar characteristics. The children can also explicitly tell Merlyn that an activity on the MUD is interesting or uninteresting, and Merlyn will rank-order these actions accordingly when he offers things to do.

Also, through the process of offering activities, Merlyn receives feedback from the children. This feedback will be used to weight Merlyn's decisions. So, if Merlyn offers to take them to a museum, and they indicate that museums aren't interesting, he will turn to other activities in the future. This system can also be preset with weights and suggestions for a particular MUD if Merlyn is being used to achieve particular educational goals.

Merlyn operates on cycles, one of which currently occurs about every three seconds. In each cycle, Merlyn decides on an appropriate action to perform and performs it. "Actions" for Merlyn can involve either system-level activities, such as saving or loading memory or querying the environment for information, or activities in the virtual environment, such as smiling or offering a suggestion to the children.

While Merlyn is acting, he is also capable of reacting to changes in the environment or to actions taken by others. External actions are perceived by his sensors and used in deciding what to do next. At each cycle Merlyn uses his personality traits, the current values of his moods, his internal state, and any external information about the environment to choose an appropriate action to take. His actions are organized into a tree structure, with high-level abstract actions at the higher nodes and concrete actions at the leaf levels. The structure also makes a distinction between environmental activities, such as smiling and speaking, and administrative ones such as querying annotations, which are handled in different parts of the tree.

When Merlyn takes an action, it has some effect. If the action takes place in the environment, he will receive notification from the world just as an ordinary player would, and can use that in making future decisions. He can also query the environment to learn the effects of his actions in some cases (so, for example, after making a move in a game he can ask the environment what his new status is in the game). He may also modify his internal state as a result of an action. Thus Merlyn can become tired over time as he engages in physical activity such as speaking or moving. Similarly, when notified of a change in the environment, he may change his internal state, so a child that kicks him is likely to make him more irascible, while a child that smiles at him may make him more friendly.

Some of Merlyn's actions affect his memory. When he queries the environment for a description of available actions, those actions are incorporated into his action tree for as long as he remains in the current environment. When he queries the environment for a description of its content and meaning, however, that information goes into a permanent store of memory that he can later access should his action be to suggest activities to the children, or as a reaction to being asked a question. Similarly, specific factual information is stored in a database to be offered to the children spontaneously or when asked. This forms his permanent memory and is retained across interactions with them.

Implementation: First Version

Our first version of Merlyn was implemented in LPC, an object-oriented variant of C built into the MudOS MUD architecture. The work was done at Overdrive MUD, which has a large library of functions supporting actions and environmental queries by semi-intelligent autonomous characters. In this implementation, Merlyn was not operating remotely through an ordinary connection to the MUD, but acted as an autonomous program within the MUD environment. This means that he was a MUD object, rather than an avatar of a user connecting from a remote location. This was done principally because the LPC language on Overdrive is specifically designed to accomplish the kinds of communications tasks Merlyn needs to do, and it allowed rapid prototyping of his basic features.

Our experiments so far have involved Merlyn interacting with a single user, rather than a group. In addition to being an easier context with which we can experiment, it is also more demanding for Merlyn, since he is the sole focus of social attention. We believe that if we can solve the believability and annotation issues adequately to cover the one-on-one case, the hardest parts of the problem will have been solved, and that it will be reasonably straightforward to scale Merlyn up to handle groups.

In the first version our goal was to see how well a simple action hierarchy

```
> look
In the Forest Sauvage

    This is a small clearing in the heart of the vast and an-
cient Forest Sauvage. Enormous boles tower above, though the
bright sunlight streams down through the gaps in the leafy
overhead. In the center of the clearing stands a stout stone
cottage, smoke curling from the chimney. Beside the cottage is
a small well, complete with a bucket, winch, and bright red
roof. A narrow dirt track leads back off to the north, toward
Sir Ector's castle.

— There is one obvious exit: in.
Merlyn.
> examine merlyn
This befuddled old man is none other than Merlyn, the famous
enchanter. It's his job to help train young Wart to be a good
ruler when he grows up.
> say Hello, Merlyn.
You say: Hello, Merlyn.
Merlyn wonders if you were talking to him.
Merlyn scratches his head in confusion.
> ask merlyn about himself
Merlyn exclaims: Oh, yes...Me? Why, I'm the greatest wizard
the world has ever seen, that's who!
[after a pause]
Merlyn says: Wart, quit daydreaming! Hmph. Children today.
> smile merlyn
You smile at Merlyn.
Merlyn smiles at you.
Merlyn asks: Lovely day, isn't it?
> ask merlyn about well
Merlyn says: Oh, yes...Dratted old thing. I won't get decent
modern plumbing for another thousand years yet.
> kick merlyn
You give Merlyn a swift kick.
Merlyn glares furiously at you.
[after a pause]
Merlyn says: All this activity is making me sleepy.
Merlyn closes his eyes and goes to sleep.
```

Figure 2. Interacting with Merlyn, First Version.

would produce interesting behaviors, given a small amount of emotional information. Simple passive annotations explaining some objects were added
to the environment. Figure 2 shows a single user interacting with Merlyn on
Overdrive, in an area modeled on the Forest Sauvage in T. H. White's novel.
As before, user commands are in boldface.

Merlyn was capable of choosing actions, though his action tree was limited to casual conversational comments and some unobtrusive behaviors (such

as scratching his head or sneezing). He was also able to follow the user around the MUD, and although he understood how to move from location to location, he would not do this independently. He could scan the environment, but he did this only when the user requested information directly; he was passive rather than active in this respect.

When the user did ask for information, Merlyn would first examine his database, which was implemented as a keyword-based mapping, and if he failed to find a match on the given topic would ask the current environment for data. Any information he gained was stored in the database, so the user could ask later and still retrieve it. This memory did not extend to his action tree; he did not add new actions to his repertoire when he entered new areas.

Merlyn's first mood was a metric of fatigue; as he spoke or interacted with the user, he would gradually become more tired, and the likelihood that he would choose to fall asleep would grow. Merlyn could sleep for a time, during which his fatigue went down, and would eventually choose to wake up again.

In the first version, Merlyn's ability to respond to the environment was limited to stimulus-response reactions to user actions. Thus, for example, he would smile if the user smiled at him, or grimace if kicked or poked. This produced reasonably lifelike behavior, but allowed for very limited variation in his responses, and his perception of the user's actions did not modify his moods.

Merlyn communicated by speaking in the environment (by "saying" things in the same way real users would do), and was able to accept commands in a simple natural-language form when spoken to by users. However, he recognized only a limited subset of standard MUD forms of dialog, so for example the user needed to "ask merlyn about" something, rather than simply speaking a question and having Merlyn recognize it. Thus Merlyn simply assumed that there was only one user with whom to interact, and that user was the child.

While amusing to interact with for a time, this version of Merlyn was limited primarily because he had little intelligence behind choosing his actions. Because he did not use context or history to decide what to do next, he was prone to repetitive statements and *non sequiturs*. He was also incapable of offering positive suggestions to the user. His basic personality did show through in his commentary and responses to stimuli, though fatigue was the only mood that changed over time.

This version was implemented primarily to see where the obstacles would lie in prototyping Merlyn on the MUD. We were pleased to find that the limited version operated well within its design limitations, and so moved on to a more sophisticated Merlyn.

Implementation: Second Version

The second version of Merlyn continued to be an object in the MUD environment. The only major difference between this and making him a full-fledged avatar is that, when he queried the environment, he could do it by calling functions embedded in the environment directly, rather than having to send messages across an open connection. The goals of the second test were to increase Merlyn's abilities to think and act autonomously, and to make his decision-making more dependent upon his moods and background knowledge.

This version of Merlyn actively scans each new environment as he encounters it. Merlyn recognizes that he is in a new environment whenever he makes a movement action. The annotations are stored in a database, together with context information about how and where he learned them.

Merlyn's action tree has become dynamic. He takes a list of available actions in the environment and adds it to his default tree, so that there is a chance he will choose to invoke local actions rather than the standard ones. There is an interesting obstacle here in keeping the environmental information sufficiently abstract so that a variety of agents can use it, while at the same time giving Merlyn enough data that he can reasonably invoke these actions at appropriate times. Currently, the range of additional actions he is given is limited to game-playing and information retrieval, which can very effectively be integrated into his action tree.

Instead of being passive, Merlyn can now actively suggest information or things for the user to do. Again, we have focused on game-playing and imparting facts about the world so far. His suggestions are weighted by his current moods and energy level, so they are less active ones when he is tired, for example, and he is less prone to suggest something fun to do when he is feeling unhappy.

Merlyn is now fully capable of playing games with the user in the environment. This is due largely to adding annotations to the environment to give him directions about how to play and what moves to make. In this implementation, we have annotated an environment that allows Merlyn to play tic-tac-toe against the user. Figure 3 shows an example interaction with Merlyn in which he suggests a game of tic-tac-toe, and then plays it with the user.

Merlyn's integration with the environment for game-playing is smooth. In this shot, when Merlyn entered the room, he first scanned it for features and activities. The environment informed him that there was a game (called "tic-tac-toe") available for playing. At this point, Merlyn added options to his action tree for starting a game, making moves, quitting the game, and commenting on his progress in the game.

Most of these choices were initially invalid, so Merlyn did not consider

```
Merlyn pats his vest pocket absently.
Merlyn clears the tic-tac-toe board to start a new game.
Merlyn says: Well, Wart, let's try a game of tic-tac-toe.
Merlyn says: You can go first.
Merlyn mutters something in Latin.
> play A 1
Merlyn runs his hand through his hair, frowning.
You make your move at A 1.
Merlyn says: Now where did I put my glasses?
Merlyn fishes around in his pockets, looking for his glasses.
Merlyn plays an O at B 2.
> play A 2
You make your move at A 2.
Merlyn whistles happily.
Merlyn plays an O at A 3.
Merlyn compliments himself on his game-playing skills.
> play B 2
Merlyn takes off his hat and looks inside for his glasses.
That square is already taken. Choose another.
> examine board
The tic-tac-toe board has the following configuration:

              A   B   C
            +---+---+---+
          1 | X |   |   |
            |---+---+---|
          2 | X | O|   |
            |---+---+---|
          3 | O |   |   |
            +-----------+

The game is in progress; it is X's move.

> play B 1
You make your move at B 1.
Merlyn brushes hair from his eyes.
Merlyn plays an O at C 1.
Merlyn wins the game!
Merlyn dances a little jig.
> smile merlyn
You smile at Merlyn.
Merlyn smiles happily.
Merlyn says: Oh. Silly me.
Merlyn realizes his glasses are on his nose.
```

Figure 3. Playing Tic-Tac-Toe with Merlyn, Second Version.

them. However, when he observed that no one was currently playing, he had the choice of starting a game with the user. Once the game is in progress, in addition to his usual actions Merlyn has the option to stop the game, to make a move (when it is his turn) or to comment. He asks the environment whether it is currently his turn, what moves to make, and also whether he is ahead or behind, so that he can make appropriately positive or negative comments; when he is ahead, he chortles or compliments himself; while when he is behind he can sulk or wish he were playing other games.

As a result, most of the "brains" of the operation are contained in the environment itself, but none of them is tailored specifically for Merlyn; any other agent with different goals or a different personality could use them equally well. Merlyn's internal structure uses the results of his queries to guide his own unique decision-making. Currently, the environment provides the best available move to Merlyn when requested, but it would be straightforward to allow him to request sub-optimal moves to create more believable play, as well as making him more or less challenging for each individual child.

In addition to atomic actions, Merlyn is now capable of following "trains of thought" over longer spans of time. For example, during the game in Figure 3, Merlyn begins a train of thought that involves searching for his glasses. While that train is active, he may choose to proceed down the line of thought by executing another action in it. He does not need to do so, and in fact depending on the mood values associated with each action, it might take a considerable amount of time to finish a train of thought. In Figure 3, Merlyn continues to hunt for his glasses while he is playing tic-tac-toe with the user. In parallel, the sequence of actions seems believable and perfectly normal for a human being. He is capable of running several trains simultaneously, and optionally choosing to further any one at any time. Each train of thought can also spawn new trains of thought.

Trains of thought give Merlyn coherent long-term behavior. A noticeable problem with the first implementation was that Merlyn often made random, repetitive comments that didn't appear to lead up to a point. While following trains of thought he can focus himself in particular directions, and by reincorporating earlier comments or activities in his later actions, a sense of continuity is created for the user.

Future Directions

These prototypes have proven highly encouraging, and we are looking forward to a full implementation. This version will make Merlyn an independent program operating here on the Virtual Theater site, and connecting to the MUD as other users do. He will support a wider range of emotions, more and more detailed personality actions, and trains of thought that are dynamically reconfigurable, so that they may be deflected from one thought to another while they are running.

The annotation language will be formalized and extended to describe actions, consequences, and appropriate times to invoke them. It will also contain hierarchical factual information about the environment, allowing Merlyn to tailor his descriptions to the user's level of interest or experience. Building an adequate annotation language without forcing the agent to follow a certain set of actions in order to use them effectively is one of the major research issues we are undertaking.

We are also considering adding a special kind of functionality to the environment, called *endowment*. In particular, Merlyn, using these functions in the environment, could *endow* the children's avatars with certain special abilities in the virtual world, so that they could do things not normally possible. So, for example, Merlyn might be able to give the children wings to fly in certain places, or even go so far as to turn the children into other creature altogether. In a virtual world, we can give the children the same kinds of experiences that White's Merlyn gave to Wart.

This requires a more detailed annotation of the environment, so that Merlyn knows what kinds of endowments are available and what their effects are. We are working on adding information to the annotations, and the next version of Merlyn will be able to perform endowments. By invoking endowments intelligently Merlyn's function as a guide and mentor will really begin to shine, as he can give the children experiences that they wouldn't ordinarily be able to have, and he can give them based upon the children's expressed desires as well as spontaneously through his own decisions.

Currently, Merlyn offers a simple range of suggestions to the children. With more sophisticated annotations, we intend to give him greater flexibility in choosing suggestions. We also want to make him more responsive to natural-language queries from the children (e.g., "Merlyn, where can I learn about pyridoxine hydrochloride?"). Early work has concentrated on Merlyn's believability and companionability; we now need to increase his utility as a guide and mentor.

We also want Merlyn to record the children's actions and interests over the longer term. In this way, he can build a model of the kinds of things they do and do not like to do, and with more exposure to the children he will be able to make more appropriate suggestions for activities. It will also allow him to tune his personality to the their actions, so that he will become more satisfying to interact with the longer they explore.

We will also allow Merlyn to save and recall different databases of actions and learned information, so that he can interact with many children over time, and their interactions will remain distinct. Since the emphasis of his interaction with the children is on exploring, he should know about only those things he has learned while with the children.

As virtual environments become larger, more elaborate, and more sophisticated, we anticipate they will become excellent arenas in which children can simultaneously learn and play. By providing a companion and guide that grows and explores along with the children, we can enhance both aspects of the children's experience in the virtual world.

Related Research

For some time research has been done on the social aspects of virtual communities and on MUDs in particular (Curtis, 1992; Curtis and Nichols, 1994). In addition to studies of how human beings interact in text-based virtual environments, research has been done specifically on the issue of agents in MUDs. Mauldin (1994) created Julia, an agent that freely wandered on a TinyMUD, exploring the environment, having limited conversations with other users, providing directions, and occasionally fooling users into believing she was a real human.

Julia was tailored specifically for existing in a MUD environment. Other projects, most notably Bates's Oz project at Carnegie Mellon University and Maes's autonomous agents at MIT have focused on creating believable (Bates, 1994) and lifelike (Maes, 1995) intelligent agents, both for entertainment and general purposes. Maes has concentrated on immersive virtual spaces in which the user sees him or herself projected into a virtual environment, while Bates has experimented with more traditional text-based and graphical worlds.

We are attempting to unify these lines of research, by combining the naturally computer-based interaction of virtual communities with a believable, lifelike agent. Our Virtual Theater architectures allow us to create intelligent, behavior-driven characters that have the autonomy and complexity to behave in useful and entertaining ways. We can put these characters in virtual communities which are themselves expanding and developing, and allow them to interact with other people and new situations, so that they are not locked into prescribed scenarios, but can advance with their environments.

As a side issue of interacting in unknown environments and providing useful data about those environments to the user, data the agent could not create itself, we are interested in allowing that agent to acquire knowledge from its environment via annotation, and present what it learns in an easily-digestible format to the user. In this respect our work is similar to the Guides project at Apple that sought to use interactive, though non-intelligent, guides to present information from *Grolier's Encyclopedia* that related to early American history.

Social Interaction as an HCI Paradigm

Some recent research in human-computer interaction (Nass et al., 1994; 1995) has suggested that human interaction with computers is fundamentally social. Nass describes this as the "computers are social actors" paradigm. That is, the social rules we use in dealing with humans are applied in our interactions with computers as well.

Merlyn as an intelligent, believable agent provides an excellent opportunity for exploring this paradigm. In children's interaction with the computer, the interaction is explicitly social. The computer, in the form of Merlyn with his querulous comments, provides conversation and choices relying upon ordinary rules of social interaction for them to be sensible. While children are exploring the MUD, they have the option of interacting with other users as well as with Merlyn. By presenting his actions through a traditional social interface, we are making their interaction with the computer explicitly as social as their human interactions.

Social interaction is naturally more comfortable for users than typing arcane commands at a prompt. This is especially true of our target users, who are children. By providing a social atmosphere as a means of interaction, we can increase their sense of direct engagement with the world. We can also strengthen the tendency to anthropomorphize Merlyn, making him into a real character with far more detail than we could ever provide explicitly.

The social atmosphere we provide comes in the form of Merlyn's spoken feedback, and also the nature of the text we provide when presenting options to the children. Obviously much of Merlyn's real utility comes from his ability to offer information already provided by the MUD, but in a way that is easier to grasp and is actively tailored to the interests of the children, rather than passively waiting to be sought. Since the goal of the project is to provide children with a friendly, familiar, and believable guide, we are hopeful that our interface provides this experience.

Conclusion

In this chapter we have introduced Merlyn, an intelligent and lifelike computer agent whose purpose is to be a guide and companion to children in their exploration of virtual worlds. Merlyn has an integrated personality and variable moods to create the illusion of life in his actions. Through the use of annotations in the environment, he can understand the meanings of actions and of available facts, and these guide his presentations and activities, ranging from lectures to game-playing. By monitoring the children's interests, he can tailor his personality and actions to support engaging learning in the virtual world, thus supporting the goals of world designers as well as enhancing the exploratory experience for the children.

Acknowledgments

Our work has been supported by ARPA Contract N66001-95-D-8642-Sub-contract #137-1 through Teknowledge, Inc., a gift from Intel, and Seed Grants from Stanford's Center for the Study of Language and Information and Office of Technology Licensing. We thank Lee Brownston, Daniel Huber and Daniel Rousseau for insightful discussions on our design.

This paper is a revised and extended version of Computer-Aided Exploration of Virtual Environments, which appeared in Entertainment in AI/A-Life: Papers from the 1996 AAAI Workshop, AAAI Technical Report WS-96-03, AAAI Press, August 1996.

ProjectH: A Collaborative Quantitative Study Of Computer-Mediated Communication

Sheizaf Rafaeli, Fay Sudweeks, Joe Konstan, Ed Mabry

A large group of people from several countries and many universities collaborated for a period of two years (1992-1994) on a quantitative study of electronic discussions. The research group was coordinated by Sheizaf Rafaeli, Hebrew University of Jerusalem, Israel and Fay Sudweeks, University of Sydney, Australia. Members of the group included researchers from several dozen universities, representing numerous academic disciplines, who got together to use the net in order to study use of the net.

This appendix, (which is a modified version of the Technical Report bearing the same name at the Key Centre of Design Computing, University of Sydney) describes the design of the study and the methodology used to create the first, and perhaps only, representative sample of international, public group computer-mediated communication (CMC).

Aims

The alternatives in studying group CMC are numerous. One can use quantitative or qualitative methods. One may study societies, organizations, groups, coalitions in groups, individuals, or single messages. One may study cross-sectionally, or across time. The choice, of course, should be informed by intellectual interest, availability, reliability and validity concerns.

In our case, we perceived the largest opportunity residing in three facts: (a) we were a large group; (b) one-shot, one-list studies have been done numerous times; and (c) a focus on the self-reports of participants (which typifies much of the literature) still needs validation from less obtrusive studies of the content. The aims of the study were:

- To randomly sample a sizable chunk of publicly available, archived computer mediated group discussions
- To analyze the content of messages contained in the sample
- To focus on the single message, authors, aggregate thread and the lists as units of analysis
- To empirically test hypotheses of interest to members
- To collect descriptive data to document the state of the medium and the communication over it
- To create a shared database to serve future cross-method, cross-media or historical analyses
- To conduct research in a manner unprecedented so far — working with a group of people diverse in interests, time, age, status and location.

We focused on the single message, the aggregate thread and the lists themselves. We randomly sampled a sizable chunk of publicly available, archived computer mediated group discussions and analyzed the content of the messages within the sample.

We chose a quantitative methodology because we viewed it as dovetailing the large number of experimental (laboratory based) studies of CMC, and the plethora of nongeneralizable surveys of single groups. We chose a content analysis method that is less sensitive to self report. We chose to harness our numbers to produce a cross-list, cross-time account; and we chose to not limit the range of research questions and hypotheses that can be accommodated within the study.

Computer-Mediated Discussion Groups

Decades ago, Marshall McLuhan (1964) foresaw a global network creating a global village. It turns out that the "global village" is neither global nor village. The organizing principle is a loosely coupled entity or group, which we will call "list." Each list is a virtual neighborhood, defined by common interest not geography. The networks within which the lists reside come in several flavors. Bitnet, an interuniversity network, has operated since the early eighties and its constituents are mostly academics and students. Internet, an amorphous network connecting thousands of regional networks, is the most rapidly growing and widest spread network. It has a mixed audience of both universities and a growing set of commercial affiliates. CompuServe is a commercial, privately-owned network. Following is a description of lists and their manifestations on different networks.

Discussion groups on Bitnet are called "lists" because most groups are handled by a Listserv program which holds a subscription list of electronic mail addresses. Mail sent by a subscriber to the list address is distributed to all other subscribers by the program. Access to Listserv (or similar) software is usually the only prerequisite for creation of a new list. As lists can be created at the whim of a single network user, a one-layer structure and a "free-for-all" attitude characterizes Bitnet groups.

CompuServe groups have a two-layer structure: special interest groups and sections. Discussion groups are called "SIGs" (special interest groups) and each SIG has a collection of subgroups called "sections." There are approximately 10-20 sections in each SIG on a diversity of subtopics. Creation of a new group is an expensive and complicated procedure so there is usually a substantial user base before a new group is formed.

Usenet groups, primarily on Internet, are generally referred to as "newsgroups." Newsgroups are multilayered and hierarchically structured. Whereas individual users can subscribe to any Bitnet or CompuServe group and receive messages in their personal mailbox, access to newsgroups varies at each site. A site has to receive the news "feed" and users read messages with some kind of reader software. The number and types of newsgroups held, therefore, is influenced by administration and censorship policies, and amount of storage space. The creation of new core newsgroups (i.e. those in the comp, misc, news, rec, sci, soc and talk hierarchies) is more structured than Bitnet, requiring 100 signatures and a demonstrated substantial audience. In addition to the core hierarchies, there are alternative and special-purpose ones (e.g. alt, k12, iee, bionet) in which groups are created under different, and sometimes looser, guidelines.

The depth of interactivity varies widely among discussion groups. Some groups are like cocktail parties with many conversations (threads) competing, rather like CB radio; some focus around specific topics ranging from postcard collecting to yacht design; some are like noticeboards in the local grocery store where messages are pinned and left for others to read and comment on; and some groups merely function as newspapers, disseminating electronic journals or computer programs, and advertising conferences or job vacancies. Many people are content to just read and listen, even in the most interactive groups, while a relatively few dominate conversations.

Ethics

A quantitative analysis of the aggregate of publicly available, archived content of large group discussions that occurred voluntarily is subject to fewer ethical concerns than other types of analyses. Nevertheless, ethical issues were raised: is there an ethical obligation to inform list owners and/or subscribers prior to sampling? is public discourse on CMC public? does the

---

Ethics Policy

1. Members of the ProjectH Research Group acknowledge and affirm the individual rights of informed consent, privacy, and intellectual property. We are all committed to reducing censorship and prior restraint. We believe the issue of informed consent of authors, moderators and/or archiving institutions does not apply to the ProjectH quantitative content analysis, as we intend to analyze only publicly available text. We believe public posts are public and their use is governed by professional and academic guidelines.

2. Each member of ProjectH will ensure that his/her participation in this project, data collection and analysis procedures does not violate the standards of his/her own institution's Human Subjects Committee or equivalent.

3. In this project, we will use only texts:
   - that are posted to public lists
   - that are publicly available

4. In the quantitative content analysis data collection process, the ProjectH group as a whole will observe the following policy regarding "writers" (authors of messages in our sample), "messages" (obvious), and "groups" (the collections of contributors and readers of content in computer-mediated contexts.
   - Informed consent will not be sought in advance for the quantitative content analysis of publicly available messages.
   - No individual writer will be identified by name in either data collection or data set, unless that writer has been contacted, and her/his consent was obtained in writing.
   - Except for short excerpts of 1 or 2 sentences, no messages will be quoted, in any data set, paper or publication, unless the author of the message was contacted and her/his approval was obtained in writing.
   - Statements and findings about groups of contributors will avoid identifying individuals.

5. We will take all measures necessary to separate names of authors and groups from any data collected, measured, or assessed. Individual authors will be identified only by a number. The association of person and identifying number will be kept confidential.

Figure 1. ProjectH Ethics Policy.

principle of "expectation of privacy" apply?

We invested extraordinary effort to compromise on a policy that all could accept as a framework for ethical and scholarly research. An Ethics Committee drafted a policy (figure 1) and initiated a formal online voting process in which an overwhelming majority of members voted in favor of the policy.

Copyright

Questions were also raised about intellectual ownership and copyright: who owns the messages that are sent to a discussion list? who holds the copyright? As we were using public data, we were committed to conducting the study publicly and making the data, eventually, available to all. The processed data is the intellectual property of members participating in the work and the ProjectH

Research Group holds the copyright. Access to and use of the data set was on a hierarchical basis according to contribution rates. After a two-year exclusive access period by ProjectH members, the data set is available to the public at ftp.arch.usyd.edu.au/pub/projectH/dbase or via the web at http://www. arch.usyd.edu.au/~fay/projecth.html.. A Copyright Committee drafted a formal policy (figure 2) which was accepted unanimously by members.

Conceptualization

The initial, conceptual stage of the study comprised deliberating on the unit of analysis, generating hypotheses and writing a codebook. We decided to focus on three units of analysis: the single message, the aggregate thread, and the list themselves. Research questions were many and varied, and included:

1. What are the characteristics of longer and lasting threads? Does longevity relate to number of participants, pace of discussion, interconnectedness of messages, amount and nature of metacommunication, emotic communication, interactivity/resonance/chiming?

2. Are "communities" formed on CMC lists, and if so, how? Can social "density" be measured? Can it be predicted, and/or manipulated by structural qualities of the list? Are any of the previously mentioned variables related to community formation? How? Can one discern the emergence of leadership in CMC groups? Is leadership related to talkativity?

3. How do "free" or "subsidized" lists compare with costly ones.

4. Are there measurable differences between professional, academic and recreational lists.

5. How does editorial intervention (moderation, collation, leadership, censorship) affect the nature of CMC?

6. The gender issue, and all of the above questions. Historically, CMC studies documented almost only male participation. This has clearly (and positively) changed.

7. The metacommunication concept/problem: How big is it? Is this the real downside of e-groups? Is it really a problem? How does it relate to social vs. task breakdowns? How does metacommunication interact (statistically) with length of thread, intensity of social connection? Do all threads disappear down the metacommunication drain?

8. What is the relative role (in collaboration, community formation, thread length, etc.) of asking vs. telling, of information provision vs. information demand?

9. When and where does "flaming" occur? Is it dysfunctional? If so, how is it dysfunctional?

Copyright Policy

The content analysis data produced by the collaboration of ProjectH members is subject to the following conditions.

1. The processed data, defined as the data that is pulled together, cleaned, and in any way compiled from the raw data, is the result of considerable effort by members of the ProjectH Research Group, and is the intellectual property of ProjectH members participating in the work.

2. The data is copyright to "ProjectH Research Group" and included in the copyright notice will be "Coordinators: S. Rafaeli and F. Sudweeks; Members: [full list of current members]."

3. Any individual or group who uses the processed data, either in part or in full, must acknowledge the source of the data as "ProjectH Research Group, Coordinators: S. Rafaeli and F. Sudweeks; Members: [full list of members]" or simply "ProjectH Research Group, Coordinators: S. Rafaeli and F. Sudweeks."

4. Initial access to the processed data is dependent upon participation rate. Access is granted as follows:

   Senior ProjectH members have immediate access to and use of data, subject to conditions 3 and 5. Senior membership is achieved by substantial contribution to the quantitative research project. Substantial contribution is deemed to be coding a complete list sample (100 messages) in addition to pretest coding, development of codebook and/or membership of a ProjectH committee.

   Junior ProjectH members have access to and use of data six months after the data set is finalized, subject to conditions 3 and 5. Junior membership is achieved by minimal contribution to the quantitative research project. Minimal contribution is deemed to be participation in pretest coding, development of codebook and/or membership of a ProjectH committee.

   ProjectH members who have not contributed to the quantitative research project have access to and use of data eighteen months after the data set is finalized, subject to conditions 3 and 5.

5. The data will be made available for public access and use twenty-four months after the data set is finalized subject to conditions 3 and 5.

   ProjectH members who have access privileges may release data to their graduate research students or collaborators, subject to condition 3.

6. Access by person(s) other than specified in conditions 4 and 5 is considered on a case-by-case basis by the Copyright Committee. Appeals against Copyright Committee decisions are brought before the current ProjectH members and decisions overruled by 60% of members.

7. The processed data is stored on an ftp site with restricted (non-anonymous) access.

8. Any participant(s) who is about to commence a research project based solely or principally on the data, is required to register the general nature of the research with the ProjectH coordinators. A list of current research projects and principal investigators will be available for FTP with updates sent to ProjectH monthly. If requested by principal investigators, and approved by the coordinators, details of the research project can be kept confidential. Neither coordinators, nor ProjectH, may censor or censure any topic, or in any way interfere or hinder the academic freedom of any investigator.

9. Any person producing a paper, article, chapter, report, monograph or book from the processed data, either in part or in full, is to notify the ProjectH Research Group. In addition, it is requested that any or all papers based on this data be submitted in ASCII and/or postscript to the ftp repository.

10. The codebook, which is the product of considerable effort by members of the ProjectH Research Group, is the intellectual property of all ProjectH members. The codebook is copyright to "ProjectH Research Group" and included in the copyright notice is "Coordinators: S. Rafaeli and F. Sudweeks, Members: [list of current members]." Any individual or group who uses the codebook must acknowledge the source as "ProjectH Research Group, Coordinators: S. Rafaeli and F. Sudweeks; Members: [full list of members]" or simply "Project Research Group, Coordinators: S. Rafaeli and F. Sudweeks."

11. The annotated bibliography, which is the product of considerable effort by members of the ProjectH Research Group, is the intellectual property of all ProjectH members. The annotated bibliography is copyright to "ProjectH Research Group" and included in the copyright notice is "Coordinators: S. Rafaeli and F. Sudweeks; Members: [list of current members]."

Figure 2. ProjectH Copyright Policy.

10. Are there repeating patterns in the "life" of a group, list, thread?

11. How is the expression of emotion handled?

12. What is the role, frequency and place of shorthand, innovative forms of expression such as emoticons, smileys?

To accommodate the broad range of questions of interest, many of us chose one or more variables and described a method for measuring the quality(ies). The variables, with accompanying definition, extreme case examples, and measurement scale, were collated and formed the codebook. The codebook was pretested, assessed for reliability of measures and ambiguity of definitions and modified accordingly. The final comprehensive version of the codebook has 46 variables.

Sampling

Selecting a random representative sample of discussion groups was an important phase of the study. Initial discussions revealed divergent opinions on the virtues of random and stratified sampling. A Sampling Committee, representing the spectrum of sampling persuasions within the group, drafted a Sampling Statement (figure 3) which was adopted by the ProjectH members.

List traffic is dynamic. Some groups are highly active, generating in excess of 200 messages a day; other groups are almost dormant, generating far fewer than 200 messages a year; some groups maintain a consistent volume of traffic; other groups experience high peaks and low troughs. Sampling an equal number of messages from selected groups has the advantage of capturing threads. Sampling over an equal time period has the advantage of typifying group activity. Rather than risk having to reject a high percentage of groups because we happened to sample during a quiet period, we compro-

Sampling Statement

Objectives and Constraints

The objectives of the sampling strategy are many and conflicting. Among the more critical objectives are:

1. Maintaining enough randomness to allow conclusions about as broad a range of CMC as possible.
2. Obtaining enough data from each newsgroup or list to draw conclusions about the group.
3. Sampling a wide range of groups with diverse characteristics. Among the characteristics of interest to some of us are:
   - readership and authorship
   - list volume (messages per day or week)
   - average number of concurrent threads
   - average duration of threads
   - type of group (i.e., technical, recreational, etc.)
   - type of distribution (i.e., free vs. paid)
4. Learning about CMC and human interaction.

At the same time, we operate under certain constraints:

1. Limited human resources both for coding and for analysis of the types of groups.
2. Limited availability of data, both list contents and list statistics.

The Sampling Continuum

A sampling strategy, given the objectives stated above, lies on a continuum between random selection and stratification. We believe that the constraints posed above will limit us to 50 or 60 groups. We considered two extreme proposals:

1. Complete random sampling. Just pick any groups from any of the lists. This has the advantage of randomness, but the disadvantage of likely leading to the selection of inappropriate groups (perhaps groups with only announcements, automated postings, or test messages), and might well result in a sample that is poorly representative of the entirety of the networked experience. This is particularly the case on Usenet, for example, where there are relatively many low-volume groups and relatively few high-volume ones.
2. Heavy stratification. Select a set of strata and sample from within the strata. For example, given 60 groups, we would be sure to select 30 high-volume and 30 low-volume. Perhaps 20 each from Compuserve, BITNET, and Usenet. And so forth. This has the clear problem that we would be unable to select much randomly, and even a few strata would lead to unacceptably few measures per category.

Accordingly, we examined the following compromises:

1. Weighted random sampling with a weighting factor based on the volume, authorship, and readership. We concluded that we did not yet know enough about the domain to derive a meaningful weighting function that would capture the "normality" of a group.
2. Purely random sampling. This had the problem that we would not be likely to sample enough groups from certain domains (i.e., Compuserve) to draw conclusions about the difference between pay and free services.
3. Random sampling over a more restricted domain with stratification by the type of list. This strategy limits the groups under consideration to exclude:
   - foreign language lists
   - local lists
   - announcement lists
   - help/support lists for specific products

- test and control groups
- lists whose contents are only excerpts of other lists selected by moderators
- extremely low volume lists (i.e., lists with fewer than 25 messages and 3 authors during a selected test month)

The stratification will select equal numbers of lists from Compuserve, Bitnet, and Usenet. If the number of lists is not a multiple of three, the extra lists will be selected randomly from all groups.

It is this final strategy which we propose to adopt.

We propose to select randomly from all lists and reject those meeting the exclusion criteria above. Where possible, this rejection will be accomplished in advance by not considering clearly inappropriate groups. Otherwise, groups will be rejected as they are chosen. Lists that are primarily flames or other "degenerate" cases will be accepted and coded as long as they meet these criteria on the grounds that they too hold interesting scientific results and may be reflective of a segment of the CMC experience.

Once lists are selected, we will sample 100 messages or 3 days worth of messages, whichever is greater. This is to allow us to observe and code threads with sufficient time for e-mail lag and response. The selection period shall begin on a randomly selected Monday for which message data is available. While we considered pure random selection, we consider it unwise to try to compare weekend data with weekday data until we have a better understanding of the domain. Weekend data will be included in most low and medium volume groups. In addition, we will pre-process an additional 100 messages or 3 days worth of messages, whichever is greater, BEFORE the sampling region to provide extra thread and author information for coding.

Precoding

To assist coders and provide greater information, we will be pre-coding messages, including both messages in the sample and those before it, to identify authors and subject classifications. With each batch of messages, coders will get a list of authors with author ID numbers and a list of subjects with subject ID numbers. These numbers will be unique across the entire study to allow us to exploit the opportunity should authors participate in multiple lists or should a thread exist in or move across several lists. To the extent possible, this process will be automated and will simplify coding for each coder.

List Statistics

In addition to the message coding statistics, we will attempt to obtain list statistics. Of particular interest are the following, though additional ones are likely to be added:

- Average number of postings per day in a one-month period
- Number of authors in a one-month period
- Number of readers in a one-month period
- Average message length
- Average thread length (# of messages)
- Average length of threads longer than 2 messages
- Average thread duration (# of days)
- Average duration of threads longer than 2 messages
- % of messages in threads
- Editorial status (moderated, unmoderated)
- Topic (Academic, Technical, Social, etc.)
- Age of List (New, Old)

Figure 3. ProjectH Sampling Statement.

mised on the combination of numeric and time measures: 100 messages or 3 days worth of messages, whichever was the greater, beginning on a randomly selected Monday. Unexpectedly, few of the selected groups had 100 messages in less than 3 days so a standard numeric measure of 100 messages per list was used.

Populations of groups were compiled. A list of all known Bitnet lists was obtained from Listserv@gwuvm.Bitnet with a "LISTS GLOBAL" command. Four lists of Usenet newsgroups which are updated periodically were FTP'd from rtfm.mit.edu:

- List_of_Active_Newsgroups,_Part_I
- List_of_Active_Newsgroups,_Part_II
- Alternative_Newsgroup_Hierarchies,_Part_I
- Alternative_Newsgroup_Hierarchies,_Part_II

CompuServe groups presented a methodological complication. There is no available list of CompuServe sections so the CompuServe population is a list of SIGs, giving a deceptively low percentage of CompuServe groups.

Groups which were clearly in the categories to be excluded were filtered out prior to random sampling:

	Bitnet	Usenet	CompuServe
Pre-filtered groups	3485	1868	337
Post-filtered groups	1907	986	94

A C program generated a specified number of random numbers within a specified range and to match the generated numbers against post-filtered populations of groups. Twenty groups were selected from each of three network.

The sampling period began on Monday 15 March 1993 and volunteer members shared the task of downloading. Bitnet lists were sampled using a DBase program. Internet newsgroups were downloaded from Usenet news. Articles were collected from news servers at the Royal Institute of Technology, Stockholm, Sweden; University of Minnesota, USA; University of Western Sydney, Nepean; and University of Sydney, Australia. Articles were collected according to the date and time of arrival at each news server.

Many of the selected groups did not fit the restricted domain nor meet the set criteria so we dipped into the population hat again (and again). In all, 77 Bitnet lists, 39 Usenet newsgroups and 23 CompuServe SIGs were selected to get samples of 20 groups for each network. For CompuServe, the unavailability of section lists accounts for the high "hit rate." As each SIG contained a dozen or more subgroups, a secondary random process was applied. A section was selected from each SIG using a random number procedure. CompuServe corpora, then, are randomly selected sections from randomly selected SIGs.

Coding

Each batch of 100 messages downloaded from selected groups was prepared for coders. Programs were written to:
- split files of 100 messages into individual files
- renumber, if necessary, in numeric alphabetical order
- precode the first six variables: CODERID, LISTID, MSGNUM, AUTHORID, MSGTIME and MSGDATE
- compile a cumulative database of authors across all lists
- reassemble messages in one file

Numerous universal systems for coding were considered and rejected as coders varied in technical expertise, access to technology and Internet resources, and working style. An enterprising member, using the catch phrase "if we build it will you come?," headed a technically skilled committee to develop standard coding formats for different platforms—Hypercard stack for Macintosh, FileExpress database for DOS, and templates for text editors and wordprocessors.

After coding, data was exported as ASCII and emailed to an account dedicated to data processing. A C program and a suite of *awk* scripts verified and manipulated the data. The automatic processor involved five stages:

1. *Check if incoming mail is data.* Key strings were used to identify incoming mail as a data file. If one of the key strings were found, then the file was processed as data. If a string were not found, the processor assumed the mail to be regular, and ignored it.

2. *Check for errors.* Each mail message determined by the processor to be data was checked for errors, e.g. values out of coding range, missing values, wrong message numbers, non-numeric codes. Data with errors were returned to the coder.

3. *Check for completeness.* As each new list was processed, a unique subdirectory was created and error-free coded messages were transferred to the subdirectory as separate files. When the list was complete (i.e. 100 error-free coded messages as 100 files), the codes were transferred to databases.

4. *Manipulate the database.* Data was added to databases of two format types — with and without comma-delimiters for fields. In each case, each line is one message.

5. *Report to coder and coordinator.* Mail with processable data generated automatic error and completion status reports; unprocessable data was returned to the coder. A copy of all reports was sent to the coordinator and the system maintained a log file of all incoming and outgoing mail.

For each list coded, a questionnaire was completed to gather descriptive information about the coders, the technology used, impressions of the list, and problems experienced.

	Bitnet	*Usenet*	*Compuserv*
single coded lists	BLIND-L BONSAI BUDDHA-L CJ-L EMAILMAN HOCKEY-L LAWSCH-L LITERARY	alt.cobol alt.sexual.abuse.recovery comp.ai.genetic k12.ed.math k12.ed.comp.literacy rec.arts.startrek.current soc.college	COMIC PHOTOFORUM TELECOM UKFORUM WINEFORUM
Double coded lists	CELTIC-L	rec.folk-dancing rec.humor.funny rec.nude rec.radio.swap	CARS DISABILITIES EFFSIG FISHNET JFORUM
Partially coded lists	HOCKEY-L	comp.bbs.waffle rec.arts.startrek.current soc.veterans	

Table 1. Single, double, and partially coded lists.

Reliability

Reliability assesses the degree to which variations in data represent real phenomena rather than variations in the measurement process. Once again, we followed the same procedure for attaining consensus on a methodological process. A Reliability Committee drafted a Reliability Statement (figure 4) which was adopted by ProjectH members.

For various reasons, 40% of potential coders were unable to code. Of the 37 lists (batches of 100 messages) distributed, 20 were single coded, 12 were double coded, and 5 were not coded. Of the 32 coded, 4 were unfinished, giving a final tally of 20 single coded and 10 double coded lists (table 1). The database(s), therefore, has a total of 4000 messages from fully-completed lists, of which 3000 are unique. In addition, there are 322 messages from 4 unfinished lists.

It was important to maintain independence of coding, particularly those lists that were double coded. Independent coders, working in a defined (and confined) physical work context, typically are less accessible to one another on a day-to-day basis. Email access, however, bridges distances and schedule clashes, and puts coders communicatively closer to each other.

To eliminate a possible source of invalid (inflated) reliability, coders were discouraged from discussing coding problems amongst themselves or within the group. Coder queries were directed, instead, to an advisory committee of twelve members. Each advisor, or oracle, fielded questions on a section of the codebook, responding in a nondirective manner. The more complicated questions were discussed amongst the oracles and the leader (the Commissioner of Oracles) summarized the discussions and responded to the inquirer.

Reliability Statement

The following statement on reliability represents a month of intense discussions and a compromise among the many and varied opinions of the "reliability group." We consider, however, it is sufficiently flexible to satisfy both casual inquirers and restrictive publishing standards.

There are a number of ways to collect reliability data. We considered two that are proposed by Klaus Krippendorff (Content Analysis, Sage, 1980):

1. Test-standard: "The degree to which a process functionally conforms to a known standard." This involves training all coders to a standard set by "expert" coders and accepting as coders only those who code to the preset level of accuracy.

2. Test-test: "The degree to which a process can be recreated under varying circumstances." This involves using at least two coders for the same data to establish the reproducibility of results.

Given the unprecedented nature of our project, the unavailability of an established standard, and the number of coders involved, we propose to adopt a test-test design as follows.

1. Each coder must code the nine pretest messages using the pretest codebook. Completion of the pretest is a prerequisite for real coding. The purpose of this is to provide all an opportunity to complete a practice run, ask questions, realize problems, etc.

2. Everything will be coded twice. In other words, each 'list' (or batch) of 100 messages will be coded by two coders. We now have sufficient coding power (participants) to do this. It is crucial that each coder codes independently. Communication among coders introduces errors and makes data appear more reliable than they are. Independence of coding will be maintained as follows:

   • each "list" (batch of 100 messages) will be randomly assigned to two coders
   • the list assignment will be kept confidential
   • each coder will receive assigned lists privately
   • guidelines will be posted to ProjectH for avoiding coding discussions that threaten reliability
   • everyone is requested to ensure specific comments or quotes from messages are avoided in discussions with other group members, except "oracles" (see 4 below), either privately or publicly.

   These strategies will provide us with full reliability figures.

3. We will set a threshold for an acceptable level of bi-coder agreement. In cases where this threshold is not reached, we will have a third coder deal with corpora/data. In other words, while all messages get double coded, we'll set a tolerable level of ambiguity. Any list (or pair of coders) that does not achieve that level of agreement, will be given to a third "blind" coder who will code the divergent variable(s). If the third coder codes the problematic variable(s) in a way that coincides with one of the two previous coders, then we accept the two consistent data. If the third coder's coding is different from both of the two previous coding attempts, we will use the original two coders' data and mark as "unagreed."

4. We will recruit a small number of "oracles" for sets of variables. Questions on the codebook will be directed privately to the oracle for that question. The question to the oracle may be specific and include quotes but the oracle will respond with a summary of general comments to ProjectH. We will also appoint a "Commissioner of Oracles" to coordinate this effort.

Figure 4. ProjectH Reliability Statement.

The typical practice was for an inquiry to be posted to the group, the specialist oracle (or the Commissioner if the appropriate oracle was not available) would post a recommended response, all oracles would comment on the response, and the Commissioner would summarize oracle recommendations and post the final recommendation to the inquirer and/or the group.

Requests for oracle assistance were relatively low. Inquiries could be divided into four types: technical, confirmatory, enigmatic and interpretive. Technical questions related to the group's procedures for precoding, sampling and distribution; confirmatory questions related to apprehension about and applicability of coding categories; enigmatic questions involved some form of an apparent paradox; and interpretive questions dealt with matters of coding protocol intent. Answers were couched in analytical yet open-ended terms. Turnaround time on inquiries posted to oracles was 48-72 hours.

Access

On completion of coding, the following information was compiled and archived and made available, in the first instance, to participants who coded at least 100 messages, agreed to comply with ethics and copyright policies, and outlined the precautions that would be taken to protect author identification and the database:

1. databases
2. data index (explanation of column/row numbers)
3. list of listids, coderids, listnames and network
4. corpora
5. list of authorids and author names
6. coder questionnaires
7. technical report

Acknowledgments

The ProjectH research was supported by the following:

- Comserve (vm.its.rpi.edu) sponsored the project and unwittingly endowed it with a name. Sponsorship is granted to research groups whose activities fall within the ambit of Comserve's aims to promote CMC-related research. The sponsorship includes a private "hotline," Listserv services and disk space for archiving logs.
- A grant from Compuserve provided access to archives and downloading time.
- The Recanati Fund provided funds for some computing resources and co-ordinating time.

- The network resources of the Department of Architectural and Design Science, University of Sydney, Australia was used extensively throughout the project: anonymous ftp site for archiving of ProjectH material (key documents, coding formats, database, papers related to the project), system aliases for distribution lists, an account for processing data, and disk space.

Most importantly, we acknowledge the enthusiasm, perseverance and expertise of ProjectH members who contributed their valuable time and skills to the collaborative project. Listed below are the participants of various phases of the project, and a full list of members.

Project Coordinators

Sheizaf Rafaeli, Hebrew University of Jerusalem, Israel; *Fay Sudweeks*, University of Sydney, Australia

Software Development

Joe Konstan, University of Minnesota, USA

Ethics Committee

Sheizaf Rafaeli, Hebrew University of Jerusalem, Israel; *Fay Sudweeks*, University of Sydney, Australia

Copyright Committee

Sheizaf Rafaeli, Hebrew University of Jerusalem, Israel; *Fay Sudweeks*, University of Sydney, Australia; *Jim Thomas*, Northern Illinois University, USA

Sampling Committee

Joe Konstan, University of Minnesota, USA (Coordinator); *Bob Colman,* Pennsylvania State University, USA; *Sheizaf Rafaeli*, Hebrew University of Jerusalem, Israel; *Fay Sudweeks*, University of Sydney, Australia; *Bob Zenhausern,* St Johns University, USA

Reliability Committee

Bob Colman, Pennsylvania State University, USA (Coordinator); *Joe Konstan,* University of Minnesota, USA; *Bob McLean*, Ontario Institute for Studies in Education, Canada; *Sheizaf Rafaeli*, Hebrew University of Jerusalem, Israel; *Bill Remington*, Middle Tennessee State University, USA; *Fay Sudweeks*, University of Sydney, Australia; *Phil Thompsen*, University of Utah, USA; *Bob Zenhausern,* St Johns University, USA

Mechanics Committee (Coding Formats)

Cheryl Dickie, York University, Canada (Coordinator); *Pat Edgerton,* University of

Texas, USA (FileExpress (format for DOS) Developer); *Bob McLean*, Ontario Institute for Studies in Education, Canada (Hypercard Stack (format for Macintosh) Developer); *Joe Konstan*, University of Minnesota, USA; *Ed Mabry*, University of Wisconsin-Milwaukee, USA; *Michael Shiloh*, TRW Financial Systems, USA

Downloading of Corpora

Ray Archee, University of Western Sydney, Nepean, Australia; *Joe Konstan*, University of Minnesota, USA; *Clare McDonald*, Royal Institute of Technology, Sweden; *Michael Shiloh*, TRW Financial Systems, USA; *Lucia Ruedenberg*, New York University, USA; *Sheizaf Rafaeli*, Hebrew University of Jerusalem, Israel; *Bob Zenhausern*, St Johns University, USA

Oracles

Ed Mabry, University of Wisconsin-Milwaukee, USA (Coordinator "The Commish"); *Sharon Boehlefeld*, University of Wisconsin, USA; *Pat Edgerton*, University of Texas, USA; *Nancy Evans*, University of Pittsburg, USA; *Sandra Katzman*, Stanford University, USA; *Joe Konstan*, University of Minnesota, USA; *Clare McDonald*, Royal Institute of Technology, Sweden; *Judy Norris*, Ontario Institute for Studies in Education, Canada; *Carole Nowicke*, University of Indiana, USA; *Bill Remington*, Middle Tennessee State University, USA; *Michael Shiloh*, TRW Financial Systems, USA; *Macey Taylor*, Marie Curie University,, Poland; *Michelle Violanti*, University of Kansas, USA

Distribution Committee

Bob Colman, Pennsylvania State University, USA; *Joe Konstan*, University of Minnesota, USA; *Ed Mabry*, University of Wisconsin-Milwaukee, USA; *Margaret McLaughlin*, University of Southern California, USA; *Diane Witmer*, University of Southern California, USA; *Sheizaf Rafaeli*, Hebrew University of Jerusalem, Israel; *Fay Sudweeks*, University of Sydney, Australia

ICA Panel/Conference/Workshop Committees

Ray Archee, University of Western Sydney, Nepean, Australia; *Deanie French*, Southwest Texas University, USA; *Joe Konstan*, University of Minnesota, USA; *Ed Mabry*, University of Wisconsin-Milwaukee, USA; *Margaret McLaughlin*, University of Southern California, USA; *Ted Mills*, University of Connecticut, USA; *Diane Witmer*, University of Southern California, USA; *Sheizaf Rafaeli*, Hebrew University of Jerusalem, Israel; *Myles Slatin*, State University of New York-Buffalo, USA; *Fay Sudweeks*, University of Sydney, Australia; *Bob Zenhausern*, St Johns University, USA

Coders

Shamir Ahituv, Israel; *Ray Archee*, Australia; *Ross Bender*, USA; *Bob Boldt*, USA; *Amos Cividalli*, Israel; *Bob Colman*, USA; *Cheryl Dickie*, Canada; *Patrick Edgerton*,

USA; *Kerstin Eklundh*, Sweden; *Scott Erdley*, USA: *Nancy Evans*, USA: *Sueli Ferreira*, Brazil; *Deanie French*, USA; *Stephanie Fysh*, Canada; *Peter Gingiss*, USA; *Dean Ginther*, USA; *Jay Glicksman*, USA, *Allen Gray*, USA; *Steve Harries*, UK; *Richard Henry*, USA; *Merebeth Howlett*, USA; *Sandra Katzman*, USA; *Marcia Kaylakie*, USA; *Mavis Kelly*, Hong Kong; *Ed Mabry*, USA; *Clare Macdonald*, Sweden; *Leland McCleary*, Brazil; *Margaret McLaughlin*, USA; *Robert McLean*, Canada; *Ted Mills*, USA; *Carole Nowicke*, USA; *Andriana Pateris*, USA; *Diane Witmer*, USA; *Sheizaf Rafaeli*, Israel; *Vic Savicki*, USA; *Ermel Stepp*, USA; *Michelle Violanti*, USA; *Gerry White*, USA; *Nancy Wyatt*, USA

Projecth Members (January 1994)

Ray Archee, Australia; *Lecia Archer*, USA; *Ross Bender*, USA; *Alex Black*, Canada; *Sharon Boehlefeld*, USA; *Luiz Henrique Boff*, USA; *Bob Boldt*, USA; *Ingo Braun*, Germany; *Doug Brent*, Canada; *Jeutonne Brewer*, USA; *Mark Bryson*, UK; *Bill Byers*, USA; *Paul Chandler*, Australia; *Robert Christina*, USA; *Bob Colman*, USA; *Alicia Conklin*, USA; *Brenda Danet*, Israel; *Boyd Davis*, USA; *Cheryl Dickie*, Canada; *Patrick Edgerton*, USA; *Kerstin Eklundh*, Sweden; *Jill Ellsworth*, USA; *Scott Erdley*, USA; *Nancy Evans*, USA; *Nicky Ferguson*, UK; *Sueli Ferreira*, Brazil; *Peter Flynn*, Ireland; *Davis Foulger*, USA; *Deanie French*, USA; *Al Futrell*, USA; *Stephanie Fysh*, Canada; *John Garrett*, USA; *Peter Gingiss*, USA; *Dean Ginther*, USA; *Jay Glicksman*, USA; *Allen Gray*, USA; *John Gubert*, USA; *Kate Harrie*, USA; *Steve Harries*, UK; *Anne Harwell*, USA; *Richard Henry*, USA; *Ping Huang*, USA; *Noam Kaminer*, USA; *Sandra Katzman*, USA; *Marcia Kaylakie*, USA; *Mavis Kelly*, Hong Kong; *Yitzchak Kerem*, Israel; *Mary Elaine Kiener*, USA; *Elliot King*, USA; *Lee Komito*, Ireland; *Joe Konstan*, USA; *Joan Korenman*, USA; *Herbert Kubicek*, Germany; *Stan Kulikowski*, USA; *David Levine*, USA; *Mazyar Lotfalian*, USA; *Ed Mabry*, USA; *Clare Macdonald*, Sweden; *Richard MacKinnon*, USA; *Carole Marmell*, USA; *Yael Maschler*, Israel; *Leland McCleary*, Brazil; *Margaret McLaughlin*, USA; *Robert McLean*, Canada; *Rosa Montes*, Mexico; *Ted Mills*, USA; *Michael Muller*, USA; *Rosemary Nowak*, Brazil; *Carole Nowicke*, USA; *Andriana Pateris*, USA; *Diane Witmer*, USA; *Janet Perkins*, USA; *Tom Postmes*, Netherlands; *Sheizaf Rafaeli*, Israel; *Volker Redder*, Germany; *Bill Remington*, USA; *Bernard Robin*, USA; *Alejandra Rojo*, Canada; *Roy Roper*, USA; *Yehudit Rosenbaum*, Israel; *Laurie Ruberg*, USA; *Lucia Ruedenberg*, USA, *Vic Savicki*, USA; *Steve Schneider*, USA; *Rob Scott*, USA; *Myles Slatin*, USA; *Gilbert Smith*, USA; *Ermel Stepp*, USA; *Fay Sudweeks*, Australia; *Pat Sullivan*, USA; *Philip Swann*, Switzerland; *Macey Taylor*, Poland; *Jim Thomas*, USA; *Lin Thompson*, Australia; *Philip Tsang*, Australia; *Alexander Voiskounsky*, Russia; *Dadong Wan*, USA; *Wendy Warren*, USA; *Gerry White*, USA; *Jesse White*, USA; *Sabina Wolfson*, USA; *Marsha Woodbury*, USA; *Nancy Wyatt*, USA; *Kathleen Yancey*, USA; *Bob Zenhausern*, USA; *Olga Zweekhorst*, Netherlands

Bibliography

Abbott, L. L. 1986. Comic Art: Characteristics and Potentialities of a Narrative Medium. *Journal of Popular Culture* 19(4): 155-176.

Abel, E. L., and Buckley, B. E. 1977. *The Handwriting on the Wall: Toward a Sociology and Psychology of Graffiti*. Westport, Conn.: Greenwood.

Adams, R. 1994. Total Traffic Through Uunet for the Last Two Weeks. *UUNET Communications*. August.

Alderton, S. M, and Frey, L. R. 1986. Argumentation in Small Groups Decision-Making. In *Group Decision-Making and Communication*, eds. R. Y. Hirokawa and M. S. Poole, 157-173. Newbury Park, Calif.: Sage.

Allbritton, M. M. 1996. Collaborative Communication Among Researchers Using Computer-Mediated Communication: A Study of ProjectH. Master's Thesis, Dept. of Communication, Univ. of New Mexico, Albuquerque, New Mexico.

Allen, D. F. 1987. Computers Versus Scanners: An Experiment in Nontraditional Forms of Survey Administration. *Journal of College Student Personnel* 23(3): 266-273.

Anderson, R. E.; Johnson, D. G.; Gotterbarn, D.; and Perolle, J. 1993. Using the New ACM Code of Ethics in Decision Making. *Communications of the ACM* 36(2): 98-107.

André-Leicknam, B., and Ziegler, C. 1982. *Naissance de L'Écriture: Cuneiformes et Hieroglyphes*. Paris: Ministère de la Culture, Editions de a Reunion des Musées Nationaux.

Antaki, C., and Leudar, I. 1992. Explaining in Conversation: Towards an Argument Model. *European Journal of Social Psychology* 22: 181-194.

Arestova, O.; Babanin, L.; and Voiskounsky, A. 1993. A Sociological and Psychological Portrait of a Computer Network User. In *Proceedings of the East-West International Conference on Human-Computer Interaction, EWCHI'93, Vol.3*, ed Y. Gornostaev, 68-75. Moscow: ICSTI Press.

Arndt, H., and Janney, R. W. 1991. Verbal, Prosodic, and Kinesic Emotive Contrasts in Speech. *Journal of Pragmatics* 15(6): 521-549.

Asteroff, J. F. 1987. Paralanguage in Electronic Mail: A Case Study. Ed.D diss., Teacher's College, Columbia University.

Avrin, L. 1991. *Scribes, Script and Books: The Book Arts from Antiquity to the Renaissance*. Chicago: American Library Association.

Aycock, A. 1993. Virtual Play: Baudrillard Online. *Arachnet Electronic Journal on Virtual Culture* 1 (listserv@kentvm.kent.edu; file: aycock v1n7)

Aycock, A. 1995. "Technologies of the Self:" Michael Foucault Online. *Journal of Computer-Mediated Communication:* Play and Performance in Computer-Mediated Communication 1(2) (www.usc.edu/dept/annenberg/vol1/issue2/)

Aycock, A., and Buchignani, N. 1995. The E-Mail Murders: Reflections on "Dead" Letters. In *CyberSociety*, ed. S. Jones, 184-231. Newbury Park, Calif.: Sage.

Bach, K., and Harnish, R. M. 1979. *Linguistic Communication and Speech Acts.* Cambridge, Mass.: The MIT Press.

Baird, R. E. 1991. New Questions Emerge about Computer Crime: New Computer Technology Creates New Legal, Ethical Boundaries. *Colorado Daily* 98(196) (August 29): 4, 23.

Bakhtin, M. M. 1984. *Problems of Dostoevsky's Poetics.* Minneapolis, Minn.: University of Minnesota Press.

Baldwin, J. D. and Baldwin, J. I. 1988. Factors Affecting AIDS-related Sexual Risk-Taking Behavior Among College Students. *Journal of Sex Research* 25(2): 181-196.

Balka, E. 1993. Women's Access to On-Line Discussions About Feminism. *Electronic Journal of Communications/La Revue Electronique de Communication* 3. (Send balka v3n 193 to comserve@vm.Its.Rpi.edu)

Ball-Rokeach, S. J., and Reardon, K. 1988. Monologue, Dialogue, and Telelog: Comparing an Emergent Form of Communication with Traditional Forms. In *Advancing Communication Science: Merging Mass and Interpersonal Processes*, eds. R. P. Hawkins, J. M. Wiemann, and S. Pingree, 135-161. Newbury Park, Calif.: Sage.

Balson, D. A., ed. 1985. *International Computer-Based Conference on Biotechnology: A Case Study.* Ottawa, Canada: IDRC Press.

Bandura, A., and Walters, R. 1963. *Social Learning and Personality Development..* New York: Holt, Rinehart and Winston.

Barash, D. P. 1979. *The Whisperings Within.* New York: Harper and Row.

Barlow, J. P. 1990. Crime and Puzzlement. *Whole Earth Review* 67(Fall): 45-57. (www.eff.org/pub/Legal/Cases/SJG/crime_and_puzzlement.1)

Barlow, J. P. 1996. Crime and Puzzlement. In *High Noon on the Electronic Frontier: conceptual Issues in Cyberspace,* ed. P. Ludlow, 459-486. Cambridge, Mass.: The MIT Press.

Baron, L., and Straus, M. A. 1989. *Four Theories of Rape in American Society: A State-Level Analysis.* New Haven, Conn.: Yale University Press.

Bartle, R. 1990. Interactive Multi-User Computer Games. MUSE Ltd. Research Report.

Bate, B. 1988. *Communication and the Sexes.* New York: Harper and Row.

Bates, J. 1992. The Nature of Character in Interactive Worlds and the Oz Project. Technical Report CMU-CS-92-200, School of Computer Science, Carnegie Mellon University,

Bates, J. 1994. The Role of Emotion in Believable Agents. *Communications of the ACM*, 37(7): 122-125.

Bateson, G. 1972. *Steps to an Ecology of Mind.* New York: Ballentine.

Bauman, R. 1975. Verbal Art as Performance. *American Anthropologist* 77(2): 290-311.

Bauman, R. 1977. *Verbal Art as Performance*. Prospect Heights, Ill.: Waveland Press.

Baym, N. K. 1992. Computer-Mediated Soap-Talk: Communication, Community and Entertainment on the Net. Paper presented at 1992 Annual Meeting of the Speech Communication Association, Chicago, Illinois, November.

Baym, N. K. 1993. Interpreting Soap Operas and Creating Community: Inside a Computer-Mediated Fan Culture. *Journal of Folklore Research* 30(2-3): 143-176.

Baym, N. K. 1995a. The Emergence of Community in Computer-Mediated Communication. In *Cybersociety: Computer-Mediated Communication and Community*, ed. S. G. Jones, 138-163. Newbury Park, Calif.: Sage.

Baym, N. K. 1995b. The Performance of Humor in Computer-Mediated Communication. *Journal of Computer-Mediated Communication:* Play and Performance in Computer-Mediated Communication 1(2). (www.usc.edu/dept/annenberg/vol1/issue2/)

Bechar-Israeli, H. 1995. From <Bonehead> to <cLoNehEAd>: Nicknames, Play and Identity on Internet Relat Chat. *Journal of Computer-Mediated Communication:* Play and Performance in Computer-Mediated Communication 1(2).

Bell, R. T. 1976. *Sociolinguistics: Goals, Approaches, and Problems*. London: B. T. Batsford.

Benedikt, M. ed. 1991. *Cyberspace: First Steps*. Cambridge, Mass.: The MIT Press.

Beniger, J. R. 1987. Personalization of Mass Media and the Growth of Pseudo Community. *Communication Research* 14(3): 352-371.

Berger, P. L., and Luckmann. 1967. *The Social Construction of Reality: A Treatise in the Sociology of Knowledge*. Garden City, N.Y.: Doubleday Books.

Berners-Lee, T.; Cailliau, R.; Luotonen, A.; Nielsen, H. F.; and Secret, A. 1994. The World-Wide Web. *Communications of the ACM* 37(8): 76-83.

Berryman-Fink, C. 1978. Attitudes Toward Male and Female Sex-Appropriate and Sex-Inappropriate Language. In *Communication, Language, and Sex: Proceedings of the First Annual Conference*, eds. C. L. Berryman and V. Eman, 1195-1216. Rowley, Mass.: Newbury House.

Biocca, F. ed. 1992. Virtual Reality: A Communication Perspective. *Journal of Communication* 42(4).

Blackman, B. I., and Clevenger, T., Jr. 1990. On-Line Computer Messaging: Surrogates for Nonverbal Behavior. Paper presented at 1990 International Communication Association, Dublin, Ireland, June 24-29.

Bolter, J. D. 1991. *Writing Space: The Computer, Hypertext, and the History of Writing*. Hillsdale, N.J.: Lawrence Erlbaum.

Bourque, L. B. 1989. *Defining Rape*. Durham, N.C.: Duke University Press.

Braaten, D. O.; Cody, M. J.; and Bell, K. 1990. Account Episodes in Organizations: Remedial Work and Impression Management. Paper presented at 1990 Annual Meeting of the International Communication Association, Dublin, Ireland, June.

Brennan, R. L., and Prediger, D. J. 1981. Coefficient Kappa: Some Uses, Misuses, and Alternatives. *Educational and Psychological Measuremen* 41: 687-699.

Bresler, L. 1990. Student Perceptions of CMC: Roles and Experiences. *Journal of Mathematical Behavior* 9(3): 291-307.

Bretz, R.; and Schmidbauer, M. 1983. *Media for Interactive Communication*. Newbury Park, Calif.: Sage.

Broadhead, G. J. 1980. Samuel Johnson and the Rhetoric of Conversation. *Studies in English Literature* 20(3): 461-474.

Broude, G. J., and Greene, S. J. 1976. Cross-Cultural Codes and Twenty Sexual Practices. *Ethnology* 15(7): 409-428.

Brown, G., and Yule, G. 1983. *Discourse Analysis.* Cambridge, England: Cambridge University Press.

Brown, J. S. 1952. A Comparative Study of Deviations from Sexual Mores. *American Sociological Review* 17(5): 135-146.

Brown, P., and Levinson, S. 1978. Universals in Language Usage: Politeness Phenomena. In *Questions and Politeness,* ed. E. Goody, 256-310. Cambridge, Mass.: Cambridge University Press.

Brownmiller, S. 1975. *Against Our Will.* New York: Simon and Schuster.

Bruckman, A. 1992. Identity Workshop: Emergent Social and Psychological Phenomena in Text-Based Virtual Reality. Unpublished ms. (asb@media-lab.media.mit.edu)

Bruckman, A. 1993. Gender Swapping on the Internet. Presented at The Internet Society Meeting, San Francisco, Calif., August 1993. (ftp.media.mit.edu/pub/asb/papers/gender swapping.txt)

Bruckman, A. 1996. Gender Swapping on the Internet. In *High Noon on the Electronic Frontier: Conceptual Issues in Cyberspace,* ed. P. Ludlow, 317-325. Cambridge, Mass.: The MIT Press.

Burgess, J. 1993. Internet Creates a Computer Culture of Remote Intimacy. *The Washington Post,* 116 (June 28): A1.

Burke, S. 1990. Electronic-Mail Privacy to be Tested in Court in Suit Against Epson. *PC Week* 7(33) (August 20): 124.

Caillois, R. 1961. *Man, Play, and Games.* Glencoe, Ill.: Free Press.

Calhoun, C. J. 1980. Community: Toward a Variable Conceptualization for Comparative Research. *Social History* 5: 105-129.

Cappella, J. N. 1987. Interpersonal Communication: Definitions and Fundamental Questions. In *Handbook of Communication Science,* eds. Berger and S. H. Chaffee, 184-238. Newbury Park, Calif.: Sage.

Carey, J. 1980. Paralanguage in Computer Mediated Communication. Presented at the Eighteenth Annual Meeting of the Association for Computational Linguistics, Philadelphia, Penn.

Carey, J. 1989. *Communication as Culture.* Boston: Unwin-Hyman.

Carey, J. T. 1975. *Sociology and Public Affairs: The Chicago School.* Newbury Park, Calif.: Sage.

Carter, J. M. 1985. *Rape in Medieval England: An Historical and Sociological Study.* Lanham, Md.: University Press of America, Inc.

Castleman, C. 1982. *Getting Up: Subway Graffiti in New York.* Cambridge, Mass.: The MIT Press.

Cathcart, R., and Gumpert, G. 1983. Mediated Interpersonal Communication: Toward a New Typology. *Quarterly Journal of Speech* 64(3): 267-277.

Cazden, C. B. 1976. Play with Language and Meta-linguistic Awareness: One Dimension of Language Experience. In *Play—Its Role in Development and Evolution,* ed. J. S. Bruner, 603-608. New York: Penguin.

Chayko, M. 1993. What Is Real in the Age of Virtual Reality? "Reframing" Frame Analysis for a Technological World. *Symbolic Interaction* 16(2): 171-181.

Check, J. V. P. 1985. Hostility Toward Women: Some Theoretical Considerations. In *Violence in Intimate Relationships*, ed. G. W. Russell. Jamaica, NY: Spectrum.

Chen, L. L.-J. 1995. "CHRONO: A Chronological Awareness Tool." Unpublished ms. Knowledge Science Institute, University of Calgary. (ksi.cpsc. ucalgary.ca: 8008/cgi-bin/release?7np)

Chen, L. L.-J. 1996. Chronological Awareness Tools: CHRONO and Meta-CHRONO. Presented at KAW96: The Tenth Annual Knowledge Acquisition Workshop, November 9-14, Banff, Alberta. (ksi.cpsc.ucalgary.ca/KAW/KAW96/chen/kawchrono.html)

Chen, L. L.-J., and Gaines, B. R. 1996a. Knowledge Acquisition Processes in Internet Communities. Presented at KAW96: The Tenth Annual Knowledge Acquisition Workshop, November 9-14, Banff, Alberta.

Chen, L. L.-J., and Gaines, B. R. 1996b. Methodological Issues in Studying and Supporting Awareness on the World Wide Web. In *Proceedings of WebNet96*, ed. H. Maurer, Association for the Advancement of Computing in Education, 95-102. Charlotteville, Va: AACE.

Chen, L. L.-J., and Gaines, B. R. 1997. A CyberOrganism Model for Awareness in Collaborative Communities on the Internet. *International Journal of Intelligent Systems* 12(1): 31-56.

Cherny, L. 1995. Gender Differences in Text-Based Virtual Reality. *Electronic Journal of Communication* 5(4). (cios.llc.rpi.edu/).

Christians, C. G. 1976. Jacques Ellul and Democracy's "Vital Information" Premise. *Journalism Monographs* 45.

Clark, L., and Lewis, D. 1977. *Rape: The Price of Coercive Sexuality*. Toronto: Women's Press.

Coates, J. 1992. Cyberspace Innkeeping: Building Online Community. Unpublished ms. (tex@well.sf.ca.us.)

Coates, J. 1993. Innkeeping in Cyberspace. Unpublished ms. (gopher.well.sf.ca.us, in the directory /Community/Innkeeping)

Cody, M. J., and Braaten, D. O. 1992. The Social-Interactive Aspects of Account-Giving. In *Explaining One's Self to Others: Reason-Giving in a Social Context,* eds. M. L. McLaughlin, M. J. Cody, and S. J. Read, 225-243. Hillsdale, N.J.: Lawrence Erlbaum.

Cody, M. J., and McLaughlin, M. L. 1988. Accounts on Trial: Oral Arguments in Traffic Court. In *Analyzing Everyday Explanation: A Casebook of Methods*, ed. C. Antaki, 113- 126. London: Sage.

Cody, M. J., and McLaughlin, M. L. 1990b. Interpersonal Accounting. In *The Handbook of Language and Social Psychology*, eds. H. Giles and P. Robinson, 227-255. London: Wiley.

Cody, M. J., and McLaughlin, M. L. eds. 1990a. *The Psychology of Tactical Communication*. Philadelphia, Penn.: Multilingual Matters Ltd.

Cohen, S., and Taylor, L. 1978. *Escape Attempts: The Theory and Practice of Resistance to Everyday Life*. New York: Penguin Books.

Colby, K. M. 1975. *Artificial Paranoia: A Computer Simulation of Paranoid Processes*. New York: Pergamon Press.

Collier, J., and Berkeley, E. C. 1982. The One-to-One Microcomputer: The Personality of a Genie. *Computers and People* 31(3-4): 21-23

Collins, A. M., and Loftus, E. F. 1975. A Spreading-Activation Theory of Semantic Processing. *Psychological Review* 82(6): 407-28.

Collot, M., and Belmore, N. 1996. Electronic Language: A New Variety of English. In *Computer-Mediated Communication: Linguistic, Social, and Cross-Cultural Perspectives,* ed. S. C. Herring, 13-28. Amsterdam: John Benjamins.

Contractor, N. S., and Eisenberg, E. M. 1990. Communication Networks and New Media in Organizations. In *Organizations and Communication Technology,* eds. J. Fulk and C. Steinfield. Newbury Park, Calif: Sage Publications.

Cook, K. S., ed. 1987. *Social Exchange Theory.* Newbury Park, Calif.: Sage.

Coyne, R. D., and Yokozawa, M. 1992. Computer Assistance in Designing From Precedent. *Environment and Planning B: Planning and Design* 19: 143-171.

Coyne, R. D.; Newton, S.; and Sudweeks, F. 1993. Modeling the Emergence of Schemas in Design Reasoning. In *Modeling Creativity and Knowledge-Based Creative Design,* eds. J. S. Gero and M. L. Maher, 177-209. Hillsdale, N.J.: Lawrence Erlbaum.

Crawford, C., and Galdikas, B. M. F. 1986. Rape in Non-Human Animals: An Evolutionary Perspective. *Canadian Psychology* 27(1): 215-230.

Cronbach, L. J. 1951. Coefficient Alpha and the Internal Structure of Tests. *Psychometrika* 16: 297-334.

Culnan, M. J., and Markus, M. L. 1987. Information Technologies. In *Handbook of Organizational Communication: An Interdisciplinary Perspective.* eds. F. M. Jablin, L. L. Putnam, K. H. Roberts, and L. W. Porter, 420-443. Newbury Park, Calif.: Sage.

Curtis, P. 1992. Mudding: Social Phenomena in Text-Based Virtual Realities. *Intertrek* 3: 26-34.

Curtis, P. 1997. Mudding: Social Phenomena in Text-Based Virtual Realities. In *High Noon on the Electronic Frontier,* ed. P. Ludlow, 347-374. Cambridge, Mass.: The MIT Press.

Curtis, P., and Nichols, D. 1994. MUDs Grow Up: Social Virtual Reality in the Real World. In *Digest of Papers, Spring COMPCON 94,* 193-200. Los Alamitos, Calif.: IEEE Computer Society Press.

Danet, B. (in press). Flaming. In *The Garland Encyclopedia of Semiotics,* ed. P. Bouissac. New York: Garland.

Danet, B. 1994. Hamming It Up on the Net. *Wired* 2(10): 38.

Danet, B. 1996. Text as Mask: Gender and Identity on the Internet. Paper presented at 1996 Conference on "Masquerade and Gendered Identity," Venice, Italy, February 21-24.

Danet, B. and Reudenberg, L. 1992. "Smiley" Icons: Keyboard Kitch or New Communication Code? Paper presented at 1992 Annual Meeting of the American Folklore Society, Jacksonville, Fla.

Danet, B. ed. 1995. Play and Performance in Computer-Mediated Communication. *Journal of Computer-Mediated Communication* 1(2). (www.usc.edu/dept/annenberg/vol1/issue2/)

Danet, B.; Ruedenberg, L.; and Rosenbaum-Tamari, Y. 1998. "Hmmm ... Where's That Smoke Coming From?" Writing, Play and Performance on Internet Relay Chat. In *Network and Netplay: Virtual Groups on the Internet*, eds. F. Sudweeks, M. McLaughlin, and S. Rafaeli. Menlo Park, Calif.: AAAI Press.

Danet, B.; Wachenhauser, T.; Bechar-Israeli, H.; Cividalli, A.; and Rosenbaum-Tamari, Y. 1995. Curtain Time 20:00 GMT: Experiments in Virtual Theater on Internet Relat Chat. *Journal of Computer-Mediated Communication:* Play and Performance in Computer-Mediated Communication 1(2). (www.usc.edu/dept/annenberg/vol1/issue2/)

Danowski, J. A., and Edison-Swift, P. 1985. Crisis Effects on Intraorganizational Computer-Based Communication. *Communication Research* 12(2): 251-270.

Davis, N. J. 1975. *Sociological Constructions of Deviance*. Dubuque, Iowa: William C. Brown.

Davis, N. M. 1994. CyberFacts. *Presstime* (October): 24-25.

De Hamel, C. 1986. *A History of Illuminated Manuscripts*. London: Phaidon.

De Hamel, C. 1992. *Medieval Craftsmen: Scribes and Illuminators*. London: British Museum.

Delany, P., and Landow, G. P. 1991. *Hypermedia and Literary Studies*. Cambridge, Mass.: The MIT Press.

Delener, N., and Neelankavil, J. P. 1990. Informational Sources and Media Usage. *Journal of Advertising Research* 30(3): 45-52.

Dennis, A. R., and Valacich, J. S. 1993. Computer Brainstorms: More Heads Are Better Than One. *Journal of Applied Psychology* 78(4): 531-537.

Dennis, A. R.; Valacich, J. S.; and Nunamaker, J. F. Jr. 1990. An Experimental Investigation of the Effects of Group Size in an Electronic Meeting Environment. *IEEE Transactions on Systems, Man, and Cybernetics* 20: 1049-1059.

Dibbell, J. 1993. A Rape in Cyberspace, or How an Evil Clown, a Haitian Trickster Spirit, Two Wizards, and a Cast of Dozens Turned a Database into a Society. *Village Voice* (December 21).

Dibbell, J. 1996. A Rape in Cyberspace, or How an Evil Clown, a Haitian Trickster Spirit, Two Wizards, and a Cast of Dozens Turned a Database into a Society. In *High Noon on the Electronic Frontier: Conceptual Issues in Cyberspace*, ed. P. Ludlow, 375-396. Cambridge, Mass.: The MIT Press.

Dickel, M. H. 1995. Bent Gender: Virtual Disruptions of Gender and Sexual Identity. *EJC: Electronic Journal of Communication* 5(4). (comserve@Vm.Rpi.edu; send Dickel v5n495)

Donnerstein, E. 1985. The Effects of Exposure to Violent Pornographic Mass Media Images. *Engage Social Action* 13: 16-19.

Donohue, G. A.; Tichenor, P. J.; and Olien, C. N. 1975. Mass Media and the Knowledge Gap: A Hypothesis Reconsidered. *Communication Research* 2(1): 3-23.

DuBois, B. L., and Crouch, I. eds. 1976. *The Sociology of the Languages of American Women*. San Antonio, Tex.: Trinity University.

Duck, S. 1976. Interpersonal Communication in Developing Acquintance. In *Explorations in Interpersonal Communication*, ed. G. R. Miller, 127-147. Newbury Park, Calif.: Sage.

Dworkin, A. 1981. *Pornography: Men Possessing Women*. New York: Perigee.

Eakins, B., and Eakins, G. 1978. *Sex Differences in Human Communication*. Boston: Houghton Mifflin.

Ebben, M., and Kramarae, C. 1993. Women and Information Technologies: Creating a Cyberspace of Our Own. In *Women, Information Technology, and Scholarship*, eds. H. J. Taylor, C. Kramarae, and M. Ebben, 15-27. Urbana, Ill.: University of Illinois Center for Advanced Study.

Edwards, D. 1973. *A New World Politics*. New York: McKay, 1973

Edwards, V., and Sienkewicz, T. J. 1990. *Rappin' and Homer: Oral Cultures Past and Present:*. Oxford: Basil Blackwell.

Ellis, L. 1989. *Theories of Rape: Inquiries into the Causes of Sexual Aggression*. New York: Hemisphere Publishing Corporation.

Epstein, C. F. 1986. Symbolic Segregation: Similarities and Differences in the Language and Non-Verbal Communication of Women and Men. *Sociological Forum* 1(1): 27-49.

Estren, M. 1974. *A History of Underground Comix*. San Francisco: Straight Arrow Books.

Faris, R. E. L. 1955. *Social Disorganization*. New York: Ronald Press.

Ferrara, K.; Brunner, H.; and Whittemore, G. 1991. Interactive Written Discourse as an Emergent Register. *Written Communication* 8(1): 8-33.

Finholt, T., and Sproull, L. S. 1990. Electronic Groups at Work. *Organization Science* 1(1): 41-64.

Finnegan, R. 1977. *Oral Poetry: Its Nature, Significance and Social Context*. Cambridge, England: Cambridge University Press.

Foner, L. 1993. What's an Agent, Anyway?: A Sociological Case Study. Technical Report: Agents Memo 93-01. Agents Group, MIT Media Laboratory, Massachusetts Institute of Technology, Cambridge, Mass.

Ford, K., and Norris, A. 1993. Knowledge of AIDS Transmission, Risk Behavior, and Perceptions Among Urban, Low-Income, African-American and Hispanic Youth. *American Journal of Preventive Medicine* 9(5): 297-306.

Ford, W. R.; Weeks, G. D.; and Chapanis, A. 1980. The Effect of Self-Imposed Brevity on the Structure of Dyadic Communication. *Journal of Psychology* 104(1): 87-103.

Foucault, M. 1990. Translated by Robert Hurley. *The History of Sexuality: An Introduction*. New York: Vintage Books.

Francese, P. 1991. What Business Are You In. *American Demographics* 13(4): 2.

Fulk, J. 1993. Social Construction of Communication Technology. *The Academy of Management Journal* 36(5): 921-950.

Fulk, J.; Schmitz, J. A.; and Schwarz, D. 1992. The Dynamics of Context-Behaviour Interactions in Computer-Mediated Communication. In *Contexts of Computer-Mediated Communication*, ed. M. Lea, 30-65. Herts, England: Harvester Wheatsheaf.

Fulk, J.; Steinfield C. W.; Schmitz, J.; and Power, J. G. 1987. A Social Information Processing Model of Media Use. *Communication Research* 14(5): 529-552.

Furniss, M. 1993. Sex With a Hard (Disk) On: Computer Bulletin Boards and Pornography. *Wide Angle* 15(2): 19-37.

Gaines, B. R. 1971. Through a Teleprinter Darkly. *Behavioural Technology* 1(2): 15-16.

Gaines, B. R. 1994. The Collective Stance in Modeling Expertise in Individuals and Organizations. *International Journal of Expert Systems* 7(1): 21-51.

Gaines, B. R., and Chen, L. L.-J. 1996. A Model of Knowledge Processes in Internet Communities. In Internet-Based Information Systems: Papers from the 1996 AAAI Workshop, ed. Alexander Franz & Hiroaki Kitano, 41-47. Technical Report WS-96-06. American Association for Artificial Intelligence, Menlo Park, Calif.

Gaines, B. R.; Chen, L. L.-J.; and Shaw, M. L. G. Forthcoming. Modeling the Human Factors of Scholarly Communities Supported Through the Internet and World Wide Web. *Journal of the American Society for Information Science.*

Gaines, B. R.; Shaw, L. G.; and Chen, L. L.-J. 1996. Utility, Usability, and Likeability: Dimensions of the Net and Web. In *Proceedings of WebNet96*, 167-173. New York: Association for the Advancement of Computing in Education.

Galegher, J.; Kraut, R. E.; and Egido, C. 1990. *Intellectual Teamwork: Social and Technical Foundations of Cooperative Work.* Hillsdale, N.J.: Lawrence Erlbaum.

Ganong, L. H., and Coleman, M. 1985. Sex, Sex Roles, and Emotional Expressiveness. *Journal of Genetic Psychology* 140(3): 405-411.

Garramone, G. M.; Harris, A. C.; and Anderson, R. B. 1986. Uses of Political Computer Bulletin Boards. *Journal of Broadcasting* 30(3): 325- 339.

Gaur, A. 1984. *A History of Writing.* London: British Library.

Gelb, I. J. 1963. *A Study of Writing.* Second Edition. Chicago: University of Chicago Press.

Gibson, L.; Linden, R.; and Johnson, S. 1980. A Situational Theory of Rape. *Canadian Journal of Criminology* 22(1): 51-63.

Gibson, W. 1984. *Neuromancer.* New York: Ace.

Giddens, A. 1976. *New Rules of Sociological Method: A Positive Critique of Interpretative Sociologies.* New York: Basic Books.

Godin, S. 1993. *The Smiley Dictionary: Cool Things to To with Your Keyboard.* Berkeley, Calif.: Peachpit Press.

Goffman, E. 1967. *Interaction Ritual.* Chicago: Aldine Publishing Co.

Goffman, E. 1974. *Frame Analysis: An Essay on the Organization of Experience.* New York: Harper and Row.

Goffman, E. 1981. *Forms of Talk.* Philadelphia, Penn.: University of Pennsylvania Press.

Goldman, J. A. and Harlow, L. L. 1993. Self-Perception Variables that Mediate AIDS Preventative Behavior in College Students. *Health Psychology* 12(6): 489-498.

Goldschmidt, W. 1976. *Culture and Behavior of the Sebei: A Study in Continuity and Adaptation.* Berkeley, Calif.: University of California Press.

Gombrich, E. 1984. *The Sense of Order: A Study in the Psychology of Decorative Art.* London: Phaidon.

Gonzales, M. H.; Pederson, J. H.; Manning, D. J.; and Wetter, D. W. 1990. Pardon My Gaffe: Effects of Sex, Status, and Consequence Severity on Accounts. *Journal of Personality and Social Psychology* 58: 610-621.

Gossen, G. H. 1976. Verbal Dueling in Chamula. In *Speech Play: Research and Resources for the Study of Linguistic Creativity,* ed. B. Kirshenblatt-Gimblett, 121-146. Philadelphia: University of Pennsylvania Press.

Govier, T. 1985. *A Practical Study of Argument*. Belmont, Calif.: Wadsworth.

Grice, H. P. 1975. Logic and Conversation. In *Syntax and Semantics: Volume 3. Speech Acts*, eds. P. Cole and J. Morgan. New York: Academic Press.

Griffin, P.; King, C.; Diaz, E.; and Cole, M. 1989. *A Sociohistorical Approach to Learning and Instruction* (In Russian). Moscow: Pedagogica Publications.

Groth, A. N. 1979. *Men Who Rape: The Psychology of the Offender*. New York: Plenum.

Guthertz, M., and Field, T. 1989. Lap Computer or On-Line Coding and Data Analysis for Laboratory and Field Observations. *Infant Behavior and Development* 1(3): 305-319.

Hafner, K., and Markoff, J. 1991. *Cyberpunk: Outlaws and Hackers on the Computer Frontier*. New York: Simon and Schuster.

Hahm, W., and Bikson, T. 1989. Retirees Using Email and Networked Computers. *International Journal of Technology and Aging* 2(2): 113-123.

Hahn, H., and Stout, R. 1994. *The Internet Complete Reference*. Berkeley, Calif.: Osborne McGraw-Hill.

Hamblin, K. 1978. *Mime: A Playbook of Silent Fantasy*. Garden City, N.Y.: Doubleday.

Handelman, D. 1976. Play and Ritual: Complementary Frames of Meta-Communication. In *It's a Funny Thing, Humour*, eds. A. J. Chapman and H. Foot, 185-192. London: Pergamon.

Hardy, H. E. 1993. The History of the Net. Master's Thesis, School of Communications, Grand Valley State University.

Harrison, T. M. and Stephen, T. 1996. *Computer Networking and Scholarly Communication in the Twenty-first Century*. Albany, N.Y.: State University of New York Press.

Harvey, D. 1989. *The Condition of Postmodernity*. Oxford: Blackwell.

Hayes-Roth, B.; Sincoff, E.; Brownston, L.; Huard, R.; and Lent, B. 1994. Directed Improvisation. Technical Report KSL-94-61, Knowledge Systems Laboratory, Stanford Univ., Stanford, Calif.

Heim, M. 1987. *Electric Language: A Philosophical Study of Word Processing*. New Haven, Conn.: Yale University Press.

Hellerstein, L. N. 1985. The Social Use of Electronic Communication at a Major University. *Computers and the Social Sciences* 1(304): 191-197.

Herbert, N. 1992. Does She Do the Vulcan Mind Meld on the First Date? *Computer Underground Digest* 4(17). (ftp.eff.org/pub/Publications/CuD/CuD/vol4/cud4.17.gz)

Hernandez, R. T. 1987. Computer Electronic Mail and Privacy. Unpublished ms. (www.cs.ubc.ca/spider/hoppe/ethics/email.privacy.html)

Herring, S. C. 1993. Gender and Democracy in Computer-Mediated Communication. *Electronic Journal of Communication* 3(2). (comserve@vm.its.rpi.edu: send Herring V3N293.)

Hertz, J.; Krogh, A.; and Palmer, R. G. 1991. *Introduction to the Theory of Neural Computation*. Reading, Mass.: Addison-Wesley.

Hiemstra, G. 1982. Teleconferencing, Concern for Face, and Organizational Culture. In *Communication Yearbook*, ed. Michael Burgoon. Newbury Park, Calif.: Sage.

Hilberman, E. 1976. Rape: "The Ultimate Violation of the Self." *American Journal of Psychiatry* 133:436.

Hilf, F. D.; Colby, K. M.; and Smith, D. C. 1971. Machine-Mediated Interviewing. *Journal of Nervous and Mental Disease* 152(4): 278-288.

Hiltz, S. R., and Turoff, M. 1978. *The Network Nation: Human Communication Via Computer.* Reading, Mass.: Addison-Wesley.

Hiltz, S. R.; Johnson, K.; and Turoff, M. 1986. Experiments in Group Decision Making: Communication Process and Outcome in Face-to-Face Versus Computerized Conferences. *Human Communication Research* 13: 225-252.

Hiltz, S. R.; Turoff, M.; and Johnson, K. 1989. Experiments in Group Decision Making, 3: Disinhibition, De-Individuation, and Group Process in Pen Name and Real Name Computer Conferences. *Decision Support Systems* 5: 217-232.

Hobfoll, S. E.; Gayle, J. A.; Gruber, V.; and Levine, O. 1990. Anxiety's Role in AIDS Prevention. *Anxiety Research* 3(2): 85-99.

Holsti, O. R. 1969. *Content Analysis for the Social Sciences and Humanities.* Reading, Mass.: Addison-Wesley.

Holtgraves, T. 1986. Language Structure in Social Interaction: Perceptions of Direct and Indirect Speech Acts and Interactants Who Use Them. *Journal of Personality and Social Psychology* 51: 305-314.

Holzner, B. 1972. *Reality Construction in Society.* Cambridge, Mass.: Schenkman Publishing Co., Inc.

Honigmann, J. J. 1977. The Masked Face. *Ethos* 5(3): 263-280.

Hopfield, J. J. 1981. Neural Networks and Physical Systems with Emergent Collective Computational Abilities. In *Proceedings of the National Academy of Sciences, of the United States of America.* 79: 2554-2558. Washington, D.C.: Government Printing Office.

Horvath, P., and Zuckerman, M. 1993. Sensation Seeking, Risk Appraisal, and Risky Behavior. *Personality and Individual Differences* 14(1): 41-52.

Huff, C. W., and Rosenberg, J. 1989. The On-Line Voyeur: Promises and Pitfalls of Observing Electronic Interaction. *Behavior Research Methods, Instruments, and Computers* 21(2): 166-172.

Huizinga, J. 1955. *Homo Ludens.* Boston: Beacon.

Inge, M. T. 1990. *Comics as Culture.* Jackson, Miss.: University Press of Mississippi.

Ishii, H., and Kobayashi, M. 1992. ClearBoard: A Seamless Medium for Shared Drawing and Conversion with Eye Contact. In *Proceedings, CHI '92,* 525-532. New York: ACM.

Ivy, D. K. and Backlund, P. 1994. *Exploring GenderSpeak: Personal Effectiveness in Gender Communication.* New York: McGraw-Hill.

Jacobson, D., and Dana, A. 1995. Play and Not-Play in Cyberspace: Frame and Cues in Text-Based Virtual Reality. Paper presented at 1995 Annual Meeting, American Anthropological Association, Washington, D.C., November.

Jacobson, D., and Dana, A. 1997. Contexts and Cues in Cyberspace: The Pragmatics of Naming in Text-based Virtual Realities. *Journal of Anthropological Research* 52(4): 461-479.

Jakobson, R. 1960. Concluding Statement: Linguistics and Poetics. In *Style in Language*, ed. T. A. Sebeok. Cambridge, Mass.: The MIT Press.

Jeffres, L. W.; Dobos, J.; and Lee, J. 1988. Media Use and Community Ties. *Journalism Quarterly* 65(3): 575-581, 677.

Jensen, J. 1991. *Redeeming Modernity: Contradictions in Media Criticism.* Newbury Park, Calif.: Sage.

Johansen, R.; Vallee, J.; and Spangler, K. 1979. *Electronic Meetings: Technical Alternatives and Social Choices.* Reading, Mass.: Addison-Wesley.

Jonah, B. A. 1990. Age Differences in Risky Driving. *Health Education Research* 5(2): 139-149.

Jones, E. E., and Pittman, T. S. 1982. Toward a General Theory of Strategic Self-Presentation. In *Psychological Perspectives on the Self,* ed. J. Suls. Hillsdale, NJ: Lawrence Erlbaum Associates.

Jones, R. A. 1994. The Ethics of Research in Cyberspace. *Internet Research* 4(3): 30-35.

Jones, S. 1995. *CyberSociety.* Newbury Park, Calif.: Sage.

Jones, S. 1998. Media Use in an Electronic Community. In *Network and Netplay: Virtual Groups on the Internet,* eds. F. Sudweeks, M. McLaughlin, and S. Rafaeli. Menlo Park, Calif.: AAAI Press.

Kahn, 1989. Defamation Liability of Computerized Bulletin Board Operators and Problems of Proof. Unpublished ms. (ftp.eff.org/pub/ Legal/bbs-defamation_liability.paper)

Kahneman, D., and Tversky, A. 1973. On the Psychology of Prediction. *Psychological Review* 80: 237-51.

Kalcik, S. 1985.. Women's Handles and the Performance of Identity in the CB Community. In *Women's Folklore, Women's Culture,* eds. R. Jordan and S. Kalcik, 99-108. Philadelphia, Penn.: University of Pennsylvania Press.

Kantrowitz, B. 1994. Men, Women and Computers. *Newsweek* 123(20) (May 16): 48-51.

Kaplan, H. L. 1991. Representation of On-Line Questionnaires in an Editable, Auditable Database. *Behavior Research Methods, Instruments and Computers* 24(2): 373-384.

Kapor, M. 1992. Computer Spies. *Forbes* 150(11): 288.

Katzman, S. 1993. Graphic Accents in Telecommunication. Draft Master's Project, Communications Dept., Stanford Univ., Stanford, Calif.

Kehoe, B. 1992. *Zen and the Art of the Internet.* Cambridge, Mass.: The MIT Press.

Kelly, H. H., and Thibaut, J. W. 1978. *Interpersonal Relations: A Theory of Interdependence.* New York: Wiley.

Kelly, L. 1988. *Surviving Sexual Violence.* Cambridge, England: Polity Press.

Keppel, B. 1990. Electronic Mail Stirs Debate on the Privacy Issue. *Los Angeles Times* 109 (May 23): D1.

Kerlinger, F. N., and Pedhazur, E. J. 1973. *Multiple Regression in Behavioral Research.* New York: Holt, Rinehart and Winston.

Kernan, A. 1989. *Samuel Johnson* and *the Impact of Print.* Princeton, N.J.: Princeton University Press.

Keubelbeck, A. 1991. Getting the Message. Los Angeles *Times* 110 (September 4): E1-2.

Kiesler, S., and Sproull, L. 1992. Group Decision Making and Communication Technology. *Organizational Behavior and Human Decision Processes* 52: 96-123.

Kiesler, S.; Zubrow, D.; Moses, A. M.; and Geller, V. 1985. Affect in Computer-Mediated Communication: An Experiment in Synchronous Terminal-to-Terminal Discussion. *Human Computer Interaction* 1: 77-104.

Kipling, R. 1961. *The Jungle Books*. New York: New American Library.

Kirshenblatt-Gimblett, B. 1996. The Electronic Vernacular. In *Connected: Engagements with Media at Century's End,* ed. G. Marcus, 21-65. Chicago: University of Chicago Press.

Kirshenblatt-Gimblett, B. ed. 1976. *Speech Play: Research and Resources for the Study of Linguistic Creativity*. Philadelphia, Penn.: University of Pennsylvania Press.

Kling, R. 1980. Social Analysis of Computing: Theoretical Perspectives in Recent Empirical Research. *Computing Surveys* 12(1): 61-110.

Konner, M. 1982. *The Tangled Wing*. New York: Holt, Rinehart and Winston.

Kozar, S. 1995. Enduring Traditions, Ethereal Transmissions: Recreating Chinese New Year Celebrations on the Internet. *Journal of Computer-Mediated Communication:* Play and Performance in Computer-Mediated Communication 1(2). (www.usc.edu/dept/annenberg/vol1/issue2/)

Kramarae, C. 1995. A Backstage Critique of Virtual Reality. In *CyberSociety: Computer-mediated Communication and Community*, ed. S. Jones. Newbury Park, Calif.: Sage Publications.

Kramarae, C., and Taylor, H. J. 1992. Electronic Networks: Safe for Women? The Electronic Salon: Feminism Meets Infotech. Paper presented at the Eleventh Annual Gender Studies Symposium. Speech Communication and Sociology. (ftp.clark.edu).

Kramarae, C., and Taylor, J. 1993. Women and Men on Electronic Networks: A Conversation or a Monologue? In *Women, Information Technology, and Scholarship*, ed. H. Jeanie Taylor, Cheris Kramarae, and Maureen Ebben, 52-61. Urbana, Ill.: Center for Advanced Study, University of Illinois at Urbana-Champaign.

Krippendorf, K. 1980. *Content Analysis: An Introduction to its Methodology*. Newbury Park, Calif.: Sage.

Krol, E. 1992. *The Whole Internet User's Guide and Catalog*. Sebastopol, Calif.: O'Reilly and Associates, Inc.

Krol, E. 1993. FYI on "What is the Internet?" Internet RFC 1462.

Labov, W. 1972. Rules for Ritual Insults. In *Studies in Social Interaction*, ed. D. Sudnow, 120-169. New York: Macmillan.

Lakoff, R. 1975. *Language and Woman's Place*. New York: Harper and Row.

Lanham, R. A. 1993. *The Electronic Word: Democracy, Technology, and the Arts*. Chicago: University of Chicago Press.

Lanier, J., and Biocca, F. 1992. An Insider's View of the Future of Virtual Reality. *Journal of Communication:* Virtual Reality: A Communication Perspective 42(4): 150-172.

LaQuey, T., and Ryer, J. C. 1993. *The Internet Companion: A Beginner's Guide to Global Networking*. Reading, Mass.: Addison-Wesley.

Laurel, B. 1991. *Computers as Theatre*. Reading, Mass.: Addison-Wesley.

Lea, M.; O'Shea, T.; Fung, P.; and Spears, R. 1992. "Flaming" in Computer-Mediated Communication: Observations, Explanations, Implications. In *Contexts of Computer-Mediated Communication*, ed. M. Lea, 89-112. London: Harvester Wheatsheaf.

LeGrande, C. E. 1973. Rape and Rape Laws: Sexism in Society and Law. *California Law Review* 61: 919-941.

LeGuin, U. 1969. *The Left Hand of Darkness*. New York: Ace.

Leslie, J. 1994. Mail Bonding: E-Mail is Creating a New Oral Culture. *Wired* 3(2):42,44-48.

Levy, S. 1984. *Hackers: Heroes of the Computer Revolution*. Garden City, N.Y.: Doubleday.

Lewis, P. H. 1990. On Electronic Bulletin Boards, What Rights Are at Stake? *The New York Times* 140(3,December 23): F8.

Lindlof, T. R. 1989. Media Audiences as Interpretive Communities. *Communication Yearbook* 11(81): 107.

Loebl, J. W. 1992. Law Firms, Employees May Clash Over Rights to Computerized Data. *The National Law Journal* 14(9): 30.

Losada, M.; Sanchez, P.; and Noble, E. E. 1990. Collaborative Technology and Group Process Feedback: Their Impact on Interactive Sequence in Meetings. In *Proceedings of CSCW '90*, 53-64. New York: ACM Press.

Luria, A. R. 1961. *The Role of Speech in the Regulation of Normal and Abnormal Behavior*. London: Pergamon Press.

Luria, A. R. 1976. *Basic Problems of Neurolinguistics*. Paris: Mouton.

Luria, A. R., and Yudovich, F. I. 1959. *Speech and the Development of Mental Processes in the Child*. London: Pergamon Press.

Mabry, E. A. 1998. Frames and Flames: The Structure of Argumentative Messages on the Net. In *Network and Netplay: Virtual Groups on the Internet*, eds. F. Sudweeks, M. McLaughlin, and S. Rafaeli. Menlo Park, Calif.: AAAI Press.

Mabry, E. A.; Jackson, J.; McPhee, R. D.; and Van Lear, A. 1990. Interactional Arguments and Group Decision-Making. Paper presented at 1990 Annual Meeting of the Speech Communication Association, Chicago, Illinois, 10 November.

Mabry, E. A.; Van Lear, A.; Jackson, J.; and McPhee, R. D. 1991. Constitutive Dimensions of Small Group Argument: Rethinking Argument in Persuasive Arguments Theory. In *Argument in Controversy: Proceedings of the Seventh SCA/AFA Conference*, ed. D. Parsons, 175-181. Annendale, Va.: SCA.

MacKinnon, R. 1998. The Social Construction of Rape in Virtual Reality. In *Network and Netplay: Virtual Groups on the Internet*, eds. F. Sudweeks, M. McLaughlin, and S. Rafaeli. Menlo Park, Calif.: AAAI Press.

MacKinnon, R. C. 1992. *Searching for the Leviathan in Usenet*. Master's Thesis, Department of Political Science, San Jose State Univ. (www.virtualschool.edu/mon/Economics/MacKinnonLeviathonUsenet.html)

MacKinnon, R. C. 1995. Searching for the Leviathan in Usenet. In *Cybersociety*, ed. S. Jones, 112-137. Newbury Park, Calif.: Sage.

MacKinnon, R. C. 1997. Punishing the Persona: Correctional Strategies for the Virtual Offender. In *Virtual Culture: Identity and Communication in CyberSociety*, ed. S. Jones. London: Sage.

MacKinnon, R. C. 1998. The Social Construction of Rape in Virtual Reality. In *Network and Netplay: Virtual Groups on the Internet*, eds F. Sudweeks, M. McLaughlin and S. Rafaeli. Menlo Park, Calif.: AAAI Press.

McLaughlin, Margaret L. 1984. *Conversation: How Talk Is Organized.* Newbury Park, Calif.: Sage.

McLaughlin, Margaret L., Osborne, K. K., and Smith, C. B. 1995. Rules of Conduct on Usenet. In *CyberSociety*, ed. S. Jones, 138-163. Newbury Park, Calif.: Sage.

Maes, P. 1995. Artificial Life Meets Entertainment: Lifelike Autonomous Agents. *Communications of the ACM* 38(11): 108-114.

Malamuth, N. M. 1948. Aggression Against Women: Cultural and Individual Causes, In *Pornography and Sexual Aggression*, eds. N. M. Malamuth and E. Donnerstein. New York: Academic Press.

Malamuth, N. M. 1981. Rape Proclivity Among Males. *Journal of Social Issues* 37: 138-157.

Malamuth, N. M. 1983. Factors Associated With Rape as Predictors of Laboratory Aggression Against Women. *Journal of Personality and Social Psychology* 45: 432-442.

Malinowski, B. 1932. *The Sexual Life of Savages in North-Western Melanesia.* London: George Routledge and Sons, Ltd.

Marvin, L.-E. 1995. Spoof, Spam, Lurk and Lag: Aesthetics of Text-Based Virtual Realities. *Journal of Computer-Mediated Communication:* Play and Performance in Computer-Mediated Communication 1(2). (www.usc.edu/dept/annenberg/vol1/issue2/)

Matheson, K. 1991. Social Cues in Computer-Mediated Negotiations: Gender Makes a Difference. *Computers in Human Behavior* 7(3): 137-146.

Matheson, K. and Zanna, M. P. 1990. Computer-Mediated Communications: The Focus Is on Me. *Social Science Computer Review* 8(1): 1-12.

Matheson, K., and Zanna, M. 1989. Impact of Computer-Mediated Communication on Self Awareness. *Computers in Human Behavior* 4(3): 221-233.

Mauldin, M. 1994. ChatterBots, TinyMUDs, and the Turing Test: Entering the Loebner Prize Competition. In *Proceedings of the AAAI 1994 Conference*, 16-21. Menlo Park, Calif.: AAAI Press.

Maynor, N. 1994. The Language of Electronic Mail: Written Speech? In *Centennial Usage Studies*, eds. G. Little and M. Montgomery, 48-54. Tuscaloosa, Ala.: University of Alabama (American Dialect Society Series). (www2.msstate.edu/~maynor/ index.html)

McCormick, N. B., and McCormick, J. W. 1992. Computer Friends and Foes: Contents of Undergraduates' Electronic Mail. *Computers in Human Behavior* 8(4): 379-405.

McGrath, J. E. 1990. Time Matters in Groups. In *Intellectual Teamwork: Social and Technological Foundations of Cooperative Work.*, eds. J. Galegher, R. E. Kraut and C. Egido. Hillsdale, N.J.: Lawrence Erlbaum Associates.

McGuire, M. T., and Stanley, J. 1971. Dyadic Communication, Verbal Behavior, Thinking, and Understanding: II. Four Studies. *Journal of Nervous and Mental Disease* 152(4): 242-259.

McGuire, T. W.; Kiesler, S.; and Siegel, J. 1987. Group and Computer-Mediated Discussion Effects in Risk Decision Making. *Journal of Personality and Social Psychology* 52(5): 917-30.

McHenry, W. K. 1994. Electronic Mail in Russia: An Overview. In *Proceedings of the Conference on the Future of Electronic Communications,* ed. Y. Gornostaev, 118-126. Moscow: Eco-Trends.

McLaughlin, M. L.; Osborne, K. K.; and Smith, C. B. 1995. Standards of Conduct on Usenet. In *CyberSociety*, ed. S. Jones, 90-111. Newbury Park, Calif.: Sage.

McLaughlin, M. L. 1984. *Conversation: How Talk is Organized.* Sage Series in Interpersonal Communication, Vol. 3. Newbury Park, Calif.: Sage.

McLaughlin, M. L.; Cody, M. J.; and O'Hair, H. D. 1983. The Management of Failure Events: Some Contextual Determinants of Accounting Behavior. *Human Communication Research* 9: 209-224.

McLaughlin, M. L.; Cody, M. J.; and Read, S. J. eds. 1992. Explaining One's Self to Others: Reason-Giving in a Social Context. Hillsdale, N.J.: Erlbaum.

McLaughlin, M. L.; Osborne, K. K.; and Smith, C. B. 1995. Standards of Conduct on Usenet. In *CyberSociety,* ed. S. Jones, 90-111. Newbury Park, Calif.: Sage.

Mehra, P., and Wah, B. W., eds. 1992. *Artificial Neural Networks.* Los Alamitos, Calif.: IEEE Computer Society Press.

Melbin, M. 1977. *Night as Frontier.* Glencoe, Ill.: Free Press.

Merton, R. K. 1973. *The Sociology of Science: Theoretical and Empirical Investigations.* Chicago: University of Chicago Press.

Meyer, G., and Thomas, J. 1990. The Baudy World of the Byte Bandit: A Postmodernist Interpretation of the Computer Underground. In*Computers in Criminal Justice*, ed. F. Schmalleger, 31-67. Bristol, In.: Wyndham Hall. (ftp.eff.org;/pub/cud/papers/baudy.world.)

Miller, D. 1994. The Many Faces of the Internet. *Internet World* 5 (7, October): 34-38.

Miller, M. W. 1991. Lotus is Likely to Abandon Consumer-Data Project. *The Wall Street Journal* CCXVII (16)(January 23):B1.

Miller, S. C. 1992. Privacy in Email? Better to Assume It Doesn't Exist. *The New York Times* 151(3): 8F(N), 8F(L).

Mittal, B. 1988. Achieving Higher Seat Belt Usage: The Role of Habit in Bridging the Attitude-Behavior Gap. *Journal of Applied Social Psychology* 18(12): Pt. 2, 993-1016.

Moody, J., and Darken, C. J. 1989. Fast Learning in Networks of Locally-Tuned Processing Units. *Neural Computation* 1(2):281-294.

Moore, W. J. 1992. Taming Cyberspace. *National Journal* 24(13): 745-749.

Mr Bungle. 1991. *Mr Bungle* (compact disc). Burbank, Calif.: Warner Bros. Records Inc.

Mulac, A., and Lundell, T. L. 1986. Linguistic Contributors to the Gender-Linked Language Effect. *Journal of Language and Social Psychology* 5(2): 91-101.

Mulac, A.; Bradac, J. J.; and Mann, S. K. 1985. Male/Female Language Differences and Attributional Consequences in Children's Television. *Human Communication Research* 11(4): 481-506.

Murray, D. E. 1991. *Conversation for Action: The Computer Terminal as Medium of Communication.* Amsterdam: John Benjamins.

Myers, D. 1987a. "Anonymity is Part of the Magic:" Individual Manipulation of Computer-Mediated Communication Contexts. *Qualitative Sociology* 10(3): 251-266.

Myers, D. 1987b. A New Environment for Communication Play: On-Line Play. In *Meaningful Play, Playful Meaning,* ed. G. A. Fine, 231-245. Champaign, Ill.: Human Kinetics.

Nass, C.; Moon, Y.; Fogg, B.; Reeves, B.; and Dryer, D. 1995. Can Computer Personalities Be Human Personalities? *International Journal of Human-Computer Studies,* 43(4): 223-239.

Nass, C.; Steuer, J.; and Tauber, E. 1994. Computers Are Social Actors. In *Proceedings of the CHI Conference,* 72-78. New York: ACM Press.

Neuwirth, C. M.; Kaufer, D. S.; Chandhok, R.; and Morris, J. H. 1994. Computer Support for Distributed Collaborative Writing: Defining Parameters of Interaction. In *Proceedings of CSCW 94,* 145-152. New York: ACM Press.

Newberry, M. 1995. "Katipo—A Web Lurker." Unpublished ms. Victoria University of Wellington, New Zealand: (www.vuw.ac.nz/~newbery/Katipo.html)

Newhagen, J., and Rafaeli, S. 1996. Why Communication Researchers Should Study the Net. *Journal of Communication* 46(1). (jcmc.huji.ac.il/vol1/issue4/ rafaeli.html)

Newton, S. 1992, On the Relevance and Treatment of Categories in AI in Design. In *Artificial Intelligence in Design '92,* ed. J. S. Gero, 861-882. Dordrecht, Holland: Kluwer.

Niven, D.; Wang, C.; Rowe, M. P.; Taga, M.; Vladeck, J. P.; and Garron, L. C. 1992. The Case of the Hidden Harassment. *Harvard Business Review* 70(2): 12-19.

Norman, D. A. 1993. *Things That Make Us Smart: Defending Human Attributes in the Age of the Machine.* Reading, Mass.: Addison-Wesley.

Norusis, M. J. 1993. *SPSS for Windows: Professional Statistics, Release 6.0.* Chicago: SPSS, Inc.

Nunnally, J. 1978. *Psychometric Theory 2e.* New York: McGraw-Hill.

Oldenburg, R. 1989. *The Great Good Place: Cafes, Coffee Shops, Community Centers, Beauty Parlors, General Stores, Bars, Hangouts and How They Get You Through the Day.* New York: Paragon House.

Olien, C. N.; Donohue, G. A.; and Tichenor, P. J. 1978. Community Structure and Media Use. *Journalism Quarterly* 55(3): 445-455.

Olmert, M. 1992. *The Smithsonian Book of Books.* Washington, DC: The Smithsonian Press.

Ong, W. J. 1982. *Orality and Literacy: The Technologizing of the Word.* London: Methuen.

Oren, T.; Salomon, G.; Kreitman, K.; and Don, A. 1995. Guides: Characterizing the Interface. In *The Art of Human-Computer Interface Design,* ed. B. Laurel, 367-381. Reading, Mass.: Addison-Wesley.

Osborn, A. F. 1953. *Applied Imagination.* New York: Scribner.

Palmer, M. T. 1994. Interpersonal Communication and Virtual Reality: Mediating Interpersonal Relationships. In *Communication in the Age of Virtual Reality*, eds. F. Biocca and S. Levy. Hillsdale, N.J.: Lawrence Erlbaum Associates.

Perkel, A. K.; Strebel, A.; and Joubert, G. 1991. The Psychology of AIDS Transmission: Issues for Intervention. *South African Journal of Psychology* 21(3): 148-152.

Piaget, J. 1929. *The Child's Conception of the World*. New York: Harcourt Brace.

Poole, M. S., and DeSanctis, G. 1989. Understanding the Use of Group Decision Support Systems: The Theory of Adaptive Structuration. In *Organization and Communication Technology*, eds. J. Fulk and C. Steinfield, 173-193. Newbury Park, Calif.: Sage.

Poole, M. S., and McPhee, R. D. 1983. A Structural Analysis of Organizational Climate. In *Communication and Organizations: An Interpretive Approach*, eds. L. L. Putnam and M. E. Pacanowsky, 195-219. Newbury Park, Calif.: Sage.

Poster, M. 1990. *The Mode of Information: Poststructuralisms and Contexts*. Chicago: University of Chicago Press.

Powell, J. 1983. CB: An Inquiry into a Novel State of Communication. *The Automobile and American Culture*. Ann Arbor, Mich.: University of Michigan Press.

Press, L. 1991. Wide-Area Collaboration. *Communications of the ACM* 34(12): 21-24.

Pulman, S. G. 1983. *Word Meaning and Belief*. London: Croom Held.

Quarterman, J. S. 1990. *The Matrix: Computer Networks and Conferencing Systems Worldwide*. Burlington, Mass.: Digital Press.

Quina, K.; Wingard, J. A.; and Bates, H. G. 1987. Language Style and Gender Stereotypes in Person Perception. *Psychology of Women Quarterly* 11(1): 111-122.

Quinsey, V. L. 1984. Sexual Aggression: Studies of Offenders Against Women. In *Law and Mental Health: International Perspectives, Vol 1*, ed. D. Weisstub. New York: Pergamon.

Rafaeli, S. 1986. The Electronic Bulletin Board: A Computer Driven Mass Medium. *Computers and the Social Sciences* 2(3): 123-136.

Rafaeli, S. 1988. Interactivity: From New Media to Communication. In *Sage Annual Review of Communication Research: Advancing Communication Science, Volume 16.*, eds. R. P. Hawkins, J. Wiemann and S. Pingree, 110-134. Newbury Park, Calif.: Sage.

Rafaeli, S. and Sudweeks, F. 1998. Interactivity on the Net. In *Network and Netplay: Virtual Groups on the Internet*, eds. F. Sudweeks; M. McLaughlin; and S. Rafaeli. Menlo Park, Calif: AAAI Press.

Rafaeli, S., and LaRose, R. J. 1993. Electronic Bulletin Boards and "Public Goods" Explanations of Collaborative Mass Media. *Communication Research* 20(2): 177-197.

Rafaeli, S., and Sudweeks, F. 1998. Interactivity on the Nets. In *Network and Netplay: Virtual Groups on the Internet,* eds. F. Sudweeks, M. McLaughlin, and S. Rafaeli. Menlo Park, Calif.: AAAI Press.

Rafaeli, S., and Tractinsky, N. 1989. Computerized Tests and Time: Measuring, Limiting and Providing Visual Cues for Response Time in On-Line Questioning. *Behaviour and Information Technology* 8(5): 335-351.

Rafaeli, S., and Tractinsky, N. 1991. Time in Computerized Test: A Multitrait, Multi-method Investigation of General-Knowledge and Mathematical-Reasoning On-Line Examinations. *Computers in Human Behavior* 7(3): 215-225.

Rafaeli, S.; McLaughlin, M. L.; and Sudweeks, F. 1998. Introduction. In *Network and Netplay: Virtual Groups on the Internet*, eds. F. Sudweeks, M. McLaughlin, and S. Rafaeli. Menlo Park, Calif.: AAAI Press.

Rafaeli, S.; Sudweeks, F.; Konstan, J.; and Mabry, E. 1994. ProjectH Overview: A Quantitative Study of Computer Mediated Communication, Technical Report, Dept. Communication, Univ. of Sydney. (www.arch.su.edu.au/~fay/projecth.html.)

Ratcliffe, M. 1992. Privacy Focus of Borland Case. *MacWeek* 6(35): 1-2

Raymond, E. S. 1991. *The New Hackers' Dictionary*. With Assistance and Illustrations by G. L. Steele, Jr. Cambridge, Mass.: The MIT Press.

Reed, B. S. 1990. Unity, not Absorption: Robert Lyon and the Asmonean. *American Journalism* 7(2):77-95.

Reid, B. 1993. Top 40 Newsgroups in Order by Popularity. News, Lists, Internet newsgroup. Posted August 6.

Reid, B. 1994. Usenet Readership Summary Report for July 94. DEC Network Systems Laboratory. Marlboro, Mass.: Digital Equipment Corporation.

Reid, E. 1991. Electropolis: Communication and Community on Internet Relay Chat. B.A. Honors Thesis, Dept. of History, University of Melbourne

Reid, Elizabeth 1995. Virtual Worlds: Culture and Imagination. In *Cybersociety: Computer- Mediated Communication and Community,* ed. S. Jones, 164-183. Newbury Park, Calif.: Sage.

Reid, E. M. 1991. *Electropolis: Communication and Community on Internet Relay Chat.*. B.A. Honours Thesis, Department of History, University of Melbourne.

Resnick, P.; Iacovou, N.; Suchak, M.; Bergstrom; and Riedl, J. 1994. GroupLens: An Open Architecture for Collaborative Filtering of Netnews. In *Proceedings of CSCW 94*, R. Furuta and C. Neuwirth, 175-186. New York: ACM Press.

Rheingold, H. 1991. *Virtual Reality*. New York: Summit Books.

Rheingold, H. 1994. *The Virtual Community: Finding Connection in a Computerized World*. London: Secker and Warburg.

Rheingold, H. 1993a. A Slice of Life in My Virtual Community. In *Global networks: Computers and international communication,* ed. L. M. Harasim, 57-80. Cambridge, Mass.: The MIT Press. (ftp.eff.org./pub.EFF/papers.cyber.)

Rheingold, H. 1993b. *The Virtual Community: Homesteading on the Electronic Frontier.* Reading, Mass.: Addison-Wesley.

Rheingold, H. 1993c. *Virtual Communities*. Reading, Mass.: Addison-Wesley.

Rhodes, R. 1981. Why Do Men Rape? *Playboy* . (April): 112-114, 172, 224-230.

Rice, M. L.; Sell, M. A.; and Hadley, P. A. 1990. The Social Interactive Coding System (SICS): An On-Line, Clinically Relevant Descriptive Tool. *Language, Speech, and Hearing Services in Schools* 21(2): 2-14.

Rice, R. E. 1984. *The New Media: Communication, Research, and Technology*. Newbury Park, Calif.: Sage.

Rice, R. E., and Love, G. 1987. Electronic Emotion: Socioemotional Content in a Computer-Mediated Communication Network. *Communication Research* 14(1):85-108.

Riddle, M. H. 1990. The Electronic Pamphlet—Computer Bulletin Boards and the Law. Unpublished ms. (ftp.eff.org/pub/EFF//Legal/bbs_and_law.paper)

Riley, P. 1983. A Structurationist Account of Political Culture. *Administrative Science Quarterly* 28(3): 414-437.

Ritzer, G. 1992. *Sociological Theory, Third Edition*. New York: McGraw-Hill.

Rogers, E. M. 1962. *Diffusion of Innovations*. New York: Free Press.

Rogers, E. M. 1986. *Communication Technology: The New Media in Society*. New York: The Free Press.

Rogers, E. M., and Rafaeli, S. 1985. Computers and Communication. In *Information and Behavior, Vol. 1*, ed. B. D. Ruben, 135-155. New Brunswick, N.J.: Transaction Books.

Rosch, E. 1978. Principles of Categorization. In *Cognition and Categorization*, eds. E. Rosch, and B. B. Lloyd, 27-48. Hillsdale, N.J.: Lawrence Erlbaum.

Rose, V. M. 1977. Rape as a Social Problem: A By-Product of the Feminist Movement. *Social Problems* 25: 75-89.

Rosengren, K. E. 1981. *Advances in Content Analysis*. Newbury Park, Calif.: Sage.

Rosenman, M. A., and Sudweeks, F. 1995. Categorisation and Prototypes in Design. In *Perspectives on Cognitive Science: Theories, Experiments and Foundations*, eds. P. Slezak; T. Caelli; and R. Clarke, 189-212. Norwood, N.J.: Albex.

Rucker, R. 1992. On the Edge of the Pacific. In *Mondo 2000 Users' Guide to the New Edge*, eds. R. Rucker, R. U. Sirius, and Q. Mu, 9-13. London: Thames and Hudson.

Ruedenberg, L.; Danet, B.; and Rosenbaum-Tamari, Y. 1995. Virtual Virtuosos: Play and Performance at the Computer Keyboard. *EJC: Electronic Journal of Communication* 5(4). (comserve@cios.llc.rpi.edu; command: send Rueden v5n495).

Ruggiero, G. 1975. Sexual Criminality in the Early Renaissance: Venice 1338-1358. *Journal of Social History* 8: 18-37.

Rumelhart, D. E., and McClelland, J. L., eds. 1986. *Parallel Distributed Processing: Exploration in the Microstructure of Cognition, Vol. 1: Foundations*. Cambridge, Mass.: The MIT Press.

Sabin, R. 1993b. *Underground Comics: An Introduction*. London: Routledge.

Sanders, W. B. 1980. *Rape and Woman's Identity*. Newbury Park, Calif.: Sage Publications.

Sanderson, D. W., and Dougherty, D. 1993. *Smileys*. Sebastopol, Calif.: O'Reilly and Associates, Inc.

Schaefermeyer, M. J. and Sewell, E. H. 1988. Communicating by Electronic Mail. *American Behavioral Scientist* 32(2): 112-123.

Schechner, R. 1988. Playing. *Play and Culture* 1(1): 3-19.

Schegloff, E. A. 1992. Repair After Next Turn: The Last Structurally Provided Defense of Intersubjectivity in Conversation. *American Journal of Sociology* 97(5): 1245-1295.

Schegloff, E. A. 1987. Between Macro and Micro: Contexts and Other Connections. In *The Micro-Macro Link*, eds. J. C. Alexander, B. Giesan, R. Much and N. J. Smalser, 207-234. Berkeley, Calif.: University of California Press.

Schlenker, B. R. 1980. *Impression Management.* Pacific Grove, Calif.: Brooks/Cole.

Schmidt, K., and Bannon, L. 1992. Taking CSCW Seriously: Supporting Articulation Work. *Computer Supported Cooperative Work (CSCW)* 1(1): 1-33.

Schmitz, J. A., and Fulk, J. 1991. Organizational Colleagues, Information Richness, and Electronic Mail: A Test of the Social Influence Model of Technology Use. *Communication Research* 18(4): 487-523.

Schonbach, P. 1990. *Account Episodes: The Management or Escalation of Conflict.* New York: Cambridge University Press.

Schopler, J. 1965. Social Power. In *Advances in Experimental Social Psychology, Vol. 2.*, ed. L. Berkowitz. New York: Academic Press.

Schudson, M. 1978. The Ideal of Conversation in the Study of Mass Media. *Communication Research* 5(3): 320-329.

Schwarz, J. 1993. On-line Lothario's Antics Prompt Debate on Cyber-Age Ethics. *The Washington Post*, 116 (July 11): A1.

Schweitzer, J. C. 1991. Personal Computers and Media Use. *Journalism Quarterly* 68 (4): 689-697.

Schwendinger, J. R., and Schwendinger, H. 1983. *Rape and Inequality.* Newbury Park, Calif.: Sage Publications.

Scott, M. B., and Lyman, S. M. 1968. Accounts. *American Sociological Review* 33: 46-62.

Selfe, C. L., and Meyer, C. A. 1991. Testing Claims for Online Conferences. *Written Communication* 8: 165-192.

Shade, L. R. 1993. Gender Issues in Computer Networking. Paper presented at 1993 Community Networking: The International Free-Net Conference, Carleton University, Ottawa, Canada.

Shapiro, N. Z. and Anderson, R. H. 1985. Toward an Ethics and Etiquette for Electronic Mail. Technical Report, R-3283-NSF/RC,The Rand Corporation, Santa Monica, Calif. (www.rand.org/areas/r3283.html.)

Shaver, K. G. 1987. *Principles of Social Psychology, Third Edition.* Hillsdale, N.J.: Lawrence Erlbaum Associates.

Shea, V. 1994. *Netiquette.* San Francisco: Albion Books.

Sheldon, T. 1992. *Windows 3.1 Made Easy.* New York: McGraw-Hill.

Sherblom, J. C. 1990. Organizational Involvement Expressed Through Pronoun Use in Computer Mediated Communication. *Communication Research Reports* 7(1): 45-50.

Sherr, L.; Strong, C.; and Goldmeier, D. 1990. Sexual Behaviour, Condom Use and Prediction in Attenders at Sexually Transmitted Disease Clinics: Implications for Counseling. *Counseling Psychology Quarterly* 3(4): 343-352.

Shields, W. M., and Shields, L. M. 1983. Forcible Rape: An Evolutionary Perspective. *Ethology and Sociobiology* 4(2): 115-136.

Short, J.; Williams, E.; and Christie, B. 1976. *The Social Psychology of Telecommunications.* New York: Wiley.

Siegel, J.; Dubrovsky, V.; Kiesler, S.; and MaGuire, T. W. 1986. Group Processes in Computer-Mediated Communication. *Organizational Behaviour and Human Decision Processes* 37(2): 157-187.

Sitkin, S. B.; Sutcliffe, K. M.; and Barrios-Choplin, J. R. 1989. Determinants of Communication Media Choice in Crganizations: A Dual Function Perspective. Paper Presented at 1989 National Meeting of the Academy of Management, Washington, D.C., September.

Smith, C. B.; McLaughlin, M. L.; and Osborne, K. K. 1998. From Terminal Ineptitude to Virtual Sociopathy: How Conduct Is Regulated on Usenet. In *Network and Netplay: Virtual Groups on the Internet,* eds. F. Sudweeks, M. McLaughlin, and S. Rafaeli. Menlo Park, Calif.: AAAI Press.

Smith, E. E., and Medin, D. L. 1981. *Categories and Concepts.* Cambridge, Mass.: Harvard University Press.

Snoeck Henkemans, A. F. 1989. Analyzing Argumentative Texts; The Normative Reconstruction of Multiple and Coordinatively Compound Argumentation. In *Spheres of Argument: Proceedings of the Sixth SCA/AFA Conference on Argumentation,* ed. B. E. Gronbeck, 331-334. Annendale, Va.: SCA.

Snoeck Henkemans, A. F. 1991. The Analysis of Dialogical Elements in Argumentative Texts. In *Proceeding of the Second International Conference on Argumentation,* eds. F. Van Eemeren, R. Grootendorst, J. A. Blair, and C. A. Willard, 365-370. Amsterdam: SICSAT.

Solomon, J. 1990. Electronic Mail: Is it For Your Eyes Only? *The Wall Street Journal* CCXVI (25) (August 6): B1.

Spafford, G. 1993. Rules for Posting to Usenet. Unpublished ms. (ftp.rtfm.mit.edu/pub/usenet/news.answers/posting-rules.)

Specter (1995). *WebWatch.* Specter Communications. (www.specter.com/)

Spitzer, M. 1986. Writing Style in Computer Conferences. *IEEE Transactions on Professional Communications (PC)* 29: 19-22.

Sproull, L. and Kiesler, S. 1991. *Connections: New Ways of Working in the Networked Organization.* Cambridge, Mass.: The MIT Press.

Stamm, K. 1985. *Newspaper Use and Community Ties: Toward a Dynamic Theory.* Norwood, N.J.: Ablex.

Steiner, P. 1993. On the Internet, Nobody Knows You're a Dog? *The New Yorker.* (July 5): 61.

Steinfield, C. W. 1986. Computer Mediated Communication in an Organizational Setting: Explaining Task Related and Socioemotional Uses. In *Communication Yearbook 9,* ed. M. L. McLaughlin, 777-804. Newbury Park, Calif.: Sage.

Steinfield, C. W. 1987. Computer Mediated Communication Systems. In *Annual Review of Information Science and Technology, 21,* ed. M. E. Williams, 167-202. Newbury Park, Calif.: Sage.

Stoll, F. C.; Hoecker, D. G.; Krueger, G. P.; and Chapanis, A. 1976. The Effects of Four Communication Modes on the Structure of Language Used During Cooperative Problem Solving. *Journal of Psychology* 94: 13-26.

Stone, A. R. 1992. Will the Real Body Please Stand Up?: Boundary Stories About Virtual Cultures. In *Cyberspace: First Steps,* ed. M. Benedikt. Cambridge, Mass.: The MIT Press.

Strate, L. 1995. Experiencing Cybertime: Computing as Activity and Event. *IPCT—Interpersonal Computing and Technology: An Electronic Journal for the 21st Century* 3(2) (Strate ipctv3n2 from listserv@guvm.georgetown.edu).

Sudweeks, F., and Rafaeli, S. 1996. How Do You Get a Hundred Strangers to Agree: Computer Mediated Communication and Collaboration. In *Computer Networking and Scholarship in the 21st Century*, eds. T. M. Harrison and T. D. Stephens, 115-136. New York: SUNY Press. (www.arch.usvg.edu.au/~fay/papers/strangers.html)`

Sudweeks, F.; Collins, M.; and December, J. 1995. Internetworking Resources. In *Computer-Mediated Communication and the Online Classroom: An Overview and Perspectives, Vol. 1*, eds. Z. Berge and M Collins, 193-212. Cresskill, N.J.: Hampton Press.

Symons, D. 1979. *The Evolution of Human Sexuality*. New York: Oxford University Press.

Tabachnick, B. G., and Fidell, L. S. 1989. *Using Multivariate Statistics*, Second Editon. New York: Harper Collins Publishers, Inc.

Tabori, P. 1971. *The Social History of Rape*. London: The New English Library, Ltd.

Tannen, D. 1982a. The Myth of Orality and Literacy. In *Linguistics and Literacy*, ed. W. Frawley, 37-50. New York: Plenum.

Tannen, D. 1982b. The Oral/Literate Continuum in Discourse. In *Spoken and Written Language: Exploring Orality and Literacy*, ed. D. Tannen, 1-16. Norwood, N.J.: Ablex.

Tannen, D. 1989. *Talking Voices: Repetition, Dialogue, and Imagery in Conversational Discourse*. Cambridge, England: Cambridge University Press.

Tannen, D. 1990. *You Just Don't Understand*. New York: Ballantine.

Tannen, D. 1994. Gender Gap in Cyberspace. *Newsweek* 123(20) (March 16): 53.

Thiessen, D. D. 1986. The Unseen Roots of Rape: The Theoretical Untouchable. *Revue Europeanne des Sciences Sociales* 24: 9-40.

Thomas, F., and Johnston, O. 1981. *Disney Animation: The Illusion of Life*. New York: Hyperion Books.

Thomas, W. I., and Znaniecki, F. 1927. *The Polish Peasant in Europe and America, Vols. I and II*. New York: Knopf.

Thornhill, R., and Thornhill, N. W. 1983. Human Rape: An Evolutionary Analysis. *Ethology and Sociobiology* 4(2): 137- 173.

Thornhill, R., and Thornhill, N. W. 1987. Human Rape: The Strengths of the Evolutionary Perspective. In *Sociobiology and Psychology: Ideas, Issues, and Applications*, eds. C. Crawford, M. Smith, and D. Krebs. Hillsdale, N.J.: Lawrence Erlbaum Associates.

Tichenor, P. J.; Donohue, G. A.; and Olien, C. N. 1980. *Community Conflict and the Press*. Newbury Park, Calif.: Sage.

Tichenor, P. J.; Olien, C. N.; and Donohue, G. A. 1970. Mass Media Flow and Differential Growth in Knowledge. *Public Opinion Quarterly* 34: 159-170.

Tipton, R. M.; Camp, C. C.; and Hsu, K. 1990. The Effects of Mandatory Seat Belt Legislation on Self-Reported Seat Belt Use Among Male and Female College Students. *Accident Analysis and Prevention* 22(6): 543-548.

Trevino, L. K.; Daft, R. L.; and Lengel, R. H. 1990. Understanding Manager's Media Choices: A Symbolic Interactionist Perspective. In *Organizations and Communication Technology*, eds. J. Fulk and C. Steinfield, 71-94. Newbury Park, Calif: Sage.

Troll, D. A. 1990. The Illiterate Mode of Written Communication: The Work of the Medieval Scribe. *Oral and Written Communication: Historical Approaches,* ed. R. L. Enos, 96-125. Newbury Park, Calif.: Sage.

Trudgill, P. 1983. *Sociolinguistics: An Introduction to Language and Society.* London: Penguin Books.

Truong, H. 1993. Gender Issues in On-Line Communications. Paper presented at 1993 Third Conference on Computers, Freedom, and Privacy, Burlingame, California, March. (ftp.cpsr.org/Gender)

Turkle, S. 1984. *The Second Self: Computers and the Human Spirit.* New York: Simon and Schuster.

Turkle, S. 1995. *Life on the Screen: Identity in the Age of the Internet.* New York: Simon and Schuster.

Turner, J. A. 1991. Messages in Questionable Taste on Computer Networks Pose Thorny Problems for College Administrators. *Chronicle of Higher Education* 36(19) (September 14): A13-A14.

Turner, V. 1967. *The Forest of Symbols.* Ithaca: Cornell University Press.

Turner, V. 1974. From Liminal to Liminoid: An Essay in Comparative Symbology. *Rice University Studies* 60(3): 53-92.

Turner, V. 1986a. *The Anthropology of Performance.* New York: PAJ Publications.

Turner, V. 1986b. Carnaval in Rio: Dionysian Drama in an Industralizing Society. In *The Anthropology of Performance*, ed. V. Turner, 123-138. New York: PAJ Publications.

Turner, V. 1986c. Performing Ethnography. In *The Anthropology of Performance.* New York: PAJ Publications.

Tversky, A. 1977. Features of Similarity. *Psychological Review* 84(4):327-52.

Ulrich, A. 1992. Here's Reality: "Mower" is Less. *San Francisco Examiner* (March 7).

Valacich, J. S.; Paranka, D.; George, J. F.; and Nunamaker, J. F. 1993. Communication Concurrency and the New Media. *Communication Research* 20(2): 249-276.

Van Gelder, L. 1986. The Strange Case of the Electronic Lover. In *Talking to Strangers: Mediated Therapeutic Communication*, eds. G. Gumpert and S. L. Fish, 128-142. Norwood, N.J.: Ablex.

Vasu, M. L., and Garson, G. D. 1990. Computer-Assisted Survey Research and Continuous Audience Response Technology for the Political and Social Sciences. *Social Science Computer Review* 8(4): 535-557.

Voiskounsky, A. 1992. Speech in Computer Mediated Communication. In *Proceedings of the East-West International Conference on Human-Computer Interaction, EWC-HI'92*, ed. Y. Gornostaev, 240-243. St. Petersburg, Russia: ICSTI Press.

Von Rospach, C. 1993. A Primer on How to Work with the Usenet Community. Unpublished ms. (ftp.rtfm.mit.edu/pub/usenet/news.answers/usenet-primer.)

Vygotsky, L. S. 1962. *Thought and Language.* Cambridge, Mass.: The MIT Press.

Vygotsky, L. S. 1978. *Mind in Society. The Development of Higher Psychological Processes.* Cambridge, Mass.: Harvard University Press.

Walker, C. B. F. 1990. Cuneiform. In *Reading the Past: Ancient Writing from Cuneiform to the Alphabet,* 15-74. London: British Museum.

Wallich, P. 1993. Electronic Envelopes? The Uncertainty of Keeping Email Private. *Scientific American* 268(2): 30-31.

Walster, E. H.; Walster, G. W.; and Berscheid, E. 1978. *Equity: Theory and Research.* Boston, Mass.: Allyn and Bacon.

Walter, R. 1992. *The Secret Guide to Computers.* Sixteenth edition. Boston: Russ Walter.

Walther, J. 1992. Interpersonal Effects in Computer-Mediated Interaction: A Relational Perspective. *Communication Research* 19(1): 52-89.

Walther, J. B., and Burgoon, J. K. 1992. Relational Communication in Computer-Mediated Interaction. *Human Communication Research* 19(1): 50-88.

Wambach, J. A. 1991. Building Electronic Mail Coalitions: Network Politics in an Educational Organization. Paper Presented at 1991 Western States Communication Association, Organizational Communication Interest Group, Phoenix, Ariz. February.

Watzlawick, P.; Beavin, J. H.; and Jackson, D. D. 1967. *Pragmatics of Human Communication: A Study of Interactional Patterns, Pathologies and Paradoxes.* New York: Norton.

We, G. 1993. Cross-Gender Communication in Cyberspace. Unpublished manuscript Dept. of Communication, Simon Fraser University. (we@sfu.ca.)

Weisband, S. P. 1992. Group Discussion and First Advocacy Effects in Computer-Mediated and Face-to-Face Decision Making Groups. *Organizational Behavior and Human Decision Processes* 53: 352-380.

Weizenbaum, J. 1966. Eliza — A Computer Program for the Study of Natural Language Communication Between Man and Machine. *Communications of the ACM* 9(1): 36-44.

Weizenbaum, J. 1976. *Computer Power and Human Reason. From Judgment to Calculation.* San Francisco: W. H. Freeman.

Werman, R. 1993. *Notes from a Sealed Room: An Israeli View of the Gulf War.* Carbondale, Ill.: Southern Illinois University Press.

Werner, C. and Latane, B. 1976. Responsiveness and Communication Medium in Dyadic Interactions. *Bulletin of the Psychonomic Society* 8(1): 13-15.

Wertsch, J. V. 1991. *Voices of the Mind: A Sociocultural Approach to Mediated Action.* London: Harvester Wheatsheaf.

White, G. 1991. Suit Says Nissan Fired Pair Over Privacy Issue. *Los Angeles Times* 110(January 8): D3

White, T. H. 1958. *The Once and Future King.* London: Collins.

Wilson, D. L. 1993. Censoring Electronic Messages. *Chronicle of Higher Education* (May 12): A2.

Winer. B. J. 1971. *Statistical Principles in Experimental Design.* Second Edition. New York: McGraw-Hill.

Witmer, D. W. 1998. Practicing Safe Computing: Why People Engage in Risky Computer-Mediated Communication. In *Network and Netplay: Virtual Groups on the Internet,* eds. F. Sudweeks, M. L. McLaughlin, S. Rafaeli. Menlo Park, Calif.: AAAI Press.

Witmer, D. W., and Katzman, S. L. 1998. Smile When You Say That: Graphic Accents as Gender Markers in Computer-Mediated Communication. In *Network and Netplay: Virtual Groups on the Internet*, eds. F. Sudweeks; M. McLaughlin; and S. Rafaeli. Menlo Park, Calif: AAAI Press.

Wittgenstein, L. 1968. *Philosophical Investigations*. New York: Macmillan.

Yates, S. 1992a. Computer Conferencing: A Written or Spoken Environment? In *Report No. 151*. Milton Keynes, England: Centre for Information Technology in Education, The Open University.

Yates, S. 1992b. Conflict and Ambivalence Over Oral and Literate Boundaries: An Examination of "Literacy Events" *Computer-Mediated Communication*. Milton Keynes, England: Centre for Information Technology in Education, The Open University.

Yates, S. 1996. Oral and Written Linguistic Aspects of Computer Conferencing. In *Computer-Mediated Communication: Linguistic, Social, and Cross-Cultural Perspectives*, Ed. C. Herring, 29-46. Amsterdam: John Benjamins.

Zack, M. H. 1993. Interactivity and Communication Mode Choice in Ongoing Management Groups. *Information Systems Research* 4: 3.

Zillman, D. 1984. *Connections Between Sex and Aggression*. Hillsdale, N.J.: Lawrence Erlbaum Associates.

Zimmerman, D. P. 1987. Effects of Computer Conferencing on the Language Use of Emotionally Disturbed Adolescents. *Behavior Research Methods, Instruments, and Computers* 19(2): 224-230.

Index

accounts, 98-111

action tree structure, 253

activation rule, 195

active documents, 221

addiction, 74

advocacy sequences, 16

agents, 243-263
  believable, 247
  see also Merlyn

aggression, 72. 73

agon, 69

alea, 69

alphabets
  Cyril, 38-29
  Latin, 38-39

America Online, 78

annealing schedule, 197, 202

annotated environments, 248

anonymity, 165
  in CMC, 3-4, 165
  see also identity

argument framing, 13

argumentative message structure, 14-16

argumentative responses, 16

ASCII art, 47

asterisks, 61

asynchronous update, 197, 199, 205

asynchrony, 16

audience behavior, 63

autoassociative neural networks, 195-198

awareness hierarchy, 226

awk, 194

believable agents, 247

Bitnet listservs, 179-183, 193

brainstorming, 177, 181

browsing, chronological, 233

camouflage, principle of, 49

capitalization, 46

categorization, 191-193

charades, 59

Christians, Clifford, 89

CHRONO, 233-235

chronological browsing, 233

clamping, 200, 205-207, 211

CMC, 3-11, 13-14, 227, 22-224, 266-267
  anonymity in, 3-4
  dimensions of, 223-224
  ethics of, 267
  human-technology interface in, 16-18
  origins of, 27
  pioneering researchers in, 421
  playfulness in, 41-47
  self-communication in, 37

codebook, 181

collective stance, 236

comic strips, 61

communication, 175
  comparisons, 175, 177
  face-to-face, 175
compliments, 63
CompuServe, 78, 188
  SIGs, 179-183, 193
computer-mediated communication *see* CMC
computer-mediated groups
  agreement in, 179, 183
  description of, 174
  in organizations, 178, 182
Comserve, 188
connectionist model, 191-193
consensus formation, 177
conspicuous markings, principle of, 49
content analysis, 180, 182
copyright, 268-269
Creole, 33
cross dressing, 50, 72-73
CSCW, 31
cybersex, 127

deindividuation, 177
Delphi, 113
digital writing, conventions of, 46
discourse, 4
  gender differences in, 4, 5
  patterns, 226
discussion groups, 14
disinhibition, 177
Dungeons and Dragons, 51

e-mail, *see* electronic mail
electronic mail, 27, 129, 132
  features in, 27
  message structure, 14-16
  reproaches, 101, 106-110
  usage of, 38
electronic supervision, 132
ELIZA, 247
Ellul, Jacques, 89

emoticons, 30, 42 178
emotions, 5
ephemerality, 44
Esperanto, 32
Euclidean cluster model, 193
EUnet, 114
extensional awareness, 225, 227, 232
external entrainment, 226
external validity, 177

FAQ, 96
FAW, 97
field research, 177
flames, 13-26
  see also flaming
flaming, 6, 10, 43, 98, 102, 110, 128, 177
flow experience, 45
frames, 52
  blurring of, 66-67
  party, 53, 55
  play with, 52
framing, 15
  perceptual, 15
  argument, 13
  party, 53, 55
  play, 43
  pretend, 53
gender, 99-100, 110
  issues of, 133
  markers, 3-11
  masking of, 49-50
graphic accents, 5
  use by females, 9-10
group CMC
  characteristics of, 179, 183-184, 186

Hamnet Players, 71
HCI paradigm, 261-262
Hebbian learning rule, 201
hieroglyphs, 27
hypertext, 45

icons, 65

identity, masking of, 47

improvisation, 64, 71

information exchange, 113, 116

intensional awareness, 225, 232

interactivity, 45
    constructs, 191
    definition of, 173, 175-176
    logs, 63
    outcomes, 175, 185
    theory, 185

internet relay chat, see IRC

Internet, 13-14
    communities, 224-225

interpersonal communication, 29
    media simulated, 29
    human-computer, 29
    mediated, 29

interrupting, 35, 174, 176

IRC, 130, 131, 230, 244

Julia, 248

Katipo, 235

Klyosov, 113

laboratory research, 177

LambdaMOO, 151-153

LAN, 37

legal responsibilities, 134

list server discourse, 228

logs of interaction, 63

Los Angeles *Times,* 88

LUDUS, 68-69

masks, 49
    textual, 49

McLuhan, Marshall, 266

media richness, 177

mediated mental acts, 28

mental development, 28

Merlyn, 246, 248-263
    abilities of, 252-253
    implementation of, 254

message structure, 14
    argumentative, 14-16

monitoring service, 124

Mr Bungle case, 150-153, 169-170, 171

MudOS MUD architecture, 254

MUDs see multi-user domains

multi-user domains, 3, 244-246
    environments, 250

multimedia, 40

mutual entrainment, 226

netiquette, 14, 97

network users, 37
    growth rates of, 174

newsgroups, 106
    standards of conduct, 97
    Usenet, 29, 34, 179-183, 193, 231

nicknames, 46-47, 48, 50

nonverbal behavior, 178

norm of reciprocity, 236

oracles, 182

PAIDIA, 68-69

party frame, 53, 55

passwords, 129

perceptual framing, 15

performance, 47, 59-60
    frame, 53, 60

pictorial simulation, 64

pidgin, 32
    attributes of, 37-38
    defined, 28
    formation of, 33

play, 43, 249
    categories of, 68
    definition of, 43
    frame, 43
    pretend, 59
    theorists of, 43
    theory of, 68

playfulness, 42, 43, 44, 46

polylogue, 30, 35

posting, 105

pretend frame, 53

privacy, 129, 131, 133, 138, 140

ProjectH, 6-8, 32, 173, 193, 265-281
  acknowledgments, 278-281
  aims of, 265-266
  coding, 275
  conceptualization of, 269-270
  copyright policy of, 270
  reliability statement, 277
  sampling statement, 271-272

puns, 51

rape, 31
  and social construction, 153-154
  attitude towards, 155-159
  in cyberspace, 147-172
  in virtual reality, 161-162
  climate for, 162-163
  social construction of, 159-160
  social history of, 154-155
  virtual, 151-153

reality, virtual, *see* virtual reality

rec.arts.tv.soaps.abc, 97

recounting, 15

RELARN Association, 116

Relcom network, 114-117, 126
  characteristics of, 115-116, 126
  geographic dispersion, 118, 126
  users' experience, 119, 126
  users' competence 119, 126
  users' motivations, 121, 126
  occupations of users, 122, 126

Relcom users
  age range, 118-119, 126
  competence, 119-121, 126
  experience, 119, 126
  geographic dispersion, 118, 126
  occupation, 122-124, 126

reliability, 182, 194

remediation, 37

reproaches, 108
  characteristics, 106
  messages, 101, 106-110

rhyme, 51

risky CMC, 127-141

Russia, network users in, 113-125

sampling, 180

science fiction, 51, 52

security, 130, 138, 140

semiotic systems, 28, 31

sexual harassment, 133

sign systems, 27-31

smiley faces, 5, 51, 65

soc.culture.yugoslavia, 79-89

social context cues, 177

social entrainment, 226, 230

social exchange model, 259

social exchange theory, 236

social influence, 178

social learning theory, 238

social needs, 138

social presence, 177, 178

socioware, 240, 259
  comparison with groupware, 240

speech, 31-36
  dialogical, 31-32, 34, 43-44
  oral, 31, 34, 35
  monological, 31-32, 34, 36
  written, 31, 34, 35

Star Trek, 51

status leveling, 177

student culture, 50

stylization, 47

synchronous update, 196

technological determinism, 74

telelogue, 28
  attributes of 39
  defined, 28

theater, virtual, 71, 244, 252

threads, 180, 186, 191, 211, 213-215

threshold, 195-196, 199, 202, 207

Times-Mirror, 87

Toronto *Globe and Mail,* 79
totalitarian society, 113
turn-taking, 36, 174, 175, 177
typicality set, 203, 207, 208, 211, 218
typographical errors, 62-63
typographical simulation, 59
tyranny of materials, 44, 45

UNESCO, 113
UNIX, 194
URL-Minder, 235
USA Today, 79
Usenet newsgroups, 29, 34, 179-183, 193, 231

virtual cooperative interaction, 221-241
virtual environments, 244-246
virtual party, 48
virtual persona, 225
virtual pubs, 70

virtual rape, 151-153
virtual reality, 147-150, 184
virtual theater, 71
    project, 244
    system, 252
virtual worlds, 243-236
Vreme, 81, 84

WAN, 37
Washington *Post,* 88
WebWatch, 235
weight matrix, 202-204, 214
Wilks' lambda criterion, 103
word play, 51, 56, 63, 70
word processing, 45
World Wide Web, 40
writing, 72
    digital, 46
    history of 72

youth culture, 56